INVENTING
WOMEN

SCIENCE, TECHNOLOGY AND GENDER

This book is the third in a series of four published by Polity Press in association with The Open University. The complete list is:

Knowing Women: Feminism and Knowledge
edited by Helen Crowley and Susan Himmelweit

Defining Women: Social Institutions and Gender Divisions
edited by Linda McDowell and Rosemary Pringle

Inventing Women: Science, Technology and Gender
edited by Gill Kirkup and Laurie Smith Keller

Imagining Women: Cultural Representations and Gender
edited by Frances Bonner, Lizbeth Goodman, Richard Allen, Linda Janes and Catherine King

The books are one component of the Open University course *U207 Issues in Women's Studies*. Details of the course are available from the Central Enquiry Service, The Open University, PO Box 200, Milton Keynes MK7 2YZ. Telephone: 0908 653078.

The Open University U207 *Issues in Women's Studies* Course Production Team

Amanda Willett, Barbara Hodgson, Catherine King (Chair), Diana Gittins, Dinah Birch, Felicity Edholm, Fiona Harris, Frances Bonner, Gill Kirkup, Harry Dodd, Helen Crowley, Joan Mason, Judy Lown, Kathryn Woodward, Laurie Smith Keller, Linda Janes, Linda McDowell, Lizbeth Goodman, Maggie Riley, Maureen Adams, Meg Sheffield, Melanie Bayley, Randhir Auluck, Richard Allen, Rosemary Pringle, Siân Lewis, Susan Crosbie, Susan Himmelweit, Susan Khin Zaw, Tony Coulson, Veronica Beechey, Wendy Webster

External Assessor: Elizabeth Wilson, Professor of Policy Studies, Polytechnic of North London

Cover illustration by Christine Tacq

INVENTING WOMEN

SCIENCE, TECHNOLOGY AND GENDER

Edited by Gill Kirkup and Laurie Smith Keller

POLITY PRESS   in association with    The Open University

First published in the United Kingdom by Polity Press
in association with Blackwell Publishers Ltd and The Open University.
Reprinted 1998

Editorial office:
Polity Press
65 Bridge Street
Cambridge CB2 1UR, UK

Marketing and production:
Blackwell Publishers Ltd
108 Cowley Road
Oxford OX4 1JF, UK

Published in the USA by
Blackwell Publishers Inc.
350 Main Street
Malden MA 02148, USA

Edited and designed by The Open University.

ISBN 0–7456–0977–5
ISBN 0–7456–0978–3 (pbk)

A CIP catalogue record for this book is available from the British Library
and has been applied for from the Library of Congress.

Typeset in 10 on 12 pt Palatino
by Photo·graphics, Honiton, Devon
Printed in Great Britain by TJ International, Padstow, Cornwall

This book is printed on acid-free paper.

CONTENTS

INTRODUCTION

Technology touches us all, in every aspect of our lives. Every artefact we make or touch or use is the product of technology; most foods have been processed by some form of technology; even raw food is grown, harvested and transported by technological means. Yet how that touch feels – how we use technology, what technologies we think appropriate, whether a particular technology brings benefits or burdens, and to whom, whether it is useful or out of reach – is very much influenced by who we are: what gender, class and race we are and where we live.

Since the seventeenth and particularly the eighteenth centuries in the West, science has contributed increasingly to technology and technology has demanded answers from science. This has had a particular influence on science – how it is perceived, how it is carried out, by whom and why, and who pays for it and to whose benefit.

The aim of this book is to introduce students of women's studies to some of the most important areas of debate of women's studies scholars in the fields of science and technology. The articles selected have been chosen, as far as possible, for their accessible style as well as their content. There is still a mystique around scientific and technological material, and an expectation that women will find it hard to understand; we hope to demonstrate that when it is written by women's studies scholars this is not true.

Compared with the numbers of women's studies books that have been published in the fields of arts and social sciences, there have been relatively few in science and technology. One of the first edited collections to make feminist debates about science accessible to an interdisciplinary women's studies audience was *Alice through the Microscope*, edited by the Brighton Women and Science Group (1980). Since then the number of edited collections which have dealt with the wide range of issues to do with gender and science and technology has been small. Jan Zimmerman's *The Technological Woman* (1983), Joan Rothschild's *Machina Ex Dea* (1983), Wendy Faulkner's and Eric Arnold's *Smothered by Invention* (1985) and Cheris Kramarae's *Technology and Women's Voices* (1988) are well worth reading alongside this collection.

In this volume we have tried to present a wide variety of voices and informed comment about science and technology with particular reference to their influence on us according to our gender, but also with reference to race, class and place. We have sought to include those who 'make' science and technology: a woman who is a Nobel laureate, a working-class Jewish woman who became an important scientist at a time when science was virtually closed to women, and an Indian woman, Sarin, engaged in helping rural poor women to lighten their crushing burden of work and ameliorate the effects of deforestation. We have included military technology, household technology, medical science, but also Third World technology and appropriate technology.

All these voices speak from different experiences of life and in different styles. Most speak in prose and non-fiction, but some speak in poetry and one speaks in fiction of a vision of a Third World woman's science and technology. We consider this diversity to be an especial strength of this volume and have sought, in our editing, to maintain the styles of these different voices.

There are themes that run, like bright threads, through the book. Science, mostly done by men, seeks to define women in particular ways; not surprisingly, these definitions are often selective in the 'facts' they use and support cultural notions of male superiority and dominance/female inferiority and submission. Women, of whatever class, race, caste and in whatever part of the world, are deeply affected by technology, yet they are often the last to benefit, if at all. Often a technology which benefits men and affects work typically undertaken by men will not benefit the women at all, and it is not unusual to find that some technologies add to the burdens of women rather than relieve them. Whether a particular technology is done primarily by men or women almost always depends upon where that technology fits into pre-existing cultural notions of what is appropriate to each gender. Women can be and are excluded from certain technologies for a variety of reasons and rationalizations: women are thought to 'lack' such characteristics as bodily strength or intellectual capacity; certain activities may be thought to threaten the moral welfare of women; other activities are seen as threatening a woman's 'natural role'; women have less access to education, tend to be less experienced and less assertive until they gain experience and training (a Catch-22 if ever there was one!); education and training may be unfriendly. How men and women approach the same technology, and the reasons for their approaches, may also differ greatly.

The first chapter introduces the topic of what science is and what technology is. It attempts to draw some distinctions between the two – now so closely associated with each other in the West that we have difficulty knowing where one stops and the other starts – and to place them in a general historical and social context. Once the general context is established, science and technology are then viewed in relation to gender. This relationship with gender is two-way: science and technology assume certain things about gender, and notions about gender affect science and technology. The question is asked: can feminist illuminations of gender affect science and technology – for the better?

Chapter 2 focuses more specifically on the relationship between science and gender at the physiological, anthropological, medical and genetic levels. Science defines biological sex (and sex defines gender), but the definition of sex is more complex and less straightforward than we may imagine at first glance. The definition of gender and the anthropological evidence for and against the 'natural' gender division of labour is also examined. Being defined as female places one in a particular category as medicine uses the scientific definition of biological sex to set a model of female illness and health against a male 'norm'. Aspects of the female experience have been taken over and defined as needing medical supervision. This has extended to the role of women as the bearers of children. Medicalization of the female role of gestation has expanded to include the detection of foetal genetic disease, but the techniques used and the outcomes of various tests are neither ethically nor emotionally straightforward. We become engaged with the conflict between a desire for health and perfection and a partial rejection of at least some of the logical outcomes of prenatal screening at both broadly social and very specific psychological and emotional levels.

The third chapter steps back to look at women (and men) producing science and technology: how women have achieved what they have and what has kept them from full participation. Women have had a long and arduous fight to gain entry to the sciences, particularly since they became professionalized in the nineteenth century. Despite this struggle and its lessons for collective feminist action, much of science remains – at best – uncongenial to girls and women. This begins with science education at the lowest levels. It is here that feminist insight has much to offer. In return, female scientists may contribute to science in ways that men have not, with different approaches and different insights. The fight to 'get in' is by no means over, particularly in respect to technology. We have to ask the question: how have men kept technology, at both the craft and the professional level, to themselves and why? Gender, class, caste, race and location enter into our dialogue between science, technology and our daily lives, both in paid employment and in the ways in which we carry out common tasks. The impact of high technology in the West on Western women and the impact of various types of high and intermediate technologies on women in the Third World illustrate this.

Whatever other relationships we may have individually and collectively with technology and its associated sciences, we are all consumers. The final chapter looks at this aspect of our lives. How much has technology actually helped Western women in their daily tasks? For that matter, what can technology do for women and their work in the Third World? What kind of technology is appropriate? How can a better technology be disseminated and made available to the women who need it? How can women come to control this major influence on their lives? What happens when women take a stance with respect to science and technology and its impacts – many of them negative – on our lives? What sort of relationship do we make for ourselves with our world? In the final analysis, what dreams can we dream?

Gill Kirkup

Laurie Smith Keller

1
THE NATURE OF SCIENCE AND TECHNOLOGY

We need an appreciation of what science and technology are – at least at this historical moment within this culture – in order to understand feminist critiques of science and technology. As Evelyn Fox Keller (1986) asserts in Article 1.3:

> Modern science, as we know it, has arisen once and only once in cultural history. That is, we cannot say of [modern] science what we can say of gender – namely that all cultures do it . . . The point to keep in mind, however, is that this inability reflects not so much the failure of other cultures, but precisely the social character of the process by which science gets named – even, or especially, good science.

To some people this might sound like a piece of ethnocentric arrogance, especially to those who associate science with intellect, rationality and a search for truth. But Fox Keller's statement is just the opposite; it is in fact, an assertion that one particular way of searching for truth – through experimental method and abstract theory building, often grounded in mathematic models – is not the *only* way. All cultures try to make sense of the material world around them, predict cause and effect and develop techniques and knowledge to make artefacts, but many of the methods they use would not qualify as 'scientific' in our terms. (See Plate 1.)

Since Thomas Kuhn wrote *The Structure of Scientific Revolutions* in 1962, most historians and philosophers of science no longer view science as progressing historically through better and better theories by which to understand reality. Kuhn demonstrated, with examples from early modern Europe, that 'old' theories were often discarded and replaced by 'new', different theories, not simply because the new theories had better explanatory power, but because events within society made the new theory more acceptable. This was often to do with the nature of ideological and political change. The internal logic of science itself was seen to be a less powerful agent of change than previously believed, and certainly never an autonomous agent.

This kind of critique of science fits well with a Foucauldian[1] analysis:

> [O]ne could say that truth is not a collection of insights or information floating about, parts of which are sooner or later revealed or discovered, nor does it lie deep within us waiting to be freed. Truth is produced through discourse (based in science upon 'proper' scientific methods and investigations) and its production is involved with relations of power.
>
> *(Bleier, 1984, p. 195)*

An understanding of the historical and cultural relativity of modern science frees us to be open to other methods and systems of thought which can now be seen as valid explanations of the world within their own context. It also enables us to see science as a product of a gendered culture and to speculate about the possibility of a 'gender-neutral' or feminist science. It gives us firm ground, as feminists, on which to stand in order to do a job of deconstructing science. During the 1980s that ground has been inhabited by a growing number of feminist theorists and feminist scientists. It is, however, important also to be able to evaluate what has been and is useful about science rather than occupy this ground simply to propose anti-science or anti-technology positions.

Fox Keller discusses this when arguing that it is important that the 'personal' should be incorporated into any kind of new science:

> Faced with the charge that 'women always get personal', Mary Ellman counters: 'I'd say men always get impersonal. If you hurt their feelings, they make Boyle's law out of it.'
> . . . The fact that Boyle's law is not wrong must, however, not be forgotten. Any effective critique of science needs to take due account of the undeniable successes of science as well as the commitments that have made such successes possible. If individuals tend to be drawn to science by the desire (or need) to escape the personal, or by the promise of quasi-religious communion, they are also drawn by another, equally personal but perhaps more universal ambition: namely, the search for reliable, shareable knowledge of the world around us. Indeed, scientists' shared commitment to the possibility of reliable knowledge of nature, and to its dependence on experimental replicability and logical coherence, is an indispensable prerequisite for the effectiveness of any scientific venture. What needs to be understood is how these conscious commitments (commitments we all share) are fuelled and elaborated, and sometimes also subverted, by the more

parochial social, political and emotional commitments (conscious or not) of particular individuals and groups.

Boyle's law does give us a reliable description of the relation between pressure and volume in low density gases at high temperatures, a description that stands the tests of experimental replicability and logical coherence. But it is crucial to recognize that it is a statement about a particular set of phenomena, prescribed to meet particular interests and described in accordance with certain agreed-upon criteria of both reliability and utility. Judgements about which phenomena are worth studying, which kinds of data are significant – as well as which descriptions (or theories) of those are most adequate, satisfying, useful, and even reliable – depend critically on the social, linguistic and scientific practices of those making the judgements in question.

(Fox Keller, 1985)

The first article in this chapter – 'Discovering and doing' by Laurie Smith Keller – sets the context for the chapter, and the book. It analyses the historical formulation of science and technology, to uncover how, when we use the words in a commonsense fashion, we often convey erroneous, exaggerated or fictional notions of the nature of science and technology. Many of us women, even those with post-school education, stopped doing formal science in our early teenage years (and never did 'technology' activities at all). Smith Keller describes in simple language the process of experimental method, as well as the history of it.

She also examines the nature of technology and its relationship to science, a debate of considerable interest to feminists. For many people technology is simply 'the appliance of science', a view promoted through the formal teaching of technological subjects as applied science. However, if we accept that modern science is an historically and culturally specific activity, we are left with the question of whether cultures without science can have technology which is both rational and systematic. And, since they patently can and do, then the relationship between technology and science is not the simple cause and effect that might be presumed. The association of technology with modern science has had negative as well as positive effects. Women have always engaged in technological activities, making containers, clothing and various domestic artefacts, but their exclusion from industrial, technical processes has caused them to be seen as non-technological, and their technological activities to be redefined as art and craft.

The second article, 'Women's voices/men's voices: technology as language' by Margaret Lowe Benston, discusses technology as a language in a way different from a Foucauldian analysis. She describes the use of technology by people living their lives and 'doing' as a kind of language. Access to this language is through the ability to use and understand tools and artefacts. The analogy here is with words. Having limited access to the vocabulary of a language is at worst silencing and at best allows only limited participation in the discourse. This is the position women are in with respect to tools and technology and, although she does not say it, with respect to modern science too. Access to technology, and science, is access to a variety of sorts of power, some real and some symbolic.

This issue of access has sometimes been confused with the activity of 'fixing things'. Because many feminist workshops of the 1970s and 1980s contained 'hands-on', confidence-building activities based around demystifying common mechanical objects, such as car engines, bicycles or washing machines, this was sometimes interpreted as a notion that liberation entailed doing your own mechanical repair jobs. This was countered by the argument that if women could and did fix cars and washing machines this would simply add to their already onerous list of domestic tasks. But if access to skills is seen as access to a particular kind of power, then it becomes unarguable that access for women is a good thing. Whether we choose to use it to 'fix things' is a different question. Benston is the first of many authors in this book to argue for the importance of women's access to technology and science. She also opens the argument, which runs through many of the articles in this book, that male and female experience of the world is different and that some of this experience is mediated by technology. This different, gendered world view means that men and women bring to science and technology different visions.

Evelyn Fox Keller – the author of Article 1.3, 'How gender matters, or, why it's so hard for us to count past two' – has been influential during the 1980s in conceptualizing how a feminist science might be different from 'malestream' science as it exists at present. In an important book about the work and life of geneticist Barbara McClintock (discussed in more detail in Article 3.3), she argued that women, because of their gendered location in the world, could bring new and useful methods of thought to a male science. Fox Keller herself originally worked as a mathematical biophysicist, and she retains a commitment to a feminist revolution in science that will ultimately make science better at achieving its own aims.

Fox Keller analyses what the question about women and science means for different people. The most basic version of this question, and one which certainly is not part of the feminist agenda, is: what is wrong with women that they can't do science? The next simplest version, and one which still has many feminist adherents today, asks: since men and women are equals, what are the barriers which keep women out of science and how can they be removed so that women can join (a presumed gender-neutral activity) on the same grounds as men? She then identifies a shift – certainly within modern feminism – to arguments that because women and men are not the same, then there is masculine science and could-be feminist (or feminine) science. Fox Keller is obviously worried about this position. She sees it as giving up on attempts at objectivity, which she values, for a relativism which asserts that there are as many different kinds of science as there are people. She argues for shifting the focus of inquiry into how ideas of gender have shaped the construction of science and how ideas of science have shaped our construction of gender – a more complex agenda altogether. She argues that we must move away from dualisms – male/female, mind/nature, self/other – and look instead for difference. She is also very careful to say that she doesn't see this way of thinking as being biologically determined – by being female – although she argues that women have more to gain by thinking this way than men. She ends her piece with a discussion of the language of evolutionary theory, in which she argues that debates about competition or co-operation disguise the richness of what is actually happening through the use of a gendered language that romanticizes both competitive masculinity and co-operative femininity and forces theorists into one camp or the other. This for her is an example of the unhelpfulness of allowing gender to play a crucial role in science.

Sandra Harding in Article 1.4, 'How the women's movement benefits science: two views', is also concerned about the different arguments adopted by feminists working for change. She sees a core of solidarity in the struggle that all feminists have against scientific conservatives who believe that change originating from the women's movement must be bad. She identifies feminist positions differently from Fox Keller, and in a way that is perhaps initially simpler to grasp. She identifies feminist empiricists as critics of bad science interested in improving its practices, and feminist standpoint theorists as critics of all modern science who believe the whole enterprise should be dismantled. The first position she relates to liberal political and moral theory and the second to Marxist epistemology. Harding, like Fox Keller, feels that the agenda of modern science as well as some of its practices are worth defending and that it is regressive to discourage women from learning to do it, or from working in it. And yet she argues at the same time that radical critiques are necessary. The important thing is to bring the two positions close enough together to co-operate on a 'science of science'. She sees both positions as claiming benefits from the involvement of more women in modern science: the empiricists see the missing talents and abilities of women as having the potential to make new contributions; the feminist standpoint theorists see women as bringing a wholly different perspective to science stemming from their particular social location. Harding argues that it is very important to all feminists to have a theory about doing science, and this should connect what happens in laboratories with social relations in society at large, something that will become more apparent in later chapters of this book.

There is a more recently developed position, beyond that of feminist standpoint theory, which is likely to play a significant part in feminist theory debates of the 1990s, that is 'feminist post-modernism'. It has been described by Mary Hawkesworth, who is very critical of it, as rejecting

> ... the very possibility of *a* truth about reality. Feminist post-modernists use the 'situatedness' of each finite observer in a particular socio-political, historical context to challenge the plausibility of claims that any perspective on the world could escape partiality. Extrapolating from the disparate conditions that shape individual identities, they raise grave suspicions about the very notion of putative unitary consciousness of the species. In addition, the argument that knowledge is the result of invention, the imposition of form on the world rather than the result of discovery, undermines any belief that the Order of Being could be known even if it exists.
>
> *(Hawkesworth, 1989, p. 536)*

This is a position of epistemological relativism. It suggests that there are as many truths as individual people and that no single truth has any claim to be better than any other. This is what Fox Keller calls a step from 'the twoness of us, to the infinity of us's'. As a position it runs counter not only to the aims of science, but to those of feminism of the 1970s and '80s. Feminism as a theory, and a political movement, claims that there are 'facts' and 'realities' about the position of women, such as rape, domestic violence and unequal pay that are a key to understanding sexual oppression, and that these have been hidden or distorted. For people like Fox Keller, Harding and Hawkesworth, science and feminism have similar agendas in that they are both concerned to remedy distortion and move closer towards a more accurate description of how things are. Both feminism and science claim that there *are* things that can be known. This position brings us back full circle to Smith Keller's paper about the activity of science. Science is a systematic attempt to know about the material world; it presumes that there is an external reality that we can know in some form – that Boyle's law works.

Gill Kirkup

Note

1   Michel Foucault (1926–84), French philosopher and historian. His writings contain two main themes – how to theorize the relationship between general history and the history of thought, how individuals become knowing and self-knowing. His work is discussed in detail in the first volume of this series, *Knowing Women: feminism and knowledge* (Crowley and Himmelweit (eds) 1992).

Article 1.1
DISCOVERING AND DOING: SCIENCE AND TECHNOLOGY, AN INTRODUCTION

Laurie Smith Keller

téchnophób|ia *n.* (Morbid) fear of or aversion to technology, which is the application of science or the practical or industrial art(s).

My purpose in this chapter is twofold: to explain what science and technology are and how they are related to each other and to the social systems in which they are embedded, and to overcome to some degree the technophobia and alienation from science and technology that many people, particularly women, feel. The attitude held by many women and some men towards increasingly common devices like microwave ovens and video recorders provides an example. Such machines can provide a great deal of flexibility – for example, video recorders can be used to record a favourite television programme for viewing at a more convenient time – but users often find themselves frustrated by the difficulty of operating the machine. This is often a problem of the 'interface' between the machine and the user: frequently the tasks that the instructions require the user to do ('press the time button twice in quick succession, then enter the hour in 24-hour mode by pressing the set button until the correct hour appears on the display. . .') do not match what the user wants to do ('record the programme on BBC2 that starts at 8.20 pm'). The designer has made the interface convenient to the machine rather than its user. As a result, the users may transfer their feelings of frustration and alienation to 'technology' in general. This is more true of women than of men because men may be too embarrassed to admit that they cannot operate a machine and will keep trying. Often feelings of frustration and antipathy for technology are transferred by implication to science as well – isn't it science that gives us high technology? Isn't it science that promises so much and in the end apparently gives so little?

In reading about science and technology, it is easy to be put off because the terms used are 'scientific'. Many people find such terms not only beyond their immediate understanding but even beyond their ability to 'find out'. To help overcome this feeling I have deliberately not explained some of the terms I use because I know they are in general dictionaries. I hope to convince you that because a term is 'scientific' does not mean that it cannot be found in an ordinary dictionary. The term *technophobia* is not, by the way, in my dictionary, but *technology* and *phobia* are, so I combined them.

WHAT IS SCIENCE?

Science assumes a measurable, material world. It is based on the activities of observation, reason, structured experimentation in which phenomena are repeated as often as necessary, and finally, on peer review of results (hence the importance in science of publication). Science does not, however, make claims to certainty.

> The scientist has a lot of experience with ignorance and doubt and uncertainty, and this experience is of very great importance, I think ... We have found ... that in order to progress we must recognize our ignorance and leave room for doubt. Scientific knowledge is a body of statements of varying degrees of certainty – some most unsure, some nearly sure, but none *absolutely* certain.
>
> *(Feynman, 1988, p. 245)*

It is a common notion that science lacks any spiritual and emotional dimension. Its emphasis on rational thought and logical inference and deduction, and its need to be able to repeat phenomena in order to test them, appear to devalue the emotional, the intuitive, the spiritual and the unique. Yet discoveries early in this century in physics, followed by insights emerging from ethology[1] and ecology, can imbue science with a profoundly spiritual life view.

> The world view emerging from modern physics can be characterized by words like organic, holistic and ecological ... The universe is no longer seen as a machine, made up of a multitude of objects, but has to be pictured as one indivisible, dynamic whole whose parts are essentially interrelated and can be understood only as patterns of a cosmic process ... Many physicists, brought up, as I was, in a tradition that associates mysticism with things vague, mysterious and highly unscientific, were shocked at having their ideas compared to those of mystics.
>
> *(Capra, 1982, p. 66)*

The older 'scientific' view is essentially mechanistic – nature is seen as machine-like. Natural phenomena can be analysed into their constituent parts and these parts can be arranged according to causal laws. It is like looking at an old-fashioned watch. There is a spring that can be tightened, thus storing energy that can be released over time by allowing the spring gradually to unwind. The unwinding of the spring turns a cog-wheel that turns other cog-wheels causing the hands of the watch to move around its face in a measured fashion. When the spring has fully unwound, the system has no further energy to move any of its parts and the watch stops until some external agent winds the spring up again. A mechanistic model can be applied to classical physics very satisfactorily and can be very easily studied through the application of mathematics. By 'disassembling' a phenomenon to its constituent parts and seeing what causal laws drive each of the parts, we can come to an understanding of nature.

It is this view that has been seen as a particularly masculine view and therefore opposed to a feminine view because of the ingrained practice of gendering modes of thought, modes of reaction to the world around us and modes of working. It is the view that science is comprehensible only by the intellect using objectivity and reason that has labelled science as a masculine activity.

> Feminist scholars have called attention to the many ways our conception of science is tied up with our conception of masculinity. Modern science, they argue, is based on a division of emotional and intellectual labour in which objectivity, reason and 'mind' are cast as male and subjectivity, feeling and 'nature' are cast as female. In this genderization of the world, it seems 'natural' to describe science as a 'marriage' between mind and nature – a marriage celebrating not so much union between mind and nature, but a radical separation of subject and object and, ultimately, the dominion of mind over nature. The result is a particular conception of science – one that seems more suited to men than to women.
>
> (Fox Keller, 1984, p. 45)

This is reflected in the division of science into a proliferating number of specialisms, in which the scientist spends more and more time looking at smaller and smaller parts of nature. While what follows is a simplification, the changing and expanding terminology of science shows the increasing tendency to split larger units of study into ever smaller units: what was known as natural philosophy gradually became science and science divided into physics and chemistry on the one hand (dealing with inanimate nature) and natural history (dealing with the Earth and animate nature) on the other. Then chemistry subdivided into inorganic and organic chemistry and joined another stream of thought, the biology that descended from natural history, to produce biochemistry and molecular biology. Natural history became palaeontology, geology and biology (life), the last subsequently splitting into zoology (animals) and botany (plants), with zoology then dividing further into icthyology (fish), herpetology (reptiles), mammalogy (mammals) and so on as study was divided along finer and finer lines.

However, many scientists eschew the notion of a single ideology and the notion that the mind can achieve dominion over nature. Capra (1982) believes that the scientific paradigm is shifting to a model which is less mechanical and more holistic. For example, James Lovelock, with Lynn Margulis, a microbiologist, has developed the Gaia hypothesis: this is that the Earth can be viewed as a living organism, that life alters the planet's atmosphere to maintain its continued existence. Lovelock's book (1979) often surprises because it is a detailed scientific treatise and not the tract it is sometimes supposed to be. The Gaia hypothesis has considerable influence in areas such as tropospheric science (that is, the study of the lower levels of the Earth's atmosphere) and it has spawned new areas of study incorporating formerly separate disciplines, for example geophysiology. 'Some scientists who have started listening to Lovelock think Gaia is less important as a concrete theory than as a new paradigm' (Lyman, 1989).

Trying to pin science to a single ideology in the last quarter of the twentieth century is like trying to capture a moving image in text. While many scientists adhere to a belief in the older mechanistic paradigm (which, it should be noted, remains a useful paradigm yielding valid results and providing a valid basis for acquiring detailed knowledge in many spheres), many others are coming to recognize that modern, Western science and technology have not always followed a smooth path of increasing progress and enlightenment; they are seeking new paradigms which will begin to re-integrate scientific knowledge into a holistic view of nature:

> . . . modern physics has not only invalidated the classical ideal of an objective description of nature but has also challenged the myth of a value-free science. The patterns scientists observe in nature are intimately connected with the patterns of their minds; with their concepts, thoughts, and values . . . Although much of their detailed research will not depend explicitly on their value system, the larger paradigm within which this research is pursued will never be value-free. Scientists, therefore, are responsible for their research not only intellectually but also morally.
>
> (Capra, 1982, p. 77)

Science is as old as speculation and the transmission of knowledge. Until near the end of the eighteenth century it contributed little to either technology or most people's daily lives, though it has always called upon technology to help it develop its instruments. It was an activity confined largely to priests, sages, teachers and only later (in the eighteenth century particularly) to wealthy dilettantes. In the nineteenth and twentieth centuries the practice of science passed to professional scientists in universities and latterly in governmental and industrial research laboratories.

In the West, when we talk about 'science' we mean modern, Western science. We think of it as culturally universal and impartial, and '. . . these assumptions are so pervasive that we hardly notice them, much less question them' (Williams, 1990). Levidow argues that Western science 'embodies values appropriate to capitalism' (1988, p. 101) and that our science was stolen from and supplants other sciences, primarily the Greek model developed and amplified in Arabic science, and Eastern sciences developed primarily in the Indian subcontinent. He argues that Western science expropriated these Eastern sciences and then denigrated, destroyed or denied their sources.

Europeans considered themselves superior from the time they 'discovered' other cultures. However, the measure of superiority has gradually changed from general criteria (including, for example, physical appearance, social customs) to material self-improvement by means of science and technology (the eighteenth century), to 'them' and 'us' divisions based on the opposition of 'progressive' and 'traditional', West and East, and even non-white and white (the nineteenth century). In the twentieth century, struggles for national liberation and reaction to Nazi atrocities have discredited racist arguments for Western superiority, but arguments based on material superiority have remained and been strengthened.

The transformation of science in the West to what we know as modern science (and what we now think of as science) came about as a result of the development and rigorous application of the experimental approach, when ordinary, if painstaking, observation of a phenomenon came to be deemed insufficient to explain cause and effect relationships. Phenomena had to be repeatable, and repeatedly observed, under conditions which clarified the relationships between a possible cause and the effect observed – experimental science.

An example that provides an interesting perspective on this experimental approach and on its subsequent influence on technology is the development of the ploughshare. Over centuries in Europe the development of the ploughshare was a slow process, and when better designs were developed, usually by individual smiths seeking to address local conditions and requirements, the dissemination of information about plough design and the necessary design skills was slow. It was not until the late eighteenth and early nineteenth centuries that *systematic* experiments took place in which one aspect of the design of a ploughshare was varied and tried until a body of knowledge existed about the possible designs of ploughshares and how different designs behaved in different conditions (heavy soil, light soil, wet and dry, initial cultivation and recultivation and so on). By then, the dissemination of designs and skills had come to depend on a literate public with access to mass-produced sources of technical and scientific information and occurred far more rapidly than was possible under the localized master–apprentice system of knowledge transfer.

Master and *apprentice* are legal terms, limited to men; the relationship was defined by a contract, and only boys could be apprenticed. The master agreed to house and teach, the apprentice to provide labour and to learn. A qualified apprentice became a journeyman (sic), usually practising his trade as an itinerant. When he found a place and sufficient money to settle and develop his own atelier, he could become a master in his turn. Girls similarly learned by practical example and practice from an older woman, usually a mother or other adult female relative, and similarly supplied labour, but the relationship was not a legal one; girls did not become 'journeywomen', but often married into the same trade as their father practised and contributed significantly – but informally – to its execution. Women sometimes became masters, but only as a result of being the widow or daughter of a deceased master, not in their own right.

Science was originally a rather solitary occupation. Scientific societies such as the Royal Society gathered, disseminated and published information and provided a forum for the interchange of ideas. They began in earnest in the seventeenth century. They excluded women because they reflected the gendering of the larger society from which they sprang. Before the nineteenth century, most scientists did much of their experimental or observational work alone or with an assistant, corresponded with others interested in the same areas of investigation on a one-to-one basis and met occasionally in the forum of the scientific society. In the fifteenth century under Henry IV of Portugal scientists were brought together in a laboratory-like setting, but this way of doing science was not adopted more widely until the start of the nineteenth century in universities and the start of the twentieth century in industrial firms. The popular image of the lone (and possibly mad) male scientist working late into the night in a grim laboratory – for example, Mary Shelley's *Frankenstein* – is now a fictitious one: very little science is now carried out by an individual or even a small team working alone. What has not changed significantly is the image of the scientist as male. This reflects the statistical reality that women are grossly under-represented in the sciences, especially the so-called 'hard' sciences like physics and chemistry.

17

Box 1.1.1   Scientific method

Experiments try to observe the relationship between two factors, one of which the experimenter can change to observe its effect on the other. The factor that can be changed is called the *independent variable*. The factor which is observed in order to see whether alterations in the independent variable change it is called the *dependent variable*.

Let's suppose we want to determine whether the temperature of the water has any effect on how well soaking removes fruit-juice stains in 100% cotton cloth. In this case, the *independent variable* is the water temperature: we can change this and observe its effect on the *dependent variable*: the degree of stain remaining (let's say) after soaking.

A variable can be either quantitative (something which can be expressed in numbers) or qualitative (something about which the observer makes a value judgement or something based on a relative comparison with another object). In our example, temperature can be measured on a standard scale (degrees Celsius), but the degree of stain remaining will probably be a qualitative variable. We could make the experiment more quantitative by using a light meter, say, to measure the darkness of the stain on white cloth.

The values of the independent variable are usually called *the experimental conditions*. The number of conditions depends on how many values of the independent variable the experimenter wants to test. In our example, suppose we wanted to test 10°C, 20°C, 30°C, 40°C, 50°C, 60°C, 70°C, 80°C, 90°C and 100°C, we would have 10 experimental conditions.

An experiment is described in terms of an *operational definition*. This lists the steps or operations that have to be carried out to observe or measure whatever it is that is being defined. In our example, assuming that we already have lots of cloth stained with a big stain, our steps might be: cut sufficient strips of cloth for testing all the experimental conditions (plus one which will not be soaked, the *control*), heat water to required temperature, submerge cloth for set time (we don't want the time to vary, or it becomes *another* independent variable and it will no longer be possible to tell whether the temperature, the length of time or a combination of the two is responsible for the degree of stain removal), remove cloth, dry it, observe the remaining stain by comparing it to the piece of the same cloth unsoaked, upon completing testing all 10 conditions, compare results.

We've already mentioned the *subject* of our experiment, though not by name, in the paragraph above. *Subject* is also the term for people or animals who undergo an experiment or who are observed. Jane Goodall's observations were of chimpanzees interacting in the wild; the chimpanzees were the *subjects* of her study. It is important in many types of experiments to make decisions about what kind of subjects to use. For example, in biological, medical or psychological experiments and observations it is usually impossible to make every individual a subject, so experimenters must choose subjects from among the set of all possible subjects. When this is done, we say we choose a *sample*. We have to have some basis for choosing. It may be *random* (a method whereby each individual in the whole of the population has an equal chance of being chosen). If subjects come from a 'captive audience', then the sample is not random and one cannot think of these subjects as forming a sample of any general population. Experimenters may make their own subjects – in our example the experimenter may soak a cotton cloth in raspberry juice to create a stain to test.

The change in the dependent variable produced by change in the independent variable is called the *experimental effect*. (However, there may be changes produced by variables other than the independent variable.) The experimenter has to design experiments to negate, to the greatest degree possible, these other variables or the effects of these other variables. It is the attempt to do this that makes science appear so reductionist – it is too difficult to deal with multiple independent variables (possible causes for the effect observed) so as many as possible of them are eliminated. The more control the experimenter has over the conditions of the experiments, the less likely it is that the experiments will be invalidated by the interfering effects from other variables. In our example, we want to be certain that time soaking is not such another variable, so we need a stop-watch to ensure that no one strip of cloth soaks any less or more than any other subject. We also want to draw the water from the same source, so that, for example, water hardness or softness does not vary.

The penultimate step is to evaluate results and publish. The evaluation often involves experimenters in subjecting the data they have gathered to statistical or other mathematical analyses. Publication must occur in a reputable, refereed journal (a refereed journal is one where the papers submitted are sent by the journal to independent experts for opinions as to the soundness of the work and whether or not the papers should be published by the journal in question).

A last step entirely outside the experimenter's control occurs when the experimenter's peers read the journal paper. They may put forward and publish criticisms of it, or try to duplicate the experiments in their own laboratories to determine the validity of the results. Because of subtle differences in techniques, materials and so forth, they may or may not obtain results consistent with those claimed, and publish in support or in criticism of the original paper.

In addition to absorbing ideas about science based on outdated or fictional representations, the media often misinterpret scientific findings. It is common to find that a relatively small research finding carefully reported in a scientific paper can end up appearing to promise, in the popular press, a cure for cancer when in fact the finding only points to a possible avenue of exploration for a better understanding of the mechanisms involved in just one form of the disease. This has the effect of leading the public to expect more of science than it can produce. Eventually, disillusion sets in and science is 'blamed' for its failure to produce the promised miracles (Florman, 1991).

PERCEPTIONS OF SCIENCE

It is inherent in scientific practice that scientists constantly argue about the nature and value of their work. Often this argument is limited in scope to which project gets the backing of the university department in seeking resources, but much wider-ranging and more fundamental arguments occur. Below I outline some of the perceptions and concerns that inform these arguments. However, it is important to note that these perceptions and concerns do not constitute mutually exclusive categories: any one person may hold overlapping or multiple views about science itself or even about individual scientific projects.

Science for knowledge's sake

This view holds that science is the seeking of knowledge for its own sake. It assumes knowledge is value-free and the search for it should remain unfettered.

> . . . if we make *good* things [as a result of scientific investigation], it is not only to the credit of science; it is also to the credit of the moral choice which led us to good work. Scientific knowledge is an enabling power to do either good or bad – but it does not carry instructions on how to use it.
>
> *(Feynman, 1988, p. 241)*

Science and its ethics

An ethical argument can be made that scientific enquiry should not be free and unfettered because its potential application has an ethical dimension that must be determined beforehand. The direction that enquiry should take can be determined ahead of time for the greater good, which may be a social good or a religious good (science as a study of the universe undertaken to understand God's will) or a combination of both. Frequent ethical questions arise in medical research in particular: should enquiry be undertaken to determine cause and prevention as opposed to cure, and should less harmful and invasive means of treatment be explored and developed fully rather than accept the more drastic treatments? Who should be subjects of experiments, and under what conditions should experiments be conducted?

Big science and little science

A version of the ethical approach looks at the costs of scientific enquiry and the benefits which may derive. This cost–benefit analysis asks the question: can society afford a particular kind of science?

Some research results in direct benefits to human life: for example, the development of the germ theory of disease transmission provided a sound basis for arguments about the provision of clean water supplies and improved sanitation, which in turn resulted in diseases like cholera and dysentery becoming rare; the development of penicillin as a drug virtually eliminated amputations and deaths from septicaemia. Other areas of research are of doubtful or negative benefit (for example, weapons research). Still others are very expensive to undertake but do not result in any obvious benefit other than the extension of knowledge (for example, particle physics and astronomy). A cost–benefit approach assumes that we have limited resources of time, money and trained scientists and that we must make decisions about which projects to fund based on how much benefit can be achieved at what cost, and to whom.

Figure 1.1.1
Death (cholera) pumping water. The germ theory of disease transmission provided a sound basis for arguments about the provision of clean water supplies and improved sanitation.

Big science like astronomy is very costly.[2] So is research into drugs, where individual projects may provide great or little benefit, and the benefit may be primarily to a commercial organization which gets a return on its investment, or it may be of greater general benefit or both. Small science is inexpensive and may provide great or little benefit, depending on the project. Both big and little science may undertake projects of a similar nature: for example, research into drugs can be done on a large scale, as it is in the multinational drug companies, or on a small scale, for example in Nicaragua where the resource-poor health service undertakes research in herbal medicine to try to provide maximum health benefits to the population at as low a cost as possible. The hidden agenda for funding big science where little or no benefit accrues beyond the extension of knowledge is often that undertaking such research bestows prestige on the nation, the institutions and the individuals concerned.

The sociological view of science

Science can be influenced by struggles for personal, political, organizational and national power; this is especially clear when funding is in question or honour is to be bestowed. Langdon Winner (1991), speculating on modern science and technology states:

> Knowledge products, sometimes mistakenly called discoveries, are crafted within a complex, multi-centred social process . . . The credit lavished on the likes of Newton, Edison and Pasteur is better placed within the complex relations that link science and society in myriad patterns.

Another 'problem' in the conduct of science is its intensely competitive nature. While scientific teams co-operate among themselves, a team is in competition with others working in similar areas. The competition among scientists is more often for prestige than for money; however, prestige can guarantee the flow of funds to a research group. In addition, scientists may have an eye on whose name will go in the history books alongside important discoveries.

Watson and Crick, credited with the discovery of the DNA molecule for which they were jointly awarded a Nobel prize, failed to acknowledge their debt to Rosalind Franklin, whose painstaking work gave them considerable additional evidence. Watson, writing in 1968, belittled Franklin's contribution and indeed implied that she was 'difficult to work with' – he apparently did not like her cautious approach. Subsequently he added an afterword to his book, partly retracting his earlier position regarding her contribution. But his failure to credit Franklin fully grew out of both the 'great man' [sic] attitude to science and the fierce competition that prevails in much of science, where sharing credit amounts to diluting one's own contribution and lessens the likelihood of receiving a lion's share of funding and such prestigious recognition as the Nobel award.

Problems with method

Reductionism necessitated by the experimental method means that findings of experiments are often difficult to re-integrate into an understanding of more complex phenomena. The germ theory of disease, for example, makes it difficult to integrate observations that disease, even when it results from the presence of pathogens such as bacteria, often follows stress, or that changes in the environment may be responsible for changes in levels of certain types of disease (as in the example of bilharzia cited below).

It can be argued that method as currently defined in fact limits enquiry: peer review and the fear of negative peer reaction confines enquiry to 'acceptable' channels, ignoring possible valid lines of enquiry by designating them unacceptable. A science that uses all forms of ideas in its search for knowledge, rather than a science limited to acceptable 'scientific' ideas, could produce better results:

> There is no idea, however ancient and absurd, that is not capable of improving our knowledge. The whole history of thought [could be] absorbed into science and ... used for improving every single theory. Nor [should] political influence [be] rejected. It may be needed to overcome the chauvinism of science that resists alternatives to the status quo.
>
> *(Feyerabend, 1975, p. 47)*

A problem here is that the earliest hypothesis to be published which adequately explains the phenomenon observed becomes the 'working' hypothesis, no matter how many other hypotheses that can fully explain the phenomenon follow it. The first hypothesis must be *disproved* before it loses its primary position.

Further, there are subtle, unconscious influences on scientific methods:

> Science bears the imprint of its makers; the empirical and conceptual constraints familiar to objectivists underdetermine virtually all scientific conclusions leaving considerable scope for the influence of such supposedly non-cognitive variables as gender ideology.
>
> *(Harding, 1986)*

TECHNOLOGY: WHAT IS IT?

Technology is both older than science and has had a much greater influence on the daily lives of people. *Tekhne* means art (in the sense of 'way of doing') and *logike* means reasoning – therefore reasoning about the art of doing. Technology is about coping with needs for food, shelter, health, communication and so forth in a practical way, by reasoning about available or possible materials and by using that reasoning to design and make practical objects, including tools used to make new materials, objects and tools. Many of these basic concerns for food, shelter, health and communication are, at the most fundamental level, domestic and therefore commonly fall into the sphere of women's work. Technology encompasses everything from the simplest stone, wood and bone tools and the modification of animal skins for purposes of clothing to automobiles, trains, systems for delivery of power, water and sanitation to homes, television, computers, the telephone system, textiles, cosmetics and modern weaponry.

Technology was frequently appropriated from the Third World by the West. The British, for example, considered Indian steel to be the best in the world in the 1790s and expropriated their techniques, making improvements on them. The result of this appropriation and improvement (and particularly of mechanization) is that indigenous industries become less economically competitive, wither and eventually die. The 'colony' comes to depend on the 'imperial' centre (Levidow, 1988). As less economically viable activities wither and die, the colony becomes a net importer of cheap manufactured goods and in turn supplies raw materials, cash crops and cheap labour.

How is technology different from science? Doing rather than discovering

Technology differs from science in that science is about discovering and explaining and technology is about designing and making. So technology encompasses design and method, though modern technology borrows heavily for its knowledge base from modern science. Science, for example, may investigate the properties of steel and plastics and build a body of knowledge about these materials whereas technology uses that knowledge, plus practical knowledge acquired in practice, to mould steel and plastic to practical ends like providing strong joists for buildings or tools for the kitchen.

MODELS OF TECHNOLOGY

Long and Dowell (1989) describe three models of technology which are generally applicable to understanding what technology is and how it works. Like all such models, there are no hard and fast boundaries between one model and another, and examples can be found which show instances where the models are combined.

The craft model

The craft model of technology most closely characterizes the older technologies such as potting, hand-weaving, wood-working, cookery and so on; it is the 'master–apprentice model' of technology. It makes use of practical rules of thumb, develops with experience, is specific and cannot be easily generalized. It is not often written down, though. For example, these days it is more common to see cookery books which include recipes with lists of ingredients and notes on method, but older cookery books were memory aids, merely listing ingredients; they often assumed that their readers

25

knew a great deal about method and included only the sketchiest of notes. It is much more common nowadays to find manuals for all sorts of craft work, though most acknowledge that they are not substitutes for direct teaching by an expert and practical experience with materials. The craft model characterizes the technology of early periods and the early industrial revolution and technology in many Third World countries.

The engineering model

The engineering model of technology began to emerge in the late Middle Ages. It seeks to apply the practice of hypothesizing (asking 'what if' type questions) and testing to develop the practice of technology. Technology developed with this model is somewhat generalizable and forms a slowly changing body of practical, tested knowledge normally enshrined in writing. This model of technology characterizes nineteenth-century engineering and is still commonly applied today, particularly in established areas like civil engineering (and its concommitant art, architecture) and mechanical engineering. This model has, in the past, excluded women, who are only now gaining some entry as a result of changes in education and training. Past exclusion was either an unconscious result of attitudes about male aptitude for certain tasks or was a matter of explicit policy.

The applied science model

The applied science model of technology applies both prescriptive scientific knowledge and the scientific method to the solution of technological problems. This model characterizes twentieth-century, 'high' technological development, especially in areas such as electrical and electronic engineering, materials science and the systems approach to complex products. It is this form of technology which is most likely to seek to change nature to fit perceived needs. For example, this model of technology applies to the situation where scientific knowledge and experimentation is applied to, say, steel, to force the material into new forms that transcend its normal properties, making it available for new uses. This model tends to have excluded women less than the previous two because the rise of the fully professional technologist has very roughly coincided with women's battles to gain access to universities and the professions for which a university education is the ticket of entry.

Low, high, intermediate and alternative technologies

Low technology can best be defined as the most basic technologies of food production and preparation, shelter-building and body-sheltering (such as simple textiles), health maintenance and communication. These needs tend to be ranked in importance so that food production and preparation and shelter-building and body-sheltering are more immediately important than, say, communication.

High technology is what is usually meant in the West by the term *technology*. High technology encompasses large *systems* for the production of food, the building of shelter and communication, and far more than basic needs are met. (In fact, many needs must be artificially stimulated, as present-day high technology in the West depends upon high demand to achieve economies of scale for production.)

Intermediate technology (sometimes called *appropriate technology*) is a concept which has grown out of attempts to apply technological solutions to problems of underdevelopment in many parts of the world. It was observed that high technology solutions failed partly or wholly to alleviate hunger, poverty and poor health. In many cases, high technology solutions have created more problems than they have solved. Large hydroelectric dams have, for example, created considerable social upheaval, taken land out of agricultural production, had unforeseen environmental impacts and greatly increased the incidence of certain water-borne diseases like bilharzia. This is caused by a parasite which at an intermediate stage in its life-cycle parasitizes a snail found in sluggish or still waters. Dams decrease the flow of water and encourage the spread of the snail which, while acting as a host to the parasite, spreads the disease to humans who wade, bare-footed or -legged, into the water. Bilharzia is not a problem in areas where water flows freely. The main benefit of the dams – the electricity produced – has not improved the lot of local people, who have little need for it and often cannot afford it.

Westerners and their institutions assumed the superiority of a technological way of life and based their models of development on it. However, to modernize along either Western capitalist or Soviet lines would be disastrous in ecological terms, and probably social terms as well. Intermediate technology seeks to *build* on low technology, local materials and local interest and knowledge by applying a more scientific approach to the development of tools and artefacts. Such technologies 'have often proved better suited to the actual needs and socioeconomic conditions in developing areas than programmes oriented to large-scale, capital-intensive projects' (Adas, 1990). An example of the application of appropriate technology is described by Bina Agarwal in Article 4.2, which describes the development of a more efficient wood-stove for cooking. Such technology often contributes significantly to easing women's work. The improved stove, for instance, greatly reduces the amount of fuelwood needed, and women do most of the fuel-gathering, often over great distances.

Alternative technology is also a more recent concept and is closely allied to the aims of intermediate technology. Alternative technology seeks to minimize the environmental impact of technology by seeking less destructive or resource-hungry ways of doing the same things or nearly the same things that high technology does. For example, the use of solar heating in houses to minimize the consumption of fossil fuels or the use of nuclear-generated electrical power reduces the impact on the environment of home heating. The materials used for solar heating (glass, metal, heat-holding paints) and the methods for determining how to achieve the best placement and use of the heating panels may very well draw on high technology. Calculating the best angle and placement of solar panels is a mathematically exacting exercise. The objective of an alternative technology like solar heating remains the same as that of high technology: to provide a significant measure of comfort (with some health benefits) to human life. Women have a considerable interest, and often an involvement, in alternative technologies. The Women's Environmental Network, described in Article 4.5, is a particular example.

THE ENGINES OF TECHNOLOGY

The development of Western technology as we know it began about the middle of the eighteenth century. Since then, per capita income in the West has increased tenfold, the population of Europe has increased by a factor of five, infant mortality has declined very considerably and the average life-span has doubled.

According to Rosenberg and Birdzell (1990), this cannot be attributed entirely either to imperialism (they note that prosperous European countries like Switzerland and Norway never adopted imperialist policies) or to the possession of abundant natural resources. Rather, they attribute it to a fortunate conjunction of economic needs and economic climate, access to and the dissemination of information about superior technologies, and since the 1880s the input of scientific sources of information. Productive technology has to be shaped to meet local needs, and local people have to be able to understand, experiment with and evaluate it both technologically and economically. For example, Japan in the nineteenth century had little land or capital available but was rich in labour resources. The Japanese quickly adapted techniques from land- and capital-rich (but labour-poor) America or shifted to different technologies. They substituted labour for capital, bought machinery second-hand to preserve their capital and aimed to maintain their investment by careful maintenance and repair of their machinery. The decentralized economies of the West encouraged experimentation with technology as no one institution had a veto on any particular avenue of enquiry or development.

Both the Western and the major socialist economies and technologies have had a heavy dependence on the military; indeed, the military has been an enormous engine of technological development. In the West, in deference to voters' sensibilities about the uses of their tax monies, military technology has commonly provided 'spin-offs' for civilian consumption: nuclear technology can be viewed as a militarily important technology that can be made palatable because it can also produce electrical power; computers were developed firstly for the military and only entered the civilian sphere a decade later. Much research and development in computer technology continues to be funded by the US Department of Defense and the UK Ministry of Defence. Development of lightweight but very strong materials for military aircraft and vehicles may find their way onto the domestic market in improved bicycle frames.

While the military was and remains today a major engine of technological development, individual engineers, designers, applied scientists and technicians often work in the areas they do because they feel strongly that improved and new technologies help in bettering the human condition. As with scientists, their motives may be quite mixed: they may combine a sense of mastery and power over a technology, a sense of curiosity, feelings of altruism and even a sense of the aesthetics of the things they develop.

GENDERING TECHNOLOGY

Technology is, popularly, strongly gendered. Certain technologies – textiles, manual agriculture, food preparation and storage, 'female' medicine and midwifery – are very strongly associated with women while others – hunting, mechanized agriculture, transport, weapons – are equally strongly associated with men.

There is some anecdotal evidence that, even in modern engineering and computing, women bring a different perspective to the work to their male counterparts. Turkle (1984a) notes that boys bring interests to, and use methods for, computer programming that are different from the interests and methods of girls. She fears that attempts to help girls in schools may lead to a different form of gender bias in computing – that girls' interests and methods will be seen as inferior rather than merely different. Florman (1984) notes some informal studies revealing that female engineering students are three times more likely to be interested in literature and broader social issues than their male counterparts. In the Soviet Union, only 5 per cent of women in science and engineering endorsed the party line on the dissident scientist Andrei Sakharov when he was in exile, while 24 per cent of their male colleagues supported the party line, indicating that the women were more willing than men to maintain links with people who are 'out of favour' with the establishment.

Women as scientists and engineers

Three factors are important in an individual's career choices: ability or inclination, access to education and training, and the perceived opportunity to practise a particular career. Women have been excluded from science and engineering careers on all three counts. Most women have met the assumption that 'women are not good at maths'. In the United States, university entrance is based partly on success in the Scholastic Aptitude Tests and it has been observed for years that there is a sex difference in maths scores, with boys achieving an average 45 points (out of 600) more than girls. However, investigation into the reasons for this discrepancy showed that it was not a lack of ability in girls that accounted for lower scores, but the fact that they were very likely to have had a half a year less maths than their male counterparts. In the past, universities also practised subtle and not-so-subtle sex discrimination: not having sufficient residential places available for female applicants, closing certain courses off to them (sometimes with the excuse that chaperoning on field trips would be a problem!). Women are less likely than men to receive public and institutional support even where the women come from families with fewer resources than their male counterparts. Perceptions of opportunity for careers further discourage women from taking up science or engineering – women see few role-models in such areas.

Hornig (1984) argues that, though educationalists feel it is important to reach girls in secondary education to interest them in careers in science and engineering, it is the universities that educate scientists and 'act as gatekeepers to the professions'. According to Hornig, women *appear* to constitute a smaller number of scientists and engineers because they constitute a smaller proportion of these than they do of other fields. In the United States in 1982, for example, about *50,000* women held PhDs in science and engineering, compared with about 20,000 in the humanities. However, science and engineering are very large fields, while humanities departments in universities (who mainly employ women with humanities PhDs) are relatively very small. Thus women constitute a larger proportion of the humanities (over one-quarter) than they do the sciences and engineering (where they constitute about 12 per cent).

While the picture is changing slowly, Hornig comments that scientists are not noted for their objectivity and unbiased judgement where social observations and decisions are called for. Science and engineering remain predominantly male and the university departments are still run by the men who made or enforced discriminatory rules in the recent past.

A similar gender gap exists in jobs. Fewer women than men who pursue a scientific or engineering career are likely to end up as managers, while more women are likely to end up in the less well-paid and less secure support activities: acting as librarians, collecting data and writing reports. Women scientists and engineers argue that the personal and psychological costs of pursuing a career beset by curtailed opportunity, token status and discriminatory employment practices are so high that they find it difficult to function in their chosen field, or even at times to function at all. The male 'mould' imposed on science and engineering, particularly in such fields as high-energy physics, makes them especially alien to women. Traweek (1984) observed that the traits required for entry into the world of high-energy physics were especially masculine: 'aggressive individualism, haughty self-confidence and a sharp competitive edge'.

Harassment exists in all workplaces: a very senior environmental engineer found that men tried either to treat her as something of a joke or to 'father' her. One man, accompanying her at a particularly toxic site, expressed concern lest she jeopardize her childbearing potential. She pointed out, much to his embarrassment, that he was equally jeopardizing his potential to father children (Hynes, 1984).

CONCLUSION

I have in this article laid some foundations for the debates and issues taken up in the following articles and chapters. Science is not a single ideology: it is a relatively broad church admitting a variety of practices and objectives. While it is critical of itself in its own terms, only recently have both scientists and non-scientists begun to question the historical origins of knowledge, the Western 'scientific miracle', the sociological, political and personal influences on who does science, who gets funding, and how science is done. As with many institutions, science was, almost from its outset, a strongly gendered institution, though some women have always been able to undertake science usually because they were either rich, determined or related to a male scientist. The issue today is how to change this.

Technology is older than science and in many places exists without scientific input. It encompasses virtually everything that human beings make: from prepared, preserved and stored foodstuffs of the most basic kind to the most complex systems for transport and communication. Much of technology, particularly of the domestic variety, has always been in the purview of women, but strongly gendered notions of the relations a human being should have with a machine or tool have tended to exclude women from participation in modern, high technology. Technology can be carried out as a craft, as an engineering discipline or as applied science. Since a participant in technological design, at whatever level, has to be able

31

to appreciate the technology and evaluate it, women may be excluded even from simple technologies that have enormous impact on their daily lives.

The articles that follow discuss how women and feminists are changed by science and technology or seek to change practice by challenging underlying, often unspoken, gender assumptions. Outright rejection of science is an extreme position based on Foucauldian analysis; feminist scientists and technologists seek to keep objectivity as the centre of science but to show how conscious and especially unconscious attitudes to gender *and* race distort science. Women are now finding an increasing interest in technology, particularly in appropriate (intermediate) and alternative technologies because they are either concerned to lighten their crushing labour burdens or to carry out the function of living without unduly degrading the environment.

Notes

1   The study of animal behaviour. Women like Jane Goodall and Dian Fossey have been pre-eminent in modern ethological studies.

2   Whether a particular science is costly or not may depend upon the type of project undertaken; while the Hubble Space Telescope is enormously expensive, valid astronomical observations continue to be made by unpaid amateurs using relatively inexpensive telescopes and cameras.

Article 1.2
WOMEN'S VOICES/MEN'S VOICES: TECHNOLOGY AS LANGUAGE

Margaret Lowe Benston

Men and women in our society have very different experiences in nearly every aspect of their lives, so it is not surprising to find that their experiences with respect to technology are also very different. Boys and men are expected to learn about machines, tools and how things work. In addition, they absorb, ideally, a 'technological world view' that grew up along with industrial society. Such a world view emphasizes objectivity, rationality, control over nature and distance from human emotions. Conversely, girls and women are not expected to know much about technical matters. Instead, they are to be good at interpersonal relationships and to focus on people and on emotion. They are to be less rational, less capable of abstract, 'objective' thought. (See Chodorow (1978), Benston (1982) and articles in Rothschild (1983).)

These differences have consequences in two different areas: first, technology itself can be seen as a 'language' for action and self-expression with consequent gender differences in ability to use this 'language'. Second, men's control over technology and their adherence to a technological world view have consequences for language and verbal communication and create a situation where women are 'silenced'.

The ideals for men and women are communicated in a variety of ways and are acted on from early childhood. By my early teens, while boys my age were discovering cars and pinball machines, I discovered books and horses. Later in adolescence, Friday night . . . would be spent with the boys discussing cars or football and the girls discussing clothes or gossiping about friends. In school, [technical courses were] required for boys and home economics for girls but even if any of the girls had had a choice we would never have ventured into a world of tools and grease.

Unlike most of the girls I knew, however, I liked science in . . . school and took chemistry . . . in college. I was odd enough to enjoy mathematics and theoretical work but still I avoided or skimped labs. In graduate school, as a physical chemist, I was in one of the 'hard' sciences and my husband was in English, yet he was the one who did the plumbing repairs and tuned up the car. We both liked music but he was the one who discussed needle and speaker characteristics endlessly with his male friends; I would simply let them talk while I listened to the records. Still avoiding lab work, I did a theoretical problem rather than an experimental one for my PhD thesis and later, when I switched to computing science, it was to explore the social implications of this new technology.

There is a clear pattern here. Even though I like mathematics and scientific theory, I have never felt at home around machines and technology. I am not alone in this – it is typical for women. In fact, even with my history of avoidance, I am considerably more at home in the world of machines and equipment than are many women. I have, after all, done laboratory work, however reluctantly, and I do teach technical courses.

This is not to say that women do not use tools and machines in our society. *Everyone* interacts with the underlying technological system. . . Sometimes machines or systems are used by both women and men – we both use the same means of transportation and we both use telephones and TVs. But there *are* important differences. . . [M]uch equipment tends to be gender-typed. There are machines and tools 'suitable' for men – saws, trucks, wrenches, guns and forklifts, for example – and those 'suitable' for women – vacuum cleaners, typewriters and food processors. Even on assembly lines, men make cars and women assemble electronic components or pack fish. Most often, women are excluded from control of large or powerful pieces of equipment. More importantly, women are excluded from an understanding of *technique* and of the physical principles by which machines and tools operate (see, for example, articles in Kelly, 1981).

This exclusion is important because technique is often over-looked as a major component of technology. To simply refer to the machines and tools involved is not a sufficient definition of any system of technology; often the underlying knowledge or technique is more important than the actual machines. After all, if all the machines are destroyed, they can still be rebuilt as long as the human beings who built them retain the knowledge that was used to build them in the first place. Technique includes not only this knowledge of how to construct equipment but the knowledge of how to use it. It further includes much basic scientific knowledge, such as that required to control the chemical processes involved in refining or the physical principles involved in electronics. Scientific principles, mathematical techniques and even techniques for organizing production, such as assembly lines, can all be important parts of 'technique' and hence part of technology.

The exclusion of women not only from active practice in scientific and technical fields but from training in basic physical and mechanical principles means that even when women use tools or machines, they are marginal to a male-created and male-dominated technology. (Note: all of this describes the usual situation for most Western women, not the invariable rule for each individual. . . Note also that, although this paper is concerned with gender differences in technology processes, it is important to recognize that there are other ways in which access to tools and technique is not equal for everyone. We live in a society of institutionalized hierarchy and sexism; in addition to gender, race and class are also factors in determining such access.)

Besides gender differences in access because of experience and training, there are differences because of the very logic of the tools and techniques of our society. As a social force, technology has moved far beyond a relationship between an individual and their tools. It is now deeply intertwined with major institutions of the society, most notably industry, government and the military. As Dickson notes, 'the institutionalization of technology has meant that the choice of particular machines [and techniques], or at least the control over this choice, remains in the hands of a dominant social class' which exercises fundamental power in the society (1974, p. 177). This dominant class, which is almost exclusively white and male, operates on a logic of profit and of maintaining their control over society. The technical world view, mentioned earlier, is a straightforward reflection of their world and their interests (though it is also shared by white, working-class and minority men who are not so well served by it. . .

For those of us seeking a more egalitarian, co-operative society, many fundamental tools and techniques – such as those to support democratic decision making and communications – simply do not exist. The telephone system, for example, makes communication between two people easy but it is very difficult to arrange a group discussion. This situation is quite appropriate to an individualistic society but not necessarily in one where co-operation is more highly valued. . .

The logic of ruling-class men then leads to a technology that reflects ruling-class men's experience and view of reality. As mentioned earlier, this view of reality is, to a large extent, shared by other men in the society. The fact that much of the technology of modern industrial society is more compatible with male habits of mind and experience than it is with those of women thus imposes a second kind of limit to women's access to this technology.

TECHNOLOGY AS A LANGUAGE OF ACTION

Introduction

As Dickson (1974, pp. 176–7) points out, technology can serve as a 'language' of social action. The technology available at any specific time provides a range of options for acting on the world. Dickson's point is primarily that these options function rather like words in a language. In the case of language itself you must use the words as given in attempting to speak; in the case of technology, you must use what tools and techniques are available in any attempt to carry out a particular action.

The direct analogy falters because while one can usually find words and or combinations of words to express new meanings, actions are more constrained by the available technology. We can carry out only those activities where suitable techniques or machines are available. One cannot travel by public [transport] to places that don't have service, for example, and, as I have painfully learned in doing simple household maintenance, simple jobs become impossible if you don't have a Phillips screwdriver when you need one. . .

The 'language' for action provided by the technological options available to a person must be understood then as one that imposes limits on what can be 'said'. The range of options for any person at any given period reflects the characteristics of the society of that period. As we saw above, men and women have different access to training, knowledge and confidence around technology. One result of this difference is that men have access to much more of the technological realm than women have and their potential for action is correspondingly much larger . . . Women's domain contains fewer and less powerful machines, and women typically do not engage in behaviour that changes the physical world or involves much control over it.

A second consideration is that the technology itself may not be suitable for things that women would like to 'say'. Expressions of community through group conversations on the telephone are, as we have seen, nearly impossible. As another example, if one should want to live in some kind of co-operation with nature rather than in a relationship of exploitation and domination, then very little technology exists to help (Dickson, 1974; Merchant, 1980).

Technology and power

Differences in the ability to act, to express oneself, are not neutral. Use of any of the different options communicates a great deal of information about the one who is acting. Men not only have access to a much wider range of action around technology than women do but that action implies a great deal more control over the physical and social world.

This question of control is, I think, a central one in understanding why the logic of present technology makes it inaccessible to women. Domination over nature, i.e. control over the physical world, is a central feature of much of present-day technology. Part of the technical world view . . . is the belief in one's *right* to control the material world. Part of successful socialization as a man in our society involves gathering confidence in one's actual *ability* to

36

exercise that control. Women generally do not think they have the right to control the material world and have little confidence in their ability to; as long as they doubt either, it is very difficult for them to use a technology created by those who accept domination/control as a given.

This does not necessarily mean that women must learn to accept the technical world view unquestioningly. Increasingly feminists have been raising the question as to whether or not this kind of domination over nature *is* in fact legitimate (see Griffin, 1978, and Merchant, 1980). From this might follow the development of new technologies based on different assumptions about the world and on a changed relationship to nature. Keller (1983), Arditti *et al.* (1980) and Easlea (1978) all discuss these issues. Such alternatives to present technology could provide a 'vocabulary' that is more compatible with experiences and issues outside the mainstream technical view of the world.

In the present situation, however, power is the most important message that male use of technology communicates. Power over technology and the physical world is just one aspect of men's domination of this society. Patriarchy in the West means that not only is it white men (and a minority of these) who hold political power and the prestige positions but that individual men have control over individual women. Male power over technology is both a product of and a reinforcement for their other power in society. Even at the household level, every time a man repairs the plumbing or a sewing machine while a woman watches, a communication about her helplessness and inferiority is made. . .

Technology as self-expression

A specific machine or tool can be used as an individual statement or means of expression. For example, men seem to identify with their cars as expressions of themselves more than women do and often are explicit in using them as symbols. As one of the most obvious examples, the very existence of 'muscle cars' and the image these cars project comes out of a particular ideal of macho masculinity. (And it would seem that the working-class or black men who most often drive these cars are using this image as a substitute for the actual power and control over their lives that they lack.)

Ghetto blasters are also obviously used, most often by young males, black and white, to make a statement that seems to include an aggressive claim to public space and a hostility to any other claims on that space. Guns are widely regarded as symbolic penises, and military technology can be an expression of male potency. . . The lead guitarist in the local rock band, like the owner of a muscle car or an MX missile, can use his instrument to communicate a particular vision of male sexuality and power. For years, executives expressed their eminence by their *refusal* to use a technology, i.e. executives did not type since the typewriter was a female tool. However, with the advent of electronic office systems, it's now called 'keyboarding' instead of 'typing' and, since a computer is involved, it's okay for executives to do it. In each of these cases, the technology is used by men to express something of their perceived relationship with the social world.

Because of the gender differences discussed above, women use technology much less as a means of symbolic self-expression. Clothes and cosmetics are the traditional means of expressing femininity and an association with anything technological is definitely unfeminine.

[···]

EFFECTS OF TECHNOLOGY ON VERBAL COMMUNICATION

Women's silence

Gender differences around technology have consequences for verbal communication as well. In her book *Man Made Language*, Dale Spender (1980) is concerned with differences in the ways that women and men use language. In particular, she introduces Edwin Ardener's concept of women as a 'muted' and men as a 'dominant' group with respect to language, meaning and communication. Ardener (1975) argued that in patriarchal cultures, men create the general system of meanings for the society and then validate those meanings by asking other men if they are correct. Women are muted because they have no part in the creation and validation of meaning. The result is that it is difficult for women to express themselves: the concepts and vocabulary available to them are those that come out of male experience.

Inherent in this analysis is the 'assumption that women and men will generate different meanings, that is, that there is more than one perceptual order, but that only the "perceptions" of the dominant group, with their inherently partial nature, are encoded and transmitted' (Spender, 1980, p. 77).

Men's perceptions are heavily influenced by technology and a technological world view. Men are expected to be rational, objective and able to keep emotions out of most parts of their lives. The characteristics of stereotypical scientists or engineers are only a slight exaggeration of the traits of normal men. It is not clear whether the technical world view with its emphasis on facts, control, rationality and distance from emotion or personal considerations is a cause or an effect of the definition of normal masculinity but it is clear that the two are deeply interwoven. Even the ideal businessman, operating according to objective logic and the latest principles of scientific management, represents the technical world view in action.

Men and women have access to different vocabularies, experiences and concepts around tools, machines and technique. Women are excluded from education and action in the realm of technology. They do not have the same access to technique or the same experience with concepts and equipment that men do. They are not expected to act from a technical view of the world. Instead, women's world is one of people, nurturance and emotion. Ideal women are expected to be experts in human relations and, in relations with men, to supply emotional depth and insight. The highly technological world of men is one of single cause and effect, of order and control, of rationality; the human world of women is more complicated and less logical. It involves resolution of conflicts between the world of facts and the world of emotion, commitment and responsibility to others. It often involves contradictions arising out of conflicting duties and conflicting loyalties (see Gilligan, 1982).

[· · ·]

Besides men's control over the creation of meaning, they also have control over styles of communication. Articles in Thorne *et al.* (1983), along with material in Spender (1980), outline a variety of ways in which male control over the terms of communication can lead to women's inability to participate. Of interest for our argument are, first, the insistence, particularly in public discourse, on the separation of the 'personal' from the 'scholarly', 'scientific' or 'rational', and, second, the emphasis in public styles on verbal competitiveness and dominance.

The terms of the discourse as given by men put women at an immediate disadvantage. Men are *experts*; women are not. The TV images of a male authority figure using pseudo-scientific terms to sell detergent or orange juice or headache remedies to women is merely an exaggeration of the ordinary terms of communication between men and women. Men see themselves as authorities; their real power in society, their scientific/technical world view and the fact that men do have more expertise in a wide variety of 'male' areas make this inevitable. Control over and understanding of technology is only one facet of that expertise but it is an important one in a society increasingly technologically based. The areas of male expertise are defined by them as the only legitimate areas of concern; women's whole realm is dismissed as unworthy of serious notice. The resulting communication between men and women is then largely asymmetric and women's contribution is often mainly that of finding topics that men want to discuss (Spender, 1980).

[· · ·]

Communicating about technology

The inequality resulting from male control over the terms of communication can be seen clearly when technology itself becomes the subject matter of the discourse. Men, in general, relate to other men as equals around technology: they exchange information and discuss points of interest. Where men have interests in some common technical area, either at work or as a hobby, such discussion is a way of relating to peers and a common language to share interests and knowledge.

Men and women do not, however, communicate as equals about technology. The information flow is almost entirely one-sided: men may *explain* a technological matter to women but they do not discuss it with them; that they do with other men. The education process in technological fields, for example, is heavily dependent on learning from fellow students and this asymmetry becomes a major problem for women. It is very difficult to discuss technical problems, particularly experimental ones, with male peers – they either condescend or they want to simply do whatever it is for you. In either case, asking a question or raising a problem in discussion is proof (if any is needed) that women don't know what they are doing. Other male students, needless to say, do not get this treatment – whatever it is becomes a joint problem to be solved.

Generally, because they lack knowledge, women do not discuss technology with other women at all. When they do, my experience in scientific work has been that since most women scientists have learned male styles, the discussion is most often conducted in terms indistinguishable from male conversations. . .

Tunnel vision

The general inequality in communication is unfair to women but it also has consequences for men. Spender points out that men frequently 'don't know what women are talking about' (1980, p. 96). In part, she says, this results from the kind of *tunnel vision* that comes from total acceptance of the dominant definition of reality. Women must at least recognize that there are different points of view and must know enough of the dominant one to survive within it. When men have uncritically accepted the scientific/technical world view, they tend to view the kinds of issues important to women and the solutions they find to problems as absurd and illogical. With no perception of the assumptions underlying the non-technological world view that comes out of women's experience and women's responsibilities, they are literally unable to understand what is being said.

CONCLUSION

Men and women seem to inhabit different worlds. All too often they speak to each other only across a gulf of misunderstanding or inequality. Women have lost a great deal from this state of affairs: the whole realm of technology and the communication around it reinforces ideas of women's powerlessness. Men lose by this too: they lose touch with a reality outside their own technical world view. In addition, both men and women lose the chance to develop a technology that would serve other goals than those of a small group of privileged white men.

There is no easy solution to the problem. Yes, women do need to learn more about technology and gain more confidence. Yes, men do need to be more sensitive to other perceptions. But these are only preconditions. Fundamental change can only come about by an attack on all the structures of domination in the society. As a part of this, we will have to change science and technology to give more primacy to the kinds of approaches now considered feminine. If we can do that, the consequences will be new kinds of technology as well as new kinds of people. Both of these will be necessary for ending the barriers that now exist between men and women.

Article 1.3

HOW GENDER MATTERS, OR, WHY IT'S SO HARD FOR US TO COUNT PAST TWO

Evelyn Fox Keller

I often think that the juxtaposition of the terms gender and science serves as a kind of Rorschach test[1] – by which I mean that the responses and associations it evokes can be read as a key to deep conflicts and confusions about both gender and science that almost all of us live with. These conflicts and confusions are manifested in a number of ways – perhaps all of them variants of what we might call the one-two step (or sometimes the two-one step).

One version goes like this: . . . I tell an anecdote illustrating a rather typical response I get from people when I tell them that I work on gender and science: 'How interesting', they say. 'What is it that you've learned about women in science?' The replacement of 'and' by 'in' is clear enough, and perhaps not too indicative, because we all tend to be pretty sloppy about the little words in our language, but the replacement of gender by women is both less clear, and, I think, finally more significant. But even accepting this replacement, there are still roughly three variants or stages – like stages of cognitive development. In the first stage, the reality – both social and cognitive – that is implicitly presupposed is fixed. Gender is determined by biology, and science, by nature. People (along with other animals) manifest in their behaviour their inner natures as determined by the presence of an X or Y chromosome. In this framing of the world, where there are two genders, and one science, the subject of gender and science becomes fairly boring – it immediately reduces to a discussion of 'why women are unfitted for science'. Such a discussion may in fact be no longer fashionable these days, but it is nonetheless still logically compatible with the basic assumptions that are, if anything, newly fashionable – at least in some quarters (particularly sociobiology and certain kinds of brain research).

A slight increase in sophistication leads us to see these claims as referring to 'stereotypes' about gender. We can call this stage two. Now, the subject of gender and science becomes translated into 'Women aren't really unfitted for science; they are only said to be so' – or, with yet a little more sophistication, 'Women aren't unfit for science by nature, only by nurture – i.e. they are made so'. That is to say, the world is truly unitary, divided only in appearance – either (merely) by language or (merely) by social convention. Our task, therefore, as enlightened critics, is to restore its natural unity. This is the two-one step – it is the move that has historically been taken by women in science, and for good political reasons. Women had observed that the division of the world into two serves them poorly – it serves to exclude them from the domain of public life, of power, and of science. The claim that we are different meant that we are less. Quite reasonably, therefore, women fighting for admission into the world of science countered with the claim, no, we are not different. But, there's a hidden kicker in this move, that only becomes evident with the question: different, or not different, from whom? . . .

The problem of the hidden referent in this strategy appeared not to concern most of these early feminists – certainly not nearly as much as it has begun to worry modern feminists. We are speaking, of course, of the problem that inheres in the fact that the universal standard is after all not neutral – of what happens to our strategy, and our thinking about gender and science when we begin to notice that the universal man is, in fact, male. The first thing this recognition enables us to do is to begin to make sense of the failure of the promise of equity. To be included in the big 'one' means not to be equally represented, but to be unrepresented. It is to be swallowed up whole, negated in the quest for assimilation – as it were, a hole in 'one'.

A simple story may serve to illustrate. A committee . . . was charged with the task of determining the causes of continuing inequity of women in the biological sciences. After reviewing possible claims of ongoing discrimination, the Committee rejected these as explanations, and concluded that the problem lay elsewhere. 'Women', they felt obliged to conclude, 'are not sufficiently aggressive to successfully compete at the forefront of modern research'.

This is a point worth pausing at in order to take note of the fact that it did not occur to anyone on the Committee that there was in fact more than one possible response to this judgement, namely, 'How can we train (or remake) women to be more aggressive?' When I tried to suggest the possibility of alternative responses to a member of the Committee, she proved remarkably resistant, until, all of a sudden, she turned to me: 'Do you mean to say there would be a female science?'

This is the one-two step. Gender has become abruptly collapsed back into sex, reminding us that there really are two. But now, instead of, as in the first stage, two sexes and one science, the suggestion is that there are two sexes and two sciences. Men and women are once again born, but now science is made. This I might call stage three.

When it comes, this shift – from no difference, or universality, to absolute difference, or duality – comes surprisingly fast. Certainly, it came very fast in the recent history of the subject of gender and science. My own first attempts to discuss these issues (as recently as 1978) met with absolute resistance, even – or perhaps even especially – among feminists. Just a few short years later, the notion of a feminist science – by which people usually mean a feminine science – has become something of a rage. It is rather like the invertible figure/ground diagrams,[2] the ease and rapidity of the shift suggesting that universality and duality are, in some basic sense, two sides of the same coin.

Figure 1.3.1
A well-known example of a reversible figure/ground diagram showing either a vase or two faces in profile. If you continue to stare at the figure, the figure/ground relation will spontaneously change back and forth.

(Because confusion is so easy here, let me make it absolutely clear that this is not an argument for duality – for a female science either to replace or supplement a male science. That is, I do not believe that science is written in our chromosomes . . .)

We can see a somewhat different version of the same one-two step when we look at another tack people have taken in their thinking about gender and science – a tack which focuses not on the sociology of sex and gender but on its biology. Which is to say, where the issue of concern becomes the biology of sex (in biological terms, there is no language for distinguishing sex and gender). Note also though, that the biology of sex in turn, again tends to be translated into the biology of women.

Here, feminists – many of them the very same feminists who fought against forms of stereotypic socialization that work to exclude women from science (and other domains of power) – now turned their attention to the uses of biology in perpetuating the exclusion of women – where biology is not any longer understood as biological nature, but as a scientific construction. That is to say, these critics put a wedge between science and nature rather than between sex and gender.

In short, feminist scientists began to think about the political and social contributions to sexual segregation made by their own profession, giving rise to such critiques as *Alice Through the Microscope* (Brighton Women and Science Group, 1980), *Women Look at Biology Looking at Women* (Hubbard, Henefin and Fried, 1979), *Woman's Nature* (Hubbard and Lowe, 1983) or, more recently, *Science and Gender* (Bleier, 1984). In much of this work, we find a view on the subject of gender and science that might be represented by the translation of science and gender to the science of gender, and more specifically, to the biology of women.

What emerges from these extremely important and valuable analyses is the inescapable conclusion that the science of gender is not very scientific, whether we are talking about hormonal studies, brain studies or sociobiology. Indeed, the science of gender appears to be no more scientific than the science of race has been. The claims of sex differences, like those of race differences, are more often properly seen as the starting points of these studies, rather than the conclusions. But where, in the past, critiques of bias and ideology in the science of race led to a repudiation of this work – by scientists and liberals alike – as scientifically flawed, i.e. racist science was bad science, here a major strain of the feminist critique of the science of gender does not remain content with the equation of androcentric or misogynist science with bad science, but goes beyond the repudiation of the science of gender as failing in objectivity, to a repudiation of objectivity itself as an androcentric value. The need, it is now concluded, is not simply the upholding of more rigorous standards but a different kind of science, perhaps a 'gynocentric' science. This is an extraordinary move for a number of reasons.

First, like the one-two step before, it takes us from a position predicated on the denial of sex differences to one which affirms sex differences, with hardly a blink. Second, it is a move which effectively undermines the very critique that led to it. That is, step two is a step which undoes step one. If objectivity is a male value, a code word for domination and therefore not good science, then subjectivity is a female value and good science is one which affirms good values. Or, unpacking this move a little more, it goes from showing that science is not always value-free to the position that all science is inescapably value-laden. Hence the equation between good science and value-free science breaks down and can be replaced by another equation: good science is science that embodies good values. If science does not mirror the oneness of nature, then it must mirror the twoness of us. But now our critique of the science of gender has in fact become redundant. What matters is not that that work is not objective, but that it embodies the values of patriarchy. (Parenthetically, we might note a step which appears to follow quite easily – namely from the twoness of us, to the infinity of us's. That is, having given up on objectivity, we might be tempted to say that there are as many sciences as the perspectives we might hold – indeed, infinitely many . . .)

What I suggest is that the ease of the transition from one to two, or even from two to infinity, is indicative of a more general problem or paradox latent in much of contemporary perceptions about science, not only in discussions of gender and science. Many people, including scientists themselves, seem to believe, at one and the same time, that 'of course' the practice of science is not objective, and 'of course', what distinguishes science, and accounts for its triumphs, is precisely its objectivity. The first of these beliefs owes a large debt to a pair of ideas emerging from the philosophy of science in the early 1960s, and then rapidly rising to favour: one is that 'observation is theory-laden', and the other that theories are value-laden. Half assimilated, these ideas co-exist, more or less uncomfortably, with the continuing claim that the practice of science justifies itself by 'progressive' discovery and successful prediction.

In other words, the same kind of schizophrenia plagues our thinking about science as plagues our thinking about gender: both fixed, natural categories in one moment, and constructed, perhaps even indefinitely plastic, categories in another. Having no good way of mediating between these two sets of insights, we manage to slip readily from one to the other – back and forth between objective realism and relativism on the one hand, and between universality and duality on the other. The question is: how can we get past this impasse?

I suggest that a better understanding of the insights from both feminist theory and the social studies of science, and even more an integration of these insights, points us in the direction of resolving these paradoxes – towards learning to count past two, and in the process towards a radically expanded meaning of what the subject of gender and science is about. Feminist theory has brought home to us that gender is neither simply the manifestation of sex, nor simply an easily dispensable artefact of culture. It is, instead, what a culture makes of sex – it is the cultural transformation of male and female infants into adult men and women. . .

46

Similarly science is neither a mirror of nature, nor simply a reflection of culture. It is the name we give to a set of practices and a body of knowledge delineated by a community – constrained although certainly not contained by the exigencies of logical proof and experimental verification.

The relationship between gender and science is a pressing issue not simply because women have been historically excluded from science, but because of the deep interpenetration between our cultural construction of gender and our naming of science. The same cultural tradition that names rational, objective and transcendent as male, and irrational, subjective and immanent as female also simultaneously names the scientific mind as male and material nature as female. Beginning with Francis Bacon and continuing into our own times, the very same sexual division of emotional and intellectual labour that frames the maturation of male and female infants into adult men and women also simultaneously divides the epistemological practices and bodies of knowledge we call science from those we call not-science. Modern science is constituted around a set of exclusionary oppositions, in which that which is named feminine is excluded, and that which is excluded – be it feeling, subjectivity or nature – is named female. Actual human beings are of course never fully bound by stereotypes, and some men and some women – and some scientists – will always go beyond them. But at the same time stereotypes are never idle. To a remarkable degree, to learn to be a scientist is to learn the attributes of what our culture calls masculinity. It is to learn how to perform in (or on) a (conceptual) world definitively cleft in two. This core observation – of the historic naming of science as male and nature as female, and of scientific as masculine and unscientific as feminine – causes an immediate expansion of the subject of gender and science. From the comparatively simple questions about women in science, or about the biology of women, grows a much larger set of questions about how our ideas of gender have helped shape our construction of science, and how our ideas about science have influenced our construction of gender – in short, it becomes a study of the simultaneous making of men, women and science. And it is to this study that much of my own work – as well as that of a growing number of other feminist scholars – has been devoted.

By now, we have a considerable literature that has documented an extensive interpenetration between scientific, philosophical and gender discourse. This literature has emerged in a critique of traditional notions of objectivity as deeply intertwined with traditional notions of masculinity. I would argue that in the effort, important aspects of the social, historical and psychological dynamics of this intertwining have been illuminated. But in many ways, the question that must inevitably be of greatest interest to scientists –

namely, what difference does such a gendered discourse make to science – that question has only begun to be addressed. It is easy enough to say, and to show, that the language of science is riddled with patriarchal imagery, but it is far more difficult to show – or even to think about – what effect a non-patriarchal discourse would have had or would now have (supposing that we could learn to ungender our discourse). In short, *what does language have to do with science?* This, I suggest, is the real task that faces not only feminist critiques of science, but all of the history, philosophy and sociology of science.

The major problem that confronts us in this task derives from the fact that modern science, as we know it, has arisen once and only once in cultural history. That is, we cannot say of science what we can say of gender – namely that all cultures do it. We cannot look to other cultures, with other gender systems, and ask how their science is or was different for the simple reason that the knowledge practices of other cultures do not conform to what we call science. . . The point to keep in mind, however, is that this inability reflects not so much the failure of other cultures, but precisely the social character of the process by which science gets named – even, or especially, good science. And in fact, attending to this process shows us a way out of our difficulty.

What all social studies of science see when they look closely at the process by which good science is named is a variety and range of practices, visions and articulations of science far in excess of any ideological prescriptions. As in the case of gender stereotypes, ideological norms may be formative but they are never fully binding. In every period of scientific history, in every school of science, we can see a rich diversity of meanings and practices. In fact, it would appear that where ideology makes its force felt most crucially is in its role in the process by which some theories, methodologies and explanations are selected as representative of good science and others are discarded. Scientific proof – be it logical or experimental – is rarely if ever enough to make this judgement. Indeed, even the criteria of proof are themselves selected in a complex social process that includes social, political and psychological factors.

This is, in fact, the real point of the McClintock story [see also Article 3.3]. The success of Barbara McClintock, the 1983 Nobel Laureate in medicine and physiology, forces our acknowledgement of the existence and the value of deviance in science. As such, her example stretches our conception of science, teaching us to count past two in our division between scientific and non-scientific. Her success serves to legitimate a vision and practice of science that contemporary standards had almost lost sight of. In short, what McClintock brings home to us is a lesson in diversity.

In turn, the particular character of her vision and practice of science teaches us to count past two in our thinking about nature, as well as in our thinking about the relation between mind and nature. McClintock offers us a vision of science that begins not so much with the search for generality as with a primary interest in and respect for difference. For her, the important thing is the capacity to see one kernel – she is a corn geneticist – that is different, and make that difference understandable.

[· · ·]

What McClintock in effect offers us is a philosophy of science in which difference – rather than division – constitutes the fundamental principle for ordering the world. Instead of aiming toward a cosmic unity of paired opposites – a unity typically excluding or subsuming one of the pair – respect for difference remains content with multiplicity as an end in itself.

Nor, in this world view, is division between subject and object posited as a prerequisite for knowledge. For McClintock, the *sine qua non* of good research is a feeling for the organism. . . Respect for individual difference here invites a form of engagement and understanding not representable in conventional scientific discourse. What might look like privileged insight, and is readily misdescribed as a kind of mystical experience, is in fact a result of close, intimate attention and patient observation, maintained over days, weeks and even years. Even Freud, who added so much modern credibility to the number three in his thinking about man, seemed himself only able to count to two in his thinking about subject–object relations; Freud too seemed only able to think in terms either of objectivity or of what he called oceanic oneness. But McClintock's practice of science offers another possibility: it teaches us about a world in which self and other, mind and nature, survive neither in mutual alienation nor in symbiotic fusion, but in structural integrity. Her feeling for the organism need not be read either as sentimentalism or as mysticism: it is a mode of access – honoured by time and human experience if not by prevailing conceptions of science – to the reliable knowledge of the world around us that all scientists seek.

Finally, McClintock also teaches us to count past two in our thinking about gender. Many people have read this story as a story about a feminist science – by which they usually mean a feminine science. And it is easy enough to see why. Virtually all of the aspects of McClintock's science that seem so distinctive – the value she places on feeling, intimacy, connection and relatedness – all seem to confirm our most familiar stereotypes of women. She is – on this I would agree – bringing to science precisely those attributes that have traditionally been devalued as feminine.

49

Indeed, some people might say that the celebration of these traits is indicative not so much of the ability to count past two, but of an inability to count to two (if one is inclined to be negative) or (in a more positive vein) a special capacity to count between one and two. That is, women, it is often thought, tend to live in a domain between one and two, where self and other are never – again, the negative account would have it – fully differentiated, while the positive view would put it, cast in opposition. Many kinds of accounts of why this might be so are offered. One roots it in the biology of pregnancy – a kind of paradigmatic experience of a nether world between one and two. Other accounts would root this capacity, or inability, in the dynamics of the early mother–daughter relationship (notably, as experienced by the daughter), a relationship which fosters identification if not more than, at least along with, separation. And still other accounts would root it in the emphasis on relationship and attachment demanded of parenting, a task usually performed by mothers. In the feminist version of these accounts, the space between one and two is celebrated, while in the traditional version it is denigrated. That is, recent feminist writings have sought to restore a domain of values lost by a numeric scheme limited to the numbers one and two. But while I support such an effort, I also have a problem with this view as stated. Perhaps one move that would help to reconcile it with the position I am arguing here would be to suggest a structural homology [agreement or likeness (eds)] between the space between one and two on the one hand and between two and infinity on the other, and I do make this suggestion. The capacity to count between one and two may in fact foster the capacity to count beyond two.

But that move will not do all the work of reconciliation that is required. Even though I do not want to repudiate these insights – and have in fact argued for some of them in my writing – I do want to register some reservations about these accounts as representations of women in general, and about the implication that only men get stuck in the one-step. Indeed, the examples I began with are illustrations of the difficulty in counting past two among feminists themselves. Furthermore, and more specifically germane, I need to point out that none of these accounts is relevant to McClintock herself. McClintock was never pregnant, never parented, and although she was a daughter, she had a rather anomalous relation to her mother, certainly not one that conforms to stereotypic accounts. Furthermore, her entire life was devoted to a repudiation of all feminine stereotypes and this repudiation may even have been necessary to her survival as a scientist. What relevance then, if any, can we say that McClintock's gender has to this entire story?

. . . I [would] suggest that the real relevance of gender in this story is to be found not in its role in McClintock's personal socialization, but precisely in the role of gender in the construction of science:

> In a science constructed around the naming of object (nature) as female, and the parallel naming of subject (mind) as male, any scientist who happens to be a woman is confronted with an a priori contradiction in terms. This poses a critical problem of identity: any scientist who is not a man walks a path bounded on one side by inauthenticity and on the other by subversion. Just as surely as inauthenticity is the cost a woman suffers by joining men in misogynist *jokes*, so it is, equally, the cost suffered by a woman who identifies with an image of the scientist modelled on the patriarchal husband. Only if she undergoes a radical disidentification from self can she share masculine pleasure in mastering a nature cast in the image of woman as passive, inert and blind. Her alternative is to attempt a radical redefinition of terms. Nature must be renamed as not female, or, at least, as not an alienated object. By the same token, the mind, if the female scientist is to have one, must be renamed as not necessarily male, and accordingly recast with a more inclusive subjectivity. This is not to say that the male scientist cannot claim similar redefinition (certainly many have done so) but, by contrast to the woman scientist, his identity does not require it.
>
> (*Keller, 1983, pp. 174–5*)

More generally, I suggest that as long as gender is the axis along which our world is subject to division, women will have more of an incentive to count past two – or perhaps between one and two – than most men will, even though they may still have trouble doing so. That extra incentive derives from the particular costs they bear in a world limited to either unitarity or duality. In the one case, they risk being subsumed, unrepresented, while in the other they face exclusion. In short, I am arguing that because she is not a man, in a world defined for men, McClintock's survival as a scientist with an intact integrity required that she learn to count beyond two.

[· · ·]

But . . . one example will hardly suffice to make the case for a substantive influence of a gendered discourse on science. Nor will two, and indeed, the case for what the subject of gender and science can tell us about science, like the case for what the social studies of science in general can tell us about science, will not be a strong one until a great deal more work has been done on unpacking the relation between language and science. By way of indicating the range of effort that I think is required, let me conclude with a somewhat different example drawn from my current work on the language of evolutionary discourse.

Here, the focus is not so much on the influence of a gendered discourse in analyses of a de-animated nature that has been cast as female, as in analyses of animate nature, inviting more complex and ambivalent forms of projection. In particular, I am thinking of the long history of debate about the role of competition, co-operation and altruism in evolutionary biology, and the ways in which these debates have – and continue to – reflect our cultural romances about male and female nature.

Ever since Darwin, critics have registered protest over the severity of Darwin's picture of nature ('red in tooth and claw') and the primacy he gave to competition in his description of evolution. At the turn of the century (1902), the Russian anarchist Peter Kropotkin wrote,

> Happily enough, competition is not the rule either in the animal world or in mankind. It is limited among animals to the exceptional periods, and natural selection finds better fields for its activity. Better conditions are created by the elimination of competition by means of mutual aid and mutual support. . . [N]atural selection continually seeks out the ways precisely for avoiding competition as much as possible. (*p. 74*)

'Sociability', Kropotkin argued, 'is as much a law of nature as mutual struggle' (*p. 5*).

The history of the vicissitudes of this generic debate is a long and complex one, and I will touch on only a couple of its key moments. One is a particularly interesting move that came relatively early on and appeared to deal effectively with the kind of objection that Kropotkin raised. The focus of Darwin's attention, it was said, was not so much on armed combat, dog-eat-dog overt competition, but on covert competition – the struggle for survival against the drought – struggle, now, 'in a large and metaphoric sense'. In an attempt to avoid its most offensive social implications, competition was redefined to mean the simultaneous reliance on an essential resource in limited supply. In this redefinition, competition is conflated with scarcity and, at the same time, scarcity comes to be represented as competition – both mathematically and linguistically. That is to say, the consumption of resources is represented [as]: my dinner means your starvation, and ultimately, my survival means your extinction [termed zero-sum].

This relatively more benign formulation of competition in this model – one made eminently reasonable by reference to the economic sphere – appeared to resolve debate. But it also helped to keep people from noticing the fact that it effectively excluded all interactions that cannot be accommodated by a zero-sum structure.

In particular, any co-operative interaction that could lead to a more efficient use of resources or to the *de facto* creation of new resources would conflict with this representation of scarcity. Excluded from our models, such a possibility becomes yet more effectively excluded from our consideration, almost from our imagination – even if not from the range of solutions explored by living organisms. The net effect is that this ... equation of scarcity with competition serves to maintain a conception of organisms, not quite as isolated individuals, but as individuals capable of only one kind of interaction – win or lose. By pre-empting the field of social dynamics for zero-sum interactions, it obstructs recognition of and attention to the entire range of co-operative or symbiotic phenomena. This tacit restriction amounts to a kind of zero-summing of the world that, I suggest, has had significant consequences for the kind of research that appears to be legitimate, productive etc. As one example of such an effect, I think of the history of research on cellular symbiosis. Through most of this century, the role of symbiosis in cell evolution has been regarded as uninteresting, implausible or, as E.B. Wilson once wrote, 'too fantastic for mention in polite biological society'. As it happens, it is only quite recently that this subject – in part due to the efforts of such mavericks as Lynn Margulis – has begun to gain legitimacy in the scientific community.

Box 1.3.1 Symbiosis

Symbiosis refers to the mutual interdependence of two different species of plant or animal. An example is the bacteria that live in the human gut. These bacteria help the human host by breaking down complex foodstuffs so that they are more easily absorbed by the gut wall and also by producing important substances such as vitamin K. In turn, the human provides a protective environment for the bacteria. There are many, many examples of symbiosis in the natural world.

A larger point is that evolutionary theory is in fact rife with concepts that frame the world in zero-sum terms – in a number system of base two. Very briefly, let me mention the rather obvious example of altruism, technically defined to mean behaviour that benefits the fitness of another at the cost of one's own fitness. This definition has caused endless problems for evolutionary biologists, essentially deriving from the fact that, in evolutionary terms, it makes of altruism a logical impossibility. Extraordinary ingenuity has been exercised to resolve the contradiction this fact appears to pose with biological experience, but as yet, a redefinition of the concept – one reflecting a less oppositional relation between self and other – has not been seriously pursued.

Similarly, and closely related, problems can be identified in the entire debate over individual vs. group selection in evolutionary theory. In a recent review of this debate, David Sloan Wilson (1983) observes,

> Group benefit and individual cost together determine the group size at which a character can evolve . . . We therefore arrive at a crucial question: What are the trade-offs between group benefit and individual cost? When is a socially desirable character necessarily costly to the individuals possessing it?
>
> This question is so simple and so fundamental that one might think it would have been carefully examined. On the contrary, it has been almost universally ignored. In almost all discussions of group selection, group benefit is simply assumed to require extreme self-sacrifice . . . This fact is perhaps the largest irony in the history of group selection and its development is well worth tracing. (p. 182)

How come, our question is, all those questions about the middle ground between my gain and your loss, between self-interest and self-sacrifice, between individual cost and group benefit – questions so simple and fundamental – are not being pursued? And does our language – even (or especially) our technical language – help to keep these questions and the wide range of phenomena to which they point out of our vision?

Without question, the story of ideological presuppositions in evolutionary biology is a long and complex one, and I certainly do not mean to hang it all on gender. At the same time, I suggest that that story cannot be properly understood without attention to the ways in which our thinking – or perhaps I should say our absence of thought – about male and female nature have crept into our thinking about nature.

One does not need to be familiar with recent developments in feminist theory to notice how well the proclivity toward zero-sum descriptions of relations between self and other conforms to an ideal of masculinity that is deeply embedded in our culture. In fact, one does not need to be familiar with anything but the literature of evolutionary biology itself – perhaps especially the recent literature.

To illustrate the presence and function of a covertly gendered discourse in these debates, I will read to you – in closing – a brief selection of quotations from the recent literature. Throughout this literature, competition, conflict and individualism are almost invariably associated with maturity, hard realities, what life is really like, in short with truth, while on the other hand co-operation, harmony, group selection and altruism are associated with a childish desire for comfort and peace, with romanticism – even worse, with sentimentalism, with warmth and security, indeed with motherliness itself.

George Williams, for example, in his epochal 1966 book that is often credited with the vanquishing of group selection, writes:

> There is a rather steady production of books and essays that attempt to show that Nature is, in the long run and on the average, benevolent and acceptable to some unquestionable ethical and moral point of view. By implication, she must be an appropriate guide for devising ethical systems and for judging human behaviour. (*p. 255*)

To explain this rather lamentable shift, Hamilton (1975) suggests:

> 'Benefit of the species' can thus serve as euphemism and as an escape from inner conflict, permitting us to pay no more emotionally than (for) our childhood acceptance that most forms of life exploit and prey on one another.

By contrast, Ghiselin offers us a view that he claims to be free from any such euphemism, free from all sentimentalism – indeed a view that constitutes something of a challenge, designed to expose the latent sentimentalism residual in even the toughest amongst us. He writes:

> The economy of nature is competitive from beginning to end . . . No hint of genuine charity ameliorates our vision of society, once sentimentalism has been laid aside. What passes for cooperation turns out to be a mixture of opportunism and exploitation . . . Scratch an 'altruist' and watch a 'hypocrite' bleed. (*p. 247*)

It appears to be with some justification, then, that Dawkins (1982) can write, in his characteristically uncompromising prose:

> 'Genteel' ideas of vague benevolent mutual cooperation are replaced by an expectation of stark, ruthless, opportunistic mutual exploitation . . .
> This kind of unsentimental, dog-eat-dog language would not have come easily to biologists a few years ago, but nowadays I am glad to say it dominates the textbooks. (*pp. 55–6*)

Finally, to make it absolutely clear in just what terms the alternative to stark, ruthless exploitation is conceived, Lynn Margulis is described for her work on symbiosis and cell evolution, as 'introducing feminism to Darwinism', and W. Ford Doolittle's recent review is titled 'Is Nature really motherly?' Doolittle (1981) begins his review with:

> The good thing about this engaging little book by Jim Lovelock[3] is that reading it gives one a warm, comforting feeling about Nature and man's place in it. The bad thing is that this feeling is based on a view of natural selection ... which is unquestionably false.

My point is not that Lovelock's understanding of natural selection is not wrong – although I don't think it is – or that nature *is* motherly – I don't believe this either. In fact I don't even think that mothers are motherly. Rather, it seems to me that what we have here is a kind of projective sentimentalization. Co-operation, mutualism, altruism are projected onto women – endowed with the romance of women's culture – and then readily dismissed as romance and sentimentalism ... [O]n the other hand, competition, conflict and individualism are associated with the harsh realities of mature men's lives. Given this alternative, between romantic sentimentality and harsh reality, there is no contest. But the fact of the matter is that this framing, this vision of male culture, is equally romantic – it is a romance about a certain kind of masculinity. Real women may or may not be co-operative, mothers may or may not be motherly, Lynn Margulis may or may not be a feminist, men may or may not be warriors. But Nature is oblivious of all our romances, and knows nothing of our gender roles and distinctions. Most probably, the very division that has been set up in theoretical ecology between competition and co-operation is itself unrealistic – loaded in similar ways to the loading of a definition of altruism that excludes the possibility of mutual benefit. A whole world of interactions might be seen between organisms that could not easily fit into a category either of co-operative or competitive. Perhaps, I am suggesting, if we were more attentive to our tendencies to project our own romances onto nature, we might discover new kinds of stories, not yet written in our own scripts. Instead of zero-sum games ... we might discover what we never imagined possible – games that require us to count past two, or between one and two.

Notes

1   A Rorschach test is a psychological test using cards printed with symmetrical ink blots. A subject is asked to say what she 'sees' on each card. Responses are interpreted to reveal personality traits.

2   A picture can be seen as dividing into at least two coherent parts: the figure (the object of focus) and the ground (background). The two influence each other in how they are seen so that on some drawings the relationship can be reversed and the ground can be seen as the figure and the figure as the ground.

3   James Lovelock, originator of the Gaia theory of the Earth's ecosystem, is discussed in Article 4.5, 'Ecofeminism', by Cat Cox.

Article 1.4
HOW THE WOMEN'S MOVEMENT BENEFITS SCIENCE: TWO VIEWS

Sandra Harding

FEMINIST SCIENCE CRITIQUES: SOLIDARITIES AND DIFFERENCES

One focus in recent writings by feminists working in and around the natural sciences has been on the resources the women's movement offers to science. Here I will be concerned with three such resources that, it has been argued, make unique contributions to the growth of knowledge in the natural sciences: women scientists, feminist politics and feminist theories about science. Feminists who think about such resources are both in solidarity and conflict with each other. They all agree that the women's movement does make important contributions to the growth of knowledge. But they disagree about just what these contributions are.

The solidarities between feminists are created by the fact that they must work together against traditionalists, who regard the very idea that a social movement could make contributions to the growth of knowledge as deeply threatening to some of their most cherished assumptions. Thus on a daily basis, all feminists in and around the sciences have to struggle together against individuals and institutions who say that – or act as if – women are not the most likely people to become really good physicists, chemists, mathematicians or engineers, and that imagining that science can learn anything from the women's movement is guaranteed to generate only political ideology and a decline in the quality of scientific activity. It certainly could not contribute to the growth of knowledge.

However, feminists who must struggle together against traditionalists also find themselves disagreeing among themselves about other important issues. One such disagreement separates those who believe that the task of feminist analysis is to object to 'bad science' from those who think that 'science as usual' – the whole scientific enterprise, its purposes, practices and functions – should be the target of feminist criticism. Indeed, feminists from one group are often surprised to discover just how different their agendas are from people in the other group who also seem to think themselves feminists. The critics of bad science sometimes see the critics of science-as-usual as undermining the former's attempts to end sexist hiring practices and sexist and androcentric biases in the sciences. On the other side, the critics of science-as-usual sometimes see the critics of bad science as a distracting and particularly difficult part of the problem with science-as-usual. They see the feminist critics of bad science as complicitous with our culture's failure to question deeply enough the ethics, goals and functions of science. Of course, not all feminists concerned about science adopt only one of these agendas. A few are concerned to explore the relationship between them; many others simply draw on whichever agenda seems appropriate at the moment and do not worry about the way these projects conflict. But many – perhaps even most – of the feminists concerned with science find compelling the projects of only one or the other of these two general approaches.

I find this situation troubling for a number of reasons. For one thing, if it is science-as-usual that is the problem, then it appears that feminism should not encourage more women to become part of this problem. But it is distressing that an apparent consequence of the success of the feminist criticisms of this field would be to alienate women from entering it when they have been so vigorously excluded from it by patriarchal culture, and when many of the women in the sciences have waged such heroic campaigns to enter and remain there. Moreover, it is not a purpose of the feminist criticisms of literature that women should stop writing, nor of feminist criticisms of the social sciences that women should abandon attempts to understand the social world. How bizarre if it is an outcome of the purportedly most radical feminist science criticisms that women should give up trying to understand the natural world. Can we work toward feminist sciences without any feminist scientists? Moreover, we live in a scientific culture; to be scientifically illiterate is simply to be illiterate – a condition far too many of us, women and men, are in already. It is regressive tendencies in science-as-usual that foster such illiteracy, as feminist critics have pointed out. If women do not become scientists, would not that fact further discourage girls and women from becoming scientifically literate and from gaining the kinds of control of our own lives that such literacy appears to make possible? Should feminism join science-as-usual in fostering scientific illiteracy among women? What, I ask myself, could be progressive about that?

For another thing, it is equally troubling that many of the critics of bad science are resistant to critically examining the way the social structure and purposes of contemporary science are created far away from scientists' daily experience; they are created in the bourgeois, racist and imperialist projects, as well as androcentric ones, of the social order. It is an important principle of that social order to maintain the separation between the laboratories that are supposed to contain scientists' experiences of science and the councils where science policy is made. Should feminism want women to have equality with the men of their respective races and classes without challenging race and class exploitation within science? Should feminism want women, too, to do research that it is only reasonable to predict will be used by the military or to increase profit? What is progressive about mounting heroic campaigns to 'add women and gender' to the social structure and subject matters of the sciences without questioning the legitimacy of science's social hierarchy and politically regressive agendas more generally?

There needs to be more dialogue between the critics of bad science and of science-as-usual ... Moreover, it is crucial that this dialogue be informed by the voices of the majority of the world's women who are not involved in criticizing the sciences at all, but simply in surviving. It is desires to eliminate, control and economically exploit them that set far too many of the agendas of science-as-usual. How can they benefit from natural sciences that are supposed to be for the improvement of 'humanity'?

One topic of such conversations should be to envision now what feminist natural sciences could look like and, most importantly, what we should do now to move toward that goal ... That is, if feminists and women around the world, could choose the structure and projects for physics, chemistry, engineering and biology, what would we choose? To begin to answer this question wisely requires dialogue between the critics of bad science, the critics of science-as-usual, and the rest of the world's women. In my opinion, the most important answers to these questions for women outside the sciences – in this culture and around the world – cannot be provided by either of the two groups of feminist critics alone. In the natural sciences, feminist energies have been devoted primarily to criticizing what exists. It would be a service to feminism (and to humanity!) to create contexts where some of our energies could also be put into such future-oriented dialogues. . .

[· · ·]

It can clarify such conversations to identify the outlines and origins of some of the differences between the agendas of the two main feminist approaches to science ... and then turn to look at the contrasting position each takes with respect to how resources for science are provided by women in science, feminist politics and feminist theories about science.

FEMINIST EMPIRICISM AND THE CRITIQUE OF BAD SCIENCE

Feminist researchers in biology and the social sciences have shown in useful detail the many ways in which sexist and androcentric results of research have resulted when scientists did not carefully enough follow principles of method and theory already well-understood in their fields [see Birke (Article 2.1) and Fedigan (Article

2.2)]. Making generalizations about humans based only on data about men violates obvious rules of method and theory.

[· · ·]

If critics ended their arguments with such attacks on bad science . . . they would be attempting to preserve principles of good research and the logic of explanation (the logic of justification, as philosophers call it) as these are widely understood today in the natural and social sciences. This understanding of science was developed at the moment when the natural sciences first became positivist but . . . science is older than its positivist era. . . Today, if there are any objections to the social values imbedded in the results of scientific inquiry, those who hold to this positivist theory think that these must be the consequence of insufficient rigour in enforcing scientific method. Those who see the problem only as bad science support the goal for all scientific inquiry of value-neutral objectivity and impartiality; they assume that there is an [ideal] vantage point from which the relations of the natural and social world could appear in their proper perspective.

In this theory, the subject of knowledge – the scientist, the knower – is always an individual; the knower cannot be a group such as a social class or gender. And this individual is abstract – it cannot have any particular historical social identity. The authors of the results of scientific research are supposed to be socially anonymous. To put this point another way, it is not supposed to make any difference to the 'goodness' of the results of research if the researcher is Chinese or British, black or white, a woman or a man. Scientific method is supposed to be powerful enough to eliminate any social biases that might find their way into scientific hypotheses because of the social identity of the scientist.

Though its defenders rarely recognize it as such, this theory of knowledge is in fact part of a world view that includes as other central elements liberal political and moral theory. I have called the feminist form of this theory about science and its procedures for producing knowledge 'feminist empiricism'.

FEMINIST STANDPOINTS AND CRITIQUES OF SCIENCE AS USUAL

The other major theory about science uses the structure of a Marxist epistemology. Knowledge is grounded in experiences made possible by historically specific social relations. In societies where power is organized hierarchically – by class, race or gender – there is no possibility of [a] perspective that is disinterested, impartial, value-free or detached from the particular, historical social relations in which everyone participates. Instead, each person can achieve only a partial view of reality from the perspective of his or her own position in the hierarchical social relations. Moreover, such a view is not only partial but also distorted by the way those relations of dominance are organized. Further, the view from the perspective of the powerful is far more partial and distorted than that available from the perspective of the dominated; this is so because the powerful have far more interests in obscuring the injustice of their unearned privileges and authority. The cost of these unearned privileges for the few is paid for by the injustice of the misery for the many. As Hegel [1770–1831] (1979) formulated the point that structures this theory, masters see the activity of slaves as an expression either of slaves' 'natures' or of masters' wills. From the perspective of the slaves, the situation looks very different. The two perspectives are not scientifically or epistemologically equal.

The feminist standpoint theorists argue that the men's experiences and activities on which Western knowledge has been based are only partial; they represent only masculine experience and activity, not the distinctively and admirably human, as men perennially claim. Moreover, they are a particularly poor grounding for knowledge claims since, as masculine, they represent the ruling part of society. Women's experiences and activities provide a far preferable starting point for scientific research as well as for politics. Indeed, they argue, the most important feminist research and politics of the last two decades have emerged precisely from the gap between the dominant conceptual schemes and women's experience. The conceptual schemes, based as they are primarily on gendered masculine experience, do not fit women's experiences of our own lives (Hartsock, 1983; Rose, 1983; Smith, 1987).

Thus, in this theory the subject of belief and of knowledge is never an individual, let alone an abstract one capable of transcending its own historical location. It is always a particular social group. I always see the world through my culture's eyes; I think within its assumptions. To say the same thing in other words, our society can see only through our eyes and think its characteristic thoughts with our minds. There is no impartial, disinterested, value-neutral . . . perspective. Nevertheless, it is possible to make reasonable judgements about which beliefs are and which are not better supported by empirical evidence. No one can tell one eternally true story about the way the world is; but we can tell some that can be shown with good evidence to be far less false than the dominant ones.

Although this theory of knowledge, like feminist empiricism, has emerged from biological and social science research, in its challenge to the practice of grounding only in masculine experience scientific problematics, concepts, evidence, interpretations and purposes of research, it has the consequence of challenging the natural sciences, too. As I asked earlier, what would a physics, chemistry, engineering and biology look like if they were driven by purposes of research and problematics identified by feminism rather than only by those identified by a patriarchal culture that is also racist and bourgeois? Of course, one could hold that there are two sciences with different 'logics' of inquiry and explanation: in the social sciences and parts of biology, the social origins of research can play a positive role in the growth of knowledge; in the natural sciences they have no role to play. However, this position is difficult to defend in the light of the fact that almost all natural science research these days is technology driven. Scientists may not be motivated by visions of new technologies of control or for profit, but funders of scientific research are. The point is that the feminist standpoint theorists challenge not bad science but science-as-usual; they challenge the fit of science, in history and today, with the gender projects of its surrounding culture. I attribute a standpoint approach here to many of the feminist critics of science's technologies and applications, though they do not always articulate their position as a standpoint approach (compare, for example, Arditti, Duelli-Klein and Minden (1984) and Spallone and Steinberg (1987)).

FEMINIST SCIENCES OF SCIENCE

The two approaches to science can be thought of as ways to shape the projects of a 'science of science', since the goal for both is to describe and explain the regularities and underlying causal tendencies of the practices of science. I have only been able to provide their broad outlines, but this is sufficient to reveal why it is that one finds within the feminist discussions alternative analyses of the resources for science to be found in women scientists, feminist politics and feminist theories about science. I turn to identify how the two approaches shape different interpretations of the value of the women's movement to science.

FEMINIST EMPIRICISM:
HOW WOMEN SCIENTISTS BENEFIT SCIENCE

For the critics of 'bad science', justice demands that women, too, be given the same opportunities available to their brothers for science educations, degrees, lab appointments, publication, teaching positions, membership in scientific societies, awards and the other benefits that participation in science can provide. The perceived radicalness of this apparently modest principle of equal opportunity becomes evident the minute one looks at the heroic struggles that were necessary to eliminate the formal barriers against women's equality in science, mathematics and engineering. [See Article 3.1.]

Similarly vigorous struggles are still going on; they are unlikely to fade away as long as informal barriers succeed in ensuring unequal opportunity. The issue is not that there are few women in science, for there are vast numbers of women with science degrees working in the scientific enterprise. The issue, instead, is why there are so few women directing the agendas of science (Haas and Perrucci, 1984; Rossiter, 1982).

The grounds for the demands for equal opportunity have always been that women can do just as good science as their brothers, and that they should be given the same opportunities to demonstrate their abilities. Women are an overlooked segment of the 'manpower' pool from which science draws its workers. Thus, women scientists' contribution could be considered to be simply that they enlarge the pool of talents from which good scientists can be made. From this perspective, there would appear to be no political or conceptual space to argue that women scientists have a *special* contribution, as women, to make to the growth of scientific knowledge.

Feminist empiricism clarifies why women natural scientists are resistant to the possibility that they should, somehow, be doing science as women rather than as the impartial, disinterested, value-neutral observers and thinkers that they were trained to be and that feminist empiricism legitimates. The women's movement creates the possibility for more women scientists as it attacks the formal and informal barriers that make it difficult for women to gain the opportunities in science that are available to their brothers. But there is no claim here that women scientists provide any special resources as women for the growth of scientific knowledge. Consequently, the claim other feminists make about women's special contributions to the growth of knowledge *should* be troubling to women who, in order to gain the precarious positions they have achieved, have had to insist that they were 'just one of the boys', that in the labs they certainly were not functioning as women. Whatever maternity leaves, child care or other accommodations to women's reproductive and family roles they might think it appropriate to ask for, feminist empiricism tells them that the way they do science and the content of their work is not, and should not be, affected by the fact that they are women.

[· · ·]

How feminist politics benefits science (empiricism)

The position becomes a little more complex when we turn to ask if – in addition to generating more scientific 'manpower' – there are other benefits to science that the women's movement provides. Could the women's movement improve the logic or content of science?

One could argue that presumably the kind of quantitative change discussed above that the women's movement generates should have qualitative results. . . But the question here is a different one: does the women's movement contribute to increasing the growth of knowledge by changing its content or logic in other ways?

Here is a reply given by two empirical sociologists that states particularly clearly the feminist empiricist position:

> Everyone knows the story about the Emperor and his fine clothes: although the townspeople persuaded themselves that the Emperor was elegantly costumed, a child, possessing an unspoiled vision, showed the citizenry that the Emperor was really naked. The story instructs us about one of our basic sociological premises: that reality is subjective, or rather, subject to social definition. The story also reminds us that collective delusions can be undone by introducing fresh perspectives.
>
> Movements of social liberation are like the story in this respect: they make it possible for people to see the world in an enlarged perspective because they remove the covers and blinders that obscure knowledge and observation. In the last decade no social movement has had a more startling or consequential impact on the way people see and act in the world than the women's movement. Like the onlookers in the Emperor's parade, we can see and plainly speak about things that have always been there, but that formerly were unacknowledged. Indeed, today it is impossible to escape noticing features of social life that were invisible only ten years ago.
>
> (Millman and Kanter, 1975)

Echoing empiricist themes here are the claims that the child has 'unspoiled vision' in comparison to the townspeople; that the child's unspoiled vision brings 'fresh perspectives'; that the townspeople 'persuaded themselves' to believe a delusion; that the women's movement 'removes blinders' from our eyes, enabling us to 'see things' that have always been there but were not visible to us earlier.

While the empiricist theory of how good science is done is still presented in technicolour here, it appears to be slipping out of focus in spite of the authors' intent. Evidently, scientific claims do have historical authors since sometimes their reality is and sometimes it is not defined by such a social movement, and the former are better than the latter. Before the women's movement, our eyes were covered; the women's movement opens them for us. The assumptions of abstract individualism – that I can see reality all by myself, that

64

scientific method alone is powerful enough to remove the blinders that obscure knowledge and observation – begins to itself appear a foolish delusion. But this passage suggests that Millman and Kanter still think that there is nothing special about women *as women* for science to use as a resource. Men and women can both lose our blinders as we learn from the unspoiled vision and fresh perspectives the women's movement provides.

Moreover, it does not appear to be necessary to good science for individual scientists, or even any scientists at all, to go out of their way to engage in the politics of the women's movement in order to increase these kinds of benefits that the movement brings to science. Someone has to do such politics for these benefits to science to accrue, but it doesn't have to be scientists. Feminism appears available as a discourse and as an identity to people of good will if they open their minds to what the women's movement reveals to us all, if they get rid of their superstitions, ignorance, and prejudices and, of course, if they have a humane attitude toward the disadvantaged and participate when asked in attempts to gain justice for them. Feminist science here is no more than the science that such people – men and women – do. And, in the case of physics, chemistry, and parts of biology, it hardly seems worthwhile to attach the label 'feminist' to the science done in the presence of a women's movement. Maybe physicists will have to speak up on equity issues and watch their language a little more carefully to avoid offensive sexist metaphors. But nothing fundamental to how description and explanation of the natural world are produced will be done differently from the ways in which sciences are practised when no women's movement is around.

Is feminist theory about science a scientific resource?

Finally, what does feminist empiricism have to say about the role of social theories of science as a resource *for* science? Very little. If pressed, feminist empiricists tend to be reluctant to own that they have a theory of science at all. Empiricism presents scientific research as following a formula or algorithm. . . This tendency goes back to Newton's hesitation even to admit that he made hypotheses: 'I frame no hypotheses; . . . hypotheses, whether metaphysical or physical, whether of occult qualities or mechanical, have no place in experimental philosophy', said Newton (1687). This empiricist tendency holds that the products of the mind (in contrast to the products of 'nature') constitute obstacles for science; hypotheses and theories, like all products of the mind, should be regarded with suspicion.

Supporting this position is the assumption, widespread in the sciences and in philosophy, that while false beliefs often require social explanations, true beliefs are the consequence only of natural processes. . . Recently, this assumption has been the target of criticism from the 'strong programme' in the sociology of knowledge. These sociologists call for causally symmetrical accounts of both true and false, legitimate and illegitimate beliefs. Otherwise, they point out, the sociology of knowledge is really only the sociology of error (Bloor, 1977). Feminist empiricists appear ambivalent about whether the explanations of the results of good science research should or should not refer to social causes; but – my point here – they do not think it important to doing good science to have a distinctive *social theory* of how to do good science. For example, they do not give their implicitly held theory of science a name – I, not they, have called it feminist empiricism.

The Millman and Kanter passage quoted earlier is the closest to a statement of the benefits feminist social theory can bring to science that I have found in this literature. Presumably they would say not just that such movements of social liberation do enlarge the vision available to science whether or not scientists realized it (the point I discussed above), but also that the *understanding* of the positive effect of such social values on the growth of knowledge – an understanding advanced by the very fact that they write this passage – should be useful to science. Of course to say this clearly is to challenge directly and deeply the 'positivist' grounds of empiricism. Either scientific method in fact leaves a great deal to the 'wit and imagination', or else scientific method should be taken to include processes of deciding how we should shape the entire moral and political order. In their passage, there is, as I have noted, an unselfconsciousness about the way the parts of their statement fit together that appears paradoxical. Is it really an 'unspoiled vision' that the women's movement brings, and not one shaped by interests in improving women's condition? Are there no interests, benefits to men as men, that might account for the 'covers and blinders' over women's as well as men's eyes? Did we all really 'persuade ourselves' of the truth of the partial and distorted sexist vision of the world? Why haven't our lives improved as rapidly as the story about the townspeople would predict, since women's movements have been removing covers and blinders from eyes in the West at least since Christine de Pizan wrote *The City of Ladies* in the late fourteenth century (published 1404), and yet we still live in a world ruled by powerful, old, naked, patriarchal emperors?

I make these comments not as a criticism of Millman and Kanter (1975), for I think I would have said much the same thing to the audience they were addressing. In fact, I still hear feminist empiricist claims not too different from theirs emerging from my very own lips when I am initially presenting feminist materials to audiences that I judge to be friendly to empiricism but hostile to what they consider feminism. I make these points, instead, to indicate how difficult it is for feminists to maintain a theory of science that is coherent with the sciences' own visions of their projects. The attempt to explain within empiricist constraints the resources that the women's movement generates for the growth of scientific knowledge reveals the flaws in the paternal empiricist discourse. That discourse was developed to explain the successes of the natural sciences. If it is flawed as an explanation of the successes of the growth of knowledge in biology and the social sciences, then should it not be regarded as problematic also as an explanation for the growth of knowledge in physics?

To conclude this discussion, the critics of bad science appear caught between two loyalties. On the one hand, they try to respect the empiricist dogma that one can explain 'good science' without referring to social causes. On the other hand, they think that the women's movement is a social cause of better science; an understanding of this process should inform scientific practice at least in that scientists should welcome the women's movement and listen to what it says in order to increase the growth of knowledge.

FEMINIST STANDPOINT: HOW WOMEN SCIENTISTS BENEFIT SCIENCE

The logic of the Marxist epistemology in which the feminist standpoint is grounded does not lead to advocating the advancement of women in the existing scientific enterprise – that is, leaving science otherwise unchanged. From this perspective, at best it makes no difference at all to women's situation in general if women are added to the social structure of a science that appears to be so thoroughly integrated with misogynist, racist and bourgeois projects in the larger society. More likely it is a bad thing, since it diverts women's attention and energies from struggles against the sources of male domination, not just their effects in the social structure of science. Moreover, adding women to an institution that is highly stratified by class and race as well as by gender has the effect of strengthening class and race divisions between women. The women who achieve the top of the race and class hierarchies in science tend not to criticize or work against those other forms of domination that oppress their sisters in other classes and races. From the standpoint perspective, intentionally or not, women scientists are in this way complicitous with male domination since it is a system that is inseparable from race and class domination for all women in the world except for white, Western, economically privileged women. Only for women of their class and (typical) race do gender issues appear separable from class and race issues. So, on balance, adding women to science strengthens an institution that should be weakened.

However, the Marxist theory of science argued that if its bourgeois shell could be stripped away, a 'pure science' could emerge that would be useful to the proletariat. In a certain way, the feminist standpoint theorists borrow something of this notion. Looked at from this perspective, women *do*, or at least could, provide a special resource, as women, to science – that is, to the science to be created (a feminist science?). For it is the gap between women's experience and the dominant conceptual schemes from which both so many issues of the women's movement as well as the most important feminist research in social science and biology have emerged. . . All of the issues about women's bodies arise from this gap – issues about reproduction, child care, the assignment to women of the care of everyone's bodies and the local places where they exist, sexuality, rape, incest, wife-battering, the mutilation caused by standards of beauty. So, too, does the focus on gender itself; gender appears, emerges, as a phenomenon we can all see only from the perspective of women's experience. So, too, is this gap the source of all the criticisms of the exclusion and distortion of women and our lives in dominant patterns of Western thought – including scientific thought.

[· · ·]

Historians of science and of theories of scientific knowledge such as Evelyn Fox Keller (1984), Carolyn Merchant (1980), Donna Haraway (1986) and Susan Bordo (1987) have argued that extremely abstract elements of Western scientific thought gained legitimacy because they both reflected and reinforced certain historical aspects of men's experiences. So from the perspective of the standpoint theorists' criticisms of science-as-usual, women scientists can bring certain benefits to the growth of knowledge if they can find ways to use their experience as women to create a critical perspective on the dominant conceptual schemes. (I am not suggesting that the historians are standpoint theorists, but that their analyses permit such accounts of the natural sciences.) I hasten to mention that these theorists do not argue that all women scientists automatically bring such benefits to science, or that only women can look at the world from the perspective of women's activities. They argue, instead, only that powerful critical theories *can be developed* out of the gap between the half of human experience that is assigned to women and the conceptual schemes grounded only in masculine experience.

Thus the feminist critique of science-as-usual provides a different assessment of the resources for science that women scientists can provide. Where it is primarily their numbers and their gender-free talents and abilities that the critics of bad science think make an important contribution to the growth of knowledge, it is their ability to speak from the perspective of their specific activities as women that is important to the standpoint theorists. I think that men, too, can speak from the perspective of women's activities; these theorists might say that John Stuart Mill, Karl Marx, Friedrich Engels, Frederick Douglass and other 'male feminists' have done so. But men can do so only after women have articulated what that experience is, and after men, too, have engaged in those political struggles to which I next turn.

How feminist politics benefits science (standpoint theories)

Standpoint thinkers believe that political struggle is a necessary part of learning how to criticize the dominant conceptual schemes from the standpoint of women's activities. It is overtly inside science for this approach – not out there somewhere in the environment for our mental appreciation. 'His resistance is the measure of your oppression', said an early guide to the politics of housework (Redstockings, 1971), pointing to the way it was only through political struggles that women could get the chance to observe the depth and extent of masculine privilege. Feminist struggle has direct scientific value.

[· · ·]

[S]cience is like sculpture in that it is a 'craft' activity. Only working with (and against) the material reveals its true character – its internal relations and structure, the deepest, most enduring and most powerful sources of its strength, its surprising weaknesses. The 'material' whose regularities and underlying causal tendencies feminist politics can reveal is male dominance.

This claim can call on historical precedents. The feminist politics of the women's movement provides the kinds of resources to science that were provided for the emergence of modern science by the political struggles necessary to bring Europe from the medieval world to modernity. That is, modern science itself was created through a movement of social liberation. The new physics advanced precisely because it both expressed the ethos of an emerging class (materialism, anti-elitism, progress) and also provided the means for expressing that ethos in technologies that could materially advance that class. Its very 'method' – experimental observation – required the performance of both head and hand labour by one and the same person, new kinds of persons who did not exist in the feudal aristocracy (Merchant, 1980; . . . Zilsel, 1942). Are not women sociologists and other women scientists just such new kinds of persons created through politics of a social liberation movement?

69

This theory has a more robust analysis of the positive role that feminist politics plays in the growth of scientific knowledge. Feminist struggle is a fundamental part of gaining knowledge – of science. People, men as well as women, who do not engage in it, who do not risk in their daily activities offending or threatening the legitimacy of male dominance, in important ways cannot *know* how the social and natural worlds are organized. A woman who could say 'I've never been discriminated against as a woman' has not taken the risks that patriarchy finds so threatening – an unsettling thought for the token women that so many of us professional-class women are. Taking those risks is an activity that is inside science for the standpoint theorists.

Is feminist theory about science a scientific resource?

Finally, for the standpoint theorists, good theory about science is crucial to doing good science. What happens in the lab begins far away, out in the moral, economic and political projects of the society. The absence of an explicit theory about the causes of the patterns of everyday life in the labs or the sociology department insures that scientists will be simply 'fast guns for hire', myopically pursuing the production of information – for whom and for what purposes they haven't the slightest idea.

This argument has been made forcefully by feminist biologists and critics of the sexist production of scientific technologies. They point out that one needs an adequate theory about science in order to begin to eliminate the ways in which science and its technologies victimize women. The problem is not that there are sexist and androcentric 'misuses and abuses' of scientific technologies, such that the misuses and abuses could be ended leaving pure, gender-impartial sciences and technologies. Instead, it is inevitable that women will be victimized by the sciences and their technologies in a society such as ours where women have little power, where almost all scientific research is technology driven, and where political issues are posed as requiring merely technological 'solutions'.

However, within the natural sciences there is immense resistance to social theory about science. . . Natural scientists are trained to think that they should be the experts about what their own projects are 'about'. From the perspective of the standpoint theorists, because the social processes that eventuate in 'everyday life' in the laboratories begin far away from the laboratories – in a sluggish economy, in the desire to win a war in Asia, in attempts to control blacks in cities, in desires to limit population growth in Asia – firsthand expertise in the laboratories won't get anyone very far in providing an explanation of laboratory life. Thus, feminist theory about science must be seen as inside the process of science since it can help to explain why some problems are selected for inquiry rather than others, what counts as a reasonable hypothesis, whose observations will get to count as evidence, why some theories get accepted by the scientific community but not others.

CONCLUSION

I have explored two views of what the resources are that the women's movement provides for science. For the feminist empiricists who object to the bad science that they think is responsible for sexism and androcentrism in the results of research, these resources are more good scientists, a fresh perspective that enables everyone to see aspects of nature and social life that were invisible before, and, perhaps, an understanding of those ways in which movements for social liberation, such as the women's movement, do have the effect of contributing to the growth of knowledge. In contrast, the standpoint theorists and others who criticize science-as-usual think that sexism and androcentrism are unlikely to disappear in science until they are eliminated in the societies for which science is just one way of perpetrating and legitimating male dominance. For them, the women's movement contributes the possibility of articulating a critical causal account of the dominant social order through bringing women into science who subsequently become alienated from the dominant conceptual schemes in their disciplines. It contributes a feminist politics and feminist theories about science that are inside science. The politics are inside science in the sense that if researchers engage in these politics they will change their assumptions and hypotheses about what are the regularities and underlying causal tendencies of nature and social relations. The theories about science are inside science because if researchers believe these theories, they will work to undermine the fit of science with the dominant modes of exploitation and oppression, and to create sciences that have emancipatory purposes, projects and modes of research.

I suggest that feminists who hold these views have different audiences for their feminisms. Each of us may well find one of these sets of beliefs more congenial to our own projects and the institutional worlds in which we carry them out . . . I think it would be a great loss for the women's movement to abandon either strand of these scientific projects.

The feminist empiricists support efforts to get more women into science. While the benefits of having more women in science may not be great, there are important reasons to want more feminists in science, and women do seem to turn into feminists more quickly and more thoroughly than do men. So why not encourage the entrance into this institution of the social group most likely to produce feminists? We need feminists in the presently existing sciences for many reasons: to blow the whistle from within the sciences on the failures of scientists to adhere to their often-expressed principles of impartiality, disinterest, value-neutrality; to draw into these agendas 'pre-feminists' in the sciences (male and female) who are open to such criticisms; to gain for women access to the status and authority such positions bring; to explain for women what we need to know about the regularities and underlying causal tendencies of nature and social life; to generate, within equal opportunity justifications, scientific projects that are specifically in women's interests. These projects do not appear to me to be significantly different from the feminist agendas of women who work within other powerful institutions in our society – such as, for instance, the government or higher education. There, too, there should be limits to what kinds of projects one will work on. . . Under such circumstances, it becomes an important feminist project within the sciences to help locate the trail of social relations that connect what occurs in the laboratories with the social relations of the larger society, to contribute to the demystification of science, to increasing science literacy, to generating projects that can benefit women – strategic as well as substantive.

On the other hand, the women's movement needs feminists 'outside science' who take as their project a critical examination of the regularities and underlying causal tendencies in the fit of science with other social projects. The study of science is itself a science, and people inside a culture or institution are never in the best position to see those causes of their daily activities that originate far outside their daily world. These understandings can have an effect on how people inside science think about their activity, and make intellectual, practical and political choices as scientists. But to have this effect, feminists inside and outside the sciences need to think of themselves as working together in spite of the occasionally contradictory aspects of their conjoined projects.

To paraphrase a metaphor familiar to philosophers, the women's movement finds itself in the middle of the ocean, having both to redesign and rebuild the leaky ship of modern science one plank at a time. In other words, we are forced to remake science, but not in conditions of our own choosing.

2
OUR BODIES, OUR MINDS, OUR SELVES

Western science has had a confused attitude towards the female body. 'Nature' (the material world) is often symbolized as a woman, and the activity of scientific enquiry represented as uncovering the secrets of the naked body (see, for example, Plate 3). And yet – or perhaps because of it – the bodies of real women have been regarded with fear, and a great deal of intellectual effort has gone into searching for evidence of their inferiority to the male body.

Susan Griffin in *Woman and Nature: the roaring inside her* condenses these scientific arguments into a long prose poem:

> And it is observed that woman is less evolved than man. Men and women differ as much, it is observed, as plants and animals do. And men and animals correspond just as women and plants correspond, for women develop more placidly, like plants, and have an 'indeterminant unity of feeling'.
>
> That her evolution resulted in a higher and shriller voice, a smaller larynx, fewer red corpuscles and a less complex nervous system.
>
> *Our voices diminish*
>
> (That the later development of the abbreviated foot in women must have been a throwback, since the short foot is clearly 'unworthy of a noble animal'.)
>
> *We become less*
>
> And it is observed that the woman's brain mass is smaller.
>
> *We become less*
>
> That lacking in reason and morality, women are a kind of middle step between the child and the man, who is the true human being.
>
> *And they say that muteness is natural to us.*
>
> (*Griffin, 1984, p. 26*)

Griffin argues that the masculine analogy of 'Woman' and 'Nature' has been destructive of both. She asserts a different kind of essential relationship – biologically and spiritually – between women and 'Nature', which she believes is empowering of both. However, feminists in general have preferred instead to deconstruct the Woman/Nature relation, arguing that women's bodies have few, if any, biological differences from men that are significant enough to merit the sexual divisions in society or the claims of a special relationship to the rest of the natural world. During the 1970s and '80s feminist debates about gender placed most emphasis on its social construction, arguing against any necessary connection with biology at all. This cast doubt on whether biological theory could play any appropriate role in understanding either gender difference or the experience of being a woman. A social determinist position avoids debates about the accuracy of biological evidence and theory, and tends to be critical of medical solutions to problems. But it also denies for many women the particular bodily experience of being female.

> There are undoubtedly powerful social divisions in our society; and feminists must insist that these are not caused by the biological attributes (sex, or colour of one's skin, for example) with which they are sometimes associated. But at the same time, feminists must also insist that we experience those divisions as embodied persons. Refusing to see our biology as primary and controlling is essential: human behaviour and social organization are not caused by biology *or* by the social/cultural environment, and we are puppets of neither. But we do have bodies.
>
> (Birke, 1992, p. 77)

Lynda Birke's shrewd statement is a timely reminder that any serious search to understand the experience of being a woman must give consideration to scientific discourse in biology and the practice of medicine which is based on this discourse in particular.

Defining biological sex and gender as connected but different did not originate in feminist writing but in sexology, in particular in trying to understand the phenomenon of transsexualism, that is individuals classified on every biological measure as one sex, who declared themselves to be subjectively the other. This is described as 'gender dysphoria' and is likely to be dealt with in this half of the twentieth century by chemical and surgical modification of an individual's biological sex characteristics to match her/his subjective gender. Jan Morris, a celebrated transsexual of the 1970s, wrote: 'I regard sex merely as a tool of gender' (1974, p. 99). And yet the phenomenon of transsexualism illustrates how resilient biological sex differences are to social and environmental modification. If physical sexual characteristics could be altered, either through an effort of will or through adopting a changed social environment such as dressing and living as a member of the opposite sex, transsexuals would not need to resort to medicine. Transsexualism

74

in its present form, necessitating extensive surgery and long-term hormone treatment, can in fact be seen as a product of modern biological science and medical technology.

What biological criteria distinguish male from female human beings, and how are these measured? These are the questions addressed by Lynda Birke in Article 2.1, 'In pursuit of difference: scientific studies of women and men'. The focus of biology is not the individual, but the group or population and how certain characteristics are distributed within populations. At the most fundamental level, that of chromosomal difference, individuals exist who are not neatly classifiable as male or female compared with the characteristics of the majority of the population. Birke demonstrates that biological differences are not absolute, and with respect to some characteristics such as height or weight the overlap between men and women is large and may be even further extended by training. It is these characteristics such as strength and stamina that are most often used to justify the differential social treatment of men and women.

Birke also introduces the debate about biological differences in the brain. Brain function has only been accessible to biological measurement with the development of electronic scanning devices and is a relatively new area of study. She argues that very little can be said with confidence about sex differences in brain function, and yet the importance accorded to these is out of all proportion to their biological significance. Birke demonstrates how the desire to prove the existence of significant sex differences continues to be strong enough to override the empirical evidence; the ideological foundations of scientists have made it difficult for them to allow the empirical evidence to speak.

Anthropology is a science based – as is much of biology – on evolutionary theories (evolution in the sense of structured change and development). While biology studies the physical characteristics of living things, not just across populations but across species, anthropology does the same for social organization and behaviour. Anthropology and biology have been the sciences most used to justify continuing gender inequality in society. In Article 2.2, 'The changing role of women in models of human evolution', Linda Marie Fedigan traces the historical development of evolution back to Darwin who placed primary importance on sexual selection and the different roles of males and females in propagating species. She points out that Darwin projected onto other species models of behaviour which reflected forms of British Victorian social organization. The popular twentieth-century version of this, 'Man the Hunter', has lodged firmly in the common consciousness, despite ridicule from feminists and others. Fedigan re-examines the evidence for Man the Hunter and describes the way an alternative model,

75

Woman the Gatherer, was articulated. She demonstrates that not only was the debate carried on 'scientifically' over the evidential base for the models, but that there was also a polarization amongst anthropologists reflecting their subjectivity, with men preferring the original formulation and women the later.

Evolutionary arguments have been used to justify oppressive conformity since they assert not only that a non-conforming individual is 'unnatural' but that she/he is also somehow jeopardizing evolutionary 'progress' and the future of the species. They have also been used to support racist ideology and eugenics movements which in Europe in the 1930s and '40s led to the attempted extermination of groups such as Jews, gypsies and homosexuals.

Since biology and anthropology both identify human beings as a species of mammal with evolutionary connections to other species such as chimpanzees, it is justifiable to look for features in other species which might help cast light on our own. Feminism has preferred to stress the social, cultural and intellectual aspects of human sex and gender. Fedigan argues that anthropological evidence from the study of non-human beings can generate insights and give direction to questions and investigation helpful to understanding gender in human societies. But it is also important that it is not seen as prescriptive or encapsulating 'the truth'.

Medicine is the application of biological theory, but it is also more than that: it is a flexible social construct and encompasses a varied set of activities. Catherine Kohler Riessman in Article 2.3, 'Women and medicalization: a new perspective', examines how aspects of life have become defined as medical issues, accessible to medical solutions. A feminist critique of medicine argues that women's power and control over our own bodies has been removed from us, and has become a professionally guarded area of expertise for doctors who, it sometimes seems, think that they know more about what's good for us than we do for ourselves! Campaigns such as the one against the automatic hospitalization of childbirth, which redefine childbirth as 'natural' rather than 'illness', have been supported by feminists. But such campaigns are not necessarily feminist ones. Reissman describes how demands for 'scientific birth', especially the use of pain relief, came in the nineteenth century from middle-class women who saw it as a way of *taking control* over the difficult process of childbirth. She is also very clear about the nature of class difference with respect to what benefits women gained from the increasing medicalization of childbirth. Self-help health groups were important parts of the women's movement of the 1970s; they disseminated information about health issues and remedies (see, for example, Boston Women's Health Collective, 1971). However, Riessman suggests that this is often 'deprofessionalization' of medicine rather than the 'demedicalization' of women's bodies. She describes the whole issue of medicine as one of a 'contradictory reality' for women, in which it is important that scientific claims are treated with scepticism, without dismissing the life-enhancing – and sometimes life-saving – potential that medicine has.

The power of medicine is not restricted to the profession of medical practitioner but is part of an international industrial and financial superstructure. The development of drugs for contraception, weight loss and depression reinforce the notion that there are medical – that is chemical – solutions to perceived personal problems. The multinational pharmaceuticals industry is huge and much of what they produce is directed at women. For example, psychotropic drugs (such as tranquilizers) for the treatment of depression were 17 per cent of all National Health Service prescriptions in 1984, and it is estimated that twice as many psychotropic drugs are prescribed for women than for men. 'In this context public health [or perhaps more critically women's health] may have more to do with a "healthy" pharmaceutical industry than had been previously considered', writes Betsy Ettore (1985).

Whereas Riessman is concerned with the impact of medicine on women in the developed world, the three maps from Seager and Olson's *Women in the World Atlas* illustrate global inequality with respect to contraception, infant mortality and general health (see the colour plate section in this book). Map 2 shows the difference in the use and availability of contraception worldwide in the mid-1980s. It illustrates not only the low proportion of women with access to contraception in most poor countries, but, in the small pie-charts at the bottom of the page, also the major reliance on sterilization in underdeveloped countries. (The figures do not reflect any changes that have taken place in the use of condoms since the spread of Aids.) The map also shows the decreasing investment from private industry in research and development of contraceptives. Drug companies have been criticized for their use of underdeveloped countries as a test-bed for new products:

> Before the Pill was marketed, it was not initially tested on Western women but taken to countries like Puerto Rico for experiments. At that time the dosage was much higher than is allowed today, but as the priority was to establish the contraceptive effectiveness of the preparation, other effects were not assessed. The racism which made Third World women more 'suitable' than white women was exacerbated by the fact that legal restrictions on trials of untested drugs were far less stringent in the Third World than they are in richer industrialized counties.

This discrepancy still operates today, with the result that

when a particular brand or dosage or method is determined to be unsafe and is partially or wholly withdrawn from the market in Western countries, it turns up in clinics in the Third World. Called 'drug dumping', this practice is an exercise in not losing profits on already-produced drugs and devices.

(Newman, 1985, p. 137)

Governments of underdeveloped countries have much less money to spend on the kind of health services usual in rich countries. They are dependent on international aid funds and also on the largesse of contraceptive companies, some of whom donate or provide contraceptive technology at very low cost to these governments. The fact that men dominate the research, development and policy of contraception globally illustrates the power of masculine science and technology:

Men hold the top positions in most international companies and agencies, as well as most national governments. Thus, decisions about the distribution of birth-prevention methods and the provision of services are generally made (and changed) by men, as are laws concerning contraception, abortion and sterilization. Similarly, most of the research into birth control is done by men. Women, of course, are the guinea pigs for new methods since most are intended for use by them. Some male techniques have been developed, but here the dangerous effects tend to be played down far less than is the case with female techniques. Disadvantages considered 'tolerable' for women are deemed an unacceptable burden for men. In fact men have been reluctant to volunteer for experiments with male methods of any kind, just as they have been generally reluctant to be sterilized. The World Health Organization recently decided not to put much money into research on male methods in the future – they simply cannot persuade enough men to try them! (In any case, women are understandably reluctant to rely on male birth control methods especially when these are 'invisible'.)

(Newman, pp. 141–2)

The availability of contraception along with the incidence of maternal and infant mortality – shown in Map 1a and b – illustrates the huge international inequalities between the life chances of women and our children. The maps also illustrate race and class inequalities within countries. The pictograms at the bottom of Map 1a show the threefold difference between the maternal mortality rates of the white population of the United States and other ethnic groups, and between these rates and the mortality rates of racial groupings in South Africa where the difference between whites and homeland blacks is almost *thirtyfold*. One of the saddest parts of this collection of diagrams is the seesaw diagram in Map 1a which illustrates the neglect of girl children, in particular in India, where three times as many girls as boys die between the ages of one and four. Environmental conditions and nutrition are more important factors with respect to maternal and infant mortality than medical provision, but there can be no doubt that a more equitable distribution of medical provision globally would contribute to improvements in these figures.

Map 3 is perhaps one of the simplest indicators of the quality of women's lives, that is their life expectancy. In industrialized countries women live on average six years longer than men, and even in non-industrialized countries women on average live longer, although the difference is smaller. There are very few countries where women's life expectancy is less than men's, and the worst case is India where women have low status and their health is neglected. Life expectancy rates in the UK are 76 years for women and 69.7 years for men; in India they are 50 years for women and 51.2 years for men (Seager and Olson, 1986). It is important to keep these kind of global figures in mind as a background to feminist debates about medical technology. Campaigns for less medical intervention by women in rich countries make little sense to women in poor countries who do not have even basic medical services.

The final article in this chapter deals with one of the newest and most controversial issues of the 1980s, at least in the developed world: reproductive technology. One of the demands of the women's movement of the 1970s was for free abortion and contraception. Liberation was seen as a positive choice to limit childbearing. The problems of women who, because of problems with fertility, were unable to become pregnant tended to be seen as one of 'false consciousness', that is that somehow the desire to have children was a socially produced desire and could be countered by resisting it. It was only when white, middle-class feminists listened to black women and working-class women who were being coerced into sterilization, or into using contraception that they did not want, that the issue began to be seen as one of choice to have – as well as not to have – children. A combination of advances in reproductive technology for contraception, with critiques of the notion of reproductive choice, has led to the development of the concept of 'reproductive rights'. The article by Lynda Birke, Susan Himmelweit and Gail Vines, 'Detecting genetic diseases: prenatal screening and its problems', examines in some detail the technology of one particular aspect of new reproductive medicine and some of the political and ethical issues involved in its use.

The first published feminist responses to developments in reproductive technology were critical and negative: an analysis of the power of male medicine (such as that quoted from Newman above) to control women's sexual and reproductive functions identified the new techniques of in vitro fertilization and genetic screening as progressing the male desire to take reproductive control from women. It is ironic that a move towards extra-uterine gestation – Firestone's (1980) technical solution to women's inequality – was viewed with horror when it appeared. It was seen as either bad for all women or only advantageous to a few rich and higher-class women; by channelling resources into these potentially few women it was thought that the reproductive needs of others would continue to be ignored. Birke *et al.* take a more reflective view of genetic screening in particular, and they have some optimism for the potential of genetic screening for improving our understanding of the causes of various disabilities. They are also clear that there must be some way of separating the individual ethical decisions a woman might need to make about abortion from scientific decisions about what is technically possible.

Over the last two hundred years biology, anthropology and medicine have contributed to the construction of sex and gender in the way empirical data have been assembled and used and in the construction of theories which contained implicit ideological bias. This construction includes a model of women as weak and deficient. Feminism has attacked this both by criticizing it from outside in terms of the uses to which the theories have been put, but also from the inside, engaging in technical arguments about data collection and analysis, and research design. The articles in this chapter have, we hope, demonstrated the value in doing this. Biology, medicine and feminism all contain distinct and different models of 'Woman'; each is separately incomplete, but when the three are articulated and informed by each other then we begin to have a more critical understanding of what constitutes sex and gender.

Gill Kirkup

Article 2.1
IN PURSUIT OF DIFFERENCE: SCIENTIFIC STUDIES OF WOMEN AND MEN

Lynda Birke

The fact that women and men are different has long fascinated people. Explanations for the origin of these differences have been plenty: evidence, on the other hand, has been in rather shorter supply. Aristotle suggested that a source of gender difference was that females were biologically defective. Their role in reproduction was merely, and passively, to give the foetus a home and some nourishment. The greater activity and importance of male seed (sperm) in reproduction was, in turn, related to the greater heat of males; women were imperfect because they lacked bodily heat (Tuana, 1989a).

In the following centuries there have been many claims of difference between the bodies of women and men. For some, like Aristotle's idea of heat, there is no evidence. Yet there clearly are anatomical differences between women and men. My concern is not so much to list the various – and sometimes obvious – ways in which the two sexes differ as to ask what we mean by the idea of *difference in how bodies work*. What is meant, for instance, when we read of sex differences in the way that human brains work? What does it mean to talk of sex differences in muscular strength? And why do we focus on sex as a source of difference rather than some other physical attribute?

This article will also address the question of how sex differences originate.[1] In part, this question can be answered in terms of human development: the chromosomes that we inherit from our parents largely determine what sex we become, for example. But human development does not cease at birth, and one theme running through this chapter is how we change throughout our life-spans – and, accordingly, what kinds of sex differences we see between people at different stages of their lives. In part, too, the question of where sex differences come from can be answered in terms of what causes the differences: why, for example, do men tend to have heavier arm muscles than women? There are many answers to these questions: but to begin to address them, we need to go back in our lives, to before a baby is even born.

SEX DIFFERENCES BEFORE BIRTH

Immediately a baby is born, we allocate it to one sex or the other, on the basis of what its genitals look like. We take this allocation very much for granted; so much so, that most people are horrified when mistakes are occasionally – if rarely – made, and a child is allocated to the 'wrong' sex. Culturally, we attach great importance to the existence of two, different, sexes: a child is brought up as either one or the other, and we expect that everyone we meet will be *either* male *or* female. But biology is not always as clear-cut as that simple dichotomy would imply.

The first step, then, in how sex differences develop is that we inherit particular sets of sex chromosomes. A person with two X chromosomes will be female: one with an X and a Y will be male. Occasionally, however, it is not so straightforward as that, and an individual is born who is neither XX nor XY.[2] Just how this happens does not concern us here. What is more important is that even the chromosomes are not as dichotomous as appears at first sight; even chromosomes cannot always indicate whether a person is 'male' or 'female'.

Indeed, women who are deemed to be too masculine in competitive sports may be subjected to 'sex tests' based on analysis of chromosomes in order to determine whether they are 'genuinely' female (tests are never done to see if men are genuinely male, however). The middle-distance Czech runner Jarmila Kratochvilova, for example, was alleged to be 'not really female' in the mid-1980s. An American doctor commented, 'This is not a normal physiological female body. I've treated Olympic female athletes in 34 countries but I've never seen a body like that' (quoted in Donahue and Johnson, 1986, p. 66). Despite medical misgivings, Kratochvilova passed the test. Chromosome tests were introduced in 1966 and Ewa Klobukowska, a Polish athlete, was the first to 'fail' the test; the doctors declared that she had 'one chromosome too many to be declared a woman for the purposes of athletic competition' (she had two Xs and one Y chromosome) (ibid., p. 77).

The next step in development depends upon the chromosomes. During the first few weeks of gestation it is not possible to tell the foetus' sex from its appearance. Even inside, the reproductive systems of male and female start out the same way. But, if a foetus has a Y chromosome, then these internal structures will begin to develop into testes and the tubes which carry sperm from the testes to the outside.[3] If the foetus has no Y chromosome (usually, this means it will be XX), then ovaries and uterus develop (see Figure 2.1.1). Again, while this may hold true for most people, a few individuals are born whose internal reproductive systems are not

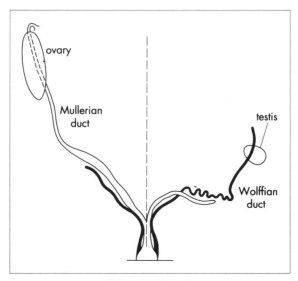

Figure 2.1.1
The development of anatomical difference in foetuses. Very early in their lives, foetuses have two sets of internal tubes, or ducts; only one of these will develop. If a foetus has a Y chromosome, then testes will develop (right-hand side). The testis produces a hormone which causes one set of ducts to develop (shaded black) and the others to shrivel. If there is no Y chromosome, ovaries form and the other set of ducts will develop.

straightforwardly 'male' or 'female' – a female born without ovaries, for example, or someone born with one ovary and one testis.

Ovaries and testes produce hormones, even at this early stage of foetal development (by this time, the foetus is still less than six weeks old). The third stage of sex development depends upon these hormones. Testes produce higher levels of certain hormones (androgens) than do ovaries; how the external genitals of the foetus develop next depends upon these levels. If the levels of androgens are high (as they would normally be if testes are present), then a penis and scrotum will develop; if they are low (for example, if the foetus has ovaries rather than a testis), then labia and a clitoris will develop: see Figure 2.1.2.

Most people would think of the structure of the external genitals as one of the most basic differences between women and men; it is, after all, genital structure that allows us to assign newborn babies to one or other sex. Yet even here the differences are not absolute, and some individuals are born with ambiguous genitals

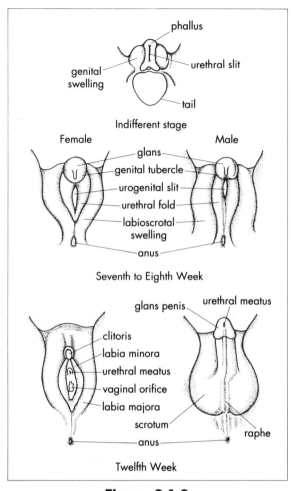

Figure 2.1.2
The development of the external genitals. Both male and female
foetuses look the same before the seventh week.

(perhaps because they are producing higher or lower levels of
particular hormones than might be expected). Babies that are
chromosomally female, for example, may have a condition that
makes them produce excess levels of androgens before they are
born (the hormones are produced by the adrenal glands, adjacent
to the kidneys). Because of the higher-than-usual levels of androgens,
the baby's external genitals are relatively masculinized by the time
she is born. Usually, this condition is recognized at birth and the
child raised as a girl (perhaps with surgery to alter her anatomy if
it has become masculinized).

Box 2.1.1
Chromosomes, genes and inheritance

One source of differences between members of any species is the genes. Each human being has thousands of genes, inherited from their parents, and arranged into 23 pairs of chromosomes. (Chromosomes are usually arranged in pairs, although different species may have fewer or more pairs than we do.)

One of these pairs is called the sex chromosomes. When the body produces eggs or sperm (called gametes), each chromosome pair is split into two: thus a human gamete contains 23 single chromosomes. When sperm and egg fuse during the process of fertilization, chromosomes are once again paired up and the full 46 (or 23 pairs) are restored.

Sex chromosomes in mammals are called X and Y. Females usually have two Xs: so each egg they produce contains one X. Males usually have one X and one Y chromosome, so that each individual sperm can have either an X or a Y chromosome. This means that it is the sperm's sex chromosome (X or Y) that will determine what sex chromosomes the resulting child will have.

Because chromosomes are in pairs, the genes they contain are usually also paired. Often, the joint action of many pairs of genes influence the emergence of a particular characteristic – through interaction with the environment, of course. Skin colour, for example, is affected by the action of many genes.

Sometimes, however, a single pair of genes controls the manifestation of one particular trait. The ability to taste a particular chemical called PTC (which is bitter to those who can taste it) is one trait depending on a single pair of genes. But we inherit two copies of the gene – one from each parent: these can be the same as each other, or slightly different. So, we could either inherit two copies that are identical – two genes for tasting (call these TT) or two genes for non-tasting (call these tt) – or we could inherit one of each type of the gene (Tt). Having two identical genes means that we will be tasters (TT) or non-tasters (tt), but if we inherit one of each – Tt – then we will also be able to taste the chemical. The effect of the T gene is said to be *dominant* to the effect of the t gene, because, when the two occur together, only T affects the outcome. The t gene is said to be *recessive*. People who have both a dominant and a recessive gene for a particular trait are said to be *carriers* of that trait: that is they can pass on the recessive gene to their children but it does not have any effect in the parent who carries it.

Most genetic diseases, such as cystic fibrosis, are recessive. So, if both parents are carriers, there is a chance that a child will inherit the two recessive genes and so develop the disease. But any of their children who inherit only one recessive gene will not develop the disease. Genetic diseases based on dominant genes are rarer: Huntington's chorea is an example. If either or both parents has this gene, there is a much greater chance of the children developing the disease, since the gene for it is dominant.

The Y chromosome carries very few genes; these include a gene called the 'testis determining factor' that promotes the development of testes in the embryo. This usually means that the embryo will develop as a male; without that gene, the embryo will develop as a female. But because the Y chromosome carries so few genes, the genes on the X chromosome in a male are not usually paired; so in a boy a recessive gene on the X chromosome acts like a dominant gene. This is why only boys develop Duchenne's muscular dystrophy; the faulty recessive gene is on the X chromosome. A woman who inherits a faulty gene on the X chromosome is likely to have a normal gene on her second X chromosome; that is, she will be a carrier for the faulty gene which may then be passed on to some of her sons. Haemophilia and Lesch-Nyhan disease are two examples of genetic diseases passed on in this way.

GROWING UP

With the exception of the external genitals, there are rather few differences between girls and boys until they reach puberty. There are small differences in height, and there are differences in the rate at which children become mature: girls reach half their eventual adult weight at an earlier age than boys, and their adult teeth come through slightly earlier, but there is considerable overlap and similarity between girls and boys in their first decade of life.

Somewhat more pronounced differences emerge as puberty approaches, and the amounts of sex hormones produced by the child's ovaries or testes increase. The age at which different children enter puberty varies enormously; what varies much less is the sequence in which the different events occur. These are summarized in Figure 2.1.3.

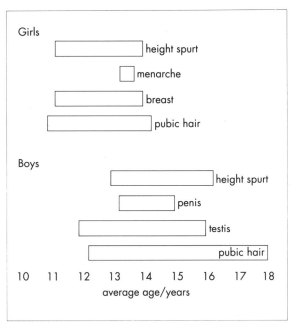

Figure 2.1.3

The major events of puberty, showing the range of ages that different individuals go through each stage.

Some of these differences reflect basic differences in the reproductive roles of males and females. Men, for example, develop larger testes as the testes begin to produce sperm; women begin to menstruate as their ovaries begin to produce mature eggs in preparation for pregnancy. Other differences are less directly concerned with pregnancy, but depend upon hormonal differences

– the growth of breasts in women, for example. (These hormones are, of course, indirectly involved in reproduction.)

Even the hormonal differences are not absolute, however. There is no one hormone that is produced uniquely by either women or men. Men produce more of the hormones called androgens than women do, whereas women produce more of the hormones called oestrogens and progestins. These hormones are produced by both ovaries and testes; they are also produced by the adrenal glands, situated above the kidneys. It is thus not strictly accurate to refer to male and female hormones as though each belongs specifically to one sex. Strictly speaking, what is meant by 'male hormone' is that the hormone stimulates the development of male characteristics. Unfortunately, however, the everyday use of terms such as 'male (or female) hormones' often implied that they belong specifically to one sex or the other.

Yet it is not only in reproductive anatomy and secondary sexual characteristics such as breasts or facial hair that women and men tend to differ physically. Accompanying the spurt of growth that takes place during puberty are changes in the child's skeleton, particularly the shoulders and hips. As boys grow into adolescence, the width of the shoulders increases particularly, whereas in girls it is the width of the hips that increases. One reason for this is that some joints of the skeleton contain cells that are particularly sensitive to hormones. Cells in the hip joint of a girl respond particularly to oestrogens, one of the major hormones produced by her ovaries, whereas cells in a boy's shoulder joints respond preferentially to androgens from his testes.

Muscles, too, begin to develop noticeably more in boys than in girls: Figure 2.1.4 shows, for example, the change in the width of muscles in the upper arm and the calf (the two measurements are combined in the figure) for boys and girls at different ages. Not surprisingly, this is associated with greater differences in muscle strength.

All of these are differences that most of us have seen for ourselves; it is, after all, fairly obvious that boys tend to become bigger and to have narrower hips than girls. But there are other differences that are less obvious; these are shown in Figure 2.1.5. Women tend, for example, to have smaller hearts than men, and to have lower concentrations of haemoglobin in their blood. Haemoglobin is the chemical in our blood that carries oxygen around to wherever it is needed. Men's blood therefore tends to carry more oxygen: for every hundred millilitres of blood, the average amount of oxygen carried in a man's blood is 19.2 millilitres compared to 16.7 for a woman's.

Further differences emerge as we get older. Women's reproductive systems go through fairly dramatic changes at the meno-

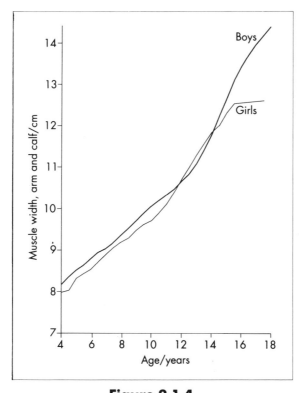

Figure 2.1.4
The growth of muscle width in upper arm and calf (combined
measurement) during childhood and adolescence.

pause, as the ovaries cease to produce mature eggs. Men's
reproductive system, by contrast, slows down less dramatically. One
of the consequences of the menopause is that women's ovaries start
to produce smaller quantities of oestrogen; some of the less pleasant
problems of the menopause, such as hot flushes, are at least partly
due to the decline in hormone levels.

As levels of these sex hormones decline in older people, the
balance of hormones may shift. In women, for example, this can
sometimes result in increased growth of bodily hair (a 'masculinizing'
effect of the balance of hormones). Another consequence of declining
hormone levels is a change in the way that bones are remodelled.
Throughout our lives, bone is constantly being broken down
and rebuilt. During early adulthood, the loss and rebuilding
approximately balance each other; but, as we age, so the amount
lost begins to exceed the amount built. As a result, bones can
become thinner and more fragile as we approach old age (a condition
called osteoporosis), and so more likely to fracture.

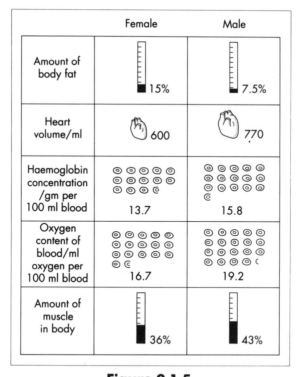

Figure 2.1.5
Some physiological differences between average men and women.

Women are more commonly associated with high risks of bone fracture due to osteoporosis than men, however. Partly, this is because women seem to lose bone at a faster rate after the menopause, owing to the more dramatic change in their hormone levels. Partly, too, they are collectively at higher risk because there are simply more older women than men in the population. So, towards the end of our lives, other differences emerge between women and men: women are more likely to suffer fractures because of osteoporosis, and they are likely to live longer.

WHAT IS A 'DIFFERENCE'?

Those, then, are some of the characteristics that someone might mention if asked what the physical differences are between men and women. But *what do we mean by difference?* I began the last section by outlining some aspects of human biology that show quite clear-cut differences (the possession of X or Y chromosomes, say, or having ovaries versus testes), and I have emphasized that even these are not absolute. But what is an absolute difference? *Are* there

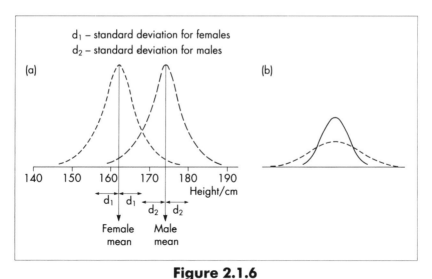

Figure 2.1.6

(a) The hypothetical distribution of human height: the number of people of each sex in the population (*y* axis; left-hand side) for each height (in centimetres); (b) Two hypothetical distribution curves with the same mean, but with different spreads.

many ways in which women are absolutely different from men? To answer that, we have to distinguish between what characteristics *an individual* has, and those exhibited by the *population*. Figure 2.1.6 illustrates how height is distributed among the population, showing different curves for men and women. There are differences between the mean height for each sex, but there are more individuals in the middle range of height for that sex than very tall or very short individuals. But there is clearly overlap between the populations. So, to state that a difference is not absolute is to say that there is some degree of overlap between two populations, even if there is a marked difference in the mean (or average) values.

When we compare two populations, we can look at the mean (average) values of each population. If they are markedly different, then we can probably conclude that the two populations really are different. (We would say that the two populations are significantly different, statistically.) If they are very similar, then there may be little difference between the two populations. But we cannot be sure just from the mean values. Look at Figure 2.1.6(b). Here there are distributions for two populations with the same mean values, but the spread of the two populations is clearly different. To assess statistically whether a difference is significant, we would need to know both the mean values for the two populations, and the amount of spread (which statisticians call *variance*).

For many of the sex differences mentioned in this article, the degree of overlap between the two populations is considerable. So, although there are differences in the mean value for men and women (in the amount of fat on the body, for example), there are clearly many people who have very little – or a great deal – of body fat and are therefore far from the average. What we should remember is that not all differences between the sexes are necessarily statistically significant.

Yet these statistics tell us nothing about individuals. Individuals could fall anywhere on the curve. Thus, there are many very thin women, and many very fat men. It is important to remember that statements about 'sex differences' in some measurement are differences between populations. Yet it is all too easy to assume that the statement is saying something about 'typical' men and women; thus, the statement that 'the typical woman is less muscular than the typical man' could refer to hypothetical individuals who are 'typical' of their sex. That is, they have a roughly 'average' amount of muscle. But within the population as a whole, there are clearly individuals who deviate markedly from that average, women who are very muscular, for example, or unmuscular men.

A third problem with the notion of difference is that it seems to imply something rather fixed and unchanging, especially if the characteristic is a physical one (such as muscle width). Yet this may be true of neither populations nor individuals. Consider first a statistical description of sex differences in muscle mass (the weight of muscles); the data referred to above were obtained from a study of growth and development in British children. But this sex difference does not apply in all human societies. In some human communities, there is very little difference in the weight of men's and women's muscles: Oakley (1972) gives an example from Bali, where men do not usually engage in heavy work so there is little difference between them and women. Some characteristics, moreover, may change with time: children's heights at any given age have increased over this century in the United Kingdom, while the age at which young girls experience their first menstrual period has decreased. As we have seen in the previous section, the extent and nature of sex differences varies throughout the life span. To talk about 'average sex differences' for the population usually means talking about people of very different ages.

Many physical sex differences seem even more variable when we consider how individuals' bodies work. Obviously, anatomical differences – the structure of the genitals, for instance – cannot be changed (except, perhaps, by surgery!). What can be, however, are physiological differences – differences in the ways that our bodies work. This includes the amount of oxygen that the blood can carry, or muscle strength and weight, for example. Differences between males and females in muscle width of arms and calf seem to increase at puberty, as shown in Figure 2.1.4, although this is less true of other muscles; there is only a small difference between women and men, on average, in the size or strength of muscles in the thigh (allowing for differences in body size; a bigger person obviously has bigger muscles). That thigh muscles do not show the large differences we saw for arm muscles may be due to the fact that all children have to exercise their thigh muscles to about the same extent during childhood, as these muscles are particularly important in standing and walking – which all children do.

Exercise can also reduce the size of some of the sex differences in bodily function in adults. In studies which have compared highly trained athletes of each sex, differences in heart size or the capacity of the blood to carry oxygen are much less than they would be for equivalent men and women who were not athletic. This effect is shown in Figure 2.1.7. In this figure, the height of each person represents the quantity of each measurement (relative to untrained men). So, for untrained people, the amount of oxygen that the blood can carry in women is smaller than that for men. But for trained athletes, the difference is very much less.

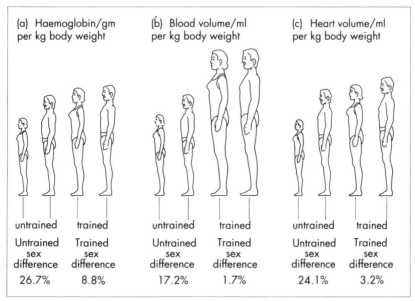

(a) Haemoglobin/gm per kg body weight	(b) Blood volume/ml per kg body weight	(c) Heart volume/ml per kg body weight
untrained trained	untrained trained	untrained trained
Untrained sex difference	Trained sex difference	Untrained sex difference	Trained sex difference	Untrained sex difference	Trained sex difference
26.7%	8.8%	17.2%	1.7%	24.1%	3.2%

Figure 2.1.7
The effects of athletic training on some physiological features: (a) the amount of haemoglobin in blood; (b) the volume of blood; and (c) the volume pumped by the heart. The size of each of the figures represents the value of each factor relative to untrained men. So, the blood volume of trained women is greater than that of untrained men, and roughly equal to that of trained men.

Another example of a way in which training can affect physiology comes from a study of the effects of carrying heavy loads. Until recently, scientists believed that doing hard work, such as carrying a load, causes a person's metabolic rate (the rate at which they burn up energy) to increase: the more work you do, the faster you burn up the energy. This is true for most of us and in one study applied to the young army recruits who were asked to carry very heavy loads in backpacks. But it did not apply to the women to whom the army men were compared. These were women from an African community who traditionally carried loads on their heads. The metabolic rate of the women in the study did not increase, even when they were asked to carry very heavy loads (Maloiy *et al.*, 1986).

One reason for this difference may be that these women were carrying heavy weights on their heads even when they were small girls; this 'training', the researchers suggest, could affect how the body uses energy. So, even something as obviously 'biological' as the rate at which we use energy can change with training.

Exercise also affects sex differences in older people. After about age 35, the rate at which bone material is lost begins to exceed the rate at which it is gained. So, during our 40s and after, we are all losing bone, although in women, this seems to speed up after the menopause, leading to osteoporosis in many women. Yet osteoporosis (very brittle and fragile bones) is not inevitable. Bone loss undoubtedly exceeds gain in later life, but the amount lost depends upon how much was there in the first place. If a person has very dense bone in their early adulthood, then their bones will retain much of their strength into old age. The density of our bones, in turn, depends upon the stresses that are put upon them through exercise. Our muscles are attached to our bones. So, as a muscle contracts, it pulls upon the bone, causing it to move. Long bones such as the femur (the thigh bone) have large, powerful muscles attached to them, and the pull exerted on the bone is considerable. Frequent stresses on the bone make its cells respond by producing more hard bone. Thus, hard exercise in early adulthood helps to build up denser bone.

The sex difference, then, in the fragility of older people's bones may be partly due to the fact that women in our culture tend to take less strenuous exercise than men throughout their adult lives. (This is not true of all cultures: women in traditional African societies are no more prone to osteoporosis than men, for example.)[4] In Britain women's bones are, consequently, less dense than men's on average, even before they reach the menopause. As one researcher commented, '[Osteoporosis] has reached epidemic proportions as a consequence of increased longevity, compounded by lifestyles that have led to women's reaching their menopause with an inadequate bone mineral reserve' (Notelovitz, 1986, p. 224).

A fourth problem with focusing on sex *differences* lies in how to interpret them. For example, when researchers discovered that men tend to sweat more than women during exercise (whereas women tend to go red), they concluded that women regulate their body temperature inefficiently. Yet women seem to be no more likely to overheat than men during strenuous exercise, and their tendency to lose heat by 'glowing' may even lessen the risk of dehydration during prolonged exercise (Ferris, 1980). Another example is running speed. On the whole, men's speeds in athletic races are faster than women's, but, if the results are adjusted for body size – women are usually smaller than men – then women actually run faster than men on average (Dyer, 1982). Similarly, the fact that women tend to have more body fat has sometimes been seen as a disadvantage in relation to sport – more weight to carry, and smaller muscles, for instance. But this difference can also be interpreted another way: fat is an excellent source of stored energy and is a good insulator. So for long-distance running, such as marathons or ultra-long-distance (races of 24 hours or longer), women might have an advantage over men in having more ready access to long-term stores of energy (Dyer, 1982). The insulation provided by fat might also be an advantage in long-distance swimming. Sex differences, then, can be interpreted in different ways.

Before leaving the issue of physical differences, however, we should ask why it is that *sex* differences are deemed to be so important. Why, for instance, is sport organized around differences between men and women? The usual answer to this is that men have an intrinsic advantage – greater physical strength, say. But that may be an advantage in only some sports. In sports requiring stamina (such as long-distance swimming) or fine control of movements (such as fine-bore rifle shooting), gross physical strength may actually be a disadvantage. In some sports, height may be a more appropriate way to distinguish between people. In basketball and rowing, for example, there is considerable advantage to being tall; true, this will apply to more men, but there are also some very tall women.

ON DIFFERENCES IN THE BRAIN

Just as male dominance in sport is sometimes justified in terms of sex differences in physical strength, so male dominance in intellectual pursuits has been justified by explanations that men's and women's brains are different. In the late nineteenth century there were two forms of such explanations. Some scientists simply pointed to the

95

greater weight of the average male brain: 'the skulls of a notable proportion of women', opined the French writer Delauney, 'more nearly approach the volume of the skulls of certain gorillas than that of better developed skulls of the male sex' (Russett, 1989, p. 36).

An alternative explanation lay in the alleged greater variability of men. Men's mental abilities were said to fit a wider bell-curve (or normal distribution) of the sort shown in Figure 2.1.6(b), women's the narrower. The focus here was not on whether the average values differed, but in the overall spread of the distribution. Men were more likely, the theory went, to be found at both ends of the distribution: there were more very stupid men and more male geniuses (an idea that is still around: people still use this to explain why 'there has never been a female Mozart'). This led to beliefs that one writer summarized as: 'Girls' minds [were said to] excel at the common or pedestrian, whereas boys' ideas are wider ranging. Because girls are more like one another than boys [in this theory] they are, as a group, closer to the "ordinary"' (Shields, 1987, p. 191).

Evidence for both these theories is lacking. Critics have pointed, for example, to the fact that the weight of the brain depends upon the size of the whole body. If comparisons are made of brain weights adjusted for total body size, the sex difference disappears. Theories which simply assert that male brains are superior at all intellectual functions are much less evident today. They have been superceded by theories that focus on the different qualities and abilities of men's brains and women's brains.

Before going into the details of recent theories, I should emphasize that there are likely to be *some* – albeit slight – differences in how women's and men's brains work. One important reason for supposing this has to do with the fact that a tiny portion of the brain (called the hypothalamus) organizes how our hormones work – and there are some ways in which these are different in women and men. Obviously, women's sex hormones usually follow a monthly cycle associated with the pattern of menstruation. Men's sex hormones do not follow such a pattern. (This is not to say, however, that men's hormones are produced at a steady level. They, too, fluctuate – with time of day, for example, or because of stress. They also rise in anticipation of sexual activity.)

During the early development of a foetus, at about the time that the external genitals are developing into characteristically female or male form, the hormones responsible also enter the brain of the foetus. Here, they affect permanently how the hypothalamus works. As before, high levels of the hormones known as androgens will stop the hypothalamus from ever organizing hormone cycles. If there are low levels, then it will be cyclic. This difference will be present at birth (although obviously undetected until puberty). But clear evidence for other intrinsic differences in the way that women's and men's brains work is scarce.

There are various ways in which researchers could, in principle, find out if the sexes differ in the ways that their brains actually function. These include:

(a) studying the gross anatomy of the brains of people after death;

(b) investigating how particular parts or cells of the brain respond electrically or chemically, say;

(c) studies looking at people's skills in relation to what we know about how the two halves of the brain work.

Each approach has been used to provide evidence that male and female brains work differently. And each has its problems, which I will deal with in turn.

An example of (a) was a study of the nerve fibres connecting the two halves of the brain. Female brains, the researchers found, had relatively thicker fibres in this area (called the corpus callosum) than men's brains: see figure 2.1.8. An obvious problem, however, with focusing on gross anatomy in this way is that the person is dead: brain function during life cannot be directly assessed.[5] Gross anatomical differences, moreover, tell us nothing about the causes of those differences: we cannot tell whether they might be due to some biological factor, such as hormones, or to some difference in, say, lifestyle. So, even if we accept that men and women differ in

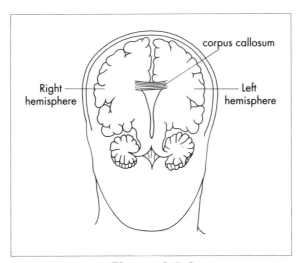

Figure 2.1.8
The two hemispheres of the human brain, connected by a band of nerve fibres, called the corpus callosum.

the thickness of this part of the brain, we are far from knowing what it means.

Direct investigation of what nerve cells in the brain are doing (b) might be informative, but it is obviously something our society considers unethical in humans (although some limited assessment of this kind has been done during brain surgery in people). Scientists do, however, use non-human animals for such purposes. Studies of how brains work in animals may combine, for example, anatomical investigations (a) with electrical or chemical investigation of the animals' brains.

It is from these, and by making inferences from observations of humans who have suffered brain damage, that scientists found out that different parts of the brain specialize in particular ways. In humans, for instance, a large area of the left side of the brain specializes in speech; so, if someone's brain is damaged in this area when they are adult, their speech will be impaired in some way (in very young children, other parts of the brain may take over the job of the damaged area).

One important aspect of this specialization is that the two halves of the brain – the right and left hemispheres – have somewhat different functions. One example of such asymmetry is handedness; the right hand is controlled particularly by the left side of the brain (see Figure 2.1.8).

If we cannot directly investigate human brain function, then we have to make inferences (c) based on observations of people's skills. Doctors faced with a person who loses the ability to speak after a road accident, for example, would have to infer that the person's brain was damaged, probably on the left side. But inference can be a problem if it is stretched too far. In relation to sex differences, the inference is made in the following way: if scientists believe that a particular skill is associated with the left side of the brain, say, then they might infer that someone who is very good at that skill, but less good at something associated with the right side, had a dominant right hemisphere.

The starting point for inferences about men's and women's brains is that there seem to be sex differences in certain cognitive (or thinking) skills. Because some of these skills are believed to be associated with one side or other of the brain, some researchers have argued that men and women differ in the degree of symmetry of their brains (that is, whether one side 'dominates' the other).

There have long been claims that women and men think differently – and perhaps they do. But the claims about brain symmetry are based largely on the results of a set of psychological tests. Some of these were designed by psychologists to test for verbal abilities (tests might include, for example, questions asking you to supply a missing word in a sequence). Females, psychology textbooks tell us, do better on these tests than males. Other tests are designed to assess spatial ability, such as the ability to imagine how a flat shape on a page would look if folded in three dimensions. Here the sex difference reverses: males, we are told, are consistently superior to females. Spatial ability may be important in learning science, some people have claimed: so sex differences in spatial ability may be the reason why so few women become scientists or engineers.

There are various, and contradictory, theories about how sex differences in cognitive abilities are linked to asymmetry of the brain, and I am not going to go into them all here. The central part of the argument, however, rests on the claim that language ability concerns the left side, whereas spatial abilities are focused more on the right side of the brain. From here, it is easy to infer that males are somehow more 'right brained' and females 'left brained'.[6]

It is also easy to go beyond the available evidence. There may be enough weight of evidence to make inferences about brains in relation to handedness, say. But when it comes to sex differences, the scales are heavily loaded; the mass of inferences and assumptions far outweighs that of clear evidence.

One important strand of criticism concerns the psychological skills themselves, and how they are tested. Of all the tests designed to measure spatial ability, only a few show a difference between males and females. Tests may measure only a very limited range of appropriate skills; verbal skills, for example, include a wide range of abilities, such as reading, and may depend upon other abilities, such as reasoning.

If it is unclear just what is being measured, it is even less clear that there is evidence of a marked difference based on sex or gender. As we saw with physical characteristics, there is enormous overlap. Indeed, the overlap is such that spatial ability alone simply cannot explain why, for instance, there are still so few women engineers. Yet the difference is often *portrayed* as much greater. One 'popular' book claims, for instance, that – unequivocally – 'men's brains are more specialized' and that 'A woman may be less able to separate emotion from reason because of the way the female brain is organized' (Moir and Jessel, 1989, pp. 43, 48). Overstating the case is not unique to popular accounts, however: Hugh Fairweather noted how little evidence there was of clear-cut sex differences, yet how often the textbooks reported it. He concluded that this was 'stuff indeed to make a myth' (Fairweather, 1976).

A second strand of criticism is that the alleged links between brain asymmetry and sex differences often contradict themselves. At one time women were said in some theories to have dominant right brains – a claim flying in the face of assertions that women were better at verbal (left side) and men at spatial (right side) skills.

Rogers (1988) notes two reasons why this claim should be made: first, some researchers have claimed that emotions have to do more with the right side (again, a claim made largely without evidence: and if we can locate 'emotion' in the brain at all, it probably has more to do with the bits of the brain lying underneath the two hemispheres). And second, she points out, '. . . it is obviously not acceptable for females to have left hemispheric dominance as analytic ability is a property of the left hemisphere' (Rogers, 1988, p. 48; also see Birke, 1992).

The third strand of criticism is that we should not automatically assume that any difference between women and men in performance of psychological tests is due to biology. It is, moreover, a strange kind of biology – for these theories portray the differences as somehow etched into a fixed kind of brain. Yet surely the human brain is anything but fixed: on the contrary, it shows amazing capacities for learning and memory. If there *are* differences between populations of women and of men in performance on certain psychological tests, then this may have little or nothing to do with their biology at all.

It has much more to do with gender, and how that is perceived. Females tend to gain higher scores on some tests of verbal ability; but boys learn early in life to associate reading with femininity (Rogers, 1988). Parents, however, usually recognize the importance of acquiring verbal skills and try to ensure that sons *learn* them (McGuinness, 1976).

Such compensation is less evident, however, in relation to girls and learning mechanical/spatial skills. But neither parents nor schools have traditionally tried to give girls compensatory education specifically aimed at developing these skills.

Yet there is evidence that the sex difference in spatial abilities is not found in all human societies. It largely disappears, moreover, if girls and boys are taught science in ways that encourage initiative and appropriate cognitive skills. Jane Butler Kahle studied a group of American biology teachers whom she had selected as being particularly successful in encouraging children to study science – including the girls. These teachers made particular efforts to encourage all children to participate, and were more likely than most teachers to include plenty of opportunities for the children to do 'hands-on' work in the laboratory. The students of these teachers were given various psychological tests, including tests of spatial ability and tests designed to measure students' anxiety about doing science. Sex differences virtually disappeared (Kahle, 1985, p. 64).

CONCLUSIONS

There are undoubtedly differences between women and men, both physically and psychologically, and our society attaches a great deal of importance to them. So much so, indeed, that they are often exaggerated out of all proportion. Such differences as exist are easily portrayed as absolute instead of statistical (that is they imply that the difference is between all men and all women, rather than only some). The question of what is meant by 'difference' in these discussions is clearly of some concern to feminists: but so is the widespread tendency, which I have tried to outline here, to attribute difference to 'biological' causes. There are two major problems with this: the concept of 'biology' it invokes is one of fixity – 'biology' is not seen as something which might change. And, secondly, other factors that might contribute are excluded. Even such obviously biological parts of the body as your bones are subject to change. The psychologist, Helen Thompson Woolley, said in 1910 that,

> There is perhaps no field aspiring to be scientific where flagrant personal bias, logic martyred in the cause of supporting a prejudice, unfounded assertions, and even sentimental rot and drivel, have run riot to such an extent as here.
>
> (Quoted in Sayers, 1980, p. 58; also see Rosenberg, 1982)

She was referring to research into sex differences. Feminist critics might well wonder how much has changed in 80 years.

Notes

1   In this chapter, I have relied upon the distinction between sex and gender (although it is problematic – see Birke, 1992). Thus, to refer to biological difference in, say, muscle size, I use the term sex difference. Gender is more usually applied to behavioural/social differences.

2   A person may be born, for example, with only one X chromosome and no other sex chromosome, or with two Xs and one Y, or two Ys and one X. In the first case, the person would appear to be female at birth, although she would lack ovaries. At puberty she would fail to develop secondary sexual characteristics, such as breasts and pubic hair, and would fail to menstruate. Some degree of 'intersex' is apparent in most individuals with sex chromosome anomalies; they are usually infertile.

3   Scientists have identified a gene situated on the Y chromosome (in humans and other mammals) which promotes the development of testes. If that gene is absent, the internal structures will develop into ovaries, uterus and so on. In that sense, the gene on the Y chromosome could be called 'male-determining' gene. Interestingly, many scientific reports referred to it as did newspaper accounts as

a *sex*-determining gene, as though differentiating into two sexes is equal to becoming male. (See Fausto-Sterling, 1989).

4   There are many reasons for women's lack of strenuous exercise, of course, that do not concern us here. Women may not wish to participate in organized sport, for example because of its image of trenchant masculinity, or because – unlike most men – they lack the leisure time. See the special issue of *Women's Studies International Forum* (edited by Ann Hall) on the 'The gendering of sport, leisure and physical education' (Vol. 10, No. 4, 1987). There is, however, rather more interest among women in taking exercise now than there was, say, twenty years ago – so the sex difference may be declining.

5   There were other problems specific to this study: the number of brains dissected was small, the significance of the thickness of this part of the brain not really understood. Later research failed to find the sex difference (see Bradshaw, 1989; and Rogers, 1988), yet the study was widely popularized.

6   For critical feminist analysis, and further details of these theories, see Rogers (1988), Bleier (1984) and Genova (1989). The theories agree that males and females differ in the degree of specialization of the two halves of the brain; they differ, however, in whether they see this as due to dominance of one half over the other (for example, male spatial ability seen as resulting from dominance of the right half of the brain), or due to one sex being less 'lateralized' (that is the two halves of the brain show more 'cross-talk' and less dominance of one by the other).

Article 2.2
THE CHANGING ROLE OF WOMEN IN MODELS OF HUMAN EVOLUTION

Linda Marie Fedigan

INTRODUCTION

Imagine three anthropologists:

A primatologist observes a ... chimpanzee fashioning ... crude tools from grass stems, which she will use to fish termites from an underground nest over many hours, in the presence of her sometimes intrigued, sometimes impatient offspring. An ethnographer lives with a group of ... foragers at one of their campsites on the edge of a waterhole, recording in detail the daily patterns of adult women and men as they go about their lives, obtaining and preparing food, caring for their children, enjoying their leisure, interacting with their neighbours. An archaeologist and a team of bone hunters fan out across an escarpment..., squatting every now and then to peer and scratch carefully at the surface; they walk and look and listen for the call that will signal a 'find'.

Probably the primatologist and ethnographer would deny that the objective of their research was the reconstruction of the lives of our earliest human ancestors. The latter is there first and foremost to understand the lives of these contemporary human beings before their way of living disappears entirely, and the former works to explicate the animal species for itself... Nonetheless, the information obtained from all these studies will be gathered up ... and woven into a scientific story of the origins and evolution of early human behaviour. For we have a powerful urge to know our origins – scientists and public alike – allied to a strong cultural imperative to justify our present social arrangements through reference to historical precedents. And what more significant guide to comprehending the structure of our own underlying nature could we discover than the original blueprint for human society?

That is why the practice of modelling the life of early humans, although shunned by many anthropologists, is ... a scientific game played with great determination; its reward is the right to propound a view of human nature. Some of these models are widely disseminated, in ... textbooks, in popularized scientific writings, in fiction, on film. And in a society which tends to believe that what is natural is good, or at least acceptable, 'scientific' statements about the original nature of human society represent applications of data which even those who disapprove of such modelling can ill afford to ignore.

Reproduced with permission from the *Annual Review of Anthropology*, Vol. 15, © 1986 by Annual Reviews Inc.

In this review, I take one aspect common to models of early hominid life, namely, the reconstruction of sex roles, examining in particular the part that women are seen to have played in human society and in the evolution of those characteristics that distinguish us from our primate relatives, ... [examining] not only how the perceptions of women's roles in human evolution have changed, but also [describing] how women lately have come to play a part in the very construction of models of their origins. As anthropologists, we might have expected that women, with their distinctive life experiences, would have origin stories to tell that would differ in significant ways from those of men.

[···]

HISTORICAL CONTEXT

Although evolution as a concept was in use ... long before Darwin's time, it was in scholarly treatises of the second half of the nineteenth century that the idea of gradual, adaptive change came to be widely applied to the place of humans and human societies in the natural world. Evolutionary models became something of a fashion among European and North American scholars, including those interested in explaining the social nature of humans. . .

After publishing *On the Origin of Species* in 1859 ... Darwin was left with several puzzles. Two of these were: the explanation of secondary sexual characteristics in a wide range of species, and the extent to which evolutionary theory could be applied to human behaviour and biology. He set out to explore both of these topics in his 1871 book, *The Descent of Man and Selection in Relation to Sex*. The book has two intertwining objectives: the development of a theory of sexual selection applicable to the entire animal kingdom, and the establishment of the human species as subject to the laws of both natural and sexual selection. In the process of demonstrating that the characteristic features of the human phenotype and the human way of thinking and living show rudimentary similarities with those of other animals, Darwin also provided sketches of his own view of early human life. Especially in the course of discussing the application of sexual selection theory to humans, he provided us with a clear picture of how he saw the roles and the interrelationships of men and women in human society. First let us look briefly at Darwin's conclusions on sexual selection and the human place in nature, the two platforms on which he was to build his scenario of early human social life.

Darwin's reasoning was that secondary sexual characteristics, which neither are directly necessary for reproduction nor for survival, were the result of two types of interactions involving the sexes: competition and choice. Competition, Darwin believed, generally occurred between males for access to female mates, and choice, he reasoned, was exercised by females from among the male mates available to them. Thus, certain traits in males which enhanced their ability to win in competitions and/or to be chosen by females were sexually selected. It seemed obvious to Darwin that sexual selection had occurred in humans, because he believed the human male to be more courageous, energetic, inventive, pugnacious and sexually assertive than the female. The human male is also bigger than the human female, because, Darwin argued, in primitive times men fought to the death for access to women, and in modern times his size advantages are maintained because he has to work harder than woman for their joint subsistence. Women are more nurturant, more reclusive and more altruistic than men, traits which occur because of the lack of selection for the assertive, selfish male traits listed above, and also because of an extension of 'maternal instincts' toward other members of the group as well as toward infants.

Several authors ... have pointed out that Darwin projected onto the large screen of nature his own images of appropriate role behaviour for men and women, images which were clearly drawn from upper-class Victorian culture in Britain in the 1800s. Not so often pointed out are certain inconsistencies in the conceptualization and application of sexual selection theory itself. For example, Darwin saw selection as operating almost entirely on males. Competition selected for male armaments (size, strength, weapons) and choice selected for male ornaments (colours, elaborate headdresses, beautiful voices). Females of the species were seen to be, as a general rule, similar in appearance and behaviour to juveniles, their traits occurring in the absence of sexual selection. Darwin weakened his principle of female choice by equivocating about the actual power of females to exercise choice in determining which males would mate. At times he thought females had the selective power to bring about elaborate male features such as the peacock's tail. At other times he thought that females could do no more than accept the least distasteful male available, or accept the winner of a previous male-male competition, a lack of selective power ... I have likened to 'Hobson's choice'.

Having ... equivocated about the power of female choice to bring about sexual selection in animals, Darwin then contradicted himself when applying the theory to humans. For Darwin believed that the human female was sexually selected by males. Since this is the opposite of his principle of female choice, it is odd that Darwin argued repeatedly that men in various societies around the world exercise choice among possible female mates on the basis of the latters' appearance and behaviour. He did seem to believe that female choice had operated on human progenitors, but apparently at some point in human evolution he saw the process reversing. The human species appears to be the only one for which Darwin argued that males presently exercise both the mechanisms of competition and of choice, although nowhere does he discuss the matter of how or why the process of intersexual selection reversed, with choice as well as competition becoming the prerogative of the human male.

Darwin's second objective in *The Descent of Man* was to demonstrate that many human features, then thought to be unique, had simple analogues in other animal species. Thus, he ... [discussed] the evidence for rudimentary beginnings of higher mental powers in animals: faculties of mind such as reasoning, imagination, aesthetics, ability to produce material objects, and religious beliefs. He also argued that humans shared with many animal species the 'social instincts': desire for company, sympathy for others in the social group, altruism, love of praise and fear of blame. However, the most important characteristic to distinguish early humans from animals was a sense of morality. Once humans had developed the 'self-regarding virtues', which Darwin saw as self-control and awareness of good and evil, they began to develop societies based on higher mental faculties than those of other animals. He believed that early men developed their tool-making skills to produce weapons and to become efficient hunters. They also began to accumulate property which helped to bring about social stratification. To alleviate sexual jealousy and because of their ability to exercise self-control, marriage practices were instituted which would regulate sexual behaviour, primarily of women. In some societies, powerful men could take more than one wife.

... In the absence of an understanding of how traits are biologically transmitted to the next generation, Darwin used a concept he called 'equal transmission of characters' to explain how women were not left totally behind in the process of human evolution. In this way, Darwin helped to pioneer what I call the 'coat-tails' theory of human evolution: traits are selected for in males and women evolve by clinging to the men's coat-tails. This model became, and remains, the predominant image of human evolution, though rarely so candidly stated as by Darwin:

> Thus man has ultimately become superior to woman. It is indeed fortunate that the law of equal transmission of characters to both sexes prevails with mammals. Otherwise it is probable that man would have become as superior in mental endowment to woman as the peacock is in ornamental plumage to the peahen. (1871, p. 874)

[· · ·]

Darwin's views on the evolution of human behaviour were reinterpreted by Herbert Spencer to support his views of appropriate political action in Britain in the late 1800s. A coverage of social Darwinism is beyond the scope of this review. However, it is fair to say that whereas Darwin's ideas on the biological mechanisms of evolution throughout the plant and animal kingdom were to have continual and increasing influence on the life sciences of the twentieth century, his ideas specifically on human social and racial evolution were largely dropped or forgotten. Even when aspects of his thoughts on early humans reappear in modern models, his work often is not cited and apparently not remembered.

[· · ·]

Overview of twentieth-century models

For the first half of the twentieth century, sociocultural anthropol-ogists laboured . . . to collect . . . information on non-industrial societies before the latter transformed entirely under the impact of contact with colonizing or emergent nation-states . . . [S]ocial evolution remained very much out of favour. Physical anthropol-ogists for their part, largely under the influence of Ales Hrdlicka, also occupied themselves greatly with data collection, primarily in the area of anthropometry . . . [N]ot until the 1960s [did] a strong interest among physical and some social anthropologists [reappear].

When models of human social evolution and origins began to reappear widely. . . , they shared one powerful theme: 'Man the Hunter'. The lines of thought . . . by mid-century seem to have . . . [focused] on one distinguishing human trait: the pursuit, killing and eating of animals with the use of tools. The most influ-ential . . . expression of this new model was . . . Washburn and Lancaster's 1968 paper on the 'Evolution of hunting'. In it they argued that hunting demands all those qualities . . . that separate man so sharply from the other primates . . . [T]he hunting model was premised on the idea that this means of procuring food was the catalyst for all of the technological, social and intellectual achievements of human beings. Just a short list of traits believed to have resulted from hunting . . . would include: bipedalism, elaborate tool kits, development of language, appreciation of beauty, male aggressiveness and pleasure in killing, division of labour, the nuclear monogamous family, loss of female oestrus, the invention of incest taboos, and bonding between males. Furthermore, Wash-burn and Lancaster argued that the killing of animals with tools dominated human history for such a long time that it became the shaping force of the human psyche for all time . . . This argument was repeated in so many articles and introductory textbooks that it took on something akin to the status of a received truth.

[· · ·]

The picture of human sex roles that emerges from the hunting models is . . . little changed in essence from that drawn by Darwin a century earlier. Men are still seen as actively and aggressively engaged in procuring food and defending their families, whereas women are seen as dependants, who remain close to home to trade their sexual and reproductive capacities for protection and provisioning. Some authors such as Sahlins (1960) retained Darwin's concern over the control of human sexuality, which at least implied a consideration of two sexes. However, many . . . effectively omitted the female half of the human species from any consideration whatsoever.

In retrospect, there are two significant peculiarities of the [influential] book *Man the Hunter* [Lee and Devore (eds) (1968)] . . . The first . . . is that [there is no agreed] . . . definition of hunting . . ., a failure which could not help but weaken any resultant theorizing, and which inevitably led to later disagreements . . . about the importance of hunting in human foraging patterns. The second . . . concerns its title and its . . . promotion of the hunting model. For it was the very same ethnographic information . . . and the interpretations made by the collectors for this volume which were to turn the minds of many researchers . . . toward alternative explanations of human origins, that is, to the significance of human gathering, carrying and sharing of mainly vegetable foods. For example, Lee (1968) argued . . . that plant and marine resources are far more important than game animals . . . and Deetz (1968) cautioned of hunting that we must not let the label overdescribe the subject. From this perspective, the papers in *Man the Hunter*, championing as they did the explanatory power of hunting, also provided the insights and the data that . . . lead to its undoing.

In 1971 Sally Linton . . . pointed out various shortcomings and examples of androcentric bias in the Washburn and Lancaster paper, and then drew on a variety of sources to develop a model of early hominid females gathering, carrying and sharing foods with their young. It seemed to her that these three patterns exhibited by hominid females would have been a logical extension of the intense mother–infant bond found in all primates, and she suggested that the first cultural inventions were containers to hold the products of gathering and the infants. According to Linton, the hunting of large animals by males was a late development, after the matrifocal sharing-family was well established. She argued that the first hunters shared food not with sexual partners, but with their mothers and siblings who had shared with them. Such a scenario would obviously set human sex roles on a very different foundation from the 'male as husband and provider/protector' model that has come down . . . from Darwin. Men would still hunt and women would still gather, but sexual bonds and sexual exchange would not be the cornerstone of society, and the activities of women as autonomous individuals in society would play for almost the first time a significant part in the story of how we evolved those traits that make us uniquely human.

Linton's ideas . . . obviously struck a chord with a number of women anthropologists, because several of them . . . began to focus simultaneously on the question of what women did in early human societies. Zihlman . . . produced a series of elaborations on what came to be called the 'Woman the Gatherer' model, in which she stressed that obtaining plant food with tools was the 'new' or catalytic event in human evolution. She argued that bipedal locomotion and the invention of carrying devices first enabled women to walk long distances with babies in slings in order to exploit the resources of the more open savannah areas, and to carry these gathered plant foods back to safer familiar areas for shared consumption with their children. Plants and not meat were the focus of technological and social innovation for the emerging hominids three million years ago, and females, ever responsible for the nourishment of themselves and their young, were the providers and the inventors. It might be said by critics that males have now become the inconsequential sex in the story of our origins, because they may bring in meat, but these modellers see it as being of little importance, and it is shared with the matrifocal unit to which the males belong rather than with dependent female sexual partners. Indeed, in some early versions of the Woman the Gatherer model, the male's role was so little described that he might be said to have evolved clinging to the apron strings of the women. In more recent versions Zihlman and Tanner (1978) called simply the 'gathering model', the male's role is elaborated, but still considered to be secondary to the part played by women in unique human inventions.

In retrospect, it may seem discouraging that the choice had to be seen as either hunting *or* gathering, with either men *or* women inventing the cultural patterns that make us distinct. However, at the time, it must have seemed necessary to establish that a credible scientific origin story could be constructed in which women invented tools, chose mates, developed social systems, provided for themselves and their offspring, and generally participated in the evolution of significant human abilities.

[· · ·]

The response of some of the proponents of the hunting model was to superimpose the new model on the older hunting scheme, and to emphasize a mixed economy in which early hominid men and women were mutually interdependent. . . . Many authors now emphasize the importance of *sharing* between gathering women and hunting or scavenging men as the key human invention, i.e. the sexual division of labour. Isaac (1982, 1984) has done the most to develop a model in which food sharing is the 'central platform'. He argued that the archaeological evidence from East Africa demonstrates that the earliest hominids carried food and tools to certain locations where we now find their remains. In his view, this is evidence that the unique human social and economic arrangement of sexual division of labour had already begun to take place, and the reason they carried food to consistent locations was in order to share it. He hypothesized that males and females ranged in separate groups, engaging in specialized activities, and brought food back to a home base to share, as do contemporary foragers.

Unfortunately . . . models are constructed on a foundation of assumptions about causal chains and about human sex roles. It may not be possible to simply superimpose one on the other like so many building blocks without resulting faults in the logic of the whole. Gould (1981) for example, has said that food-sharing models are really about meat sharing, and both Hayden (1981) and Isaac (1978, 1982) have stated that neither sharing nor social living would have been particularly advantageous to foragers living largely on vegetable foods. Indeed, Isaac in his later version (1984) still tended to see meat-eating, now scavenged rather than hunted, as the key factor in the development of human intelligence, language and social patterns. And since he saw women as encumbered with children and handicapped in meat-obtaining activities (Isaac, 1978) females still do not seem to be credited with full partnership in the 'sharing' model. The recognition that simple choppers and hand axes would have facilitated scavenging, but not hunting, has been slow to find its expression and implications in the sharing model (e.g. Leakey, 1981). There has been no 'scavenging model'; rather, scavenging has replaced or been added to hunting, without any concomitant changes to other aspects of the model or consideration of its implications for sex roles.

[· · ·]

In 1981 Owen Lovejoy published a paper . . . in which the postulated sex roles and division of labour of early hominids were described precisely as Darwin had imagined them. . . : women remained around home bases to bear and rear children and were dependent on men to protect and provision them. The arguments as to why women had to remain dependent and sedentary were new, but otherwise the origin story remained familiar. Lovejoy's argument drew from several new and diverse sources (such as life history theory) and can be summarized as follows. The earliest hominids were able to become successful as a lineage, especially in comparison to their ape relatives, by facilitating higher fecundity and lower infant mortality rates than the present chimpanzee life history pattern of one infant every four years and only five live offspring in a female's lifetime. Hominids increased their reproductive success by reducing the mobility of lactating mothers and inventing the provisioning of the sedentary females by mobile, bipedal males. Lovejoy's scenario began with the assertion that hunting was not the crucial human technological invention, but rather that gathering was the key innovation. It did so without any reference to the published Woman the Gatherer models, which had accumulated the major body of evidence and arguments for gathering (and against hunting) as the 'master behaviour pattern'.

Further, Lovejoy attributed the collecting of plant food items, and all the ramifications of gathering and sharing in hominid evolution, to the early hominid men. Since male anthropologists had shown no previous signs of wishing to associate their sex with gathering, and since all of the ethnographic evidence points to women as primary gatherers, this sudden enthusiasm for gathering has been seen as the co-opting of the gatherer model. . . . The core assumption of Lovejoy's scheme is that for hominoid females, successful rates of reproduction *and* productive activities are incompatible, and thus men produced the impetus for hominid success by inventing the provisioning of vegetable foods to sedentary, monogamous female mates.

No extended analyses of Lovejoy's model have yet appeared . . . ; however, his view of early hominid sex roles is cited in many recent editions of physical anthropology textbooks and popular accounts. Appearing as it did in an invited article in the prestigious journal *Science*, Lovejoy's model could be said to represent the current orthodoxy about human evolution.

Another recent, but much less widely noted, model of human origins (Leibowitz, 1983) began with a similar question to that of Lovejoy's (how were early humans able to survive and succeed?), but offered a very different, even opposing answer. Leibowitz argued that a sexual division of labour was a very late human invention, and that for much of hominid evolution both males and females engaged in the same sorts of productive activities. . . Females simply combined productive activities with reproductive activities, as do many contemporary women. In Leibowitz's view, the key human invention was production, by which she means food-getting with tools, and which was initially unspecialized and undifferentiated by age or sex within the group. She drew an analogy to the manner in which every weaned member of a monkey or ape social group is an independent foraging unit.

Like Lovejoy, Leibowitz interpreted the material evidence to mean that early hominids were 'hovering precariously on the edge of extinction' (1983, p. 135), and argued that their major hedge against a marginal replacement rate was to invent the practice of accumulating surplus food through production. All individuals in the group participated in gathering surplus and in the resultant sharing or exchange. In her view, it was only with the invention of fire and projectile weaponry at the time of late *Homo erectus* that a sexual division of labour began to appear. The sexual division of labour also served as an instrument for stabilizing and extending both intragroup sharing and intergroup exchange. However, for most of human history, production alone (and not a specialization of roles by age and sex) was necessary and sufficient to create the characteristic human patterns.

Leibowitz's idea ... shows again how the same data can be interpreted in quite different ways, and it is one of the very few attempts ... to strip away the remaining assumption common to all models, that sex differences must have been significant in the earliest stages of human evolution. It seems that one of our own cultural patterns is to oppose male to female characteristics and to assume and emphasize sex and gender differences rather than similarities. That human technological and social success can be attributed to a specialization of tasks by sex is an often repeated assumption of anthropology, and some type of sexual division of labour seems to be universal in human societies today, although the importance accorded it is variable. Yet it can be very enlightening to think through what we have assumed to be the less probable solution. Could characteristic human societies have originated without a sexual division of labour beyond that directly related to insemination, gestation and lactation? Could some behavioural invention, characteristic of neither males nor females and requiring equivalent participation, have been the catalytic event that set humans moving along their own distinctive evolutionary path? Given that primate females are able to combine foraging with infant care, and that women in most societies contribute at least as much as men to subsistence in addition to their reproductive activities, Leibowitz's scenario may be no more or less data-based and plausible than the many models that seek to give preeminence to one or the other sex in the story of human evolution.

... [T]he following sections review these 'data bases' or the sources of evidence from primatology, ethnography and paleoanthropology for the models just described.

THE PRIMATE EVIDENCE

Primatologists ... not infrequently study their infrahuman subjects with an eye to casting some light on the behaviour and evolution of our own species. It is reasoned that since humans are members of the order Primates, the study of our nearest animal relations can help us to understand both the ways in which we are similar to other species and the ways in which we are distinctive. Although many primatologists are uncomfortable with inferences drawn from animals to humans ... there exists considerable pressure from colleagues and the public alike to make primate studies more directly relevant to the study of humans.

Such was the intent of one of the earliest and most widely publicized field studies of a nonhuman primate, the baboon. Washburn and DeVore (1961) observed common baboons in East Africa in 1959–60 and constructed a model of early human life based on baboons. They argued that early hominids, like baboons, differentiated from other primates by exploiting the resources of the East African savannah. Like baboons, humans would have become both predators of savannah flora and fauna and the prey of the large savannah carnivores. In order to protect themselves, ... the model proposes that both humans and baboons came to rely upon a social system of defence ... based on the bonding and co-operation of mature males organized into a rigid dominance hierarchy and employing an 'army-like' pattern of 'troop' movement across the dangerous plains ... According to the model ... human males distinguished themselves even further as exploiters of the savannah through the invention of weapons and thus hunting, which in turn led to unique human traits like language and the family. However, it was argued, this complex of distinct human characteristics initially was founded on a social system very like that which DeVore described for baboons.

[· · ·]

Today ... it is widely accepted that chimpanzees are the non-human primate most closely related to humans. ... [M]any reconstructions of early hominid life have drawn heavily from the accumulating data on the behaviour of common chimpanzees *(Pan troglodytes)* and pygmy chimpanzees *(Pan paniscus)* ... [S]ome of the recent models suggest that chimpanzees show rudimentary patterns of behaviour that also might have been exhibited by our common ape forebears ... Some of these patterns of behaviour, it is argued, were ultimately to become the distinguishing characteristics of the human lineage ... [I]t is believed that [chimpanzee] traits can give us some clues to the general 'ape-like' way of life of our hominoid ancestors, a way of life that was to set the stage for the human pattern.

[· · ·]

Most versions of the Woman the Gatherer model have used ... chimpanzee social bonding ... to argue that the matrifocal unit, and not the nuclear family, whether monogamous or polygynous, was the core of early hominid society. The intensive and extensive mother–offspring bond of the ape, it is argued, could only have become more elaborated in ... hominids... Following this argument, the initial social ties of adult males would have been to their maternal kin and not to their temporary sexual partners.

[· · ·]

[T]here clearly exists enough complexity in chimpanzee behaviour and enough diverse conclusions from the studies of these animals to give rise to many different scenarios. Specifically with reference to sex roles, some of the resultant models have tended to continue the emphasis on males . . . [O]thers, using the findings on the central significance of the female chimpanzee in social bonding and in food procurement patterns, have proposed a radical or non-traditional view of human females as prime movers in the evolution of the essential hominid traits such as tool use and sharing. . . Finally, some authors have explored the manner in which sex differences in chimpanzee behaviour might have set the stage for sexual division of labour in the first hominid societies.

THE ETHNOGRAPHIC EVIDENCE

Until the advent of agricultural practices . . . no more than 12,000 years ago, peoples around the world must have lived as foragers. The archaeological evidence of [stone] artefacts dating back some 2 million years indicates that human foragers have long acquired and/or processed their food with the assistance of tools. . . [T]he vast majority of the cultural remains of paleolithic peoples have been interpreted as resulting from the technological system of hunting and gathering.

[S]ince there are obvious technological similarities between these archaeological remains and the material culture of contemporary hunter–gatherers, and in some cases ecological/environmental similarities, some researchers have turned to the study of modern hunter–gatherers to shed light on the reconstruction of the social patterns of prehistoric foragers. The logic is that social structures respond to environmental exigencies and correspond to technological systems. Thus, it is argued that the basic social forms widely found in contemporary hunter–gatherers . . . probably occurred as well in palaeolithic hunter–gatherers.

A number of anthropologists have objected to the use of ethnographic evidence to reconstruct early human social life . . . Freeman (1968) has objected to analogies drawn between prehistoric and modern groups . . . [arguing] that to force archaeological evidence into frames of reference developed for contemporary data inevitably distorts and obscures the prehistoric analysis [and] prevents the development of frameworks based directly on the prehistoric material. Secondly, he argue[s] that like environmental stimuli do not necessarily produce like cultural responses, because

sociocultural systems have tended to regional-and-resource specialization during the course of human history. More recently . . . Testart
(1978) also [emphasizes] the particular nature of each society's
history, the importance of regional events, climate, fauna, flora, and
the 10,000 years of individual histories that separate today's
hunter–gatherers from their palaeolithic antecedents. . .

A second criticism . . . rests on ideological grounds. Berndt
(1981), for example, [objects] to the implication that the study of
modern Australian aborigines can help us to understand early
human societies . . . [suggesting] that this view is harkening back
to the nineteenth-century social evolutionist and colonialist racist
attitudes that aboriginal peoples are 'primitives' or 'survivals' . . .
Schrire (1980) has argued . . . on somewhat similar grounds . . . that
we should not regard contemporary foraging peoples as 'living fossil
groups' . . . [M]any draw the conclusion that any attempt at
reconstruction or analogy based on contemporary peoples is . . .
contrary to those tenets of anthropology based upon a nonhierarchical
view of cultural variation.

Others reply that to suggest that similar economies and similar
technologies may be associated with similar social structures, and
to construct hypotheses on the basis of such similarities, is not to
suggest social evolution in any pejorative sense.

[· · ·]

The picture . . . of the social role of women in much early
ethnographic and ethnological work on hunter–gatherers was of a
dependent, lesser, and even passive social category. Ethnographers,
mainly men, studied social phenomena of greater interest to men
and talked mainly to male informants. The emphasis on hunting,
weapons and warfare ignored the contributions of women to
subsistence and to social dynamics. Theoretical models (e.g. Lévi-
Strauss, 1949) viewed men as actors and women as objects of sexual
exchange. However, in the last two decades, many new ethnographic
studies employing female as well as male perspectives have been
undertaken (see extensive review in Quinn, 1977). Thus, a picture
of women as active, competent, contributing, and even self-sufficient
members of hunter–gatherer societies, with their own stories to tell,
has begun to emerge from the shadows of early ethnographic
scenarios.

In particular, Lee's (1968) continuing analysis of women's
contribution to subsistence in contemporary hunter–gatherer societies has been an important starting point in a reassessment of the
parts women might have played in early human society. In a survey
of 58 foraging societies from around the world . . . , Lee concluded
that on average hunted foods contributed only 35% of the diet and
thus, contrary to popular conception, men provided less than half

of the food of 'hunting' peoples. . . Thus, he concluded that . . . plant food, shell fish and fish, collected primarily by women, form the bulk of the diet. Hence his argument that foraging women generally are capable of feeding themselves and are not dependent on men for subsistence.

These conclusions were taken up enthusiastically by the various modellers of Woman the Gatherer and are also occasionally mentioned in introductory textbooks, perhaps to temper the emphasis on males as providers in descriptions of hunter–gatherers.

[· · ·]

Finally, the issues are further muddled by the fact that although women are primarily associated with gathering plant foods, they do also obtain small animals and occasionally hunt with weapons for larger ones (Estioko-Griffen and Griffen, 1981). Men, on the other hand, often help with gathering or feed themselves on plant matter while hunting. . .

The issue of differential contribution to subsistence . . . is important in assessing women's status in early foraging societies. Women's reproductive roles have never been in question (except the degree to which they are handicapping); it is their productive capabilities that are contentious. Anthropologists who have followed Engels' argument at its most basic . . . have long argued that those women who actively contribute to subsistence, and who are not economically dependent but interdependent with all the other producing members of the group, will have equivalent status to that of the men. Others . . . have modified this argument to add that women must not only contribute to subsistence but also have a measure of personal control over the disposition and distribution of the fruits of their labour in order to achieve power and prestige equivalent to that of the men. The ability to control production and distribution is more difficult to demonstrate, and possibly is less true of women than the ability to contribute to production. However, if the data continue to show that women are not economically dependent on men for provisioning in most hunter–gatherer societies, indeed that they often produce more than do the men, then the assumption of the nonproductive female, which has been a key element in most reconstructions of our earliest ancestors, must be seriously re-examined.

[· · ·]

THE MATERIAL EVIDENCE

[· · ·]

Archaeological evidence for early human social life

[· · ·]

More recently, there has been a reassessment of the archaeological evidence for, and interpretations of, early hominid behaviour. . . Although the study of human evolution often has been characterized by heated debate, . . . these recent attempts to test fundamental archaeological assumptions and to develop alternative ways of explaining the material evidence have been, in Isaac's own words, 'liberating' and an 'exciting exercising of alternating leaps of imagination with rigorous testing' (Isaac, 1980, p. 66). [T]he recognition that early hominids may have been very different in lifeway from modern humans has also been liberating from the perspective of sex role reconstruction. And the most important aspect of this minor paradigmatic revolution for women's roles concerns the new interpretations of bone-and-artefact associations, or what were traditionally known as 'home bases'.

Isaac, it will be recalled, had developed a 'sharing' model which was founded on the fact that in the early East African sites of around two million years ago, tools are found in dense patches in association with the bony remains of many animal species. Both stones and bones appear to have been transported to 'central locations'. Beginning with this . . . material evidence, Isaac suggested that humans carried food and possessions to consistent locations as part of a social system involving home bases, division of labour, hunting and gathering, substantial meat eating, food sharing and food preparation. . .

Several researchers . . . have now challenged the home base interpretation. Binford (1981) analysed some of the published evidence from Olduvai Gorge to argue that the 'so-called' living sites or home bases were in fact the remains of carnivore activities. Isaac (1984) countered that the published data sets on which Binford worked were declared by their author (M. D. Leakey) to be incomplete and preliminary, and that Binford had not accounted for the fact that the bone assemblages come from patches in which thousands of human artefacts (tools) also occur. Thus Potts' (1984) detailed, first-hand analysis of the Olduvai Gorge and Koobi Fora stone-bone concentrations was to be very influential.

Potts came to a different . . . conclusion from both Binford and Isaac. . . He argued that the animal bones at these sites were marked *both* by carnivore teeth and by stone tools, including tooth marks from gnawing and cut-marks made by slicing, scraping and chopping with stone. Somehow, both early hominids and large carnivores were active at these locations, in some cases upon the same parts of the carcass, even the same bones. However, it is not whole carcasses of animals that are represented and the bones were not completely processed for meat and marrow, suggesting that hominids were abandoning considerable portions of the available food. Finally, the incredible density of bones at some of the sites and the patterns of weathering indicate bone accumulation spanning 5–10 years. All four factors, according to Potts, argue against a home base interpretation of the sites. The presence of large carnivores would certainly have restricted the activities of early hominids at such locations, and surely campsites would never have been established in such unsafe places. Modern hunter–gatherers carry whole or nearly whole carcasses back to camp, not restricted portions, and they intensively modify the bones of animal food. Finally, hunter–gatherers rarely occupy a campsite for a long period of time, and seldom re-occupy an old site. Thus Potts concluded that it is not possible to assume that the behaviours associated with home bases (sharing, division of labour) occurred at the early sites in Olduvai.

. . . Potts argued that the sites represent stone-tool caches and meat-processing locations. Because animal carcasses attract many meat-eaters, the hominids were forced to transport parts of the animal away from the original location where it was obtained either by scavenging or hunting. These portions of meat were taken to the nearest stone-tool cache in the foraging area, where raw stone, manufactured tools, and bones remained from previous visits. . . It is hypothesized that the hominids processed the meat quickly with the stone tools in the cache and abandoned the site before direct confrontation occurred with the carnivores . . . attracted to the remains. . . Such sites could represent the antecedents of home bases, but Potts believes that until hominids gained the controlled use of fire to make home bases safe from carnivores, . . . they may well have continued to sleep in trees and to range widely during the day as do the other primate species.

One implication . . . for early hominid sex roles is clear: if there is not evidence for home bases where the sick and the dependent waited for the well and the productive, then perhaps we can finally free our minds of the image of dawn-age women and children waiting at campsites for the return of their provisioners. Even though the sharing model and many other anthropological scenarios appear to be about a division of labour in which women return to camp with vegetables and men with meat, it has almost always been assumed that women would have been more tied to the campsites. Women and homes have been inextricably linked in our cultural imagery, and thus the shaking loose from the home base focus for early hominid social life may allow our imaginations to turn to alternative scenarios.

CONCLUSION: HOW CAN WE IMPROVE OUR RECONSTRUCTIONS OF EARLY HUMAN SOCIAL BEHAVIOUR?

Given the necessarily limited evidence of social life and the correspondingly large role played by speculation in the endeavour to reconstruct early hominid society, it seems appropriate to ask if it is worth doing at all. As I have pointed out, many primatologists and anthropologists oppose such modelling, often for different reasons than the one offered by Evans-Pritchard (1965) . . . , that it is a waste of time to speculate upon unanswerable questions. Yet origin myths exist in all societies, leading me to suspect that humans have 'wasted their time' in just this manner ever since self-awareness became one of the hominid characteristics. . .

Furthermore, it is hard to imagine other sciences such as physics attempting to restrict themselves only to non-speculative, empirically answerable questions. Pilbeam has argued that some unanswerable questions in palaeoanthropology 'still ought to be asked because they help to direct research efforts and channel thinking into fruitful pathways. The problem comes in knowing which unanswerable questions to ask' (Pilbeam, 1980, p. 268). . . Pilbeam made it clear that, in his opinion, reconstructions of early hominid behaviour would be much improved through greater reference to the actual fossil and archaeological data. Because contemporary apes are not necessarily like fossil apes, and because the hominoid fossil record in any case is virtually non-existent, Pilbeam has concluded that a comparative approach is not likely to yield fruitful theories. It should be added . . . that few reconstructions . . . take complete or accurate account of the primate and ethnographic data that are available . . .

. . . However, it is clear that the data-bases of human evolution will always remain limited . . . Isaac (1984) believed that there are two related routes to a fuller understanding of the dynamics of human evolution. The first is an emphasis on problem-oriented and experimental studies of the processes that might have led to characteristic archaeological remains by making use of analogous modern activities and environments. The second is that propositions should be expressed as a series of falsifiable, alternative hypotheses, and tests should involve attempts to overturn intuitively favoured hypotheses. His suggestion was that reconstructions would be better served by each researcher providing a series of alternative models, rather than promoting and defending a single model.

. . . [A]nother analyst (Landau, 1984) has suggested that it will probably be impossible to remove the subjective or 'storytelling' element from evolutionary accounts. Landau argued that many scientific theories are essentially narratives, that is, the creative piecing together of an organized and plausible sequence of events by application of the imagination to standard forms. Particularly paleoanthropology with its description of the events of human evolution is, in her view, a form of storytelling, open to narrative analysis . . . Landau did not address the question of the part played by 'fiction' in human evolution models which would be one implication of a literary analysis to which many scientists would object. But surely any modeller would agree that it takes creativity as well as data to create a plausible account of human evolution. And neither creative nor scientific minds function in a cultural vacuum. Landau's narrative analysis attempts to make some of the implicit structural guidelines of any human origins model explicit. . .

Landau took a structural approach that looks for common elements in the different versions of the human evolution story. For example, she identified four major events or episodes that are consistently emphasized by palaeoanthropologists: a shift from trees to the ground (terrestriality); development of upright posture (bipedalism); the development of the brain, intelligence and language (encephalization); and the development of technology, morals and society (culture). She suggested that the question of which episode came first has been a major source of debate since Darwin, but in all versions the same episodes are recognized. She then argued that the diverse theories of what happened in human evolution actually follow a common narrative structure. This structure takes the form of a 'hero story' in which the protagonist (= hominid) starts from humble origins on a journey in which he will be both *tested* by environmental stresses (savannah predators etc.) and by his own weaknesses (bipedalism, lack of biological armaments) and *gifted* by powerful agents (intelligence, technological inventions, social co-operation) until he is able to transform himself into a truly human hominid, the hero's final triumph which always ends the story.

Landau regards this approach to human evolution accounts not as a criticism but as a demonstration to scientists that they are interpreters of text as well as of nature, and as a potentially useful tool in comparing structural and conceptual differences between theories. If she is correct that human evolution theories follow a common narrative structure and adhere to a recognizable literary model (the hero's tale), which can be traced back through many centuries of European story-telling, this approach may give us some insight into why women generally play a subordinate role in these stories. For clearly the tale of the hero is about men and not heroines; women function in such stories either as secondary characters (mothers, sisters) related to the hero, or as potentially desirable sexual partners, often in need of rescue. If the contemporary Western raconteurs of human evolution had been raised in different narrative traditions, for example learning as children the enduring

Chinese legend of the woman warrior, the female trouble-slayer who rides into adventures carrying her infant in a sling inside her armour, then perhaps women would not have been so consistently restricted to the merely reproductive/domestic roles in our origin stories.

I have argued that one recurring theme in the human evolution accounts, from Darwin to Lovejoy, is that early men were the achievers, the producers and technological innovators; whereas early women were limited by the reproductive demands of bearing and rearing children. Or as Sacks (1982) has put it: men make culture and women make babies, two mutually exclusive activities. Anthropologists have long applied sets of dichotomous attributes to the roles of men and women in human society: public/domestic, productive/reproductive, culture/nature. However, a number of women anthropologists . . . have begun to challenge these dichotom-ies as being largely a reflection of the Western cultural belief in the opposition of the sexes that has been mistakenly generalized into a universal and 'natural' human principle. These dichotomies are also present as hidden assumptions in most models of human origins, and yet we do not know how generally they express the human condition today, much less in the past. . . . Thus a discussion of public/male versus domestic/female spheres has not been a particularly insightful approach to understanding the lives of these people. . . .

A similar inapplicability may exist for the productive/repro-ductive dichotomy. Does a foraging woman or a foraging society functionally compartmentalize human lives and activities into these two supposedly opposing realms, or is this merely an abstract and possibly ethnocentric conceptualization of how lives should be arranged? Is it necessary to assume, as does Lovejoy for example, that the human female's energy is so limited that productive activities must necessarily be detrimental to reproduction, that the behaviours involved in subsistence and child-rearing are incompatible and mutually exclusive? One of the peculiar human phenomena that anthropologists have identified is that it is possible for people widely and passionately to hold cultural beliefs that are in direct contradiction to their social actions. I suggest that this is the case with our own cultural belief that the people who are reproductively engaged cannot be productively active, a tenet clearly belied by the sexual make-up of the workforce in our society today. . .

Theories of human origins do function as symbolic statements about and indeed prescriptions for human nature. By making the assumptions of any theory more explicit, one can test or debate them rather than continuing to act as though differences between models reflect only varying descriptions of the material evidence.

When the evidence changes, as when gathering replaces hunting in economic importance, but the implications for men and women are seen to remain fundamentally the same, as when Man the Hunter becomes Man the Provider, it is clear that powerful cultural sex role expectations inform these reconstructions even more strongly than does material evidence.

Some readers may find it hard to accept that cultural beliefs and narrative traditions play a significant role in scientific models of human evolution. However, I would argue that the theories reviewed in this paper do combine the realms of science and of story-telling. If this is so, we can begin the useful exercise of learning to analyse how the two realms interact and overlap in a given model and how we can evaluate the model according to the criteria appropriate to each realm. To paraphrase Kermode (1967), if we cannot free ourselves of subjectivity, then we must attempt to make sense of it. People will not stop wanting to hear origin stories and scientists will not cease to write scholarly tales. But we can become aware of the symbolic content of our stories, for much as our theories are not independent of our beliefs, so our behaviour is not independent of our theories of human society. In these origin tales we try to coax the material evidence into telling us about the past, but the narrative we weave about the past also tells us about the present.

Map 1a
Birth and death

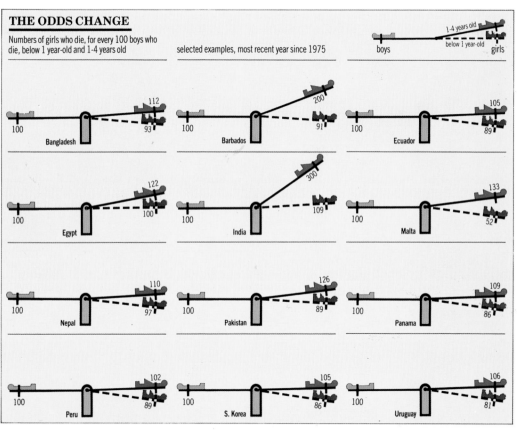

THE ODDS CHANGE

Numbers of girls who die, for every 100 boys who die, below 1 year-old and 1-4 years old

selected examples, most recent year since 1975

boys   1-4 years old   below 1 year-old   girls

	below 1 year-old	1-4 years old
Bangladesh	93	112
Barbados	91	200
Ecuador	89	105
Egypt	100	122
India	109	300
Malta	52	133
Nepal	97	110
Pakistan	89	126
Panama	86	109
Peru	89	102
S. Korea	86	105
Uruguay	81	106

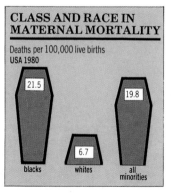

CLASS AND RACE IN MATERNAL MORTALITY

Deaths per 100,000 live births
USA 1980

- blacks 21.5
- whites 6.7
- all minorities 19.8

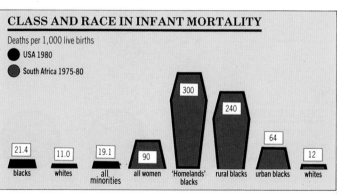

CLASS AND RACE IN INFANT MORTALITY

Deaths per 1,000 live births
- USA 1980
- South Africa 1975-80

- blacks 21.4
- whites 11.0
- all minorities 19.1
- all women 90
- 'Homelands' blacks 300
- rural blacks 240
- urban blacks 64
- whites 12

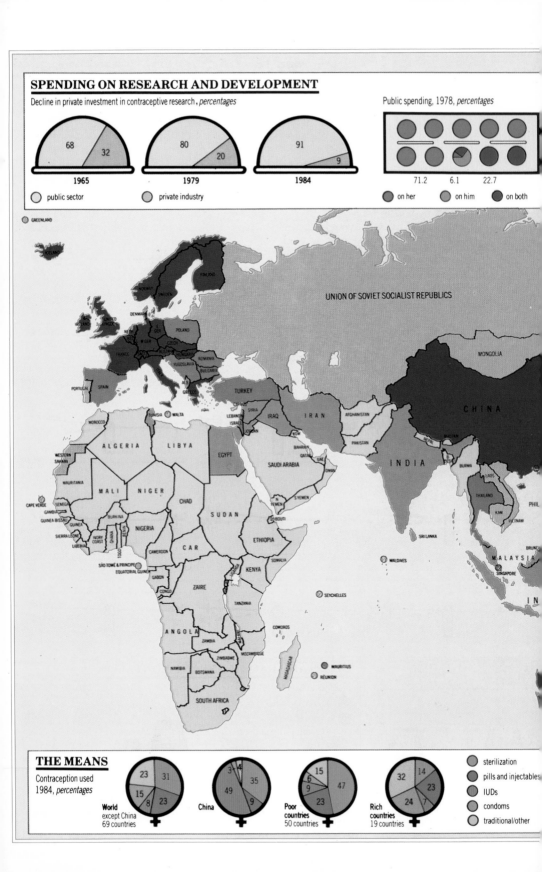

SPENDING ON RESEARCH AND DEVELOPMENT

Decline in private investment in contraceptive research, *percentages*

1965	1979	1984
68 / 32	80 / 20	91 / 9

○ public sector ○ private industry

Public spending, 1978, *percentages*

71.2   6.1   22.7

● on her   ● on him   ● on both

GREENLAND

ICELAND

NORWAY
SWEDEN
FINLAND

DENMARK

UNION OF SOVIET SOCIALIST REPUBLICS

IRELAND
UNITED KINGDOM
NETH
E. GER
W. GER
POLAND
FRANCE
CZECH
AUSTRIA
HUNGARY
YUGOSLAVIA
ROMANIA
BULGARIA

MONGOLIA

PORTUGAL   SPAIN

ALB
GREECE

TURKEY

CHINA

CYPRUS
SYRIA
LEBANON
ISRAEL
JORDAN
IRAQ
IRAN
AFGHANISTAN

TUNISIA   MALTA

MOROCCO

BHUTAN

NEPAL

ALGERIA   LIBYA   EGYPT

KUW
BAHRAIN
QATAR
UAE
SAUDI ARABIA
OMAN

PAKISTAN

INDIA

BANGLA

BURMA

WESTERN
SAHARA

LAOS

MAURITANIA

MALI   NIGER   CHAD

N. YEMEN
S. YEMEN

THAILAND

CAPE VERDE
SENEGAL
GAMBIA
GUINEA-BISSAU
GUINEA
SIERRA LEONE
LIBERIA
IVORY COAST
GHANA
TOGO
BENIN
BURKINA

NIGERIA

SUDAN

DJIBOUTI

ETHIOPIA

PHIL

KAM
VIETNAM

SÃO TOMÉ & PRINCIPE
EQUATORIAL GUINEA
GABON
CAMEROON
CAR
CONGO

SOMALIA

SRI LANKA

MALDIVES

BRUNEI

MALAYSIA
SINGAPORE

ZAIRE

KENYA

TANZANIA

SEYCHELLES

IN

ANGOLA

ZAMBIA

COMOROS

ZIMBABWE
MOZAMBIQUE

NAMIBIA   BOTSWANA

MADAGASCAR

MAURITIUS
RÉUNION

SOUTH AFRICA

THE MEANS

Contraception used
1984, *percentages*

World
except China
69 countries
31 / 23 / 23 / 8 / 15

China
35 / 9 / 49 / 4 / 3

Poor countries
50 countries
47 / 23 / 9 / 6 / 15

Rich countries
19 countries
14 / 23 / 7 / 24 / 32

● sterilization
● pills and injectables
● IUDs
● condoms
○ traditional/other

Map 2
Contraception

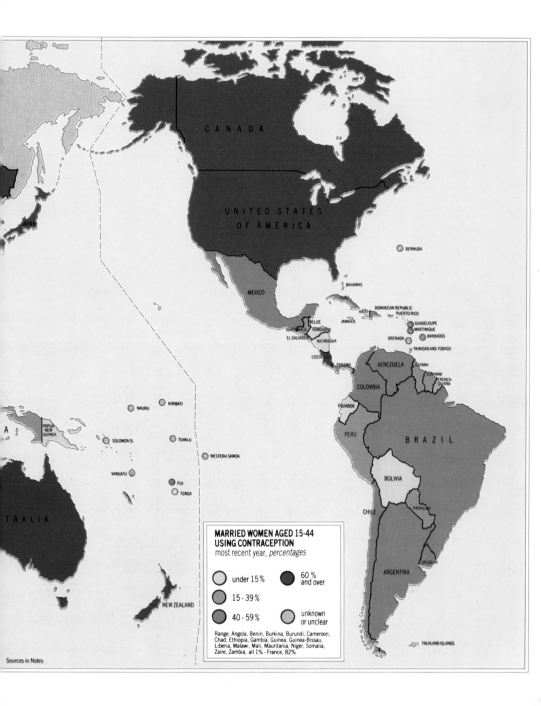

MARRIED WOMEN AGED 15-44
USING CONTRACEPTION
most recent year, *percentages*

- under 15%
- 15 - 39%
- 40 - 59%
- 60% and over
- unknown or unclear

Range: Angola, Benin, Burkina, Burundi, Cameroon, Chad, Ethiopia, Gambia, Guinea, Guinea-Bissau, Liberia, Malawi, Mali, Mauritania, Niger, Somalia, Zaire, Zambia, all 1% - France, 82%

Sources in Notes

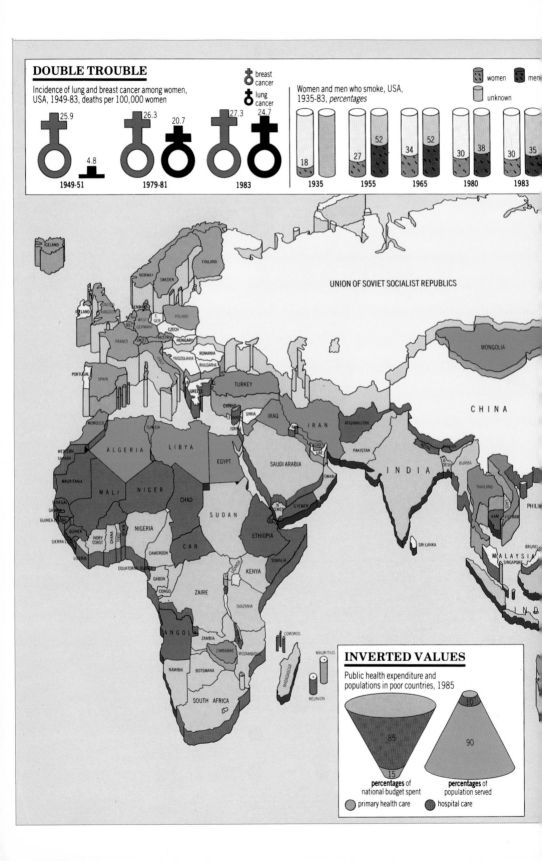

DOUBLE TROUBLE

Incidence of lung and breast cancer among women, USA, 1949-83, deaths per 100,000 women

♀ breast cancer
♀ lung cancer

25.9
4.8
1949-51

26.3
20.7
1979-81

27.3
24.7
1983

Women and men who smoke, USA, 1935-83, *percentages*

women   men
unknown

18
1935

27   52
1955

34   52
1965

30   38
1980

30   35
1983

UNION OF SOVIET SOCIALIST REPUBLICS

CHINA

MONGOLIA

INVERTED VALUES

Public health expenditure and populations in poor countries, 1985

85
15
percentages of national budget spent

10
90
percentages of population served

● primary health care
● hospital care

Map 3
Illness and health

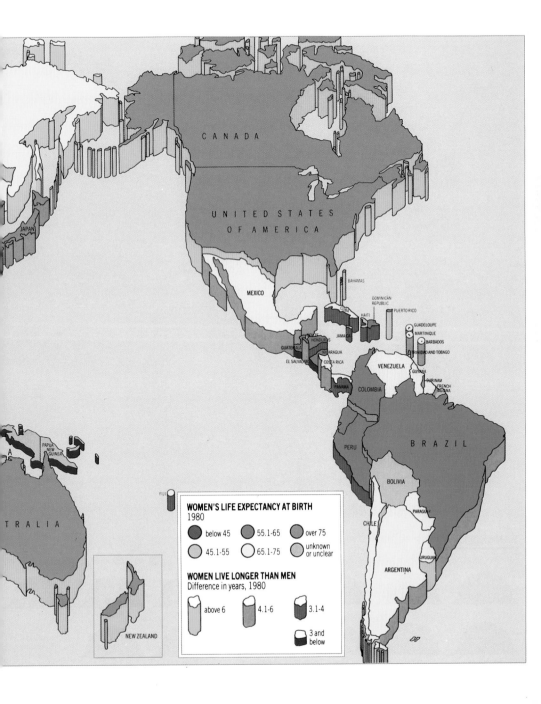

CANADA

UNITED STATES
OF AMERICA

JAPAN

MEXICO

BAHAMAS

CUBA

HAITI

DOMINICAN
REPUBLIC

PUERTO RICO

GUADELOUPE
MARTINIQUE
BARBADOS

BELIZE
GUATEMALA
HONDURAS
EL SALVADOR
NICARAGUA
COSTA RICA
PANAMA

JAMAICA

TRINIDAD AND TOBAGO

VENEZUELA

GUYANA
SURINAM
FRENCH
GUIANA

COLOMBIA

PERU

BRAZIL

BOLIVIA

PARAGUAY

CHILE

URUGUAY

ARGENTINA

PAPUA
NEW
GUINEA

FIJI

TRALIA

NEW ZEALAND

WOMEN'S LIFE EXPECTANCY AT BIRTH
1980

- below 45
- 45.1-55
- 55.1-65
- 65.1-75
- over 75
- unknown or unclear

WOMEN LIVE LONGER THAN MEN
Difference in years, 1980

- above 6
- 4.1-6
- 3.1-4
- 3 and below

WOMEN FIGHTERS

Countries where women have been combatants in revolutionary armies and civil wars, where known, 1975-85

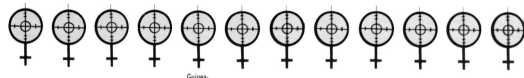

| Nicaragua | Guatemala | El Salvador | Ethiopia | Guinea-Bissau | Mozambique | Angola | Namibia | Iran | Philippines | Vietnam | Zimbabwe |

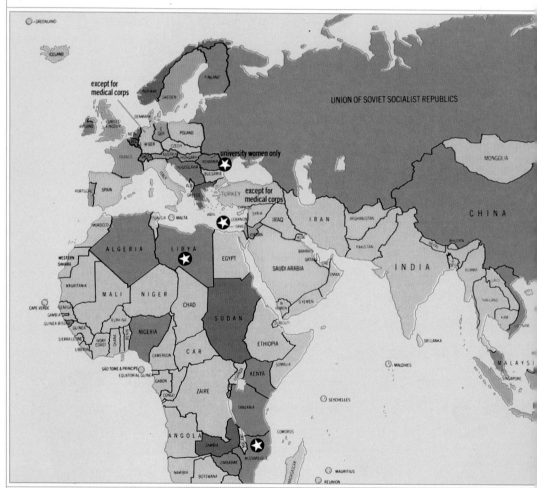

WOMEN IN NATO

Percentage of women in armed forces of NATO countries, 1983

● men ● women * medical corps officers only

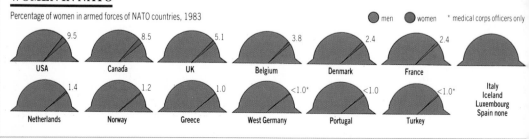

| USA | Canada | UK | Belgium | Denmark | France |
| 9.5 | 8.5 | 5.1 | 3.8 | 2.4 | 2.4 |

| Netherlands | Norway | Greece | West Germany | Portugal | Turkey | Italy Iceland Luxembourg Spain none |
| 1.4 | 1.2 | 1.0 | <1.0* | <1.0 | <1.0* | |

Map 4
Military service

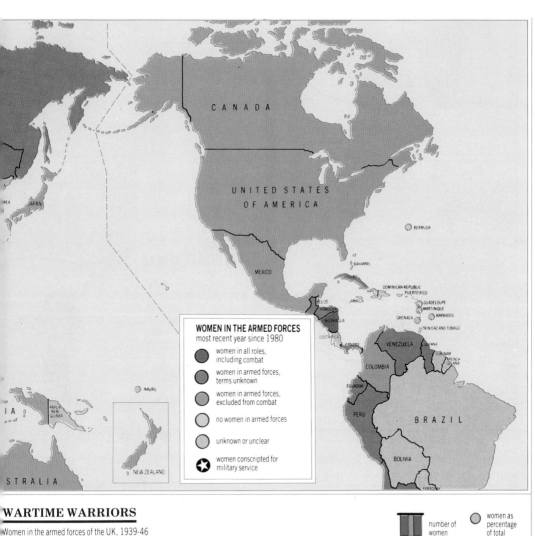

WOMEN IN THE ARMED FORCES
most recent year since 1980

- women in all roles, including combat
- women in armed forces, terms unknown
- women in armed forces, excluded from combat
- no women in armed forces
- unknown or unclear
- women conscripted for military service

WARTIME WARRIORS

Women in the armed forces of the UK, 1939-46

- number of women
- women as percentage of total

Date	Number	Percentage
Dec 1939	36,100	2.3
Dec 1940	66,900	2.3
Dec 1941	205,100	5.4
Dec 1942	386,000	8.7
Mar 1943	420,400	9.1
June 1943	445,200	9.4
Sept 1943	453,200	9.4
Dec 1943	449,100	9.2
Mar 1944	450,000	9.2
Dec 1944	436,000	8.8
June 1945	415,800	8.2
June 1946	137,400	6.7

Map 1b Birth and death (ctd.)

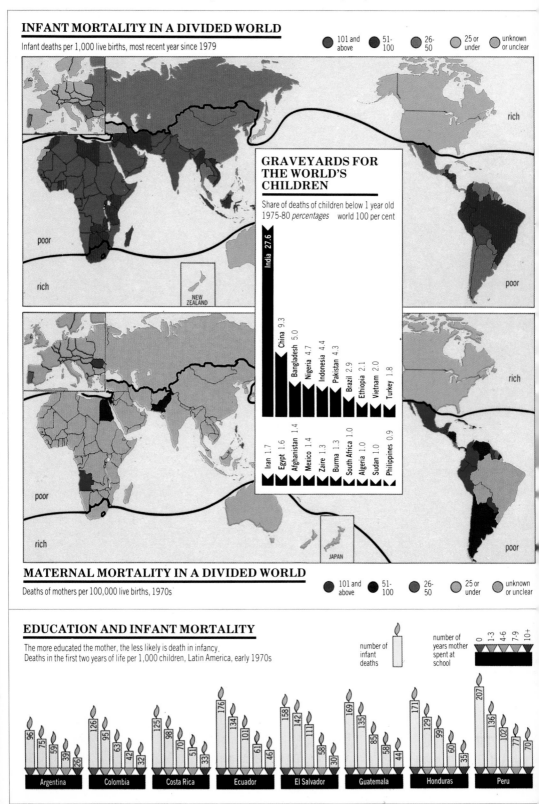

INFANT MORTALITY IN A DIVIDED WORLD

Infant deaths per 1,000 live births, most recent year since 1979

101 and above | 51-100 | 26-50 | 25 or under | unknown or unclear

rich

poor

rich

NEW ZEALAND

poor

GRAVEYARDS FOR THE WORLD'S CHILDREN

Share of deaths of children below 1 year old 1975-80 *percentages* world 100 per cent

India 27.6

China 9.3

Bangladesh 5.0

Nigeria 4.7

Indonesia 4.4

Pakistan 4.3

Brazil 2.9

Ethiopia 2.1

Vietnam 2.0

Turkey 1.8

Iran 1.7

Egypt 1.6

Afghanistan 1.4

Mexico 1.4

Zaire 1.3

Burma 1.3

South Africa 1.0

Algeria 1.0

Sudan 1.0

Philippines 0.9

rich

poor

rich

JAPAN

poor

MATERNAL MORTALITY IN A DIVIDED WORLD

Deaths of mothers per 100,000 live births, 1970s

101 and above | 51-100 | 26-50 | 25 or under | unknown or unclear

EDUCATION AND INFANT MORTALITY

The more educated the mother, the less likely is death in infancy.
Deaths in the first two years of life per 1,000 children, Latin America, early 1970s

number of infant deaths

number of years mother spent at school: 0 | 1-3 | 4-6 | 7-9 | 10+

Argentina: 96 75 59 39 26
Colombia: 126 95 63 42 32
Costa Rica: 125 98 70 51 33
Ecuador: 176 134 101 61 46
El Salvador: 158 142 111 58 30
Guatemala: 169 135 85 58 44
Honduras: 171 129 99 60 35
Peru: 207 136 102 77 70

Article 2.3
WOMEN AND MEDICALIZATION: A NEW PERSPECTIVE

Catherine Kohler Riessman

It is widely acknowledged that illness has become a cultural metaphor for a vast array of human problems. The medical model is used from birth to death in the social construction of reality. Historically, as a larger number of critical events and human problems have come under the 'clinical gaze' (Foucault, 1973), our experience of them has been transformed. For women in particular, this process has had far-reaching consequences.

Feminist health writers have emphasized that women have been the main targets in the expansion of medicine. These scholars have analysed how previous religious justifications for patriarchy were transformed into scientific ones (Ehrenreich and English, 1979). They have described how women's traditional skills for managing birth and caring for the sick were expropriated by psychomedical experts at the end of the nineteenth century (Ehrenreich and English, 1973). Feminist writers have described the multiple ways in which women's health in the contemporary period is being jeopardized by a male-controlled, technology-dominated medical-care system . . . [They] have been important voices in changing women's consciousness about their health. They have identified the sexual politics embedded in conceptions of sickness and beliefs about appropriate care. In addition, they have provided the analytic basis for a social movement that has as its primary goal the reclaiming of knowledge about and control over women's bodies.

However, in their analyses, feminists have not always emphasized the ways in which women have simultaneously gained and lost with the medicalization of their life problems. Nor have the scholars always noted the fact that women actively participated in the construction of the new medical definitions, nor discussed the reasons that led to their participation. Women were not simply passive victims of medical ascendancy. To cast them solely in a passive role is to perpetuate the very kinds of assumptions about women that feminists have been trying to challenge.

This [article] will . . . [emphasize] some neglected dimensions of medicalization and women's lives. I will argue that both physicians and women have contributed to the redefining of women's experience into medical categories. More precisely, I will suggest that physicians seek to medicalize experience because of their specific beliefs and economic interests. These ideological and material motives are related to the development of the profession and the specific market conditions it faces in any given period. Women collaborate in the medicalization process because of their own needs and motives, which in turn grow out of the class-specific nature of their subordination. In addition, other groups bring economic interests to which both physicians and women are responsive. Thus a consensus develops that a particular human problem will be understood in clinical terms. This consensus is tenuous because it is fraught with contradictions for women, since, as stated before, they stand both to gain and lose from this redefinition.

I will explore this thesis by examining five conditions that pertain to women. An examination of childbirth and [abortion] will ground the analysis historically. Premenstrual syndrome and weight will be considered in order to illustrate present-day manifestations of medicalization. Finally, I will present some beginning thoughts on the ways the analysis might be applied to mental health.

[· · ·]

THE MEDICALIZATION FRAMEWORK

The term medicalization refers to two interrelated processes. First, certain behaviours or conditions are given medical meaning – that is, defined in terms of health and illness. Second, medical practice becomes a vehicle for eliminating or controlling problematic experiences that are defined as deviant, for the purpose of securing adherence to social norms. Medicalization can occur on various levels: conceptually, when a medical vocabulary is used to define a problem; institutionally, when physicians legitimate a programme or a problem; or on the level of doctor–patient interaction, when actual diagnosis and treatment of a problem occurs (Conrad and Schneider, 1980b).

Historically, there has been an expansion of the spheres of deviance that have come under medical social control. . . Various human conditions such as alcoholism, opiate addiction and homosexuality – which at one time were categorized as 'bad' – have more recently been classified as 'sick' (Conrad and Schneider, 1980a). Currently, more and more of human experience is coming under medical scrutiny, resulting in what Illich [1976] has called 'the medicalization of life'. For example, it is now considered appropriate to consult physicians about sexuality, fertility, childhood behaviour and old-age memory problems. It is important to note that the medical profession's jurisdiction over these and other human conditions extends considerably beyond its demonstrated capacity to 'cure' them.

[· · ·]

Medicalization is a particularly critical concept because it emphasizes the fact that medicine is a social enterprise, not merely a scientific one. A biological basis is neither necessary nor sufficient for an experience to be defined in terms of illness. Rather, illness is constructed through human action – that is, illness is not inherent in any behaviour or condition, but conferred by others. Thus, medical diagnosis becomes an interpretive process through which illnesses are constructed. . .

Not only is illness a social construction, but so is science itself. Although medicalization theorists have tended to stop short of a critique of science, there are at least three ways in which scientific ideology plays a role in the medicalization process. First and most obviously, the production of scientific knowledge is a historically determined social activity. . . Certain problems are selected for study, others are not. Certain phenomena are embraced by scientific theory, others are not. Social agenda are embedded in these choices. Thus, for example, sexist beliefs about the biological roots for gender roles formed the basis for endocrinology research in the 1920s (Hall, 1980), as did racist beliefs about the genetic basis for intelligence in the 1970s (Herrnstein, 1971). To the extent that clinical practice is rooted in science, these social agenda are incorporated by physicians in their ways of thinking about the problems of their patients. Second, in the scientific mentality, complex, dynamic and organic processes are reduced to narrow cause-and-effect relationships. Clinical science locates the problem of disease in the individual body (Crawford, 1980). As a consequence, physicians use a particular framework in both seeing and solving human problems. . . Social and emotional aspects of illness that do not fit a physiological model are likely to be ignored, and uncertainty is excluded. . . Third, the assumption is that medical practice is based on scientific knowledge. In other words, science legitimates the power of physicians over definitions of illness and the form of treatment. Yet historical and contemporary evidence reveals that the assertion of therapeutic efficacy has frequently been sufficient to justify medical intervention, even when evidence was shaky (Reverby, 1981). . .

The social nature of medicine is clarified further when we note that deviance is implicit in medical definitions. As Hubbard states, 'Medical norms don't describe what is, but rather what should be.' Thus, physicians create and reinforce social norms when they define behaviours or conditions as pathological, such as hyperactivity in children or childlessness in women. . .

Finally, the medicalization framework emphasizes that the power of physicians to define illness and monopolize the provision of treatment is the outcome of a political process. It highlights the ways in which medicine's constructions of reality are related to the structure of power at any given historical period. The political dimension inherent in medicalization is underscored when we note that structurally dependent populations – like children, old people, racial minorities and women – are subject disproportionately to medical labelling. For example, children's behaviour is medicalized under the rubric of juvenile delinquency and hyperkenesis (Conrad and Schneider, 1980a). Old people's mental functioning is labelled organic brain syndrome or senility. Racial minorities, when they come in contact with psychiatrists, are more likely than whites to be given more severe diagnoses for comparable symptoms and to receive more coercive forms of medical social control, such as psychiatric hospitalization (Gross *et al.*, 1969). Women, as I will argue, are more likely than men to have problematic experiences defined and treated medically. In each of these examples, it is important to note that the particular group's economic and social powerlessness legitimates its 'protection' by medical authorities. Of course, physicians act on behalf of the larger society, thus further reinforcing existing power relations.

Although medicalization theory has emphasized power, it has tended to minimize the significance of class. Historically, as I will suggest, the medicalization of certain problems was rooted in specific class interests. Physicians and women from the dominant class joined together – albeit out of very different motives – to redefine certain human events into medical categories. Women from other class groups at times embraced and at other times resisted these class-based definitions of experience.

In sum, the medicalization framework provides useful analytic categories for examining the medicalization of women's problems as a function of (a) the interests and beliefs of physicians; (b) the class-specific needs of women; and (c) the 'fit' between these, resulting in a consensus that redefines a human experience as a medical problem. . .

CHILDBIRTH

Today, pregnancy and birth are considered medical events. This was not always the case. . . In order to understand the medicalization of childbirth, it must be analysed as the outcome of a complex sociopolitical process in which both physicians and women participated.

In mid-nineteenth-century America virtually anyone could be a doctor. As a result, there was an oversupply of healers – a series of competing sects with varying levels of training. These included 'regular' college-trained physicians, physicians trained by apprenticeship, homeopaths, botanic physicians, male accoucheurs, midwives and other healers. . . The 'regular' physicians – white, upper-class males – struggled to achieve professional dominance as boundaries between professional and lay control shifted. It is important to emphasize that this group sought control over the healing enterprise at a time when they were not more effective than their competitors in curing disease. . . [T]he diffusion of knowledge about scientific discoveries in microbiology that revolutionized medical care occurred only after medicine successfully gained control over the healing market. Thus, in the absence of superior skill, it was necessary to convert public perceptions. In order to gain 'cultural authority' (Starr, 1982) over definitions of health and disease and over the provision of health services, 'regular' doctors had to transform general human skills into their exclusive craft. Social historians of medicine have documented the political activities that succeeded in guaranteeing a closed shop for 'regular' doctors in the late nineteenth and early twentieth century. . .

A central arena for the struggle over professional dominance was childbirth. . . [T]his event was handled predominantly by female midwives who, assisted by a network of female relatives and friends, provided emotional support and practical assistance to the pregnant woman, both during the actual birth and in the weeks that followed. Over a period of more than a century, 'social childbirth' was replaced. . . The site of care shifted from the home to the hospital. The personnel who gave care changed from female midwives to male physicians. The techniques changed from non-interventionist approaches to approaches relying on technology and drugs. As a consequence, the meaning of childbirth for women was transformed from a human experience to a medical-technical problem.

A crucial historical juncture in the medicalization of childbirth occurred in the second decade of the twentieth century. In 1910 about 50 per cent of all reported births in the United States were attended by midwives. The medical profession and the laity generally believed that the midwife – essentially a domestic worker – was an adequate birth attendant. Nature was thought to control the process of birth. As a result, there was little to be done in case of difficulty. The teaching of obstetrics in medical schools was minimal, and direct experience with birth by medical students was rare. . .

Beginning around 1910, a contest began between the emerging speciality of obstetrics, the general practitioner and the midwife. Although seemingly about issues of science and efficacy, this struggle was also about class and race. Obstetricians were from the dominant class, whereas midwives were mostly immigrant and black women. Struggling to differentiate themselves from general practitioners, obstetricians fought to upgrade the image of their field. They searched for a respectable science to legitimate their work. They argued that normal pregnancy and parturition were an exception rather than the rule. Because they believed that birth was a pathological process, obstetricians often used surgical interventions as well as instruments, such as high forceps previous to sufficient dilation. These approaches, used routinely and often unnecessarily, frequently had deleterious effects on both mother and child. Over a period of several decades, obstetricians were successful in persuading both their physician colleagues and the general public of the 'fallacy of normal pregnancy' and therefore of the need for a 'science' of obstetrical practice. Their political activities, coupled with changing demographic trends, resulted in the demise of midwifery. . .

It is important to note that the medical management of childbirth did not result in greater safety for women, at least in the short run. The evidence suggests that both maternal and infant mortality rates actually rose during the period between 1915 and 1930 when midwives' attendance at birth abruptly declined (Wertz and Wertz, 1979). In the long run, there has been a steady decline in death rates, which has coincided with modern childbirth practice. However, it is not clear how much of this decline is due to improved environmental circumstances and nutrition and how much to medical care.

In light of these facts, what motivated women to go along with the medicalization of childbirth? Because childbirth is an event that occurs without complications in most cases, it is tempting to emphasize the many losses that accompanied its medicalization. In modern birth, the woman is removed from familiar surroundings, from kin and social support, and subjected to a series of technical procedures. . . A woman's experience of birth is alienated because the social relations and instrumentation of the medical setting remove her control over the experience. . . Because of these negative consequences of modern birth, there is a tendency to romanticize the midwife and pre-technological childbirth and fail to consider the contradictory nature of the process.

Women participated in the medicalization of childbirth for a complex set of reasons. First, nineteenth-century women wanted freedom from the pain, exhaustion and lingering incapacity of childbirth. Pregnancy every other year was the norm for married women and this took a significant toll on the reproductive organs. Contraception was not a viable alternative. . . For working-class women, the problems of maternity were intensified by harsh working and housing conditions. The letters of early twentieth-century working-class women vividly portray the exhaustion of motherhood (Davies, 1978). Albeit for different reasons, women from different class groups experienced birth as a terrifying ordeal (Dye, 1980).

In the early decades of the twentieth century, relief from the pain of childbirth was promised with 'twilight sleep', a combination of morphine and scopolamine, which European physicians had begun to use. Historical analysis of the twilight sleep movement in the United States reveals that it was women who demanded it, frequently pitting themselves against the medical profession who both resented lay interference and feared the dangers of the drug (Leavitt, 1980). These women – middle- and upper-class reformers with a progressive ideology – wanted to alter the oppressive circumstances of women's lives. Thus, the demand for anaesthesia in childbirth was part of a larger social movement. Pregnancy was no longer seen as a condition to be endured with fatalism and passivity. . . [P]eople believed that civilization had increased the subjective experience of pain in childbirth, and that anaesthesia would once again make childbirth natural. The upper class experienced greater pain than working-class women, who were thought to be more like primitive peoples. People believed that upper-class women had been particularly warped by civilization. . . In other words, pain had accompanied the progress of civilization. If freed from painful and exhausting labour, women could (the reformers felt) more fully participate in democratic society. . .

Second, because of declining fertility in upper- and middle-class women at the end of the nineteenth century, the meaning of birth was particularly significant to them. Because childbirth was a less frequent event, concern about foetal death was greater. In addition, women were fearful because it was common to have known someone who had died in childbirth (Dye, 1980). Thus, well-to-do women wanted to be attended by doctors not only because they were of higher social status compared to midwives but also because they possessed the instruments and surgical techniques that might be beneficial in cases of prolonged labour, toxaemia, foetal distress and other abnormal conditions. . . [P]hysicians used these fears to gain control over the entire market, including routine births.

Thus, the demise of midwifery and the resultant medicalization of childbirth were consequences of forces within the women's community as well as from outside it. Furthermore, it was a class-specific process. Well-to-do women wanted to reduce the control that biology had over their lives. They wanted freedom from pain. Most important, these women wanted control over the birthing process – the right to decide what kind of labour and delivery they would have. The contradiction was that the method these women demanded – going to sleep – put them out of control. . .

Obstetricians also wanted control. They believed that birth was a pathological process and that 'scientific birth' would result in greater safety for women. In addition, it was in the interest of physicians to capture the childbirth market, because this event provided a gateway to the family and hence the entire healing market. . . Physicians were particularly anxious to attend the births of well-to-do women, because the social status of these women lent legitimacy and respectability to the shift from midwifery to obstetrics. . . In order to control childbirth, physicians needed drugs and technology to appear indispensable. . . Therefore, they went along with twilight sleep, at least for a time. The irony for women was that this approach to the pain of childbirth served to distance women from their bodies and redefine birth as an event requiring hospitalization and physician attendance. . .

Currently, the medicalization of childbirth is taking new forms. First, there is a trend in the United States toward more Caesarean births. Although some of these are necessary for maternal health as well as infant survival, evidence suggests that many Caesareans are unnecessary (O'Driscoll and Foley, 1983). In view of medicalization, it is important to point out that the potential need for a Caesarean places childbirth squarely and exclusively in the hands of the physician. Vaginal delivery, by contrast, can be the province of non-physician experts, such as nurse midwives.

Second, there is a trend to make the birth experience more humane, for both mother and baby. Hospitals are developing 'birthing rooms' and other alternatives to the usual delivery room atmosphere of steel tables, stirrups and bright lights. After birth, maternal–infant contact is permitted so as to foster 'bonding'. Paediatricians believe that a critical period exists for the development of an optimal relationship between mother and newborn. . . Thus, paediatricians are joining obstetricians in medicalizing the childbirth experience. By defining what should be (and therefore what is) deviant, paediatricians create social norms for parenting.

The contradiction is that the recent changes in the hospital environment of birth have both helped and hurt women. Birthing rooms and early contact between mother and newborn are a welcome change from previous oppressive obstetrical and paediatric practices (which poor women still face because these reforms are more characteristic of élite hospitals than of public ones). Yet the contemporary feminist critique of childbirth practice has been cut short by these reforms. As in many reform movements, larger issues are silenced. Challenges to the medical domination of pregnancy and demands for genuine demedicalization have been co-opted by an exclusive focus on the birth environment. Even when 'natural' childbirth occurs in birthing rooms, birth is still defined medically, is still under the control of physicians, and still occurs in hospitals.

[· · ·]

ABORTION

Today, abortion is treated as a medical event. Yet in previous historical periods, it was defined in non-medical terms. Physicians brought specific professional and class interests to the abortion issue in the nineteenth century. To realize their interests, they needed to alter public beliefs about the meaning of unwanted pregnancy. Well-to-do women formed an alliance with doctors in this redefinition process because of their own needs.

. . . [A]bortion before quickening (the perception of foetal movement) was widely practised in the mid-nineteenth century and was not seen as morally or legally wrong. Information on potions, purgatives and quasi-surgical techniques was available in home medical manuals. As auto-abortive instruments came on the market, women became skilful in performing their own abortions, and they shared information with one another. In addition, midwives, herbal healers and other 'irregular' doctors established lucrative practices in the treatment of 'obstructed menses'. It is estimated that by 1878 [in the United States] one in five pregnancies was intentionally aborted. The growing frequency of abortion was particularly evident in the middle and upper classes (Mohr, 1978).

'Regular' physicians were central figures in redefining abortion as a social problem. The practice of abortion was leading to a declining birth rate, especially among the middle and upper classes who feared that this could lead to 'race suicide'. . . One physician warned that abortion was being used 'to avoid the labour of caring for and rearing children' (Silver as quoted in Mohr, 1978). In other words, women were shirking the responsibilities of their seemingly biologically determined role.

Mohr (1978) argues that physicians led the moral crusade against abortion not so much out of these anti-feminist feelings, but primarily in order to restrict the practice of medicine. They wanted to get rid of competitors ('irregulars' and 'doctresses') and gain a monopoly over the practice of medicine. By altering public opinion and persuading legislators, they succeeded in establishing their code of ethics (which specifically excluded abortion) as the basis for professional practice. These actions limited the scope of medicine's competitors, especially women doctors whose practices were devoted to the care of female complaints. By the late 1870s, anti-abortion statutes were on the books. Professional dominance was further strengthened in the 1880s when physicians became more organized. They used the scientific paradigm to force more and more folk practitioners from the field.

[· · ·]

Women's participation in the anti-abortion crusade of the 1870s also was class-specific. Feminists of the period – well-to-do women – came out against abortion, arguing instead for voluntary motherhood. These early feminists recommended periodic or permanent abstinence as methods of birth control because they did not approve of contraceptive devices (Gordon, 1976).

It is obvious that women lost significant freedoms when abortion was defined as a medical procedure and ruled illegal. Yet, from the perspective of the sexual politics of late nineteenth-century America, it is significant that women favoured abstinence over abortion. Abstinence was a more radical response to the power relations in the patriarchal family than a pro-abortion stance would have been.

Well-to-do women of the late nineteenth century had a level of hostility toward sex, both because it brought unwanted and dangerous pregnancy and because it was a legally prescribed wifely duty. Even more important, Gordon argues that these women resented the particular kind of sexual encounter that was characteristic of American Victorian society: intercourse dominated by the husband's needs and neglecting what might bring pleasure to a woman. Men's style of lovemaking repelled women. They felt that men were oversexed and violent. Furthermore, because men visited prostitutes, marital sex for women not infrequently resulted in venereal disease. Under these conditions, a woman's right to refuse was central to her independence and personal integrity.

In sum, the termination of an unwanted pregnancy underwent a series of changing definitions: it went from a human problem to a topic of medical concern to a crime.

[···]

These historical examples underscore the fact that women's experience was a site for the initial medicalization effort. Medicine 'staked claims' for childbirth and abortion . . . and secured them as 'medical turf' by altering public beliefs and persuading the state of the legitimacy of their claim. . . Physicians used science as the rationale for professional dominance. . . Women's participation in the redefinition of each experience was the result of complex historical and class-specific motives, and they not only gained but lost with the medicalization of each area.

MEDICALIZATION OF WOMEN'S LIVES

Because women's health was a site for professional monopolization in the past, it is not surprising that medicine has continued to focus on women in the effort toward medicalization. A plethora of female conditions has come to be either reconceptualized as illnesses or, if they escape medical labelling, understood in ways that connote deviation from some ideal biological standard. Because they are seen as biological events, medical solutions are applied. For example, 'sexual dysfunctions' are defined in terms of health and illness, and an industry of sex clinics and counsellors offers treatment. Pregnancy care has been broadened to include foetal as well as maternal health, which has resulted in diagnostic procedures aimed at the foetus as well as experimental treatments, such as foetal surgery. . . Menopause is understood and treated medically, with far-reaching consequences for women's health and self-esteem. Ageing has spawned a new speciality – gerontology – for which women are the primary market. Teenage pregnancy and wife-battering are being conceptualized increasingly in psychiatric terms. The medicalization of women's lives can be examined by way of two other examples – premenstrual syndrome and weight.

Premenstrual syndrome

Premenstrual syndrome (PMS) has found a place among the medical maladies of our culture. Although PMS lacks a firm definition and a base of rigorous scientific research . . . specific premenstrual signs and symptoms have come under medical scrutiny. These include physical manifestations such as oedema (resulting in weight gain and bloatedness), breast swelling and tenderness, backache and acne. Mood changes also may occur, including increased tension and irritability, depression and lethargy. . . Significantly, the diagnosis of PMS was used successfully by the defence in several . . . legal cases. . .

What are the interests and beliefs that physicians currently bring to this new disease construction? Clearly, it is more risky to analyse motives for the medicalization of contemporary problems than it is for those of the past . . . where the historical record can provide supporting evidence. Nevertheless, market conditions exist that suggest some reasons as to why the medical profession might be prospecting for new turf at this time. First, there is a declining birth rate. With fewer babies to be delivered, gynaecologists must develop other areas in order to guarantee a successful practice. Second, there are more gynaecologists per capita than ever before. As a result of US federal programmes in the 1960s, medical schools expanded and more physicians graduated. Consequently, the supply of obstetrician/gynaecologists in the United States increased from 15,984 in 1966 to 25,215 in 1979 (Theodore and Sutler, 1966; Wunderman, 1980) – an increase of 64 per cent. Finally, there are more women in the population in their thirties, as a result of the post-war baby boom. Given these conditions – lower demand, increased supply and a pool of appropriately aged women – it is not unreasonable to hypothesize that gynaecologists would actively seek out new 'disease' entities to which they could apply their skills. Premenstrual syndrome, as well as endometriosis, may represent new disease constructions that are a response to these conditions.

In addition, physicians hold beliefs about women that are likely to influence the disease construction of PMS, especially when they are joined with economic interests. In medical education, physicians are trained to think about women in ways that are anything but neutral and value-free. . . Physicians are taught psychiatric theories about the development of gender identity that reinforce existing power relations between the sexes. No doubt these beliefs also influence physicians' understanding of menstruation, although the particular ways that sexist ideology is embedded in current scientific thought about the premenstrual period needs further study.

Other communities also influence the clinical scrutiny of menstruation. The drug industry is actively looking for new markets. Corporations shape physicians' perceptions through drug advertising, personal contacts and free samples of their products. Research has shown that physicians' behaviour is remarkably sensitive to the 'educational' efforts of the pharmaceutical houses (Christensen and Bush, 1981). In addition to the drug industry, other parties that can affect physicians' perceptions include the legal profession (which has found the diagnosis of PMS useful in adjudicating clients) and the insurance industry (which will have to contend with this new diagnostic category in their reimbursement policies). . . [T]hese communities are functionally interdependent. They interact in complex ways with one another and with physicians in the creation of new technologies and disease entities.

From the perspective of women, the medicalization of the premenstrual experience is filled with contradictions. On the positive side, physicians' recognition of women's experience with menstruation is important, for it legitimates an important aspect of women's lives. Women have often observed that their moods varied over the course of their menstrual cycle and shared their observations with one another, but until recently they were discounted by the medical establishment. Doctors responded either by dismissing women's premenstrual complaints or by ascribing them to un- resolved problems with their femininity. The clinical construction of PMS acknowledges the cyclic nature of women's lives and opens up the possibility that attention will be paid to other phases of the menstrual cycle. For example, some suggest that a 'Menstrual Joy Questionnaire' be created, using the model of the 'Menstrual Distress Questionnaire' (Moos, 1963), in order to document the pleasurable feelings, increased energy and creativity that are experienced during the cycle (Delaney et al., 1976).

Women in certain economic groups are currently seeking out physicians regarding problems with menstruation just as an earlier, similar class group sought physicians for care during pregnancy.

These women are actively participating in the construction of the new medical syndrome of PMS just as they were in creating the 'new childbirth'... The contemporary feminist movement is responsible for a new consciousness that, in some ways, encourages women to be assertive regarding discomfort in menstruation, just as a previous social movement encouraged women to seek relief from pain in childbirth... [F]or the small group of women who have premenstrual problems that severely interfere with functioning, relief is possible with medical treatment (Dalton, 1977). It is also possible that scientific research can supply knowledge that might be used in nutritional, exercise and other treatment approaches (Harrison, 1982).

On the negative side, the medicalization of menstruation has disturbing implications for women's lives. Most obviously, it reinforces the idea that women are controlled by biology in general and their reproductive systems in particular. This has been used to legitimate the exclusion of women from positions of power because of supposed emotional instability and irrationality due to 'raging hormonal imbalances'... It has also been used to suggest that women are violent as a result of their biology, because of the apparent correlation between PMS and crimes committed by women. Thus, medical scrutiny of the premenstrual period serves to emphasize cyclic phenomena in women when, in fact, hormonal blood levels are episodic in both men and women... In addition, medical scrutiny also reinforces scientific assumptions about the existence of universal norms or a 'natural' menstrual history. This has been refuted by anthropological evidence, which demonstrates considerable cross-cultural variation in all aspects of menstrual cycling (Hubbard, 1981). Furthermore, labelling hormonal changes as a syndrome implies a pathological condition – something to be controlled – rather than suggesting that mood shifts and bodily changes are a normal part of everyone's life. Thus, there is a danger that medical treatments will be applied routinely to women, as oestrogen replacement therapy has been for menopause. In other words, insufficiently tested, ineffective or dangerous pharmaceutical remedies and surgical interventions may be used to treat premenstrual problems. Finally, medical labelling may create cultural beliefs and attitudes about the premenstrual period. It may create suffering in women who were previously asymptomatic. It may encourage them to perceive fluctuating bodily and emotional states differently, simply because a medical explanation for them exists. Support for this hypothesis was found in an experimental study conducted prior to the development of the diagnostic category of PMS. Women who were told they were premenstrual reported more severe physical symptoms than women who believed they were simply between periods (Ruble, 1977).

Most important, the medicalization of PMS deflects attention from social etiology. Rather than looking at the circumstances of women's lives that may make them irritable, depressed or angry, their strong feelings can be dismissed ('You'll feel better when you get your period'). The contradiction lies in the fact that the label of PMS allows women to be angry and say what's on their minds at a certain time each month, while at the same time it invalidates the content of their protest.

THE MEDICAL BEAUTY BUSINESS: GETTING THIN

Like menstruation, women's physical appearance has come under the lens of the medical establishment. Cosmetic surgeons treat everything from facial wrinkles to breast size. The medical beauty business has concentrated with special intensity on the bodily changes associated with women's ageing. Another subject of medical scrutiny is weight. 'Obesity' is now a medical condition.

Although weight is not exclusively a women's issue, it is an excellent example of the medicalization of women's experience for a number of reasons. It highlights the relationship between the social norms for femininity and medical social control. By medicalizing weight, medical science participates in programming aesthetics for women's bodies. This has far-reaching consequences for self-esteem, as women are evaluated on the basis of personal appearance more than men (Millman, 1980). Weight is also a good example of medicalization because it illustrates in a most graphic form how power relations are maintained through medical social control, how women internalize their oppression by desiring to be thin and turning to doctors for help.

As background, let me review briefly some basic information about weight – its causes, consequences for health and the efficacy of weight reduction programmes. First, adult weight is the outcome of the interplay of a complex combination of factors, including heredity, body type, childhood eating patterns and metabolism. Although amount of food intake is clearly relevant, its causal significance appears to lie in its interaction with these other factors... Also, it appears that obesity is more prevalent in lower socio-economic groups. This is true for both children and adults.

[· · ·]

[T]herapies for weight control are far from efficacious and, in some cases, are dangerous... [Most] successful are self-help groups and behaviour modification approaches to weight loss... In general, however, the pattern for most individuals is a cycle of weight loss followed by weight gain, which is repeated over and over. The cyclical process further undermines the metabolic system's ability to regulate body weight (Beller, 1977).

[· · ·]

[I]t was not until the late 1960s and the 1970s that medicine began to deal with the topic of weight with such intensity. It was in the interest of physicians to define weight as a medical problem for a number of reasons. Its apparent association with chronic disease legitimated its clinical scrutiny. More important, a market for weight control opened up as the sedentary life and associated weight gain came to characterize post-industrial society. In addition, particular medical specialities had specific reasons for going into the weight business. Surgeons, for example, facing conditions of over-supply, needed to create markets for their services. The development of surgical approaches to obesity was a logical outcome. Other specialities also needed to generate demand, as the care of infectious diseases took less and less of physicians' time. Here was a potential pool of patients who were concerned about weight and who were so desperate that they were willing to try anything to bring it under control.

Nevertheless, physicians did not act in a vacuum. The medicalization of weight graphically illustrates how medical definitions, cultural ideology and corporate interests work hand in hand.

[· · ·]

In my research on the clinical construction of obesity, I found a relationship between the extent of the medical literature on the topic and the growth of the women's movement. Reviewing the number of citations in *Index Medicus* by year, I found obesity to be an insignificant topic in 1960, warranting only slightly more than a page of entries. By 1981, more than seven pages were devoted to citations on the topic. Interestingly, articles referring to surgical remedies for obesity were insignificant in 1970 (only 8), rose to a high in 1976 (of 73) and declined thereafter.

In their research on cultural 'ideals' of feminine beauty, Garner and his colleagues also found a shift in norms that coincided with the growth of the women's movement. They studied the weights of *Playboy* magazine centrefolds and contestants and winners of the Miss America Pageant from 1959 through 1978. They found that in both contexts the women selected as exemplars of feminine beauty were significantly thinner than the norm for comparable women in the population. More important, they found that when age and height were controlled, weight declined over the twenty-year period they studied. Ideal body shape became progressively thinner in spite of the fact that the average weight of women in the general population grew slightly during the same period (Garner *et al.*, 1980).

In addition to cultural ideals and medical definitions, once again other communities shape beliefs about weight. Several industries profit from the cultural preoccupation with women's size. Pharmaceutical companies market anorectic drugs, including amphetamines and other appetite suppressants. The food industry markets low-calorie foods and artificial sweeteners: in advertising, it depicts attractiveness in terms of weight. The fashion industry simultaneously creates and reflects images of the cultural ideal – the thin woman. The beauty business provides places to realize this ideal – the health spa and figure salon.

In this context, it is not surprising that some women have gone along with the medicalization of weight. They believe it is in their interest to be thin. Yet at the same time that they have internalized this dominant value, women have also resisted it – they gain weight. This contradiction further drives the process of medicalization. Thus, economically advantaged women become the major market for a series of weight control industries. The data uniformly show that, compared to men, women are more likely to have ileal bypass surgery, to receive prescriptions for weight-related drugs, to undertake 'scientifically based' diets and to read the physician-authored diet books on the market. Women are also the primary participants in self-help groups such as Weight Watchers, TOPS (Take Pounds Off Sensibly) and Overeaters Anonymous (Millman, 1980).[1]

These women want to be thin. Some think of themselves primarily in terms of their size. . . They are responsive to cultural messages that suggest that they can be in control of how they look in part because of the powerlessness they feel in other areas of their lives. Yet, paradoxically, the feeling of being out of control ultimately takes over, as women discover they cannot really be successful in controlling weight through diet. . . In despair, they collaborate willingly with surgeons and drug-oriented physicians who offer external solutions, further reinforcing their feelings of powerlessness.

Ironically, medical science has given women some tools for understanding the psychological determinants of eating. Psychiatric thought has provided insight into the meaning that food has in their lives and the conflicts that lead them to over-eat. However, with the exception of therapies and diet groups with a feminist perspective, psychological approaches rarely question the cultural ideal of slenderness. Nor do they help women see that the internalization of this value reflects alienation from the natural self and the feminine nature of their bodies (Chernin, 1981).

It is clear that the medicalization of physical appearance has had many negative effects on women. Medical science, in collaboration with a series of industries, participates in creating social norms for physical appearance in the guise of supposedly neutral, objective, scientific standards for 'ideal' body weight. These standards are based on white, middle-class norms and neglect the diversity of women's bodies. Further, these standards do not take into account the fact that certain cultural groups value women with substantial bodies (Millman, 1980)...

In light of the class and racial bias in medical norms for weight, it is significant that resistance has tended to come from poor and working-class women, as well as from women of colour. While listening respectfully to physicians' admonitions about their weight, some of these women persist in their own beliefs about appropriate body size for themselves. As a result, they are likely to be labelled noncompliant by their doctors.

Most important, by treating weight as a medical problem, medicine diverts attention away from the social causes of poor nutrition and an obsession with thinness. Obesity is correlated with poverty. In poor communities, food preparation has been commercialized in particular ways that undermine health. Poor neighbourhoods are focal markets for fast-food chains, because there is a need for high calorie, relatively inexpensive convenience meals. Nutritional status has been compromised further by junk food; especially problematic for weight is the high sugar and salt content. Thus, the food industry has played a major role in generating poor eating habits and, as a result, disease (McKinlay, 1981). In this context, the medicalization of weight is a classic case of blaming the victim.

Furthermore, by individualizing the problem of weight, crucial questions are never asked. Why is it that women are more likely than men to be defined as overweight? Why is anorexia almost exclusively a women's health issue? What is the connection between nutritional malaise and the problems of women in this culture? Does the source of the problem lie in women's roles? Or is the problem with the norms that define appropriate appearance for men compared with women? ...

MEDICALIZATION AND PSYCHIATRY

In addition to weight, women's psychological problems are also a central focus for the drug and medical industries. Women receive more prescriptions for valium and other psychotropic drugs than do men (Cooperstock and Parnell, 1982; Koumjian, 1981). They receive more outpatient psychotherapy...

Middle-class women have been influenced in major ways by psychiatric thought. Psychiatrists as well as other mental-health professionals view emotional pain as a symptom of an illness. Middle-class women have tended to internalize these sentiments, whereas working-class women have been more likely to resist them.

In the late 1950s and early '60s, many middle-class women went into psychotherapy with a series of concerns about their lives – 'the problem with no name', in the words of Betty Friedan. But in therapy, these women came to understand their feelings as depression... [M]any highly educated women found support in psychoanalytic therapy for their private despair at being expected to find fulfilment in marriage and suburban living. The process of introspection helped individual women to voice their concerns and to act to improve their lives. At the same time these women were subjected to an ideology of femininity that made it difficult for them to realize their ambitions outside of traditional marriage. They needed the emerging contemporary women's movement to redefine their experience in structural terms.

But there is a contradiction in this, in that presenting complaints to psychotherapists is more progressive than keeping problems behind closed doors; but then issues are depoliticized... There is an ever-present danger that feminist content will be diminished with medicalization. This can occur not only with psychological problems but with physical ones as well.

For example, Stark and Flitcraft (1982) found that when battered women came in contact with hospitals, their problems were exacerbated by physicians and nurses. A purely medical definition of the situation prevailed, replacing any alternative understanding of the problem. Social workers further colluded by seeing the problem as part of a larger issue of the 'multiproblem family'...

THE FIT BETWEEN WOMEN'S INTERESTS AND PHYSICIANS' INTERESTS

These examples illustrate a general point about medical social control: there are times when the interests of women from the middle and upper classes are served by the therapeutic professions, whose political and economic interests are in turn served by transforming these women's complaints into illnesses. In other words, both historically and currently, there has tended to be a 'fit' between medicine's interest in expanding its jurisdiction and the need of women to have their experience acknowledged. I have emphasized that this 'fit' has been tension-filled and fraught with contradictions for women, who have both gained and lost with each intrusion medicine has made into their lives.

While necessary, the particular interests of women and physicians do not alone explain the expansion of the clinical domain. Other communities also influence what occurs in the doctor's office. In the context of a capitalist economy and a technologically dominated medical-care system, large profits accompany each redefinition of human experience into medical terms, since more drugs, tests, procedures, equipment and insurance coverage are needed... [S]pecific medical industries have played a direct role in influencing both physicians' and women's perceptions of repro- ductive control, premenstrual syndrome and weight. Yet it is important to emphasize that corporations, in their effort to maximize profits, work *through* both physicians and women.

Implicit in my analysis is the assumption that women's experience has been medicalized more than men's. Yet it could be argued instead that medicine has encroached into men's lives in a different but equal fashion. For example, medicine has focused on childhood hyperactivity and the adult addictions – problems more common in males than females. . . Occupational medicine has tended to focus on male jobs. In particular, 'stress management' programmes are targeting male executives. However, while not to diminish these examples, I believe that women's lives have undergone a more total transformation as a result of medical scrutiny. Medicalization has resulted in the construction of medical meanings of *normal* functions in women – experiences the typical woman goes through, such as menstruation, reproduction, childbirth and menopause. By contrast, routine experiences that are uniquely male remain largely unstudied by medical science and, consequently, are rarely treated by physicians as potentially pathological. For example, male hormonal cycles and the male climacteric remain largely unresearched. Less is known about the male reproductive system than about that of the female. Male contraceptive technology lags far behind what is available for women. Baldness in men has not yet been defined as a medical condition needing treatment, even though an industry exists to remedy the problem of hair loss. Men's psychological lives have not been subjected to psychiatric scrutiny nearly to the degree that women's emotions have been studied. As a result, male violence, need for power and overrationality are not defined as pathological conditions. Perhaps only impotence has been subject to the same degree of medical scrutiny as women's problems.

Why has women's experience been such a central focus for medicalization? In addition to the complex motives that women bring to each particular health issue, physicians focus on women as a primary market for expansion for a number of reasons. . .

[W]omen's social roles make them readily available to medical scrutiny. Women are more likely to come in contact with medical providers because they care for children and . . . are more likely to accompany sick children and aged relatives to the doctor.

[W]omen have greater exposure to medical labelling because of their pattern of dealing with their own symptoms, as well as medicine's response to that pattern. Women make more visits to physicians than men, although it is not clear whether this is due to the medicalization of their biological functions, 'real' illness, behaviour when ill or cultural expectations. . . When they visit the doctor for any serious illness, they are more likely than men to be checked for reproductive implications of the illness. They are more subject to regular checks of their reproductive systems in the form of cervical smears or gynaecological exams. Importantly, whenever they visit the doctor there is evidence that they receive more total and extensive services – in the form of lab tests, procedures, drug prescriptions and return appointments – than do men with the same complaints and socio-demographic risk factors (Verbrugge and Steiner, 1981). Thus, a cycle of greater medical scrutiny of women's experience is begun with each visit to the doctor.

Finally, women's structural subordination to men has made them particularly vulnerable to the expansion of the clinical domain. In general, male physicians treat female patients. Social relations in the doctor's office replicate patriarchal relations in the larger culture, and this all proceeds under the guise of science... For all these reasons, it is not surprising that women are more subject to medical definitions of their experience than men are. In these ways, dominant social interests and patriarchal institutions are reinforced.

... The message that women are expected to be dependent on male physicians to manage their lives is reinforced by the pharmaceutical industry in drug advertisements and by the media in general. Yet it is far too simple to portray the encroachment of medicine as a conspiracy – by male doctors and the 'medical industrial complex' – to subordinate women further... [M]edicalization is more than what doctors do, although it may be through doctors that the interests of other groups are often realized. Nor does a conspiracy theory explain why, for the most part, women from certain class groups have been willing collaborators in the medicalization process. Rather than dismissing these women as 'duped', I have suggested some of the complex motives that have caused certain classes of women to participate with physicians in the redefinition of particular experiences.

In addition, a conspiracy theory does not explain why medicalization has been more virulent in some historical periods and in some medical specialties than in others. For example, gynaecologists initially trivialized menopausal discomfort, only to reclaim it later for treatment. At the same time that gynaecologists were unwilling to acknowledge the legitimacy of women's complaints, the developing specialty of psychiatry moved in with the psychogenic account... [T]hese shifts and interprofessional rivalries over turf are explained by internal issues facing each specialty at particular points in history.

[···]

CONCLUSION

The medicalization of human problems is a contradictory reality for women. It is part of the problem and of the solution... As women have tried to free themselves from the control that biological processes have had over their lives, they simultaneously have strengthened the control of a biomedical view of their experience. As women visit doctors and get symptom relief, the social causes of their problems are ignored. As doctors acknowledge women's experience and treat their problems medically, problems are stripped of their political content and popular movements are taken over. Because of these contradictions, women in different class positions have sought and resisted medical control.

[· · ·]

Historically, establishing childbirth, abortion and birth control as medical events were critical junctures on the road to professional dominance. New areas of medical domain are needed because old ones have become saturated. Thus, expansion is occurring in such areas as menstruation, physical appearance, emotional distress, fertility, sexuality and ageing. . .

[T]he potential for medicalization increases as science discovers the subtle physiological correlates of human behaviour. A wealth of knowledge is developing about women's physiology. As more becomes known, the issue will be how to acknowledge the complex biochemical components that are related to menstruation, pregnancy, weight and the like without allowing these conditions to be distorted by scientific understanding. The issue will be to gain understanding of our biology, without submitting to control in the guise of medical 'expertise'. The answer is not to 'suffer our fate' and return exclusively to self-care, as Illich recommends, thereby turning our backs on discoveries and treatments that may ease pain and suffering. To 'de-medicalize' is not to deny the biological components of experience but rather to alter the *ownership, production* and *use* of scientific knowledge.

Ultimately, however, demedicalization may involve profound questions about the nature of science itself. The very structure of science – its system of beliefs, assumptions, methods and the description of 'reality' it offers – is problematic for understanding women's experience. . . Particularly significant for women's health is the emphasis on domination over nature that characterizes the entire scientific enterprise, especially in light of the fact that nature is seen as female (Merchant, 1980). . .

In sum, women's health is faced by a series of challenges. We need to expose the 'truth claims' . . . of medical entrepreneurs who will seek to turn new areas of experience into medical events, and instead introduce a healthy scepticism about professional claims. We need to develop alternatives to the masculinist biomedical view and place women's health problems in the larger context of their lives. . . We need to reconceptualize our whole way of thinking

143

about biology and explore how 'natural' phenomena are, in fact, an outgrowth of the social circumstances of women's lives (Hubbard, 1981).

In the meantime, because we will continue to need health care, the challenge will be to alter the terms under which care is provided. In the short term, we need to work for specific reforms and gain what we can while, at the same time, acknowledging the limitation of reform. . .

Note

1   Fox [1977] has stated that these approaches that rely on mutual aid, as opposed to professional intervention, are examples of the 'demedicalization' of a human problem in contemporary society. However, as Conrad and Schneider (1980b) note, deprofessionaliz-ation is not the same thing as demedicalization. More specifically, many of the self-help groups oriented toward weight loss share medicine's disease orientation to the problem of weight. Because many of these peer approaches to behaviour change do not challenge medicine's assumptions, they do not 'demedicalize' human problems, but rather medicalize under lay auspices.

Article 2.4
DETECTING GENETIC DISEASES: PRENATAL SCREENING AND ITS PROBLEMS

Lynda Birke, Susan Himmelweit and Gail Vines

Prenatal diagnosis is the field of medicine that specializes in attempting to detect various 'abnormalities' in the foetus. Doctors have long sought to detect [such] abnormalities. . . , but the daunting complexity of the task has long made the field an esoteric specialism pursued by only a few specialists. Now, advances in the ability both to visualize the foetus, especially through ultrasound, and to analyse its genetic material have made it possible for doctors to talk about 'routine screening' of some or all pregnant women, for many foetal abnormalities.

The medical pioneers of prenatal diagnosis divided defects into crude categories, which are still in use today. The most common serious birth defects are chromosomal abnormalities, such as Down's syndrome. Chromosomes are the structures in the nucleus of a cell that carry the genes. People normally have twenty-three pairs of chromosomes, and inherit one of each pair from each parent. Sometimes things go wrong, producing a foetus with three copies of a particular chromosome (as in Down's) or, rarely, only one copy. . .

Other inborn disorders are known as genetic diseases – or, more precisely, 'single-gene defects' – because a single faulty gene underlies the disease (see Box 2.4.1). Researchers have so far identified about 300 of these disorders, but there may be as many as 1600. . . Into this category fall a few relatively common inherited disorders, such as haemophilia, thalassaemia, sickle cell disease, cystic fibrosis and Duchenne muscular dystrophy. . . A few single-gene disorders, notably phenylketonuria (or PKU), can be effectively dealt with after birth, through diet for example. People with PKU lack a particular enzyme; undiagnosed, they build up toxins that lead to brain damage. The build-up is prevented if they eat a diet free of a particular amino acid, phenylalanine. Screening for PKU is routine in Britain even though it affects only 1 in 10,000 of the population: newborn babies are tested for PKU by a simple biochemical test on a drop of blood from a pricked heel.

Other disorders in physical development, such as spina bifida . . ., tend to be called – rather vaguely – 'congenital' because no one knows what causes them. Still other conditions fall readily into neither category, because they arise from an inherited defect that

Box 2.4.1 What can go wrong?

Some inborn defects – chromosomal abnormalities – arise when something goes awry with the sorting and swapping of chromosomes. An egg or sperm may end up lacking a particular chromosome, or missing a chunk of one. Most such chromosomal aberrations are lethal at an early age, and cause the embryo to abort spontaneously. In others, such as Down's syndrome, when the embryo has three copies of chromosome 21, instead of two, the foetus often goes to term.

A 'genetic defect' arises if there is a mutation in a single gene. A mutation is a 'mistake' in one or more of the bases that form the building blocks of DNA. The substitution of one base for another, or a deletion or addition of a base, can cause the cell to put together a faulty protein from the garbled instructions, or to make none of that protein at all. A genetic defect can be fatal, or harmless, depending upon what that protein normally does, or whether there is another, normal gene that can compensate for the mutated one.

makes the foetus more vulnerable to something else, such as a harmful chemical in the environment.

Taken together, such serious birth defects occur at a rate of 23 per 1000 births, on a global average. Very few of these disorders can be treated effectively and they account for about a third of admissions to paediatric wards in the West, and a large proportion of childhood deaths. Some epidemiologists argue that infant mortality cannot fall below the 20 per 1000 mark, now achieved by Japan and most Western countries, unless we can treat, or prevent, severe chronic disease with a genetic basis.

Until recently, doctors interested in the plethora of ill-understood disorders of the developing foetus have had only rather primitive ways of studying them. The work of cell biologists in the 1950s and 1960s led to the first breakthrough – the ability to study a foetus's chromosomes. These scientists – 'cytogeneticists' – perfected ways of detecting extra chromosomes in foetal cells. . . [They] photograph dividing cells, cut out the individual chromosomes and arrange them in an orderly group portrait, know in the trade as a 'karyotype'.

Medical cytogenetics came of age in 1959. A French geneticist, Jerome Lejeune, discovered that children with Down's syndrome have three, rather than the normal two, copies of chromosome 21. Lejeune's discovery caused a great stir, as researchers of the time, and a eugenically minded population at large, had long suspected that 'feeblemindedness' was inherited, passed on from 'inferior' parents to their offspring (Kevles, 1986). Even liberal-minded scientists were excited by the notion that we might begin to discover the genetic basis of many human ills. The search began for other abnormalities of the chromosomes, and for a way of diagnosing chromosomal aberrations before birth. Doctors soon refined a technique for harvesting foetal cells – . . . 'amniocentesis'. It became possible to diagnose disorders such as Down's syndrome in the second trimester of pregnancy.

In amniocentesis, doctors extract some of the amniotic fluid that surrounds the foetus, via a needle through the woman's abdomen. This technique exploits the fact that the foetus sheds some of its own cells into the fluid. . . In England and Wales . . . between 2 and 3 per cent of pregnant women now have amniocentesis.

In Britain doctors' enthusiasm for prenatal diagnosis was fuelled by the passing of the Abortion Act of 1967, which legalized the termination of affected foetuses, for the medics felt that there was no point in diagnosing something that they could do nothing about. Over the next two decades women's magazines and obstetricians joined forces to spread the word, focusing particularly on amniocentesis for Down's syndrome which occurs in the West at the rate of about 1 in 750 live births, and is the most common cause of mental retardation.

[· · ·]

Nonetheless, despite the success of the 'educational' campaign, amniocentesis for Down's syndrome remains a bit of an embarrassment for the advocates of prenatal diagnosis. Even within Britain, amniocentesis is not universally available on the NHS, and some regions have different [lower] age [limits] than others – thirty-eight versus thirty-five, for instance. The availability of amniocentesis has also had little impact on the number of Down's syndrome children born. This is not because most women over thirty-five or forty are rejecting the test or generally refusing to abort affected foetuses, nor even because doctors fail to offer them the test. Rather, amniocentesis for older women most at risk has little impact because 80 per cent of Down's syndrome babies are born to younger women, under thirty-five. Even though younger women are individually at lower risk, they have so many more of each year's crop of babies that they also have more Down's syndrome babies, in direct proportion.

Why not offer amniocentesis to all women then? For a start, the test can lead to the spontaneous abortion of a foetus. Much debate among medics centres on the precise risk of miscarriage –

some studies suggest it is as low as 0.5 per cent (1 in 200), others as high as 1.7 per cent. The expertise of the practitioner and the technique used, such as the size of the needle and the availability of ultrasound, probably account for some of the disagreement.

Health economists also argue that it is not cost-effective to screen all women; because the individual risk for younger women is so low, large numbers would have to be tested for each Down's syndrome foetus detected, so the cost becomes astronomical. Doctors also argue that testing younger women as a matter of course would be unethical, because the risk of producing a spontaneous abortion from the test may be higher than the risk of Down's syndrome in younger women. This seems a sensible argument on the face of it, but makes a dubious assumption: that all women will give the two probabilities the same weight, so as to equate the risk of spontaneous abortion with the risk of having a Down's baby. Depending upon their beliefs, experiences and circumstances, individual women may well balance the risks very differently.

Another drawback to amniocentesis is its timing. The amniotic fluid contains too few foetal cells before about sixteen weeks of pregnancy. Even then, amniocentesis retrieves only a few foetal cells, so technicians have to grow them in the laboratory for two weeks or more to have enough dividing ones to karyotype. It can take a month or more to get the results, forcing those women whose test results suggest something is 'wrong' to contemplate a late abortion, with all its emotional traumas and physical risks.

Amniocentesis can pick up defects other than Down's, however, notably other chromosomal aberrations . . . and a few rare 'inborn errors of metabolism'. . . Amniocentesis has also long been used to detect the failure of the spinal column to close – the so-called neural tube defects, such as spina bifida. Neural tube defects occur in about 1 in every 1000 live births, among Celts and Sikhs in particular, and so are relatively common. The causes of these birth defects are varied and largely unknown. . .

Against a background of mysterious cause, the prenatal diagnosis of neural tube defects has bloomed. Developed some fifteen years ago, its appeal is the simplicity of the first screening test: an analysis of the mother's blood. A tell-tale sign of an open spinal column in the developing foetus is an abnormal amount of alpha foetoprotein, produced by the foetal liver. The foetus normally excretes this substance into the amniotic fluid and a tiny amount enters the mother's bloodstream. High levels of alpha foetoprotein (AFP), however, suggest that something is wrong. Doctors may then offer to perform an amniocentesis to check the levels of AFP in the amniotic fluid. In the past few years, however, obstetricians have tended to use high-resolution ultrasonography, instead of amniocentesis, to confirm the presence of a neural tube defect.

In England and Wales some 60 per cent of pregnant women now have a blood test for AFP as a standard part of their antenatal care, but numbers vary dramatically from region to region (from almost all women in Oxford and North East Thames to almost none in East Anglia). In theory they are told about the purpose of the test and asked for their consent. In practice the test is often performed routinely, without informed consent.

There are technical problems with the 'maternal serum' AFP test, too. It is not foolproof, because there are marked changes in the levels of AFP during pregnancy, and between individual women. A worrying blood test may well turn out to be a false alarm, after an unnecessary amniocentesis. Or the test may falsely reassure women that all is well. Levels of AFP in the mother's blood can detect only about 60 per cent of foetuses with spina bifida, for instance. Furthermore, the severity of neural tube defects varies greatly, and it is not always easy to tell them apart, even with ultrasound scans. . .

Despite the disadvantages inherent in AFP-testing, it is growing in popularity in the United States. There, doctors are beginning to offer women the test fuelled by fears that, if they do not, they will be sued by patients who have an affected child. American commentators have already expressed concern that 'whether a prenatal screening is offered may depend as much on the patient's health insurance and the physician's perception of possible legal liability as on the physician's view of the patient's welfare' (Elias and Annas, 1987).

[· · ·]

Perhaps the most important point to emerge from decades of prenatal diagnosis is that, broadly speaking, it has not been a roaring success. Amniocentesis late in pregnancy, followed by laborious and expensive karyotyping (analysis of chromosomes), or biochemical tests for neural tube defects are not the stuff of mass screening. Such procedures cannot support a 'search and destroy' mission against severe congenital deformity and genetic disease throughout the population. Ultrasound is also still too primitive to catch many physical defects (see Box 2.4.2). 'Foetoscopy', performed at seventeen weeks of gestation or more, uses a fine fibre-optic tube to examine the foetus visually. But it is hazardous, even in experienced hands, and causes miscarriages about 4 per cent of the time. It is mostly used for extracting a foetal blood sample or a bit of liver or skin to detect rare inborn errors of metabolism in couples already known to be at risk of having an affected child.

Despite the disappointing track record of prenatal diagnosis to date, two recent developments have generated great enthusiasm among clinicians working in the field: the prospect of diagnosis at

Box 2.4.2 Ultrasound

Attempts to 'visualize' the foetus are fraught with difficulties and are not yet a great success. It began badly and in some ways is still primitive. In the early days of X-rays there was a brief medical vogue for popping pregnant women under the machines to look at the foetus – a fashion abruptly abandoned once radiologists realized the dangers of thereby causing a 'defect' themselves.

Ultrasound is now the technology of choice for such purposes. It is apparently safe, although there are still debates about whether we have enough information to assess its possible effects on young embryos in the long term. In experienced hands, an 'anomaly scan' at about twenty weeks can undoubtedly detect many major congenital defects, such as anencephaly where no brain develops. Yet interpretation is all, given the fuzzy images of ultrasound, and many medics are sceptical of some of the claims made by ultrasound enthusiasts. For instance, some sonographers advocate replacing blood tests for AFP with ultrasound scans to detect spina bifida. Other researchers claim to be able to detect 82 per cent of Down's foetuses during the second trimester through ultrasound.

Yet other doctors stress how misleading ultrasound can be, finding false positives (i.e. results that appear to indicate a positive result for, say, spina bifida, when the foetus is normal) commonplace. In Britain the Medical Research Council is conducting a trial to try to assess the strengths and weaknesses of diagnostic ultrasound. So far it has most proven its worth only in a more humble role, guiding the procedures of amniocentesis and the new technique of chorionic villus sampling (CVS) and retrieval of eggs in IVF. At the moment, antenatal clinics rely on ultrasound scans mostly to check the age of the foetus and to spot twins.

the level of the gene combined with a new way of sampling foetal tissue early in pregnancy. It is now even possible to screen embryos for some genetic diseases in the laboratory, before a pregnancy has even begun.

What is strikingly new is the ability of doctors, teamed with scientists, to diagnose many of the genetic diseases that arise as a result of a single faulty gene. Advances in the techniques of molecular biology have made this possible. Already, in theory, researchers can detect some forty single gene defects in a foetus.

The molecular diagnosis relies on one of two basic approaches. The test may detect the presence of the faulty gene itself, if we know what it is. Or it may detect some other gene nearby – usually a harmless gene that is interesting only because it is physically near enough on the chromosome to the as-yet-unknown faulty one to act as a 'genetic marker' (rather like identifying a house because you know what the neighbouring one looks like).

[· · ·]

Researchers in San Francisco were among the first to use DNA in prenatal diagnosis, in 1978, to detect a foetus with sickle cell anaemia. . . They extracted DNA from foetal cells retrieved by amniocentesis. In 1982 researchers in Oxford broke new ground by diagnosing beta-thalassaemia in the first trimester of pregnancy [using] a new technique for extracting foetal cells known as chorionic villus sampling (CVS). Since then, scores of single-gene defects have been diagnosed by the technique. It now often takes just a few months to take the discovery of a new disease-causing gene or a new genetic marker from the laboratory into clinical practice, in the form of prenatal diagnosis (Emery, 1984).

[· · ·]

EARLIER SCREENING? THE DEVELOPMENT OF CVS

Our growing ability to detect genetic diseases using DNA-based tests has fostered the development of CVS. Invented in China, this technique was refined in the United Kingdom and the United States in the early 1980s at élite medical centres. To date, more than 17,000 women throughout the world at some ninety centres have had CVS (Jackson, 1986). . .

The appeal of the test is the fact that it is a way of obtaining foetal tissue early on in pregnancy, from about nine to eleven weeks. This means that an affected foetus could be aborted much earlier than the twenty-four weeks or so necessitated by amniocentesis.

In chorionic villus sampling, doctors remove a bit of tissue from the portion of the placenta that is contributed by the foetus. Chorionic villi are finger-like projections of the chorion, the outer membrane of the gestation sac surrounding the foetus. Typically, using [an instrument] inserted through the woman's cervix, doctors snip off a few villi to obtain enough cells to test. [Sampling may also take place through the abdominal wall.] CVS via a transabdominal route is now becoming the norm between twelve weeks, the latest date for cervical CVS, and about fifteen weeks, the earliest for amniocentesis. Ultrasound imaging is essential to enable doctors to guide the instruments to the right spot, avoiding blood vessels, the foetus itself, and so on.

The foetal cells harvested by CVS can be examined directly; there are sufficient dividing cells in the villi to test immediately for chromosomal abnormalities such as Down's. This gives CVS a big advantage over amniocentesis, where technicians must grow foetal cells in the laboratory for several weeks before they can analyse any chromosomes. Equally important, these villus cells are also usually plentiful enough to enable biologists to extract DNA to test for genetic diseases such as thalassaemia. . .

Many people predict that chorionic villus sampling will soon largely replace amniocentesis. Because it can be performed early in pregnancy, it removes the need for late abortions in many cases. But the safety of the new technique compared to amniocentesis is still uncertain. . .

[· ·]

A major disadvantage of CVS, however, is that it cannot diagnose neural tube defects such as spina bifida. . . Similarly, CVS is less reliable than amniocentesis for detecting some metabolic conditions. . .

The placenta is rather odd, biologists now think; it seems to have an inherent tendency to generate cells with chromosomal abnormalities. The danger is that this ill-understood quirk of nature could lead to the abortion of a normal foetus on mistaken grounds. One way to reduce the risk is to advise a woman to wait and have an amniocentesis later in pregnancy, to double check the foetus's chromosomes. . .

ETHICS AND POLITICS

Prenatal diagnosis has already stimulated considerable debate among professionals as well as feminists. For not even all doctors agree. One highly respected African doctor, for example, wrote to the *British Medical Journal* in 1984 to denounce abortion on the grounds of genetic disease: 'I was born, in the Krobo tribe, with extra digits – a Mendelian dominant condition [i.e. due to a dominant gene] with a 1 per cent incidence at birth in Ghana. Had I been born a few miles south-east across the Volta river, there would have been great rejoicing because local tribesmen had it that I was destined to be rich. If my mother had given birth to me a few miles north-west beyond the hills, I would not be here to write to you – I would have been drowned soon after birth. Fortunately, the Krobos were neutral to extra digits but, until the government forbade the practice, some tribal elders took it on themselves to decide which genes ought to be allowed to survive . . .' Other doctors take the view, as

David Weatherall of the John Radcliffe Hospital in Oxford puts it, that 'the potential parents of genetically abnormal children should have the right to decide what kind of children they bring into the world' (1985, p. 182).

Unfortunately, little time or money has been spent trying to find out what women think of it all. Few studies tell us about the attitudes and experience of women in screening. Most ask in general terms whether patients were happy with the service they received. Such surveys tell us little, as many studies have shown that people in such situations tend to express satisfaction with whatever form of health care they receive.

Research by Wendy Farrant (1985) in Britain points to the fundamental inadequacy of provision by the health service for women undergoing prenatal diagnosis. Everything from emotional support to information on the medical techniques used is insufficient, she finds. These findings reduce women's autonomy and ability to make free and informed choices, even if women actually want the option of prenatal diagnosis.

Sally Macintyre (1987), director of the Medical Research Council's medical sociology unit at the University of Glasgow, has pointed out the need for descriptive studies that explore what actually happens to women in genetic screening programmes. Most women studied have been screened and correctly given an 'all-clear' for whatever condition they are being screened, or have had a handicapped baby and are now asked if they want screening for subsequent pregnancies. But we cannot extrapolate the experiences of these women to others. How can we compare the reassurances of the true negative, of knowing that your baby is really 'all right' with the anguish of a false negative – being told it is, and then finding out it isn't – or a false positive or a miscarriage after the test? How can we decide 'what women want'? Does the question even make sense, given the constraints on women's choices? There is a widespread tendency in the medical profession to stereotype women, says Macintyre. We need to understand, she says, that screening creates many different subgroups with different experiences – not all women are the same, nor are they all in the same situation. For instance, a woman who elects to terminate a wanted pregnancy because of a mistaken diagnosis is not readily comparable to a woman having an amniocentesis for Down's syndrome who later miscarries a normal foetus. A woman's age and the size of the existing family may also make a big difference to her feelings, say, about the risk of miscarriage after testing.

A younger woman may feel more able to abort an affected foetus or risk miscarriage, and start again; an older woman may fear for her continued fertility... In one survey of some seventy women in Leeds, reported in *The Lancet* (26 July 1986, p. 225), 70 per cent of the women 'regarded a Down's birth as worse than a miscarriage after amniocentesis', and so would have accepted amniocentesis on average even if the risk was higher. But the answers ranged from those women who would always refuse amniocentesis to those who would have it even if the risk of a Down's baby were as low as 1 in 20,000. The data on how women feel about chorionic villus sampling are equally sparse.

[· · ·]

The very existence of screening programmes creates anxiety in women and further 'medicalizes' pregnancy. For instance, most women will have had no experience of neural tube defects, so being given a test for them arouses new fears. And Barbara Katz Rothman (1986) describes how the very existence of prenatal diagnosis puts a woman into a horrifying dilemma. If she has amniocentesis for Down's, say, she must risk damaging a normal foetus, and then decide, if something is 'wrong', whether to abort a wanted child. Throughout the long wait for the results, she must regard her pregnancy as 'tentative' – even after she has felt the foetus move. Even a 'reassuring' result on amniocentesis may fail to allay a woman's fears, Rothman says, because it has raised the fears in the first place, and cannot pretend to diagnose all possible defects.

[· · ·]

Prenatal diagnosis also raises the fear that medical attention will be diverted from treatment, from caring for the handicapped and from research to find the underlying causes. No longer are paediatric wards in New York filled with children with Tay-Sachs disease, Rothman says, because most couples at risk are aborting affected foetuses. The result, she says, is 'privatization' of the tragedy of genetic disease. Abortion does not become an interim solution on the road to effective treatment and cure because 'if the loss goes unrecognized, turned around into a solution, then the pressure is off'. This may well be a real danger, especially as government funds for biomedical research grow scarcer. Certainly, there has already been more interest in studying the fashionable molecular aspects of sickle cell anaemia than in the disease in patients. Hence we know little about why the disease develops so differently under different conditions, with some people much more severely affected than others (Weatherall, 1985). Partly, this may also reflect insti-tutionalized racism: research in the UK into the cause and treatment of cystic fibrosis, a disease mainly of white northern European communities, receives about 40 times more funding than does research into sickle cell anaemia (a disease mainly of the Afro-Caribbean communities) (Rothman, 1986).

Yet prenatal diagnosis does not inevitably distort the direction of biomedical research or provisions for treatment and support for people with genetic diseases. Ed Yoxen (1986, p. 124) draws a helpful analogy with polio. Since the development of a vaccine against the disease in the 1950s, the number of children afflicted has dropped markedly. Fewer people know of anyone with the disease and medical authorities may feel obliged to support educational campaigns to encourage people to vaccinate their children. 'Surely no one would argue that we should abandon vaccination, either to remind ourselves what polio is like or to stiffen our resolve to care for future cases?' The same is true of genetic diseases, he argues: 'Prevention can lead to indifference, but this is not a valid argument for not trying to prevent the birth of children with genetic disease. It is an argument for working to prevent indifference ...' ... Furthermore, although it often sounds like special pleading on the part of molecular biologists, it must be true that research at the level of DNA does not lead only to the ability to screen prenatally for genetic disease. Such research should ultimately discover the defective proteins underlying specific genetic diseases, which are mostly unknown, and so lead to the possibility of finding a more effective treatment or cure. This is why charities devoted to various genetic diseases now fund much basic research: the worrying development is that – in the UK at least – charities now spend more money than the government does in supporting such research.

Rothman (1986), along with some campaigners for disability rights, argues that prenatal diagnosis increases the social stigma of disability, too. Taking the pressure off society to care for less able members can lead to even less material and social support for disabled people. If a woman refuses to have the test, or refuses to abort an affected foetus, society may judge that it is she who is to 'blame' for bringing a handicapped child into the world, says Rothman. With little social support for women with less than 'normal' children, women are often forced to choose abortion, she says. Rothman also argues that if you choose not to abort, the early knowledge of a defect adds nothing but anguish to the rest of the pregnancy. But some groups for disability rights support the notion of screening because if a family has decided to go on, with the knowledge of what it will entail, they may be more committed to the infant and make better parents.

At the root of much condemnation of prenatal screening is the notion that it is aimed at creating 'perfect' babies. Opinions differ about who supposedly wants such perfection: is it women coerced by society, doctors driven to excess by ambition and power, or even governments in search of a 'master race'? For instance, a leading obstetrician in London, Charles Rodeck, argues that as families become smaller, attitudes to children have changed, creating an

155

increased 'consumer demand' for perfect children.[1] Rothman speaks of 'technology-driven changes in standards'. The invention of the washing machine, she says, increased our standards of cleanliness. 'With new reproductive technology, will our standards for our children rise?', she asks. Still others argue that the quality control of prenatal screening is forced on women by the medical profession. At a conference on screening for genetic diseases organized by the King's Fund in London in 1987, Macintyre said, for instance, 'It is not true that women want perfect babies – doctors do.'

There is an element of truth in all these perspectives. In the short term, however, and given the enormous constraints on women, feminists must work to increase the choices offered to women, to make up their own minds with the best possible information, about how to run their own lives. Such a naively liberal argument acquires teeth if we look towards improving the social resources that would enhance freedom to choose. Access to information and unbiased counselling for women, now abysmally limited, is a central issue. So too is the wherewithal from government to support those affected by genetic disease.

Communication between 'expert' and 'patient' is notoriously inadequate, but is nowhere worse than in prenatal diagnosis. Macintyre points out, for instance, that some women do not really understand that prenatal tests will not enable doctors to treat an affected foetus. Doctors sometimes say that they can 'prevent' the baby being affected, and ensure that your baby is not ill. But this statement is ambiguous: doctors do not mean that they can 'cure' an affected child or prevent the foetus from being affected by some disease; they can only abort an affected foetus and so 'prevent' the baby...

'Genetic counselling' thus becomes a central issue for feminists (Farrant, 1985). Feminists need to campaign vigorously in this field to influence how a woman is given information, what she is told, and by whom. The term is a catch-all for attempts to give individuals information about their genetic status and the risks of passing on a particular genetic disease to a child (Harper, 1983). In the United Kingdom doctors dominate genetic counselling, with disastrous results. They are usually 'too busy', patronizing and downright ignorant of the social and psychological consequences of genetic disease to provide clear and undirected information. Particularly in the US, a growing band of professional genetic counsellors are becoming influential. They argue that a counsellor should provide information on the meaning of the tests, the nature of the disease and so on, and then support the woman in her choice, whether she aborts the foetus or not. The counsellor should never give advice or colour a woman's decision. Yet such ideals are extremely difficult to achieve in practice... And, as feminists such as Anne Finger

(1984) have pointed out, even counsellors have distinct stereotypes about disabilities and no claim to specialized knowledge of what it is like to grow up disabled or care for such a child.

The 'medicalization' of social and ethical questions is a real danger. As Macintyre says, 'What it is like to have a child with the condition is better answered by support groups – doctors or midwives are not likely to know.' Similarly, self-help groups may be the best help for women who decide to abort an affected foetus. One such group in London, Support After Termination for Abnormalities (SATFA)[2], offers information, counselling and support long after a woman leaves the hospital or clinic. Government funding for such support groups, to which state health agencies could refer women, may be a promising approach.

Various bio-ethics committees set up by government or the medical establishment have now drawn up guidelines to govern prenatal testing and counselling. Most stress that all information discovered about the foetus must be disclosed to the woman screened. The information must be backed up with genetic counselling. Before any screening, which should be voluntary and confidential, begins there must be an intense educational campaign in the community. Nonetheless, the issue of 'information' remains contentious. Rothman argues, for instance, that women may be ill equipped to cope with ambiguous diagnoses . . . that may have unknown outcomes for the child. . . A woman must be given the right of 'informed refusal', says Rothman – the right to decide which things she wants to know about. . . A policy of making all information available to the woman is preferable, many feel, to relying on the 'discretions' of the doctor. Already there is often pressure on a woman to abort an affected foetus, or even to agree to an abortion before doctors will agree to perform an amniocentesis. Most commentators condemn this practice; as Macintyre says, it is important to allow women to have the test and then decide what to do, because it is difficult to know how one will behave in a hypothetical situation.

But perhaps women themselves will 'abuse' prenatal diagnosis, aborting foetuses for 'trivial' reasons. [Already, the abortion of 'normal' female foetuses after amniocentesis is widespread in India, where the dowry system makes female children an expensive proposition (Roggencamp, 1984).] Rothman argues that chorionic villus sampling will only make matters worse. If it is easier to abort earlier, it becomes easier to abort for the wrong reasons, she argues, such as the sex of the child or a mild disability. What about Down's syndrome itself? Many people argue that these foetuses should not be aborted, as the children seem to lead happy, if foreshortened, lives. Who is to decide? 'Selective termination' implicitly judges the value or worth of a life, and the quality of that life. As treatment improves, as with cystic fibrosis and sickle cell disease for instance, or our knowledge of other disorders such as Down's syndrome increases, we need to reassess any judgements about the quality of those lives. . . Because it is women who are likely in our society to care for children, women are apt to consider carefully the nature of the child's life. No individual is better placed to make such a judgement. 'Science' is likely to be unhelpful in such decisions.

[· · ·]

A leading doctor in thalassaemia screening in the United Kingdom, Bernadette Modell,[3] argues that in the end we must leave all such decisions to the individual woman, for we make our best ethical choices when the course of our own lives is at stake. Psychologists have documented our tendency to underrate the moral richness of other people's lives: we often think it likely that other people will make unethical decisions, but not ourselves. This myopia may be inevitable, as we live inside our own moral world and best understand the complexity of the decisions we make ourselves. But we cannot improve on ethical decisions about abortion as a whole or prenatal diagnosis by imposing laws on individuals, Modell argues. The only right way to influence individual choice is through changes in the social context in which a woman makes her decision by, say, providing support for disabled children.

That said, we still do not know what the implications for society will be if genetic screening becomes truly widespread and we may in the future want to ban certain practices, such as the abortion of foetuses on the basis of sex. Insurance companies are already discriminating against the victims of AIDS or even people (single men) deemed to be a 'higher risk'. They would probably attempt to do the same in genetic screening, discriminating against someone with a genetic predisposition to, say, heart disease. Government legislation would be needed to make this illegal.

We might also understandably worry about the development of a 'eugenic' drive based on some criterion imposed by the government of what is 'normal'. But a more genuine danger is not a drive to recreate the racial hygiene movement of the early years of this century, but, as Edward Yoxen puts it, a temptation 'to deprive people of some of their autonomy, in the belief that one acts for their own good. What lives on is perhaps not eugenics, but a kind of genetic paternalism' (1986, p. 119). We can also gain some comfort from the abysmal track record of screening programmes that have adopted the 'top down' approach. Attempts to set up screening programmes for various minority groups work well and can enhance women's autonomy if the initiative comes from the local community and is backed by a proper educational campaign. For instance, screening for thalassaemia in several Mediterranean countries gained ground with the support of the Church... Screening for Tay-Sachs in the Jewish population of Washington and Baltimore took off after local rabbis endorsed the scheme. But in the early 1970s the US government's attempt to set up sickle cell screening was a disaster despite heavy [government] support. The black people of the US were summarily told that they were suffering from a neglected disorder, and offered screening without genetic counselling. Several states even made screening mandatory. The campaign created discrimination against blacks in jobs and health insurance and fuelled racism.

[· · ·]

SUMMARY AND PREDICTIONS

[· · ·]

It is easy to conclude from all this that society will soon slide down one or other of several slippery slopes. 'To many, eliminating genetic defects sounds like a worthy goal. But we must realize that the category "genetic defect" is one capable of infinite expansion,' says Gena Corea and her colleagues (in Spallone and Steinberg, 1987, p. 6). But can't we in fact draw a line? That is the standard solution to a slippery slope. Advances in molecular genetics could lead to horrific social changes, but they need not. As Yoxen says, a slippery slope argument is 'wrongheaded, very conservative, even reactionary, because it says so little about what we ought to do' (1986, p. 164).

In any case, the nature of genetic disease makes an organized conspiracy to create 'a more perfect human race' unlikely. Cost alone makes it difficult to imagine that any government would launch a programme to screen all pregnant women for a handful of genetic diseases, let alone the population at large. After all, doctors in Britain could routinely screen all pregnant women for diseases such as sickle cell disease or thalassaemia, but screening is in fact sporadic and patchy (Franklin, 1988, p. 592). In [the UK] today, at any rate, the risk of an imposed screening programme seems small; in fact, people at risk of passing on sickle cell disease have long lobbied Parliament for better provision for both treatment and screening. Screening newborns for the disease could be done cheaply, through a simple blood test, and would enable the children to be better protected against infection, the biggest danger for them. Not unreasonably, many have concluded that the government ignores the disease because it affects mostly black people. In Britain 5,000 people suffer from the disease – as many as from haemophilia A – yet the facilities for screening and treatment resemble the situation for haemophilia of twenty to thirty years ago.

It is worth remembering too, when we extrapolate into the future, that just as all women are not the same, neither are all genetic diseases. Many of the diseases carried on the X-chromosome, for example, arise from new mutations. In these cases, no family history of the disease alerts a couple to seek prenatal diagnosis. Screening every pregnant woman for the disease would be prohibitively expensive, as well as dangerous.

[· · ·]

The ultimate in prenatal diagnosis – detecting genetic disease in an embryo, before it has implanted in the womb – is now feasible (McLaren, 1987). [This would be carried out through in vitro fertilization (IVF)] . . . Researchers have now shown that with human embryos it is possible to remove one cell at the six-cell stage, and test that cell for the presence of a particular gene, without damaging the rest of the embryo.

Why go to all this effort? The idea is that many couples known to be at risk of passing on a severe genetic disease would want to have their embryos screened. A couple wanting children could thus avoid the trauma of repeated abortions of affected foetuses, detected later in pregnancy through chorionic villus sampling or amniocentesis. The UK Thalassaemia Society, in its submission to the Warnock Committee in the early 1980s, said that the ideal would be to be able to start a pregnancy knowing from the time of implantation that the foetus would be unaffected.

There are several stumbling blocks to this goal, however. At the moment, the technique of chorionic villus sampling causes less inconvenience and discomfort to the mother than the removal of eggs for IVF, and is less expensive. Furthermore, IVF and embryo transfer has such a low success rate that it might take several attempts to achieve a pregnancy (although success rates might be higher for fertile couples). . . The risk of an affected child from parents who were both carriers could far more simply be avoided by artificial insemination by a donor – although the husband would then not be the genetic father.

Despite these difficulties for the idea of 'pre-implantation diagnosis' many fear that the screening of embryos will become widespread and lead to the ultimate obsession with 'perfection'. Jaques Testard, a leading IVF specialist in France, has publicly withdrawn from such research for fear, he says, that soon everyone will want to have their babies by IVF, in the belief that this will ensure that they have a perfect baby. . .

It is impossible to say that this cannot happen. But it would be enormously expensive to produce all babies through IVF and difficult to prevent people from reverting to normal means. It would be far cheaper for a government to launch a eugenic drive along

160

Nazi lines, by simply killing people or imprisoning them. Why not practise infanticide, destroying affected babies cheaply at birth, rather than risk damaging an unaffected foetus through costly diagnostic procedures?

[· · ·]

[T]oday we have more to fear from the commercialization of human genetics. As Yoxen puts it: 'The excesses of the in vitro fertilization business, the surrogacy industry and the market in sex predetermination services all arise because parents' anxieties are perceived as profit opportunities by people with a skill to sell' (1986, p. 171). The solution to such excesses as 'designer children', if indeed they ever become possible, is then the control of the genetic entrepreneurs. Legislation to outlaw such services, as has been done for commercial surrogacy in Britain, is one effective approach.

But we must also work to alter the social and economic context in which women bear and rear children [in order] to enhance the autonomy of women. 'An obsession with eliminating so-called "defects" from the human population in a search for a more perfect human race could lead to an increasing intolerance for those of us who are physically challenged [(disabled)] and a reduction in the already meagre social support services for us', feminists point out (Spallone and Steinberg, 1987, p. 6). This is certainly a possible consequence of prenatal screening, but it is one that has to be fought directly rather than through a wholesale rejection of prenatal diagnosis. As Yoxen says, we must work to broaden and deepen the extent of 'environmental change' that provides support to disabled people. The notion of changing diet or wearing spectacles or hearing aids is a widely accepted solution to some perceived disabilities. But less individualistic solutions, and often more expensive ones, meet more resistance. . .

Note

1   Charles Rodeck, King's College Hospital, personal communication.

2   SATFA national office is at 22 Upper Woburn Place, London WC1H OEP.

3   Bernadette Modell, University College, London, personal communication. See also Modell (1983).

3
PRODUCING SCIENCE AND TECHNOLOGY

On Wednesday, 7 December 1989 a man in his early twenties[1] went, with a gun, into the Engineering Faculty of the University of Montreal, Canada. He systematically separated the women from the men, shot dead fourteen women, injured a further twelve, then shot himself. From what he said during the shootings and from a letter he had previously written justifying his actions, the shooting was a planned massacre of 'feminists', whom he identified as the cause of his own failures. He saw women engineers – rather than any other group – as archetypal 'castrating' feminists, despite anything the women had a chance to say themselves. Although this was the act of an insane person, for many feminists it represents one end of a spectrum of men's hatred of women. What many women saw in the Montreal massacre was the tip of an iceberg of hatred directed against women who were entering one of the most masculine professions: engineering.

Feminist analysis has argued that antipathy, as well as structural barriers, still exists against women wishing to enter the scientific and technological professions (Carter and Kirkup, 1990; Greed, 1991). This antipathy is exhibited through a range of hostile actions from simple unfriendliness (perhaps most distressing when it comes from other women) to blocked promotion opportunities and overt sexual harassment (Hearn and Parkin, 1987). But this was a minority view in the 1980s: a more commonly held belief was that science and technology, if not welcoming, were now open to women, and the barriers which remained were due to women's own lack of interest or aptitude. The struggle of the first wave of feminists for the right to qualify in and practise these professions had been won, and the struggles of the second wave of feminists for equal pay and removal of sex discrimination in employment was felt, optimistically, to be well on the way to being achieved. The massacre suggested that for some men in fact the entry of women into this most masculine of professions was perceived, at a very deep and irrational level, as an attack on their sense of themselves and their gender. In industrialized countries science and engineering are important symbols of masculinity.

Articles in the previous two chapters have discussed the nature of science and technology and how they have contributed to a

162

discourse about gender difference and a theory of the nature of 'woman' that has been restrictive and oppressive. These articles also presented the feminist attack on the empirical and theoretical foundations of this discourse. The articles in this chapter examine the structural barriers that have existed against women working as scientists and technologists and women's struggle to surmount them. Once there, women have demonstrated by the quality of their work the unfounded nature of arguments against their participation.

The first article in this chapter – Joan Mason's biography of Hertha Ayrton – deals with the well-documented period of Victorian and Edwardian feminism, but focuses on a little-known woman. At the end of the nineteenth century and the beginning of the twentieth the first wave of the women's movement in Britain included campaigns for the right of girls and women to education (particularly to scientific education), and for entry to professional associations such as the British Medical Association and the Royal Society of London. Membership of these organizations not only conferred public recognition of the quality of a woman's work, it also made it possible for a woman to practise and, most importantly, earn an income. Prior to the nineteenth century, women had been excluded in most countries from formal membership of institutions such as universities, but it had been possible for rich and aristocratic women to pursue science at their own expense or as assistants to brothers, fathers or husbands. Margaret Alic (1986) discusses some of the better known: Margaret Cavendish, Duchess of Newcastle

(1623–1673) who was the first woman to be admitted to a lecture at the Royal Society of London; Caroline Herschel (1750–1848) and Mary Somerville (1780–1872) who were the first women to be given honorary membership of the Royal Astronomical Society. But the growth of the professions as sources of livelihood for middle-class men, and the need for middle-class women, especially the unmarried and widowed, to earn an income to support themselves, meant that amateur status and honorary membership were not enough.

Hertha Ayrton's story demonstrates not only the overt resistance that existed in the male scientific establishment to acknowledging women's scientific achievements but also the power of feminist networks to support individuals and to combine around campaigning issues such as women's suffrage and education. For Ayrton and many other women scientists it was not the subject matter and methodology of science that were unfriendly to them, but the male professional establishment.

Hertha Ayrton had no scientific education as we would understand it until she was over thirty years old. At university she studied mathematics and before that a range of subjects suitable for a governess such as French and music. As Liz Whitelegg describes in Article 3.2, school education in the United Kingdom contained no science before the 1920s. Between then and the Sex Discrimination Act (1975) it was perfectly acceptable and legal to offer separate curricula for boys and girls: boys studied science and technology while girls did 'domestic' subjects. However, Whitelegg argues, although girls and boys are now offered the same curriculum, science remains for a variety of reasons an unfriendly subject for girls: one of the most important factors influencing girls against studying science is the bias in scientific method towards a white, male world view and style of thinking. Sue Rosser, in *Female-friendly Science* (1990), argues similarly that:

> The recent attention to women's ways of knowing raises the question of whether or not successful women scientists have developed approaches and theories different from those used by traditional male scientists. Extension of these theories and adaptation of pedagogical techniques could lead to courses that will attract more women and people of colour to the study of science . . . the new theories and methods may help make science more accessible, varied and humane. As more people from different races, classes, ethnic backgrounds and genders become scientists, the science they evolve will be reflective of their rich diversity of perspective. (p. xii)

Article 3.3 attempts to examine what this diverse perspective could look like through a review of Evelyn Fox Keller's biography of Barbara McClintock. McClintock has become an exemplar in feminist arguments not only because it took so long before her work received the recognition it deserved – this is a common pattern – but because, claims Fox Keller, McClintock's science is different from masculine science. It demands an empathetic relationship with the subjects of enquiry rather than a distanced, objective stance, attention to detail rather than grand theory and the development of intuition alongside reason. It is these kinds of attributes that Rosser and Whitelegg argue need to be incorporated into science teaching.

In industrialized countries increasing numbers of women have been studying engineering and technology, but only about half of them go on to work in the industry. For an increasing number of women, doing technology is a pleasurable activity with 'sensual and erotic dimensions', argues Hacker (1989), but work and technology are oppressive in the present state of the world because privileged groups (of men) oppress others. That sense of oppression is expressed wonderfully by Marge Piercy's poem *The Secretary Chant* (3.5). It is a recognition of the limited potential of such 'female' jobs, often defined by male-designed technology, that is encouraging more women to look for work that will provide autonomy and a greater sense of personal satisfaction, and to look for it in places where men had previously found it – in science and technology.

Both in the industrialized world and in developing countries more women are studying technology, but their proportions remain small. In 1990 women comprised 13 per cent of students on UK university undergraduate engineering courses but only 5 per cent of professional engineers and roughly 3 per cent of technician engineers. In Canada and the United States women were roughly 15 per cent of engineering students but only 4 per cent of professional engineers (Frize, 1991; Murray, 1991). In the US in 1989, looking at the experience of Afro-Americans, however, 31 per cent of first degrees in engineering were awarded to women – *double* the percentage of all women. This suggests that other issues are involved in career choice such as the social class and status of engineering relative to other professions.

In Article 3.4 Cynthia Cockburn uses a Marxist historical analysis to discuss the historical construction of engineering as a profession. She argues that men took control over tool-making skills and technology early in pre-capitalist societies and that they jealously guarded these transferable skills and developed them into the engineering professions that we now know. She sees the exclusion of women as the indirect outcome of a class struggle for power to control the means of production. Unlike science, which achieved status as an activity of gentlemen, engineering has never lost its class association with skilled manual trades and factory work. Industrial production strengthened and extended the sexual division of labour in employment, but it had already existed, perhaps most strongly in the military (Hacker, 1981).

The association between military objectives and science and technology has been and remains very strong. For example, engineering as a systematic body of knowledge and set of skills originated as a military activity. Even today military objectives are the engine of much scientific and technological research. However, this is rarely made explicit, especially in educational institutions. We, the editors, felt that it was very important that this volume should address some of the difficult issues that result from the symbiotic relationship of technology, the military and masculinity.

Many civilian engineers, male and female, find themselves working in jobs which have direct and indirect military outcomes. This can be very hard for women to cope with. One of the engineers interviewed by Carter and Kirkup (1990) tried to explain the conflict this caused her:

> I am working on communications and I find that relatively comfortable. I don't think I could work on missiles, although I am making communication systems for warships, which makes the rationalization a bit illogical. I don't think I am totally logical in my approach. (p. 144)

We have chosen a case study of women working in the military as a special and perhaps extreme example of the problems women face when entering 'male' jobs; this is also compounded by a conflict in feminism between an identification of pacifism with feminism (see, for example, Article 4.5) and a demand to allow women full rights of citizenship, including a career in the military. The military itself is still very much a minority profession for women, but, as Map 4 in the colour plate section illustrates, although there are few countries where women perform all roles in the military, there are also few countries where women are entirely excluded from military occupations. As Wheelwright demonstrates in Article 3.6, there is a contradiction between the masculine ideology of the military and the fact that developments in military technology, especially in command and control technology where women have been concentrated, have both increased the importance of the role of women as well as demonstrating that the distinction between combat and non-combat positions is harder to draw.

The final article in this section by Radha Chakravarthy moves away from a focus on science and technology in the West to examine its impact on women in underdeveloped countries. It is the nature of peasant society that women are engaged in productive labour; for Chakravarthy there is no easy separation between paid employment and domestic work. But, she argues, when Western technology is implemented, it embodies Western presumptions about male and female roles (presumptions that are not even accurate in the West) and, in the process, women in underdeveloped countries are severely disadvantaged. Chakravarthy draws on a wide range of examples to give a vivid picture of some of the negative impacts of technological development on women in many countries. In Chapter 4 we see how, drawing on the skills of women and local materials, technology can be developed which is appropriate to the needs of women and their families. Feminist concern with that 'rich diversity of perspective' described by Rosser must be applied to an understanding of the scientific and technological needs of underdeveloped countries.

Gill Kirkup

Note

1   The man's name is deliberately omitted in feminist discussion of the event so that he does not achieve the notoriety he so obviously desired.

Article 3.1
HERTHA AYRTON:
A SCIENTIST OF SPIRIT

Joan Mason

Hertha Ayrton was born in poverty in 1854, as Phoebe Sarah Marks. Her father, who fled the pogroms against the Jews in Tsarist Poland, was a watchmaker and jeweller in Sussex, selling watches from door to door in difficult times. Sarah was seven when her father died, leaving her mother – pregnant and with seven young children – to support the family (and pay off the debts) by her needlework. Sarah Marks' lively and original character were such that with the help of her mother's family and their circle she became one of the earliest women university students, a distinguished scientist – and a militant feminist. In 1902 she was the first woman (in 242 years) to be proposed for the fellowship of the Royal Society. Although no woman was admitted to the Society until 1945, they gave her a medal at a time when such honour was reserved in effect for women who were Nobel prize winners.

HER EARLY LIFE AND EDUCATION

Sarah helped her mother with the needlework, and in caring for her six brothers and baby sister; but her mother considered that women needed a *better* education than men, since 'women have the harder battle to fight in the world' (Sharp, 1926). With some self-sacrifice, she sent the nine-year-old Sarah to London to the school run by her sister, Mrs Hartog.

Sarah lived for seven years with the Hartogs, then worked as a governess in London, supporting her mother. Sarah learnt music and French, the latter being a great advantage in later life when she became a friend of the Bodichons and Marie Curie, and lectured in Paris. From her cousins she learnt her first mathematics and Latin – and scepticism; but as a free thinker, she was proud of her Jewish origin. It was her best friend, Ottilie Blind, who called her Hertha – after the Earth-goddess in a poem by Swinburne – and took her to suffrage meetings.

After work Hertha and Ottilie studied for the 'Cambridge Locals', advanced 'school-leaving' examinations that were opened to women after a campaign by Emily Davies, Barbara Bodichon and others. In 1869 they founded the first college of higher education for women, which moved to Girton, near Cambridge, in 1872 (Newnham College had begun in 1871). Many Cambridge professors allowed women students (with chaperones) to attend their lectures and to take the examinations informally. Hertha longed to go to college, but thought this unattainable, until she received a letter from Madame Bodichon in 1873.

Barbara Leigh Smith Bodichon was a feminist pioneer, and successful artist. In 1854, when she was 27, she published *A Brief Summary in Plain Language of the Most Important Laws Concerning Women*, expounding how a woman regained the legal status of an infant when she married, with all her rights and possessions passing to her husband. *Women and Work* (1857) argued for reasonably paid work for women, against those people to whom women's cheap labour was a threat, and against middle-class values that 'respectable' women did not do paid work. Barbara was a close friend of George Eliot, whose character *Romola* was drawn from her. They heard of Hertha's dream of going to college, and to these two childless women, she could be a surrogate daughter. Hertha went to George Eliot's Sunday evening receptions, and characteristics of Mirah, the heroine of *Daniel Deronda*, are attributed to her.

So Hertha went to Girton in 1876; she did not win a scholarship, but Madame Bodichon assembled a loan fund. Hertha's fellow students remembered her vitality – and her singing. She became leader of the Choral Society and founder of the Girton Fire Brigade, persuading Captain Shaw of the London Fire Brigade (celebrated by Gilbert and Sullivan in *Iolanthe*) to train them. (See Plate 4.)

Hertha read mathematics at Girton, and was (informally)[1] placed in the third class; she was not a good examinee and not well prepared. She might have done better to study science, but Emily Davies was a stickler for academic rigour, and most Girtonians then read mathematics or classics, natural science being a newer and less prestigious subject. After college, Hertha returned to London to teach mathematics. She held a singing class for laundry girls, and opened a working-girls' club.

HER BEGINNINGS IN SCIENCE: THE ELECTRIC ARC

Hertha came to science through invention. As a student she had constructed a simple sphygmograph, for recording the pulse in the arteries. Now she developed a device for dividing a line into any number of equal parts, which she patented, and an instrument-maker marketed it. She was invited by the Physical Society to read a paper on this, and congratulated by the feminist leader, Millicent Fawcett.

In 1884 Hertha began to study science, attending Will Ayrton's evening classes in electricity at Finsbury Technical College. They were married the following year. William Ayrton (1847–1908) was a pioneer (in India, Japan, then Britain), in electrical engineering and technical education. He founded the Finsbury college, then another (which later merged into the Imperial College of Science and

169

Technology), with his former assistant John Perry and the chemist Henry Armstrong. Their laboratories pioneered learning by doing, offering opportunities for original research for advanced students. Ayrton developed the surface contact system for electric railways, the use of higher voltages for the transmission of power, and standard instruments for electrical measurements. He was elected to the Royal Society in 1881, received a Royal Medal in 1901, and became President of the Physical Society and the Institution of Electrical Engineers.

As a housewife Hertha had little time for science, but gave lectures to women on electricity, anticipating its domestic use much later on. Her daughter, Barbara, was born in 1890. In 1891 Madame Bodichon died, leaving Hertha money for a housekeeper (and to support Mrs Marks) thus giving her time to devote to science. Her work on the electric arc arose accidentally:

> When a . . . servant lighted a fire with Prof. Ayrton's paper on . . . the Electric Arc . . . at Chicago in 1893, he little knew that he was rendering a service to science and to electrical engineering. The paper . . . had not been read in full at the Electrical Congress, and no rough copy remained . . . Mrs Ayrton took up the research and published some of the results in *The Electrician* in 1895, and her book in 1902. The book (*The Electric Arc*) was the only complete history of the electric arc . . . from the time of Sir Humphry Davy.
>
> (Nature, *12 January 1924, p. 48*)

Electric arcs were used to produce bright light, the carbon electrodes and the gas between them being heated white-hot by the high-voltage discharge. By experiment, she developed the theory connecting the length of arc with pressure and voltage, and traced the hissing noise to oxidation rather than evaporation of the electrode material. The Institution of Electrical Engineers invited her to read a paper in 1899, the first ever read by a woman. She was the first woman elected to membership, and to receive one of their prizes (with Marconi). The Royal Society invited her to demonstrate her experiments, John Perry reading her paper; and she herself spoke at the International Electrical Congress in Paris in 1900. At the British Association for the Advancement of Science, a proposal that women could serve on general and sectional committees was carried after a report that in Paris 'undoubtedly the most remarkable paper was one read by a lady, an English female electrician' (Sharp, 1926).

At the International Congress of Women, held in London in 1899, Hertha presided over the physical science section. Her speech called for the employment of women in the electrical industry:

> In . . . electrical engineering, there are . . . no women working except in the lowest and most mechanical parts . . . [A]ll the

electrical industries are advancing by leaps and bounds, and it is a great pity that women should have no great share in this advance, especially as there is one field in which they ought to prove themselves as capable as men, namely, in the making of electrical instruments . . . No great physical strength is needed, but only skill in the operative, and inventiveness, and a thorough knowledge of electrical principles in the director . . .

(Aberdeen, 1900)

WOMEN AND THE SCIENTIFIC ESTABLISHMENT

Hertha Ayrton was proposed as a candidate for the fellowship of the Royal Society by John Perry in 1902. Co-signatories included Norman Lockyer, astrophysicist and founder–editor of *Nature* (which supported the admission of women to the learned societies, then under intense debate), and colleagues who had pioneered women's classes leading to the admission of women to London University in 1878, and led the campaign for the admission of women as fellows of the Chemical Society (Mason, 1991). A notable absentee was Henry Armstrong, close colleague of Will Ayrton for 23 years, and ring-leader of the London caucus blocking the admission of women chemists.

Hertha Ayrton's Certificate of Candidature detailed her experiments on the electric arc 'leading to many new facts and explanations' and listed her publications. The Council then sought legal opinion as to the eligibility of women. This opinion was that under the Society's Charters, married women were ineligible as Fellows, the position of unmarried women being doubtful. If the Society wished to admit women they should apply to the Privy Council for a supplemental Charter.

A married woman had no legal existence (as Barbara Bodichon had complained in 1854) so could not be a Fellow of a Society incorporated by Charter. (Only in 1929 did women become 'persons' in law, by ruling of the Privy Council.) But lawyers differed on this interpretation and (chartered) Societies chose the advice they preferred, thus the Zoological Society and the Royal Entomological Society never excluded women. If the Royal Society wished to admit women they could have obtained a supplemental Charter, as had London University. But Hertha's Certificate was refused on the grounds of her ineligibility for the fellowship, and no woman was proposed for another forty-two years.

Forty-seven women have now been elected to fellowship of the Royal Society (and five to foreign membership). Most have been biologists, very few physical scientists (although women graduates made their way into astronomy and crystallography early on,

171

through low-paid data-processing – 'women's work'). Hertha Ayrton was a rare phenomenon. The proportion of women fellows is still very small (3% in 1991), and similarly in other countries, matching the small number of 'women at the top' in other male-dominated professions (Howe, 1990).

The Royal Society was not alone in excluding women for so long. In 1911 Marie Curie's candidature for the Académie des Sciences was narrowly defeated, when she was about to receive her second Nobel prize (after Pierre Curie's death). She refused to stand again, and the first woman was elected only in 1962. Marie Curie was not elected to foreign membership of the Royal Society (although foreign members have no legal liabilities); nor was her daughter Irène Joliot-Curie, who received a Nobel prize in 1934 with her husband Frédéric, for their discovery of artificial radioactivity. (He received the Hughes Medal in 1947, and was elected to the Académie des Sciences, but Irène was not.)

Hertha had invited Marie Curie to speak at the International Congress of Women in 1899, but she could not come. They did, however, become friends in 1903, and Hertha championed her when her discovery of radium was attributed to her husband: 'Errors are notoriously hard to kill, but an error that ascribes to a man what was actually the work of a woman has more lives than a cat' (*Westminster Gazette*, 1909).

A NEW DIRECTION

Hertha now had another line of research. In 1901, Will Ayrton was unwell and advised to rest. At Margate, Hertha completed her book on the electric arc. Walking on the beach, she was struck by the regularity of the ripples in the sand, noting that the ripples were produced under water, and washed out at the shoreline by the retreating tide. Their landlady, to her suprise, was asked for Mrs Ayrton's bath 'to be in the sitting room after tea', so that she could conduct experiments in the zinc bath, then in soap-dishes and baking tins. Back home, she continued her experiments in an attic room. (In the Ayrton family, her nickname was B.G. – Beautiful Genius.)

In 1904 Hertha Ayrton read a paper at the Royal Society, the first delivered by a woman, on the formation of sand ripples by oscillations of the water. The standing waves were produced by rocking a glass vessel, the wavelength depending on its size, from a 4-inch soap-dish to a 44-inch tank rocked by an electric motor. She demonstrated the growth of two distinct structures, ripples and sand bars. Her experiments were shown at the Royal Society's Conversazione, and reported to the Engineering Section of the British Association, and to the Physical Society. After Will Ayrton died in 1908 she moved her laboratory down to the drawing room, and read further papers on sand ripples to the Royal Society in 1908 and 1911.

Her proposed mechanism differed from that of George Darwin (Cambridge professor of astronomy and experimental philosophy, and son of Charles Darwin) who thought the determining factor was the friction of the sand on the bottom. Illustrations from her paper show the complexity of the problem. The water does not oscillate smoothly; turbulence develops, the sand grains being moved by little vortices or eddies within the waves. These vortices were made visible by floating particles of ground black pepper, aluminium or paint, and a coloured stream from a crystal of potassium permanganate marked the longitudinal motion of the water.

Hertha showed that sand ripples form where the longitudinal motion of the water is maximal and the water-level constant (so are half a wavelength apart) and build into mounds or sand bars. On an irregular surface ripples form on either side of a ridge in the surface, so a V-shaped depression gives V-shaped ripples.

There were disagreements over theory, and the importance of complex viscous effects emerged only later. But an authority on sedimentology, Professor Allen, FRS, of the University of Reading, has given this appraisal of her work:

> Hertha Ayrton demonstrated in an elegant manner the associ-ation of vortices with mature wave ripples, the shifting of the vortices about the ripple crests in response to the changing direction of the oscillatory wave currents, and the role of vortices in promoting the initiation of the ripples at obstacles and the spread of a pattern of ripples. It was not until the 1940s that experiments of comparable quality and range were to be performed.
>
> *(Correspondence with the author, 1990)*

Hertha was also interested in ridges in estuaries, sandbanks such as the Dogger Bank, and dunes of the shore or desert. Her interest in air vortices inspired her invention of the Ayrton fan, or flapper, used to dispel poison gas in the First World War: see Plate 5. She continued her electrical work, improving arcs used in searchlights and in the cinema: 'the flicks' were so-called because the arc flickered, and her improved electrodes, which she patented in 1913, burned more evenly (Sharp, 1926).

For her research on the electric arc, and on sand ripples, Hertha Ayrton received the Hughes Medal of the Royal Society in 1906. This is awarded annually for original discovery in the physical sciences, and she is still the only woman to have received it. Women medallists of the Royal Society are a select group. Marie Curie was the first, receiving the Davy Medal jointly with her husband in 1903 (the year of their Nobel prize, with Henri Becquerel). The third, in 1956, was Dorothy Hodgkin, who received a Nobel prize in 1964 for structure determinations of biomolecules by X-ray crystallography. To date (1991) only eight more women have received Royal Society medals.

A medal is a higher honour than the fellowship. Hertha's candidature was rejected in the presidency (1900–5) of William Huggins, whose work on stellar spectroscopy was published jointly with his wife Margaret, herself a talented scientist. Huggins wrote to his friend Larmor, after the Council meeting which decided to award her the medal:

> Dear Secretary,
>   Thanks for your information which *surprises me*.
>   There will be great joy & rejoicing in HM's gaol, among the women in prison! I suppose Girton and Newnham will get up a night of orgies on the 30th in honour of the event! ... I suppose the P[resident]. will invite her to the dinner, and ask her to make a speech. As the only lady – I should say woman – present, the P. will have to take her in, and seat her on his right hand!
>   And all this comes from what appeared as the *pure accident* of my taking a chill on Wednesday. It was considered that I should run a *considerable risk* if I had gone to town yesterday. Now, δει τα τοων Θεων φερειν* – *but*, which of the two Ds sent me the cold – Deus or Diabolus?
>   Was it Providence on her behalf or was it 'the D– taking care of his own' – which?
>   Can we now refuse the Fellowship to a Medallist?
> [* 'What the Gods send, we must bear.']
>
> *(Royal Society Archives, 1906)*

But the question of Hertha Ayrton's fellowship was not raised again.

The women in prison were militant suffragists, members of the Women's Social and Political Union (WSPU), arrested after demonstrating at the House of Commons. Hertha joined the WSPU in 1906, and helped Millicent Fawcett to organize the celebration of the prisoners' release. Clearly, if Huggins had not been kept at home he would have voted against Hertha Ayrton. The new President, Lord Rayleigh, was sympathetic to women in science, having allowed women students into the Cavendish Laboratory soon after his appointment at Cambridge in 1880, when other laboratories excluded them.

William Huggins was over 80 in 1906. His wife Margaret, 26 years younger, looked after his health – and sided with Hertha, whom she congratulated warmly. Hertha wrote:

I have had the most charming letter from Lady Huggins . . . she has done some splendid work in astronomy herself, with her husband, and has not had a bit of recognition for it because no one will believe that if a man and a woman do a bit of work together the woman really does anything. That's where the Professor has always been so generous . . . he wanted me to get the full kudos for all I did, not only for my own sake, but for the sake of all women.

(quoted in Sharp, 1926)

HERTHA AND THE SUFFRAGIST MOVEMENT

Barbara Ayrton was a WSPU organizer, and she and her mother were in the Battle of Downing Street in 1910. Hertha wrote to *The Times*:

I was marching immediately behind Mrs Pankhurst when she entered Downing Street, but was prevented from reaching No. 10 by an attempt at strangulation on the part of a policeman . . . Twice, policemen seized me by the throat . . .

and to her stepdaughter Edith Ayrton Zangwill:

Barbie shouted at the constable: 'You dare not hurt that lady; she is Mrs Ayrton!' and he let me go. We heard afterwards that there were special orders not to arrest Mrs [Elizabeth Garrett] Anderson or me. The heroism of the women, especially the old ladies, their cheerfulness and determination, were beyond all praise.

A contemporary joke was that the over-eighties would not in future be eligible for militant action.

Hertha marched in the science section of the great suffrage procession of 17 June 1911, which included 800 women graduates in academic dress (which Cambridge women could not wear until 1948). When Barbara went to prison in 1912 Hertha wrote to Edith: 'Barbie is in Holloway . . . I am *very* proud of her'. Her reading of her next paper at the Royal Society was postponed because she expected to be in prison herself.

Hertha's biographer, Evelyn Sharp, describes how she and Hertha conspired to send the funds of the WSPU abroad to prevent their forfeiture. The Pankhursts and others went on hunger strike, and the authorities were afraid of a death in prison. For eighteen months, in 1912–13, Hertha's house was a nursing home for suffragettes let out under the 'Cat and Mouse' Bill (Pankhurst, 1931/1977). The 'mice' who were seriously ill through starvation or forced feeding (which was brutal) were taken to be nursed by their friends until well enough to be rearrested. Several times Emmeline Pankhurst was brought to Hertha's house on a stretcher 'in almost a dying condition', at a moment's notice, with detectives watching the house 'and a taxi waiting to pursue, if Mrs P. should get up and run away!' (Hertha wrote to Edith). Some fled the country to avoid arrest (including Barbara, who escaped to Paris disguised as a schoolgirl).[2]

The suffragists ceased their campaign with the War in 1914. Hertha fought for the acceptance of the Ayrton fan, then helped to organize its production, over one hundred thousand being used at the Front. She worked for the rest of her life on related problems, including the dissipation of fogs, and noxious gases from mines and sewers.

By 1918 nearly two million women had replaced men in their jobs, heavy and light, most of which they lost when the men returned. Six million women were enfranchised in 1918, becoming eligible for election to Parliament in 1919. The Sex Disqualification (Removal) Act of 1919 opened the legal professions and lower ranks of the civil service to women (although they had to resign on marriage); and ensured that the charters and statutes of bodies such as the Royal Society could no longer be used to justify discriminatory policies (although no woman was proposed until 1944).

APPRECIATIONS

Hertha died in 1923. By some oversight, Henry Armstrong was asked to write her obituary for *Nature*. Typical of his views were those he gave to the Mosely Commission (1904) on the American high school system, which he considered to be schoolmarm-ridden:

> History ... proves the [female] sex to have been lacking in creative and imaginative power... And it must be so. Throughout the entire period of her existence woman has been man's slave ...
>
> (Brock, 1973)

His biographer commented:

> Such views were, of course, typically 'Victorian'. They were shared by all members of the commission with the notable exception of Ayrton, whose strange second wife was a mathematician.
>
> (Brock, 1973)

Armstrong described Will Ayrton's 'peculiar experience' that both of his wives were strong on women's rights (Matilda Chaplin Ayrton (1846–83) was a medical pioneer). He wrote of Hertha's research:

> She was an indefatigable and skilful worker. Whatever the absolute value of her observations, her husband and his good

friend Perry were the last not to make the most of her achievement, so probably the scientific halo with which they (and others who fancied that women could be as men) surrounded her was overpainted.

(Nature, *1 December 1923, p. 800*)

Robert Reid (1978) describes Hertha as:

... an extraordinarily talented, if eccentric, woman ... [being] a physicist and the recent widow of a physicist had given her a natural bond with Marie Curie. Whenever she was in Paris, a slight but distinctive figure in a flowing pre-Raphaelite robe, she would visit Marie and discuss her work with a self-assurance unusual in women scientists.

Before the First War, Marie Curie brought her daughters to spend the summer holidays with Hertha at the seaside and in London.

Hertha Ayrton showed that she could command an established, male-dominated, and complex field, in two very different researches.[3] Electric arcs are hazardous, noisy, and difficult to control closely. The 'shifting sand' experiments were difficult to interpret, for turbulence is 'chaotic', irreproducible in detail. In both, careful and imaginative experiments were needed to isolate variables which were intricately linked.

She acknowledged her debt in *The Electric Arc*, inscribed:

To MADAME BODICHON, whose clear-sighted enthusiasm for the freedom and enlightenment of women enabled her to strike away so many barriers from their path; whose great intellect, large tolerance and noble presence were an inspiration to all who knew her; to her whose friendship changed and beautified my whole life, I dedicate this book.

Notes

1   Cambridge women received only a 'certificate' until 1922, when they were granted 'titular' degrees, becoming full members of the University only in 1948.

2   Barbara Ayrton Gould became Chairman of the Labour Party in 1939 and Labour Member of Parliament for Hendon North in 1945.

3   For further reading about women in science, see Abir-Am and Outram (1987) and Ogilvie (1986).

Article 3.2
GIRLS IN SCIENCE EDUCATION: OF RICE AND FRUIT TREES
Liz Whitelegg

If you want gain in one year plant rice, in 10 years plant fruit trees, in 100 years educate women!
An old Chinese proverb

INTRODUCTION

In this article I will examine why so few girls have been involved in and motivated by science at school and hence gone onto scientific careers. I will start with an historical perspective, and offer contemporarily relevant explanations for why girls generally have not achieved as well as their brothers in scientific endeavours. I will also consider the recent policy changes in science education and examine what hopes these have for the future of girls in science.

Most of the research into girls in science over the last decade or so has focused on secondary science. Although *all* research in this area has had and continues to have very little funding and most researchers and teachers interested in this area must work in their spare time and on shoestring budgets, the latest and most exciting work has more recently been undertaken on the primary phase of education and it is with this area that I will begin in order to give a better perspective of what happens to girls at secondary school.

I will also look briefly at science education in two non-industrialized countries in order to broaden the debate and offer an alternative perspective. Although the situation and circumstances for science teaching are very different from those found in Britain and most other countries in Europe, there are some common problems and difficulties.

HISTORICAL PERSPECTIVE

Science education in primary schools is a relatively new phenomenon. Before the 1920s little or no science was taught to either girls or boys and only 30 per cent of girls attended school regularly anyway. Around this time science in the form of natural history was introduced. Most learning was by rote and many teachers using this method had no understanding of the underlying scientific principles themselves and indeed in some schools the teaching of science was specifically banned. It was not until the middle of the nineteenth century that some science training became compulsory in *teacher* education. Until then neither girls nor boys received a great deal of science education. Nevertheless, boys were still offered a broader education as the predominant view was that girls should be educated to be a social asset. (This view was not shared by the women of the time though. In the 1830s, they outnumbered men at the British Association for the Advancement of Science meetings!)

More recently science education has made significant advances and teachers are now encouraged to adopt an open-ended, enquiring, child-centred approach to science teaching. This method, however, makes considerable demands on teachers and requires them to be confident in their own science knowledge. It is still the case that infant and primary teachers are not well equipped to adopt this approach and a recent report showed that less than half of primary teachers had studied science beyond the age of 13 and less than 10 per cent of those teaching 10 year olds had science as their main subject in teacher education (*Times Educational Supplement*, 1989). (Over the period 1990 to 1993, the Department of Education and Science (DES) has made funds available for primary teachers to attend in-service training courses to gain a grounding in science knowledge and content. The funding is barely adequate to train one teacher in half the primary schools in England and Wales.)

WHAT HAPPENS IN PRIMARY SCHOOLS?

The way in which attitudes develop in the early years is vital. As Naima Browne writes:

> With the advent of the National Curriculum with its definition of science as one of the three core subjects and technology as one of the seven foundation subjects, preparation for the study of these subjects in the early years of schooling can be seen as vital, as crucial ideas about the relevance of science and technology to girls is formed in these early years and their motivation for engaging in these areas of the curriculum can be easily undermined.
>
> (*Browne, 1991*)

Until recently, before science became a compulsory element in primary schooling, it was thought that *offering* science to girls in secondary schools would solve the problem as they would engage with science in an equal way with the boys. However, as we now know, offering the same subjects to girls and boys at 11 or 13 does not alter the imbalance because of girls' exposure to the 'hidden curriculum' which has influenced their motivation and later decisions to do science. This 'hidden curriculum' in the primary school involves a complex web of taken-for-granted assumptions and procedures that can only be counteracted if there is a great deal of awareness and vigilance on the part of teachers and local authority advisers. Teachers need to recognize that they themselves are powerful agents of socialization, who also bring their own culturally acquired perspectives with them. It is recognized that attitude change does not necessarily follow presentation of information, no matter how compelling and relevant that information may be. For change to occur, teacher-educators and teachers must confront their own attitudes and perceptions and be given opportunities to challenge and change them. Teachers can then be given a repertoire of skills and strategies to deal with gender inequalities.

In the classroom, studies of children's interaction in constructional activities – those with high science, technology and maths content – have shown marked differences between boys and girls. For example, boys and girls use Lego quite differently and when playing with it show a strong preference for being with classmates of their own sex. In a recent study, Burn (1989) reports:

> Toys can be, and are, used to reinforce gender conformity. The Lego play showed that boys appear more task-oriented, have developed superior construction skills and pre-plan models independently by 6 to 7 years of age. Girls, however, see Lego [as] mainly for boys, their models are more simple in design and are not incorporated into fantasy play. They appear to gain little satisfaction from such activities. Finally, as children move from 5 to 9 years of age the separation of girls and boys becomes more evident and members of the opposite sex are frequently ridiculed in peer group play if they do not conform to gender expectations . . . [In the study] children's choice of activity was not solely influenced by interest but also by confidence – girls who played with Lego were often unconfident but boys never were. Girls rarely chose a construction toy on first entering a classroom, but boys often did. Girls adopted various strategies to play with boys and 'boys' toys', compromising themselves by adopting submissive roles or playing by boys' rules. Sometimes girls did have enough confidence to join a boys' game and play on their own terms. (p. 146)

In another study (Skelton, 1989a) the teachers gave the children a choice of activities based on the topic of 'house'. The teacher introduced the activity and left the children to proceed. The boys chose to construct an electric circuit for the doll's house whilst the girls chose to design a pattern for curtains. Some of the girls, however, would have liked to work on the electrical activity but said that the boys got there first. With some of the other activities that were offered to the same class, the girls were put off doing the construction activity (making a bird table) because it would have meant working with a group of boys. These are not isolated incidents; time and time again observations of girls' and boys' use of resources in classrooms notes similar issues.

An 'equal opportunities' approach to science teaching like those described does not ensure that girls and boys get the same experience of science learning. Simply ignoring gender in fact reinforces stereotyping because it does nothing to challenge the definition of certain aspects of the curriculum as masculine or feminine. Children (and teachers) bring the effects of socialization with them into the classroom and that affects how they interact with the teaching and resources offered in school.

Some schools have introduced a 'girls' hour' into the nursery class to try to counteract girls' lack of confidence in constructional play. In this hour, girls have unrestricted access to a range of resources without the presence of boys. This strategy enables girls to become more confident in using the resources and they use them in their own way: they don't build the same things as boys but their activities can be just as valuable in developing their spatial abilities. Development of spatial abilities is linked to increased mathematical ability and it is quite commonplace to find girls performing better at maths than boys in primary schools. Intervention strategies such as these can increase their interest and confidence in constructional play with no detrimental effect on the boys.

The learning method most favoured by teacher-educators currently is that of open-ended, child-centred learning. This method aims to treat every child as an individual and to teach each child from her or his current starting point and let the child determine where each particular topic leads. This method gives rise to the view that gender stereotyping is not an issue, as teaching is based on each individual child's needs. However, this method does not take account of the gender-power relationships that exist within the classroom or the amount of stereotyping that children experience outside the school. I do not wish to imply that this method has little to offer, as I do believe that 'starting from where a child is at' is an excellent beginning, but the current research and resulting teaching resources which are being produced with this perspective do not have a necessary (in my view) gender dimension.

Much attention has lately been paid to setting an appropriate context for children's learning and this has repercussions for the testing of children at ages 7, 11, 13 and 16 as part of the National Curriculum. Setting questions and activities that relate to children's own experience is a good way of encouraging them to engage with the question or activity; but if the context is more appropriate to a boy's world view than a girl's, it will have disastrous consequences for girls' achievement as measured by the National Curriculum levels of attainment. This, however, is a very complex area and as an Assessment of Performance Unit (APU) report says: 'Examples of gender-linked differences in performance can be found in most aspects of the assessment framework. These differences cannot be described in terms of [a single cause] . . . They are to be found in cognitive, affective and social functioning and very often any particular influence is inextricable from the others' (APU, 1988, p. 109).

The National Curriculum in general does not address the issue of equal opportunity in science although the Non-Statutory Guidelines produced by the National Curriculum Council has made some attempt to do so when they stated:

> . . . there are some groups of pupils who, according to their teachers and as shown by research, have not, in the past, realized their full potential in science. These groups include girls . . . The common, balanced curriculum which pupils will follow will help to eliminate problems of sex imbalance in the uptake of specific-science courses. Nevertheless, it is likely that the problems of low expectations of many girls, particularly in physical science, will remain.
>
> (NCC, 1989, p. A9)

Despite this rather defeatist attitude, the National Curriculum will, however, ensure that all children study science from 5 to 16 years and so girls, who have previously opted to continue with biology and drop the other sciences at secondary school, may now feel more equipped to continue with all the sciences at secondary school. Previously many girls who continued with science beyond the age of 14 continued only with biology, having built up some knowledge and confidence by being exposed to 'nature study' at primary school.

SECONDARY SCIENCE

Attitudes developed at the primary level ensure that by secondary school girls undervalue their abilities and underachieve in the sciences, technology and maths. Boys are able to obtain more teacher time and monopolize scarce resources in the classroom.

With the introduction of the National Curriculum, all children in the state sector will have to take a balanced science course from the ages of 5 to 16 years. Girls (and boys) will no longer be able to drop some or all science at 14. This may be seen as a positive outcome of the National Curriculum. However, examining this more closely, it may not have the beneficial effects for girls that could be hoped for. Firstly, there are two models for the science curriculum in key stage 4 (for students aged 14 to 16). The model that it is hoped the majority of students will follow (model A) demands that 20 per cent of the curriculum time is devoted to science. Model B allows only 12.5 per cent of time for science. It is feared that less able children and many girls will be directed towards model B. Model B will not equip students for science A-levels. The second concern over the National Curriculum is the straightjacket that it places on girls. If the science that is taught to them continues to be 'male' science then girls who do not conform to this male view will still feel alienated and will not succeed or enjoy it.

However, having stated these reservations about the National Curriculum, it will ensure a broadening in the teaching of science and it does assimilate contemporary good practice in science teaching. Attainment target 1 (AT1) – the process of science – carries a 50 per cent weighting. Good practice in science teaching will integrate AT1 (learning science as a process, learning through doing science) with the remaining fact-based attainment targets and this is seen as a step forward. Active learning is a great confidence-builder. But, as Bentley and Watts comment on Kelly's (1987) work,

> . . . confidence-building was an approach which in the early days of research into girls and science was seen to be most reasonable. Girls opted away from science, it was said, because,
>
> > . . . there must be something wrong with their perceptions of science, the world or of themselves. The corollary of this was that intervention strategies were designed to boost girls' confidence and correct their misconceptions of science. [Kelly, 1987]
>
> (Bentley and Watts, 1989, p. 191)

Kelly no longer believes that girls' lack of science achievement is to do primarily with their lack of confidence and early socialization. She now puts more emphasis on the role of schools and teachers on dissuading girls from science, and less on girls' internal states and she now thinks that it is necessary to change science. Bentley and Watts, with Kelly, 'believe that treating girls as though *they* were the problem, and designing "girl-friendly" approaches to science, is not the most successful way to ensure that women have equal opportunities to impose their ideas on existing science frameworks' (Bentley and Watts, 1989, pp.191–2):

> . . . to construe the problem as enticing girls into science may not be the most promising way of progressing. Rather, reconstructing science and in particular science education so that both are more in keeping with the experiences and explanations of the world that are familiar to women, might serve teachers better.
>
> (Kelly, 1987)

Alison Kelly has reached this view after setting up and working on the Girls into Science and Technology project (GIST) in Manchester from 1979 to 1984. GIST was the first major schools-based project addressing problems of sex-stereotyping at school, and was an example of action research; the project simultaneously took action to improve girls' achievement in science and technology and investigated their reasons for under-achievement. The final report of the project states:

> We found that boys acted [in the classroom] in a way which made science seem more masculine than it really was; the teachers also helped to create the impression that science is a very macho business. In the first lesson, teachers often pointed out the dangers of equipment and chemicals in the lab, delighting the boys, who in later sessions displayed a great deal of bravado, for instance using a magnet to have a tug-of-war, trying to give each other electric shocks with a 6V battery; for the girls the element of danger was more discouraging. Teachers and boys seemed to be unthinkingly collaborating to construct science as an area of masculine endeavour, excluding girls, who quickly took the hint.
>
> (Whyte et al., 1985, pp. 81–2)

Alison Kelly views science as masculine in four distinct senses:

- The attitudes of teachers and pupils.
- The image presented by books and other resources.
- Practitioners of science are overwhelmingly male.
- Scientific thinking embodies an intrinsically masculine world view.

The fourth point is true if we cling to an irredeemably narrow conception of science and scientific thinking. The industrial and social impact of science on health, on people and on the environment, and a focus on the beauty and complexity of the natural world were all notable omissions from the school syllabus until their introduction in the National Curriculum. But the attainment target that is concerned with the nature/philosophy of science is only available for model A students, which, as I outlined earlier, may not include many girls. This is a great pity because this is an area that is likely to interest them. Girls are not uninterested in science; they are bored by the limited version of it they meet in school.

RECONSTRUCTING SCIENCE

So, if changing the way girls interact with science does not solve the problem, how do we change science? Does feminism have anything to offer? As Helene Witcher (1985) suggests, a feminist who examines science teaching in schools does not simply note that girls are less likely to play with Lego than boys. She notes that:

- This is likely to be due to the different socialization pattern of girls and boys and she may discuss how these patterns may be challenged and changed.

- The differentiation of experience bears a relationship to girls' avoidance of mechanical and construction tasks in general and such avoidance leads directly to powerlessness and dependence.

- The lack of three-dimensional experience is significant in terms of vocational aspiration and can eliminate girls from career paths currently awarded status and power in society such as science and engineering.

- There are positive ways in which she can intervene to challenge this state of affairs, which a non-feminist researcher would not regard as a problem.

Few teachers of science would accept this feminist viewpoint. The idea that science education involves passing on a body of knowledge that is value-free has been the overwhelming and prevailing ideology of science educationalists. As Evelyn Fox Keller argues (in Article 1.3), modern science as we know it is a culturally specific activity, and what is considered 'good' science in any period is both historically and culturally determined.

> What all social studies of science see when they look closely at the process by which good science is named is a variety and range of practices, visions and articulations of science far in excess of any ideological prescriptions ... In every period of scientific history, in every school of science, we can see a rich diversity of meanings and practices. In fact it would appear that where ideology makes its force felt most crucially is in its role in the process by which some theories, methodologies and explanations are selected as representative of good science and others are disgarded.
>
> (Fox Keller, 1986, p. 174)

SCIENCE EDUCATION IN UNDERDEVELOPED COUNTRIES

In underdeveloped countries science educators face a double dilemma. Two socio-cultural factors repel girls from entering science – the unfavourable conditions created by the general economic malaise (this is also a problem for boys, of course) and the common discriminators for girls in science education: different expectations of parents and teachers for girls; unequal treatment for girls and boys in the classroom; and packaging (illustrations in textbooks etc.). Teachers who succeed in motivating girls into science are exemplary teachers who maintain well-equipped classrooms with posters on the walls, specimens and apparatus in the lab. Such learning environments are not common in poor countries. The situation in many African countries is particularly dire. In Sierra Leone, for example, there is little process-based teaching (only 10 per cent of teachers regularly use it) because of lack of time and resources (Amara, 1990). In the 1960s there was a major educational intervention programme with the objective of the dissemination of process-based learning in African countries but this is now largely defunct. Most teaching takes place via the old-fashioned 'chalk and talk' method. At the primary level, particularly, this is a further discouragement for girls. Julia Amara describes the classrooms in Sierra Leone as 'naked' – having nothing except chairs and desks in them. It is not possible for pupils to experience real science without access to equipment, especially at the primary level where experimentation is an integral part of process learning.

Pupils in underdeveloped countries often have to buy their own books – which most cannot afford to do – and there are very few libraries in primary schools. In general, all-girls' schools are disadvantaged more than boys' schools in terms of facilities. Of all the 16 girls' schools in Sierra Leone, only one is qualified to teach science in the sixth form, while there are many boys' schools which are able to teach sixth-form science. Much of the problem is to do with a shortage of educational materials.

In India the situation for urban girls and women is better. There has been some upturn in the numbers of women qualifying for and entering the professions. Science now has 31.4 per cent women, medicine has 30.4 per cent and engineering has seen a 4% increase in women between 1976 and 1987. However, the unemployment rate among qualified women in science and technology is almost 50 per cent because work often involves interacting with male colleagues and clients as well as being on call for night duty. Small numbers of Indian women often succeed well at the postgraduate level and a higher proportion do so than at the undergraduate level. Once they have broken through the barriers of prejudice they are able to continue. Having said this, education is still a middle-class concern and huge numbers of rural Indian women remain uneducated (Raghuwanshi, 1990).

These two examples indicate the problems of developing good science education for women and girls in poor countries. The lack of resources and trained teachers may force a consideration of alternative models of science, but even these cannot be taught well in a 'naked' classroom.

WHERE NEXT?

My aim in this article has been to set out the multi-layered nature of the problem for girls in primary and secondary science schooling. In the United Kingdom new policy developments – the introduction of the National Curriculum and hence the broadening of science teaching away from the content-based, active learning approach – will go some way to addressing the problem. However, there are so many other factors to take into account that a one-dimensional solution does not exist.

Only nine months after the introduction of the National Curriculum into schools, it has already been modified as it was found that teaching 17 ATs was unmanageable. Under the new proposals recommended by the Secretary of State in May 1991, science has been reorganized into just 5 ATs. AT1, scientific investigation, has been retained but AT17, dealing with the social, cultural and historic ideas in science, has been lost. This does seem a backward step as far as interesting girls in science is concerned, as this AT did hold out some hope for introducing girls to scientific ideas through real-life contexts.

Article 3.3
A FEELING FOR THE ORGANISM: FOX KELLER'S LIFE OF BARBARA MCCLINTOCK

Gill Kirkup and Laurie Smith Keller

Barbara McClintock won the Nobel Prize for medicine and physiology in 1983. [Earlier] a book about her ... written by Evelyn Fox Keller, had been published. Understandably, it became ... an inspiration for women working within science and technology, feminists and non-feminists alike. The story is heroic, made all the more enjoyable when one knows that there is a happy ending. But beware, because idealized biographies like this one can minimize and obscure the real issues which lie behind one woman's life and work.

(*Grobicki, 1987, p. 211*)

A biography is more than a picture of a person's life and work; it is a reconstruction, viewed through a particular lens. Evelyn Fox Keller's biography of McClintock has been more praised than criticized but it is worth reading what she writes about McClintock with a familiarity with her critique of masculine science.

The bare bones of McClintock's work were described as follows:

In 1951 geneticist Barbara McClintock discovered that everyone was wrong about genes and chromosomes. The scientific establishment said that genes – those building blocks of information in every cell – are attached to chromosomes in a strict, linear fashion. 'Like pearls on a string,' they explained it. People wanted to believe that, as Mendel had demonstrated with his generations of peas, inherited characteristics are predictable and logical. No one wanted to hear Dr McClintock's heretical theory that genes 'jump', that they indulge in random behaviour, and that they can even pass from cell to cell.

'They thought I was quite mad,' said Dr McClintock. In twenty years, she noted, only three people requested a copy of her paper on the phenomenon.

When Dr Barbara McClintock won the Nobel Prize in Medicine and Physiology in 1983, the award committee said it was no surprise that these theories had been rejected for decades. 'Only about five geneticists in the world could appreciate them,' stated a committee member, 'because of the complexity of the work.' Once established as a genetic dogma, Dr McClintock's discovery made it possible to study antibiotic-resistance bacteria, to seek a cure for African sleeping sickness, and to make inroads in defusing the cancer mechanism. It was 'one of the two great discoveries of our time in genetics,' said the Nobel spokesman.

(Vare and Ptacek, 1987, pp. 216–17)

Box 3.3.1
More on chromosomes and genetics

(Please see Box 2.1.1 *Chromosomes, genes and inheritance* in Article 2.1 for further details.)

Johann Gregor Mendel (1822–84) first established, after 10 years of experiments involving about 30,000 plants, that what he called 'dominant' and 'recessive' 'element pairs' passed characteristics from one generation to the next according to rules subject to exact analysis.

Barbara McClintock first established by direct observation that the chromosomes – microscopic bodies in the nucleus of a cell – were responsible for the transmission of characteristics from one generation to the next. But not all chromosomes 'obey' the rule that a parent's pair divide neatly and each gamete takes one-half of the pair and transmits it to resulting progeny (offspring) – see Figure 3.3.1.

Her work showed that chromosomes rearrange themselves. There are four forms of rearrangement:

- inversion (A-B-C-D becomes C-B-A-D)
- translocation (genes moving from one chromosome to another)
- duplication (A-B-C-D may become A-B-C-B-C-D)
- deletion (loss of some genes from a chromosome).

These rearrangements can occur as the result of radiation, infection by viruses or, McClintock showed, as a result of breaks in the chromosomes during naturally occurring mechanical stretching, particularly in the penultimate phase of cell division (the anaphase) when the nucleus is at maximum stretch as it pulls apart (see Figure 3.3.2). When breaks occur in two or more different chromosomes in the cell nucleus,

189

translocations can occur as the broken ends 'heal' together in a way different from the way the genes were organized before the break occurred. Multiple breaks tend to lead to a cycle of breaking and 'healing'. Rearrangement is the main way structural changes in chromosomes – changes visible to microscopic examination – occur in the course of evolution. (This is *not* the same as simple gene mutation.)

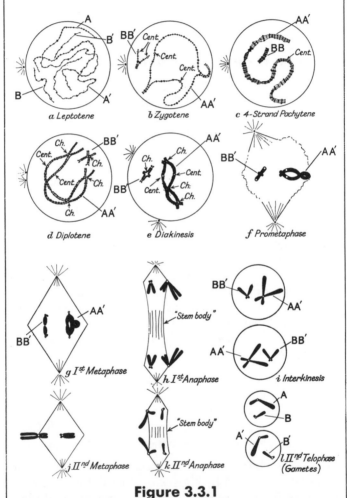

Figure 3.3.1

The main stages of cell division to form gametes (meiosis). Only two pairs of chromosomes, **A** and **A**′ and **B** and **B**′, are shown. The two cells that result in the interkinesis phase then go on to divide again to produce four gametes.

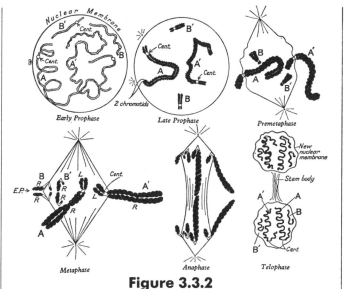

Figure 3.3.2
The main stages of cell division (mitosis). Only two pairs of chromosomes, **A** and **A**' and **B** and **B**', are shown. Note the stretching in the anaphase.

MCCLINTOCK'S SCIENTIFIC PRACTICE

Without Evelyn Fox Keller's 1983 biography *Feeling for the Organism*, McClintock's story would have been like that of many women scientists whose contributions to their field have been acknowledged long after that of their colleagues, sometimes after they have died. But Fox Keller's biography examines not only McClintock's life but the nature of her work in extensive detail. What Fox Keller sees is a particular way of working which relies on creative empathy and insight. Although different from the usual model of masculine rational science, Fox Keller argues that this way of thinking is the way to better science.

Fox Keller describes McClintock's attention to detail, which at the same time was the way she understood the whole organism.

> The tenacity with which she hunted down every observable chromosomal modification, the thoroughness and rigour that accompanied her virtuoso technique ... might lead one to think of the focus of her search as narrow. In fact, what she consistently pursued was nothing less than an understanding of the entire organism.

The word 'understanding' and the particular meaning she attributed to it is the cornerstone of Barbara McClintock's entire approach to science. For her, the smallest details provided the keys to the larger whole. It was her conviction that the closer her focus, the greater her attention to individual detail, to the unique characteristics of a single plant, of a single kernel, of a single chromosome, the more she could learn about the general principles by which the maize plant as a whole was organized, the better her 'feeling for the organism'.

(Fox Keller, 1983, p. 101)

So adept did she become at recognizing the outward signs of those structural alterations in chromosomal composition that she could simply look at the plants themselves and know what the microscopic inspection of the cells' nuclei would later reveal. *(ibid., p. 102)*

Since her days as a young graduate student, she had always carried out the most laborious parts of her investigations herself, leaving none of the labour . . . to others. In this she did as almost all beginning scientists do. But most scientists as they mature learn to delegate more and more of the routine work to others. McClintock's virtuosity resided in her capacity to observe, and to process and interpret what she observed. As she grew older, it became less and less possible to delegate any part of her work; she was developing skills that she could hardly identify herself, much less impart to others.

The nature of insight in science, as elsewhere, is notoriously elusive. And almost all great scientists – those who learn to cultivate insight – learn also to respect its mysterious workings. It is here that their rationality finds its own limits. In defying rational explanation, the process of creative insight inspires awe in those who experience it. They come to know, trust and value it.

'When you suddenly see the problem, something happens that you have the answer – before you are able to put it into words. It is all done subconsciously. This has happened too many times to me and I know when to take it seriously. I'm so absolutely sure. I don't talk about it, I don't have to tell anybody about it, I'm just sure this is it.' *(ibid., p. 103)*

McClintock's relationship with the subjects of her years of research is emotional and empathetic. She feels in some way there is a dialogue between the corn seedlings and herself, and she has to be 'open' to it.

Repeatedly, she tells us one must have the time to look, the patience to 'hear what the material has to say to you', the openness to 'let it come to you'. Above all, one must have 'a feeling for the organism'.

'One must understand how it grows, understand its parts, understand when something is going wrong with it. [An organism] isn't just a piece of plastic, it's something that is constantly being affected by the environment, constantly showing attributes or disabilities in its growth. You have to be aware of all of that . . . You need to know those plants well enough so that if anything changes . . . you [can] look at the plant and right away you know what this damage you see is from – something that scraped across it or something that bit it or something that the wind did. You need to have a feeling for every individual plant.

'No two plants are exactly alike. They're all different, and as a consequence, you have to know that difference,' she explains. 'I start with the seedling, and I don't want to leave it. I don't feel I really know the story if I don't watch the plant all the way along. So I know every plant in the field. I know them intimately, and I find it a real pleasure to know them.'

This intimate knowledge, made possible by years of close association with the organism she studies, is a prerequisite for her extraordinary perspicacity. 'I have learned so much about the corn plant that when I see things I can interpret [them] right away.' Both literally and figuratively, her 'feeling for the organism' has extended her vision. At the same time, it has sustained her through a lifetime of lonely endeavour, unrelieved by the solace of human intimacy or even by the embrace of her profession.

Good science cannot proceed without a deep emotional investment on the part of the scientist. It is that emotional investment that provides the motivating force for the endless hours of intense, often gruelling, labour. Einstein wrote: '. . . what deep longing to understand even a faint reflection of the reason revealed in this work had to be alive in Kepler and Newton so that they could in lonely work for many years disentangle the mechanism of celestial mechanics?' But McClintock's feeling for the organism is not simply a longing to embrace the world in its very being, through reason and beyond.

For McClintock, reason – . . . in the conventional sense of the word – is not by itself adequate to describe the vast complexity – even mystery – of living forms. Organisms have a life and order of their own that scientists can only partially fathom. No models we invent can begin to do full justice to the prodigious capacity of organisms to devise means for guaranteeing their own survival. On the contrary, '. . . anything you can think of you will find.' In comparison with the ingenuity of nature, our scientific intelligence seems pallid. (*ibid, pp. 198–9*)

McClintock is not a poet; she is a scientist. What marks her as such is her unwavering confidence in the underlying order of living forms, her use of the apparatus of science to gain access to that order, and her commitment to bringing back her insights into the shared language of science – even if doing so might require that language to change. The irregularities or surprises molecular biologists are now uncovering in the organization and behaviour of DNA are not indications of a breakdown of order, but . . . of the inadequacies of our models in the face of the complexity of nature's actual order. Cells and organisms have an organization of their own in which nothing is random.

In short, McClintock shares with all other natural scientists that credo that nature is lawful, and the dedication to the task of articulating those laws. And she shares, with at least some, the additional awareness that reason and experiment, generally claimed to be the principal means of this pursuit, do not suffice. To quote Einstein again, '. . . only intuition, resting on sympathetic understanding, can lead to [these laws]; . . . the daily effort comes from no deliberate intention or programme, but straight from the heart.'

A deep reverence for nature, a capacity for union with that which is to be known – these reflect a different image of science from that of a purely rational enterprise. Yet the two images have co-existed throughout history. We are familiar with the idea that a form of mysticism – a commitment to the unity of experience, the oneness of nature, the fundamental mystery underlying the laws of nature – plays an essential role in the process of scientific discovery. Einstein called it 'cosmic religiosity'. In turn, the experience of creative insight reinforces these commitments, fostering a sense of the limitations of the scientific method, and an appreciation of other ways of knowing. In all this, McClintock is no exception. What is exceptional is her forthrightness of expression – the pride she takes in holding and voicing attitudes that run counter to our more customary ideas about science. In her mind, what we call the scientific method cannot by itself give us 'real understanding'. 'It gives us relationships which are useful, valid, and technically marvellous; however, they are not the truth.' And it is by no means the only way of acquiring knowledge. (*ibid., pp. 200–1*)

Fox Keller claims that what McClintock demonstrates is a purer science, since it is not the rational masculine version, nor a feminine version.

> In her adamant rejection of female stereotypes McClintock poses a challenge to any simple notions of a 'feminine' science. Her pursuit of a life in which 'the matter of gender drops away' provides us instead with a glimpse of what a 'gender-free' science might look like. (*ibid., p. xvii*)

MCCLINTOCK'S VISION OR FOX KELLER'S?

When looking at what Fox Keller claims for McClintock, it is worth remembering that although in places she uses McClintock's own words it is Fox Keller's vision that the book encapsulates. McClintock's concern appears to be to have her work accepted and understood for what it says about genes and chromosomes, not for any particular methodology or research technique.

Fox Keller has also been criticized (by Grobicki) for having an individualistic vision of scientific theorizing: 'A new idea, a new conception,' she says, 'is born in the privacy of one man's or one woman's dreams' (p. *xii*), while at the same time 'science is at once a highly personal and a communal endeavour.'

Article 3.4
TECHNOLOGY, PRODUCTION AND POWER
Cynthia Cockburn

To understand the different relation the sexes have to technology today, we need to recognize the relevance of technology to power and to the emergence of power systems in the past. Despite the stereotype of the stone-age cave man dragging 'his' woman along by the hair and wielding a club (technology?) in his free hand, the evidence of archaeology does not point to any 'natural' distance between women and technology. Today, when explaining the emergence of human societies, the emphasis has shifted from Man The Hunter to Woman The Gatherer. [See Article 2.2.] . . . It is well established that women were the first horticulturalists, purposefully growing selected plants in and around their settlements (Martin and Vorhees, 1975). They may well have invented and used the hoe, spade, shovel and scratch-plough (Stanley, 1981). Whether hunting animals (large or small), or herding, gardening and farming, a simple division of labour may have occurred. We need not suppose, however, that it gave one sex a marked monopoly of technological skills.[1]

As human societies have developed, in different parts of the world at different times, they have tended to pass through broadly similar phases. Often these are designated by archaeologists according to the material of the dominant technology: stone age, bronze age, iron age. Associated with the technologies are successive stages in social organization. Women appear to have been central to the organization of social life until the late neolithic age. As the neolithic ceded to the bronze age, however, in many cultures of which a record exists it is possible to see a shift towards male dominance. A relatively egalitarian and peaceful community of woman-centred kinship clans gave way to an increasingly centralized society divided into hierarchical classes, based on agriculture, warfare and slavery. As this occurred, it seems, women were actively subjugated by men, excluded from many crafts and trades and displaced from their positions of political and religious authority.[2] The rise of class society is associated with a shift to patrilineality (determining descent through the male blood line) and to patrilocality (a wife moving to the domain of her husband's family on marriage). It is also associated with an increasing division of labour, the emergence of specific crafts and trades.

In particular the new occupations surrounding metallurgy were highly significant. The importance of metals and of the skills of smelter, founder and smith to the military and agricultural exploits of rulers and ruling classes can be in no doubt. It seems that in male-dominated societies these occupations are seen as male. Technological skills are a source of power and where men were in possession of all other vehicles of power, from state organization to marriage, it would have been surprising to find women in possession of mechanical powers. The 'mighty five' devices – lever, wedge, screw, wheel and inclined plane – that made it possible to move mountains and build pyramids were the technical armoury of men.

It was not in the cradles of 'civilization', however, but in the Western extremities of Europe that technology would explode in the eighteenth and nineteenth centuries AD, and it is of interest to trace the technological division of labour by sex as it progressed there. As the use of iron was rapidly expanded in the eighth and ninth centuries (see White, 1962, p. 40), it is clear that women's role in production, though of prime importance then as it has continued to be ever since . . . , was nonetheless confined to particular activities associated with domestic consumption. Apart from food preparation and childcare, women were responsible for 'spinning, dyeing, weaving, tending the garden, raising livestock and . . . cultivating land' (Wemple, 1981, p. 70). It was men who were the goldsmith, weapon-smith and blacksmith, 'making ploughshare and coulter, goad and fish-hook, awl and needle', and the carpenter, 'responsible not only for various tools and utensils but for houses and ships' (Whitelock, 1952, p. 106).

In the later Middle Ages again we find rural women involved with 'dairy work, gardening, food preparation and the textile crafts of carding, slubbing, spinning and weaving', while their male equivalents 'worked the land, reared livestock, repaired hedges, ditches and tools' (Chaytor and Lewis, 1982). Among these tools were more and more made of iron. Iron was rapidly becoming the basis of the dominant technology. 'It is the consensus among historians of agriculture that the mediaeval peasantry used an amount of iron which would have seemed inconceivable to any earlier rural population and that the smithy became integral to every village' (White, 1962, p. 41). And there were few trades more associated with manliness than that of smith.

The towns, which grew rapidly in importance in the thirteenth and fourteenth centuries, were the centres of specialized handicrafts. Under the authority of the feudal state, the craft and merchant guilds laid down the rules by which apprentices might be recruited and trained and business carried on. The guilds covered certain skilled techniques producing goods for consumption, such as printing. But they also included those that produced tools and implements: carpenter, wright and various kinds of smith. The guilds were male in character (Wilkinson, 1969; Postan, 1975). Women engaged extensively in economic life in the towns, but mainly in sex-specific areas that had by long tradition been female. They were domestic servants, washerwomen, bakers, brewers and inn-keepers, roles that were extensions into trade of the concerns of domestic life: food, drink and textiles, goods and services for domestic consumption.

The sexual division of labour was not absolutely total at this period, however. Women appear listed alongside men as engaging in certain kinds of production (shoe-making for instance) and in certain fields of commerce (as drapers, chandlers and even iron-mongers). The pattern that we [see] today, however, whereby women cluster in a few occupations and men spread across many, is evident in the Middle Ages. Poll tax returns for Oxford in 1380, for instance, mention six trades followed by women, six in which both women and men were employed, and no fewer than 81 that were followed exclusively by men. Alice Clark (1982) concluded from her study of mediaeval trades that, though women followed some skilled and semi-skilled occupations, 'no traces can be found of any organization existing' within them. Certainly women were not considered a threat to male occupational rights. A statute of Edward III expressly exempted women from the ordinance that men should not follow more than a single craft. 'But the intent of the King and his Council,' it reads, 'is that Women, that is to say Brewers, Bakers, Carders and Spinners and Workers as well of Wool as of Linen Cloth and of Silk, Brawdesters and Breakers of Wool and all other that do use and work all Handy Works may freely use and work as they have done before this time . . .' (Hutchins, 1978, p. 38).

The role of the guilds extended beyond an immediate trade to social organization within the town. A woman therefore might be a member of a guild without actually plying its trade. A daughter might take up right of patrimony in her father's guild for the civic advantages it afforded. Some are known to have become apprenticed to a master in his guild so as to work as a domestic servant to his wife. Widows frequently inherited their husbands' enterprises. Widows are therefore sometimes named even as farriers and smiths. An exceptional woman might have broken the convention to carry out this work herself, but a commoner practice was for a widow to manage the business while hired journeymen and apprentices carried out the skilled practical aspects of the work.

TOOLS THAT MAKE TOOLS

In this account of early divisions of labour we can distinguish certain skills which were of special significance in production and which yielded, as a consequence, greater influence to those who possessed them than was yielded by ordinary productive abilities. They are the skills that were required for making tools, implements and weapons. In other words, *they involved competence in the production or adaptation of other producers' instruments of labour.* Eventually we will see these skills evolve into those that make machinery and later still into those that build computer systems.

Why should these abilities afford greater power than others: than the knowledge needed to nurture children, for instance, or to weave cloth or plough the land? The answer is, first, related to systems of class power. Those who own the means of production, whether slave-owning emperors, land-owning feudal nobles or factory-owning capitalists, depend for the making of their wealth on a yoking in tandem of labour and tools, labour and machinery. They may be expected therefore to pay well, in cash or food, freedom or status, for the skills they need to effect this linkage and continually to improve its productivity. Other talents could, in another world, have been valued more highly. But from the onset of male-dominated, class-structured societies, the priority has been supremacy in a struggle for ownership and control of disposable surpluses. That priority has forced the development of technology in a certain direction. The forcing-house has often been warfare.

Secondly, however, those who possessed these skills had a source of power over everyone who did not. Such men rendered other people dependent on them for the maintenance of their own environment and instruments of labour. They were in a position to impede or enhance, direct or redirect other producers' labour processes. They acquired a degree of authority among other men of those classes who worked manually. It will be clear also that the skills enhanced men's power over women. Not only were women firmly subordinated to men in the patriarchal family, but they were also dependent on them for certain important practical processes of everyday life. The technological skills, defined as male property, were therefore both a cause and an effect of male supremacy.

[· · ·]

The history of invention represents the inventors of antiquity, the Middle Ages and the Renaissance as invariably male. . . (Strandh, 1979). The question of what part women did or did not play in technological invention is a knotty one. Women have almost always been 'hidden from history' when the historians were men. Autumn Stanley's (1983) work reaffirms women's creativeness. She suggests that we should be sceptical of the male historians of technology and look for the hidden women. We should, besides, give greater emphasis to the activities to which women notably *have* contributed their ideas: preparing food, healing, making garments, caring for children. After all, the significance ascribed to any productive practice has been largely a male choice.

Stanley (1981) proposes that 'all else being equal' we may assume that those who work in a process invent the tools by which it is carried on. While this is likely to be true for very early periods of human history, it is to miss a crucial characteristic of subsequent patriarchal and class societies. Women were systematically excluded from all sources of power, including the technologies that held sway over their own female areas of production. The development of textile technology, for instance, has been a male not a female project.

[· · ·]

Leonardo da Vinci is credited with the invention of the flyer for the spindle in 1490. Johann Jurgen, a woodcarver of Brunswick, invented a partly automatic spinning wheel employing a flyer around 1530 (Mumford, 1934, p. 144). The way of thinking that would have enabled such innovations arose not in the main from the spinning of thread but from a familiarity with other kinds of apparatus and technique. The matter of differential speeds, for instance, was being explored in clock-making at this time; the notion of the flywheel and the transmission belt were used in the developing of grinding mills. Technological knowledge is essentially a *transferable* knowledge, profitably carried from one kind of production to another. It is a field of its own . . . Computer-aided design and cutting systems built for use with metals are adapted for use with cloth; a robot developed for use in the car industry stimulates developments that will solve management problems in warehousing. Men move from industry to industry carrying know-how across the boundaries of firm and sector. Then, as now, it was men and not women who had mobility (intellectual, occupational and physical mobility) and the overview it afforded. Later of course it would be other men – Hargreave, Arkwright, Crompton, Kay – who would adapt the domestic textile apparatus for factory and mechanized use.

What is at issue here is not women's inventiveness. There is no doubt that women have the ability to be as imaginative and innovative as men. Women have frequently 'had ideas' for the improvement of tools and machinery with which they worked. They have seldom had the craft skills to effect in wood or metal the improvements they conceived. Besides, despite the frequent adulation by historians of male inventors, technological development is not in reality a series of brainwaves. A materialist understanding of history gives the personal less significance than the social. In tracing technological change, therefore, the focus needs to be 'not upon individuals, however heroic, but upon a collective, social process in which the institutional and economic environments play major roles' (Rosenberg, 1982, p. 35). The social process of technological development has been overwhelmingly a male process. It is women's lack of social and economic power that holds them 'down' to the role of producer of goods for immediate consumption. Since the bronze age, women have worked *for* men, whether the man was head of household, slave-owner or feudal lord. It is clear that they also produced *by means of* man-made technologies. They were subject to that particular form of material control that comes of men as a sex having appropriated the role of tool-maker to the world.

MACHINES THAT MAKE MACHINES

The departure that was about to change the world dramatically for both women and men, however, was not a technical invention. It was capitalism: an entirely new set of social relationships that would find the organizational means to bring science and technology together and harness them for production. During the sixteenth and seventeenth centuries the peasant economy of the countryside and the craft economy of the towns, both essentially home-based domestic forms of production, changed their character. From among the yeoman farmers and the guild masters emerged a new stratum of large-scale producers. The merchant class also grew in number and in influence. Wealth, accumulated through trade in England and overseas, sought new ways of making more wealth. Independent craft production gave way to 'manufacture' as merchants became entrepreneurs, no longer simply buying from but actively employing the producers.

At first the new capitalist class 'put out' the material to scattered producers to work on in their homes, and in this way the domestic system continued for a while within the new mode of production. Much of women's production continued to be carried on under the authority of father or husband. Eventually, however, entrepreneurs saw advantage in gathering producers into workshops and factories where an employer could enjoy economies of scale and supervise production more closely.

As the restraints of the guild system were shrugged off, the new class of employers found it possible and profitable to introduce a sub-division of the work process. Merchandise that had once been produced by a single craftsman undertaking all the varied parts of the process was now the product of a series of manual workers, each of whom repeated a part of the task over and over again with a single tool. Some of the detail tasks were more skill-demanding than others. The workforce could be differentiated: some remained relatively skilled and costly, but others could now be less skilled, and a new cheap category of entirely unskilled 'hands' was called into play. Often these were women or children, many of whom were drawn from the surplus population thrown off the land by the agrarian revolution.

A significant change began to occur in the relationship between producers and 'their' technologies. The craftsman had owned his own tools. This included the tools owned by those men who made the tools that other producers used. The craftsman guarded the 'mystery' of how to use them . . . [I]n the new factories the employer owned the instruments of labour and put the worker to work on them. For many artisans who had once purchased materials with their own money, worked with their own tools and sold to their own customers, the change was historic. Now what they sold, all they had to sell, was their labour power.

So, as the capitalist initiative (which was also, it must be noted, a masculine initiative) drew into existence this new class of wage workers, unknown in the feudal world, men of the two classes were drawn into endemic conflict. Capital might own the instruments of production but working men alone had the craft know-how to use them. How and by whom, for how long and for what reward, the tools and techniques were to be used became the basis of the struggle that has been the prime mover of history in the intervening 200 or 300 years.

The process, however, had a long way yet to go. Technology would not only set in opposition the interests of the employing class and the working class. It would also be instrumental in forming the new working class as a stratified and divided one. As the general-purpose tools of the craftsmen were put to use in a subdivided production process, the tools too were altered – simplified and multiplied – to suit the new detail tasks (Marx, 1887/1954, p. 323). Simple tools, combined and associated with a power source and a transmitting mechanism, resulted in a machine. The machine was soon associated with others in a factory system that itself had the characteristics of a machine. The groundwork was laid for vast new possibilities of accumulation for the owner of the new mechanical means of production.

Machinery offered men as a sex opportunities that were not open to women. Already certain technologies of which men had exclusive tenure had a special significance in production; now they took on an amplified importance. Those who had traditionally worked the materials from which tools were made would now adapt their skills to the new machine age. What capital needed in place of smiths and wrights were 'mechanics' and 'engineers'. It was only men, inevitably, who had the tradition, the confidence and in many cases also the transferable skills to make the leap. It was therefore exclusively men who became the maintenance mechanics and the production engineers in the new factories, governing capital's new forces of production.

Marx singled out these key employees in the new 'machino-facture'. He noted the essential division between the operators, who are actually employed on the machines, and their unskilled attendants. But, he wrote, in addition a historically new worker appears, a 'class of persons, whose occupation it is to look after the whole of the machinery and repair it from time to time; such as engineers, mechanics, joiners etc. This is a superior class of workmen, some of them scientifically educated, others brought up to a trade; it is distinct from the factory operative class and merely aggregated to it. This division of labour is purely technical' (ibid., p. 396). These technical men were the one category of worker whose earning power was not reduced by the introduction of machinery (ibid., p. 331). If one mechanic, together with a handful of unskilled, low-paid machine operators, can put out of work many craftsmen, capital could . . . afford to pay the technical newcomer relatively well.

The old-style smith and wright, new-style mechanic and engineer, however, were also to play another part in production history. Machinery was crippled in its complete development so long as machine-building itself remained a handicraft affair . . . [B]ecause of the increasing size of the prime movers and the use of iron and steel . . . huge masses of which had now 'to be forged, to be welded, to be cut, to be bored and to be shaped' – it was inevitable that machines had to be invented with which to build machines (ibid., pp. 362–3).

Skills, however, were still needed to design, develop and build these machines that were to make machines to do the work of men and women. While one kind of skilled man, therefore, had become the mechanic and engineer of the 'downstream' processes . . . where they supervised the machines that produced the means of consumption, his brother now moved 'upstream' to become the mechanic and engineer of . . . the influential machine-building or capital goods industry producing the means of production for others. . . .

THE STRUGGLE OVER TECHNICAL SKILLS

The Combination Acts, which had outlawed collective organization by workers, were repealed in 1824–5. After this, journeymen from many of the male crafts formed trade unions. At first there existed a variety of societies, local or regional in scope, representing millwrights, machinists and other categories of technical skill. The strongest of these was the Steam Engine Makers, founded in 1826, and later known as the 'Old Mechanics'. In 1851 many of the smaller societies joined together to form a new union, the Amalgamated

Society of Engineers, Machinists, Smiths, Millwrights and Pattern-Makers. It was an exclusive, skilled union, characterized by high membership subscriptions and generous benefits, and it became a model for other skilled unions... [T]he ASE ... quickly became one of the largest unions in the country and had a membership of 72,000 by 1891 (Pelling, 1976).

Meanwhile the scope of the industry itself was expanding to encompass different kinds of metal-work: the heavy sectors of ship and locomotive building, the machine-tool industry and eventually lighter sectors producing consumer goods such as bicycles. In the 1870s the employers organized themselves into the Iron Trades Employers' Association, the better to fight ... the unions. The employers, by repeated cycles of technological innovation, attempted to deskill the work of the engineering industry and divest themselves of dependence on the craft engineers. The skilled workers of the ASE and other engineering unions on the contrary struggled to maintain craft regulation of work, including an agreed ratio of apprentices to journeymen, and to prevent the employers fragmenting the labour process and using unskilled handymen on the machines (Zeitlin, 1979).

Instrumental in bringing about this sub-division of work and the deskilling of craft engineers was a new breed of formally educated professional engineers. Civil engineers – men like Isambard Kingdom Brunel – had already achieved status and acclaim as architects of the era of canal, road and rail. Now, towards the end of the nineteenth century, the new high-status industrial engineer was interposing himself between the mechanic and the employer in science-based manufacture. Entire new industries such as electrical and chemical engineering grew up, which had no craft basis. In these the engineer was not only key employee but also often manager (Noble, 1979, p. 5).

[· · ·]

From this history it will be clear that the technically knowledgeable and skilled fraternity is by no means simply a 'superior class of workman', as Marx put it. It is varied, it is hierarchically stratified and its component parts are continually shifting in relative status. Technological skills are forced by capital to adapt and change. They do not only act on others' skills, they are also acted upon. The skilled men respond by demarcating and defending areas of competence. As a result the unions at one moment join forces, at another split apart.

Some categories of technical men are always ahead of 'the state of the art', and consequently in demand. Some are running to keep up, fearful of technological redundancy, the obsolescence of their knowledge, the demise of the process they are accustomed to work at. The challenge for all of them is to keep abreast of technology, maintain marketable skills and retain a governing role over the machinery on which other people produce, at the point both of its manufacture and of its application. Those technologists who succeed, 'do well' by themselves. Their role develops more and more from control of machinery to control of labour processes and so to control of people.

[· · ·]

The advent of powered machinery was, then, profoundly contradictory for men as a sex. On the one hand many men could view it only with hatred. It was the enemy. It enabled capital to dispense with the skills of the skilled man and the muscle power of the labourer. On the other hand, mechanical skills were the property of men as a sex, much as machinery itself was the property of the dominant class. Men's power over women could only be enhanced by advances in technology.

[· · ·]

WOMEN'S RELATIONSHIP TO THE MACHINE

[· · ·]

We know that women have continuously contributed a large proportion of total production and that a very sizeable part of that has been in food and clothing, whether for immediate consumption or for sale. In addition, of course, women have been the ones to perform almost all the 'reproductive' tasks associated with child care and housekeeping that are not normally classed as work.

Women were also employed, particularly when single, in the heaviest types of manual labour, were exploited as domestic servants, as 'servants in husbandry' working in the fields, and even carrying coal, washing lead and breaking ore in the mines. More women were forced into labouring (or pauperism) as the break-up of the old feudal relationships dispossessed the least secure. Female cottagers who had scratched a living from vegetable patch and grazing rights on the commons were made landless by the enclosure movement that 'rationalized' the land into large-scale farms. More and more of the women working as independent or family producers in towns lost their livelihood as competition from outwork and factory work organized on capitalist lines in the rural areas destroyed urban craft production. At first many women, like men, became outworkers in their own homes. As industrialization advanced they followed the work to the factories. Women were unpractised in craft organization and many had the docility that results from subordination within the home. The new class of male employers could benefit by this – in a sense they stole a march on men of the working class.[3]

The effect of the industrial revolution and the special uses of women, as perceived by the new captains of industry, were contradictory for women themselves. Some results were clearly adverse. Women and children were terribly exploited and abused in the frenzy of capitalist production. Industrial methods wiped out women's small businesses – bleaching and brewing, for instance. Women's types of production were brought more firmly under the sway of a male principle. Making clothing, food and drink, for instance, as it was socialized and mechanized, became more institutionally subject to men's special knowledge of machinery than women's domestic production had been subject to individual men's knowledge of tools.

As industrialization increased and more and more women were drawn in to work, a powerful adaptation of the old ideology of 'a woman's place' evolved to ensure that women's relationship to work and earning was no more than provisional. A basic theme of this ideology was the assumption that woman's proper role was that of wife and mother. . . These were middle-class ideas that had little real relevance to the situation of working-class women, yet 'they informed the ideology of the period so thoroughly that they dominated prevailing attitudes towards working women and shaped the terms in which those women interpreted their own experience' (Eisenstein, 1983). Women, as a consequence, worked but could not aspire to the great achievement dreamed of by many Victorian men.

More positively, however, the development of a female industrial labour force did bring practical opportunities for women to evade both this gender ideology and the more material aspects of male dominance. First, it meant coming out of the enclosed sphere of the patriarchal family into the more public sphere of the patriarchal firm. This is not so simple a move as it sounds. The feudal and the early capitalist domestic system of manufacture had made the home a far from private place. In a sense the home became truly a private sphere only once production had left it. The constitution of 'home and work', the 'private and public' as we know them was in many ways a cultural artefact of the industrial revolution. The more significant factor was that an increasing number of husbands and fathers lost some of their control over their daughters and wives, as they came to depend in part on an income earned by these womenfolk in the domain of another man.

Second, many women started to earn an independent wage. Though often enough it was quickly subsumed into household income for the disposition of the head of the household, nonetheless it increasingly gave some women independent means. The population of women was greater than that of men throughout the nineteenth century, and the surplus increased from 1851 to 1901 (Hutchins, 1978, p. 75). Not all women would be able to marry and many would be widowed. By 1911, 54 per cent of single women would be working for a wage (ibid., p. 90).

[· · ·]

The third change was that women were not only following their own traditional kinds of work into the factories. They were also diversifying their roles in production. Though they were found in their greatest numbers in the spinning and weaving mills, and in jam-making, confectionery and other forms of large-scale food production, soon they were also producing other kinds of commodity. Even in the early 'domestic' years of capitalist production women had begun to do 'unskilled', heavy and dirty work in metallurgy, making nails, nuts, bolts, screws, buckles, locks, bits and stirrups. Defoe (1796) wrote of the West Midlands area in 1769 that 'every Farm has one Forge or more', and these forges were producing not for farm consumption but for capitalists. When these 'small iron trades' began to be organized into a factory system, women followed. In 1841 the number of women in the Birmingham district employed in metal manufacture was estimated at 10,000. Twenty-five years later there were 2,050 females returned as employed in Birmingham pen-works and others were employed in the light chain trade, in lacquering brass and making files and pins (Hutchins, 1978, pp. 62–3).

Women, then, were spreading into new spheres of production as production industrialized. What now became significant, however, was the particular role they played *within* these new industries. Women clustered within three types of occupation. Hutchins noted, from visits to non-textile factories early in this century, 'that men and women are usually doing, not the same, but different kinds of work and that the work done by women seems to fall roughly into three classes' (ibid., pp. 66–7). Her first class was 'rough hard work preparing and collecting the material, or transporting it from one part of the factory to another'. A second was finishing and preparing goods for sale: examining, folding, wrapping and packing. . . [T]he third group of jobs, . . . [were] the routine production jobs on machines. . . This work is 'done on machines with or without power, and this includes a whole host of employments and an endless variety of problems. Machine tending, press-work, stamp-work, metal-cutting, printing, various processes of brasswork, pen-making, machine ironing in laundries, the making of hollow-ware or tin pots and buckets of various kinds.' Hutchins did not . . . note that the mechanics who kept these machines going were *not* women. It could be taken as given that those jobs belonged to men.

THE RESPONSE OF MALE WORKERS

The final significant effect of the industrial revolution on women was that it threw them, in many cases, into direct competition with men for work. Some of the new machine-based occupations of the late eighteenth and early nineteenth centuries, while they demanded great stamina, no longer called for sheer muscle. Employers could and often did replace men with women and children. Whereas the craft guilds had been organized mainly in exclusion of other men – the exclusion of women being more or less taken for granted – the skilled trade unions were obliged to direct their energies to keeping women out. Men could do little to prevent capital engaging women to work in the new industries. Men's efforts therefore had to be geared to segregating women and maintaining sexual divisions *within* the factory. Consciously and actively, male workers hedged women into unskilled and low-paid occupations. In printing, for instance, the male compositors and machine-minders confined women to book-binding and other print-finishing operations where they were severely exploited by employers.

It is the most damning indictment of skilled working-class men and their unions that they excluded women from membership and prevented them gaining competences that could have secured them a decent living. Virginia Penny wrote in 1869 that women's lot would be greatly improved if only women might enter the trades and professions monopolized by men. 'Apprentice ten thousand women to watchmakers,' she said. 'Put some thousands in the electric telegraph offices all over the country; educate one thousand lecturers for mechanics' institutes ... then the distressed needle-woman will vanish, the decayed gentlewoman and broken-down governesses cease to exist.' Men were not misled in perceiving women as a weapon in employers' hands by which their own wages could be kept down. Where they were misled was in their response. Instead of helping women to acquire skills and to organize their strength, they weakened women (and in the long run the entire working class) by continuing to exploit women domestically and helping the employer to exploit them as a secondary labour market. Not only were women barred from men's areas of skill but women's particular skills came to be universally undervalued in comparison: undervalued and underpaid. . . .

So great a gulf had men in earlier centuries fixed between women and technology, however, that the ASE [did] not ... see women as a threat to the engineer throughout the nineteenth century. The kinds of semi-skilled work brought into being by the mechanization of engineering (in the main, machining metal) were not seen by employers as appropriate areas in which to try to substitute women for men. The stratum of 'handymen' infiltrated by the employer into engineering works was just that: men. The Victorian and Edwardian women's movements did not include in their demands technical skills for women [but see Article 3.1 and Ayrton's speech at the 1899 ICW (eds)]. It was not until the First World War, when they were brought into munitions and other heavy industries to release men for the Front, that women began to approach the masculine sphere of technical skill and consequently to be feared for the first time as 'dilutees'.

The *Labour Gazette* in 1917 estimated that one out of three working women was replacing a man (Braybon, 1987, p. 46). Women went into a number of industries besides munitions:

> They planed, moulded, mortised and dovetailed in sawmills; drove trucks in flour and oil and cake mills; made upholstery and tyre tubes; bottled beer and manufactured furniture; worked in cement factories, foundries and tanneries, in jute mills and wool mills; broke limestone and loaded bricks in steel works and worked as riveters in shipbuilding yards. They could be found in car factories, in quarrying and surface mining and brickmaking . . . only underground mining, stevedoring and steel and iron smelting were still all male.

> *(Solden, 1978, p. 102)*

Women, says this author, shattered the myth that they were incapable of skilled work.

A serious challenge was made to make exclusiveness in the ASE by the radical shop stewards' movement of the war and post-war years. Progressiveness on the woman question was a logical position for the shop stewards, whose aim was to turn the ASE from a craft union into an all-grades industrial union (Hinton, 1981; Frow and Frow, 1982). Nonetheless, the pledge the government had given the union to lay off dilutees at the end of the war was honoured. Many thousands of women were ejected from their jobs. High unemployment among women resulted, made worse by the slump of 1920.

The ASE became the Amalgamated Engineering Union in 1922, but still did not admit women members. Meanwhile women's role in the engineering industry expanded fast in the inter-war years, as they became the characteristic semi-skilled assembly-line labour force in the industries producing the new electrical consumer goods (Gluckman, 1984). In the Second World War women again replaced men in many engineering jobs, both unskilled and skilled. This time the situation for the traditionalist men in the union was past saving. Women were, with bad grace on the part of many members, finally accepted into the union on 1 January 1943. The women's section had 139,000 members by 1944 (Solden, 1978, pp. 152–3).

Acceptance into the union, however, did not mean that those

women who had acceded to skilled jobs in the war were able to consider them theirs for keeps. After the war, women were once more expected to retire gracefully to domestic life, and for the most part they did so. Those who stayed were reduced to unskilled or semi-skilled work. Women found themselves addressed by an intense ideology of 'femininity' and 'domesticity'. . . To associate women with technological competence now seemed as ridiculous as . . . ever.

Yet the situation of women was to change once again in the 1950s and '60s as the economic boom caused a demand for their labour and women themselves, even married women now, began to aspire to independence, work and careers in greater numbers than ever before. By the time the recession of the late 1970s hit the British economy, women had grown to be 42 per cent of the labour force.[4] Statements by Conservative ministers to the effect that women were expected to do the decent thing and return home, leaving the shrinking supply of jobs to men, were this time ignored by women. Women's consciousness had changed radically since the post-war period and this had influenced 'public opinion' more generally. Supportive legislation of the early 1970s had strengthened women's hand. This time they held on to work, though it was often part-time and low-paid. While the number of male employees in employment fell by 14 per cent between 1971 and 1983, the number of women rose by 7 per cent. . .

I REALLY WANTED TO BE A MECHANIC
BUT THERE WERE NO APPRENTICESHIPS FOR WOMEN

The way out of the recession for British capital, fervently promoted by a monetarist government, is [seen to be] by shedding labour, reducing the wages of the remainder and investing in superproductive new electronic technology. In such a situation, with men objectively weakened in the labour market, employers indifferent to or even positive towards employing women, and women themselves showing a new confidence in their right to work, we might expect to see women entering technical training and skilled occupations in new technology in equal numbers with men. If . . . this is not happening, it should alert us to ask more penetrating questions about how male dominance is renegotiated and how the sexual division of labour continues to be reproduced over time.

Notes

1   Eleanor Burke Leacock (1981) illustrates this point by reference to the sex-egalitarian gathering and hunting community of the Montaignais-Naskai of Canada in the period immediately preceding their conversion to Christianity by Jesuit missionaries.

2   The process was theorized by Friedrich Engels in the nineteenth century in *Origin of the Family, Private Property and the State*.

3   Painstaking accounts of women's work in the industrial revolution can be found in: Ivy Pinchbeck (1981; first published 1930); B.L. Hutchins (1978); Wanda F. Neff (1966; first published 1929); Alice Kessler-Harris (1982); and Elizabeth F. Baker (1964).

4   *Employment Gazette* figures, published in Equal Opportunities Commission *Annual Report 1983*, Table 3.3.

THE SECRETARY CHANT

Marge Piercy

My hips are a desk.
From my ears hang
chains of paper clips.
Rubber bands form my hair.
My breasts are wells of mimeograph ink.
My feet bear casters.
Buzz. Click.
My head
is a badly organized file.
My head is a switchboard
where crossed lines crackle.
My head is wastebasket
of worn ideas.
Press my fingers
and in my eyes appear
credit and debit.
Zing. Tinkle.
My navel is a reject button.
From my mouth issue cancelled reams.
Swollen, heavy, rectangular
I am about to be delivered
of a baby
xerox machine.
File me under W
because I wonce
was
a woman.

Article 3.6
'A BROTHER IN ARMS, A SISTER IN PEACE':CONTEMPORARY ISSUES OF GENDER AND MILITARY TECHNOLOGY

Julie Wheelwright

Why study the military, an institution which many people never perceive as having any direct effect on their lives at all? Whether we are aware of it or not, the military's needs make enormous demands on our society. Throughout recent decades, for example, military interests increasingly direct research funding in science and technology in the United Kingdom and the United States. Often referred to as the 'military-industrial complex', corporate research funnelled through universities ranges from advances in surgical techniques or the effects of psycho-chemical treatments, to computer software programs. While the military is far-reaching in its interests, it also takes care to preserve the perception that since its activities are highly masculine, its technology is equally gendered. The image of a sexy woman soldier/cop/terrorist with a gun may be fast becoming a Hollywood staple, but most military policy attempts to draw strict boundaries between the 'rear' – where women maintain support services – and the front – where the fighting with sophisticated weaponry occurs. As we shall see, in reality these lines are distinctly blurred and perpetuate the myth that women are the 'girls behind the men who man the guns'. Unless they were portrayed as interesting anomalies, the woman soldier was largely rendered invisible during the Gulf War in 1991, as the US Pentagon stressed the wonders of 'smart' bombs, 'surgical strikes' and 'computer-guided weapons systems'. Since handling this technology is still largely defined as a male occupation, the war preserved its traditional image.

It is important to remember that the issues affecting women in the military, especially their relationship to technology and its association of certain skills with masculinity, have parallels in civilian life. A lack of maternity leave, crèche facilities, limited advancement opportunities, sexual harassment or discriminatory expectations from their superiors affect all women in contemporary Western societies. However, given that the military has historically been perceived as the most masculine of institutions, the difficulties a woman encounters are thrown into sharp relief. While the woman soldier's position is anomalous in that she must live and work in close quarters with her male colleagues and may be subject to life-threatening situations, her struggle for equal treatment is by no means unique.

Cynthia Enloe reminds us that the pressing issues women soldiers face illuminate larger questions about the meaning of gender:

> To demystify the military and to uncover all the ways it resembles the rest of a society in which being male carries power and privilege makes it possible for women, normally excluded from military affairs, to shed light on aspects of the military ordinarily overlooked. Any woman, then, who is working to dissect and explain the myths and reality of family structures, the way sexuality is constructed or the way women's labour has been exploited can contribute to the analysis of the military.
>
> (Enloe, 1989, p. 9)

As the war in the Gulf has so clearly demonstrated, the military has the power to touch our lives in the most immediate way. Whether women are working in defence industries, losing their jobs because of the recession, fighting in the armed forces, demonstrating for peace or trying to understand international politics, militarism remains a key issue.

WOMEN'S ROLE IN THE FORCES

British women were first mobilized into army auxiliaries to perform a wide variety of services during the First World War. Although women had served throughout the eighteenth and nineteenth centuries as traders supplying food and drink to the troops, their other roles as nurses, washerwomen, seamstresses and nannies were never officially recognized. It was only when Florence Nightingale won the right to organize the first nursing units in the Crimea that an appropriate niche was carved for middle-class ladies.[1] Early experiments using female army nurses began during the British African campaigns in the late nineteenth century while at home ladies set up recruitment drives for voluntary nursing detachments. During the 1914–18 war, women in Britain enlisted in newly-formed auxiliary services and were employed in a wide variety of jobs to release men for the front. These nursing, transport and ambulance services were expanded a generation later to accommodate more than a quarter of a million women. However, even then, the military never proved the great leveller it was purported to be. Which service a woman joined – the Women's Auxiliary Air Force, the Women's Royal Naval Service, the Women's Land Army or the Auxiliary Territorial Service – was class-determined. Theoretically, women conscripted under the National Service Number 2 Act had a choice of service but in reality only the volunteers were directed into the élite corps with 'well-bred' images, such as the WRNS (Braybon and Summerfield, 1987). (See Plate 7.)

In the United States women were organized into the Women's Army Corps for the first time along British lines during the Second World War, although many had served with Belgian, British, French and even Russian auxiliaries from 1914 onwards. When the Second World War broke out, the only women in the American armed services were nurses. But labour shortages resulted in a Congressional motion allowing the formation of the Women's Army Corps (WAC) in May 1942 which was quickly followed by the Navy's Women Accepted for Voluntary Emergency Service (WAVES). In 1943 women were admitted into the Marine Corps, traditionally the most conservative service in its integration of women. At the same time, more than 800 women served as ferry pilots as the Women's Air Service Pilots (WASPs), often on hazardous missions flying military planes across the Atlantic. The Air Force became a separate service following the war and the Women in the Air Force (WAF) was created in 1948 (Moskos, 1990, p. 2). That year, a Congressional act gave permanent status to the WAC although it limited the numbers of women in the armed forces to two per cent of the total number, excluding nurses. The public's attention moved away from women soldiers but the WAC's soldiers considered themselves 'twenty-four hours a day military' (Rogan, 1981, p. 147).

However, combat exclusion policies in all three services – the Army, Navy and Air Force – were broadly drawn and strictly enforced. Within the Army, which offered only 185 out of 482 military occupational specialities (MOS) to women, they were confined to female-only units. The Navy kept all sea-going billets closed to women and restricted female strength to less than five per cent. The Air Force was no better for women who wanted to participate actively in the service: women were refused assignment to air crew duties regardless of the type or mission of the aircraft (Tuten, 1982). As we shall see, combat exclusion policies became more complex over time as military policy-makers grappled with the need to draw on women as a 'reserve army of labour', and satisfy its concerns about maintaining gendered roles for them.

Despite seemingly immovable restrictions, in the 1970s women's integration into the armed forces became a political issue in the United States. Following the bitter controversy about US involvement in the Vietnam War and the deep unpopularity of the draft, women volunteers were mooted as an alternative. Although more than 7,500 women served in Vietnam and eight died, their participation had largely gone unrecognized.[2] When the draft was scrapped in 1973, the percentages of women in all three armed services rose dramatically. From an overall 1.6 per cent, which largely represented women in medical services, the percentage of female military personnel rose to 8.5 per cent in 1980 and 10.8 per cent in 1989 (Women's Research and Education Institute, 1990, p. 1).

The political pressure to repeal the draft coincided with the rise of the women's movement in the United States and demands for the forces to update their services as a civil rights issue. However, another equally important factor in the Pentagon's change of heart about women soldiers was a realization that, given projected demographic trends, the pool of draft-age men would shrink significantly over the next two decades. Women could be used to fill the holes left behind when the all-volunteer force was implemented and, in the longer-term, supply a stable, reliable source of labour in a variety of support services (Stiehm, 1989). Another example from Britain in the 1980s when women were recruited into areas where demands were high for skilled labour – Women into Science and Engineering – reveals an identical strategy. Gender concerns are forced to give way when social policy-makers bow to pragmatism.

As the numbers of women increased, so the nature of their work changed. Flight training was opened to women by the Army and Navy in 1973 and by the Air Force three years later. Enlisted women were now eligible to operate trucks, work in chemical warfare units and conduct ship repairs. The Army selected its first general officers and admission standards were modified to apply equally to men and women. The WAC was dissolved and its officers integrated into basic officer courses; they were able to command and recruit men, admitted into officer candidate schools like West Point Academy and 430 of the 467 MOS were opened. Moreover, in recognition of women's desire to combine their service careers with a family, the policy that required pregnant women and those with dependent children to quit was scrapped.

The British Army, which has always been one of the most socially conservative in NATO, looked upon the changes within the US military with deep scepticism. In 1976 a report on the future employment of the Women's Royal Army Corps suggested that if women were to be 'an integral part of the Army' they should undergo weapons training and even be 'considered for special duties within the Special Air Service or the Intelligence Corps.' However, it was only when the infantry battallions became over-stretched in the late 1980s that discussions about the integration of women were mooted. Policy changes followed the release of a study into the wider employment of women in the Army in September 1989, but the recommendations remained inconsistent with practice. For example, while it was decided that WRAC personnel were not supposed to serve 'forward of [the] corps rear boundary' in German units, in Northern Ireland military policewomen ran considerable

216

risks that were routinely ignored (Beevor, 1990, p. 328). In a further move towards widening women's integration, it was announced in December 1990 that the WRAC would be disbanded.

Not all military women in the UK or the US welcomed these moves away from women-only units. Many American WACs worried that when their corps was abolished in 1978, leading to direct assignment of women to non-combat branches of the Army, their concerns would no longer be represented. Former WACs, interviewed in Helen Rogan's study on women in the US Army, said that integration restricted rather than liberated women because they lost their positions of leadership.

THE LIMITS OF INTEGRATION

Although 86 per cent of all MOS are currently open to enlisted women, the Army still operates a system of direct-combat-probability coding (DCPC) which many find unnecessarily restrictive. Army policy insists that once assigned to an area, female soldiers 'in the event of hostilities will remain with their assigned units and continue to perform their assigned tasks' (Moskos, 1990, p. 73). Several examples from the Gulf War illustrate the point that although women are prohibited from the highest risk positions in the infantry, artillery and armoured divisions, they face great danger. Women serving in transport, communications, supply and even medical units were risking their lives under fire as they regularly crossed into combat zones.[3] The service record of female soldiers reveals that the military's combat exclusion policy has protected women in neither peace nor war. Marine Sgt. Brenda Schroeder and Corporal Lisa Tutt were among 17 service members killed in May 1989 in two separate helicopter crashes; Sgt. Gail Elizabeth McAuley Roberts, assigned to the Task Force Bravo unit in Honduras, was killed while off-duty on Christmas Day 1986; four US Air Force nurses died in Korea and several in Vietnam (D'Amico, 1990, pp. 1–10).

During the Gulf War, as well as Army Specialist Melissa Nealy, Major Rhonda Cornum was taken as prisoner of war; combat medic Tina Garrett had her arm and leg ripped by a land mine; women helicopter pilots and reservists were killed in bombing raids and accidents (*Evening Standard*, 1991).[4] The dangers faced by the combatants on the front line were easily exaggerated by the Pentagon and the press during the war. The largest death toll followed not from the fighting or downed aircraft but from the 33 reservists killed when a Scud missile landed on their barracks. However, these casualties and deaths are hugely outweighed by the destruction wreaked on the civilian populations in Iraq and Kuwait. A former nurse in Vietnam made the point: 'There's no such thing as a safe place during a war.'

One argument against women's participation in combat

assumes that they are unable to defend themselves. As the Vietnam case illustrates, protecting women anywhere in a war-torn country may be physically impossible. The assumption of male protection also masks the reality that most women are highly aware of their own physical vulnerability – whether it is in a combat zone or walking down a darkened city street.

An interesting case in point is the controversy over how much weapons training women should be given to defend themselves in a combat zone. Speaking in Congress, in 1989, Representative Pat Schroeder asked a Pentagon official: 'So let me see if I have this straight. Army policy allows women to be shot first, but they can't be the first to shoot. The logic eludes me' (Stephen, 1990).

American servicewomen are prepared to take the risks and are frustrated if, after training for an occupational speciality, they are suddenly pulled from an operation because it is considered too dangerous. They are also concerned that the Army's policy of barring women from 'routine engagement in direct combat' in practice excludes them from about half the military jobs in the Defense Department.

A female helicopter pilot who was denied a flight assignment in Panama which she felt was due to her, told sociologist Charles Moskos, 'I was insane with anger. After nine years of training they left me out. It was the ultimate slam.' Moskos, who extensively interviewed servicewomen involved in the invasion, found the worst thing for a woman officer was to be removed from an assignment for which she was trained because of the possible exposure to danger (Moskos, 1990, p. 78).

The military's inconsistency in terms of its assignment of servicewomen has also been noted by Molly Yard, the president of America's National Organization for Women, which advocates lifting combat restrictions. According to NOW, the military operates glaring contradictions: Army women are allowed into critical positions in forward support areas but in the Marine Corps they are restricted to back-up areas, usually in administrative and personnel functions; women in the Navy are barred from aircraft carriers but assigned to the oilers which refuel them (Mitchell, 1990).

Twinned with ideological concerns – often voiced as needing to protect women from danger – are keenly guarded professional interests. A British brigadier put the matter bluntly to Anthony Beevor: 'If women are to be taken seriously in the Army, then they must be alongside the men' (Beevor, 1990, p. 339). Brian Green, congressional editor of USAF's official magazine has also noted that, 'Those with combat assignments have the inside track on promotional opportunity. Women cannot compete' (Green, 1990). The Defense Advisory Committee on Women in the Services (DACOWITS) established in 1951 to examine the role of women in

Plate 1

A symbolic representation of the 'Academy of Sciences, Arts and Trades': the frontispiece to Diderot's *Encyclopédie*.

Under a temple of Ionic architecture, Truth is wrapped in a veil and bathed in a ray of light, with Imagination to her left preparing to adorn her. To Truth's right, Reason, wearing a crown, lifts the veil from Truth, while Philosophy snatches it away. At Truth's feet, Theology, on her knees, receives light from on high. Below these are Geometry, holding a scroll; Physics, with her right hand on an air pump; Astronomy, with her crown of stars; Optics, with a microscope and a mirror; Botany, holding a cactus; Chemistry, with a retort and furnace; and Agriculture. Beneath Imagination are different genres of Poetry, along with Painting, Sculpture and Music.

Below the clouds are the arts and the professions, which emanate from the sciences and most of which are pictured as men (Schubinger, 1989).

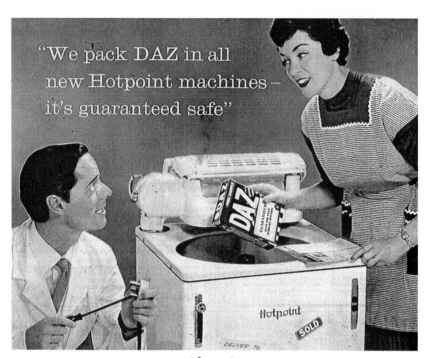

Plate 2
The (male) expert in the white coat.

Plate 3
The obverse of the Nobel medals for chemistry and physics, with both
nature and science represented as women. The inscription, however,
reads 'How good it is that man's life should be enriched by the arts he
has invented.'

Plate 4
Hertha Ayrton in the Girton fire brigade, 1880.

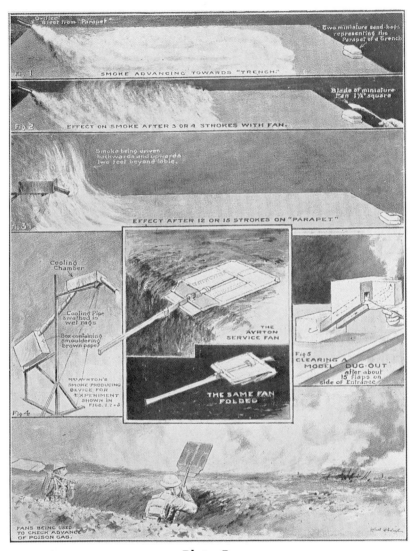

Plate 5

The Ayrton service fan.

Plate 6
Detail from mural entitled 'Modern woman' by Mary Cassatt,
showing women plucking fruits from the tree of science.
From the Women's Building at the World's Columbian Exposition,
Chicago, 1893 (demolished 1896).

Plate 7
Women pilots forming a section of the Air Transport Auxiliary Service of the Royal Air Force ferrying aeroplanes from factory to aerodrome during World War Two.

Plate 8
Tanya Luffman, one of the first group of Wrens to serve on board a Royal Navy warship HMS *Brilliant* in 1990.

AM I *the Woman*
of a YEAR AGO ?

I WONDER if you remember me — you husbands to whom I said last Christmas the things I could not say to my husband?

I was the woman whose husband gave her each Christmas some pretty trinket. The woman whose youth was slipping from her too fast. The woman whose cleaning burdens were too heavy. The woman who wanted, but could not ask for, a Hoover.

I'm not the woman of a year ago.

In one short year I have discovered that youth need not go so swiftly — that cleaning duties need not be burdensome.

For last Christmas my husband did give me a Hoover!

''GIVE HER A HOOVER AND YOU GIVE HER THE BEST''

Plate 9

The husband is encouraged to give his wife a hoover for Christmas, rather than a 'pretty trinket'.

Plate 10
Women and children who have carried woodfuel 12-15 miles into town, Kirtipur, Nepal.

Plate 11
Woman cooking using straw in a simple clay stove, in Kirtipur, Nepal.

the military, supports Green. The committee has stated that current restrictions limit the contributions women can make to national defence and advocates repealing the combat exclusion statute. Among the women Charles Moskos interviewed on active duty, he found many who acknowledged that without combat experience their career possibilities were limited. However, Moskos also found that three-quarters of the women he spoke with thought that women should not be allowed into combat. As one female transport driver described her reservations:

> I'm old-fashioned. I want to be treated like a woman. I don't want people to think I'm a man. I certainly wouldn't want to be in the infantry. A normal woman can't carry a rucksack that the guys can. Even if we could, the guys would hate us for being there. And, let's face it, we would probably make things harder on everybody all round.
>
> (Moskos, 1990, p. 78)

Concerns about being 'treated like a woman' and being a 'normal woman' stem from avoiding confrontations with male colleagues. In order for a woman to survive in this masculine environment she must avoid challenging prescribed notions about male strength and female weakness.

However, among the female officers Moskos spoke with in Panama in December 1989, many also believed that combat-exclusion rules precluded any significant number of women from becoming generals or even full colonels. US army General Pat Foote argues that limiting women's experience in warfare 'develops a whole male cadre and officer corps that doesn't know how to work with women' which prevents them from using women's full capacities. The DCPC, with few exceptions, keeps trained and qualified women from performing their assignments when they are needed (Moskos, 1990, p. 77). A 1989 study found that while the highest ranks – five-, four-, three- and two-star generals – are closed to women, only 13.1 per cent rose to the rank of captain and 15.2 per cent to 2nd lieutenant or ensign (Pentagon, 1990).

In the United States the military establishment has also fought hard in some corners to keep women from entering their top academies. In 1989 the Justice Department launched a law-suit to force the Virginia Military Institute in Lexington to abandon its 150-year-old male-only admission policy. The school is one of two publicly financed military colleges in the US that deny access to women and supporters of the exclusion policy believe standards will fall if integration is forced upon the Institute. However, the women who have entered officers' training schools since 1976, when several were integrated, have faced enormous pressure to perform better than their male colleagues.

The second ideological stumbling block servicewomen face is the male military's need to protect its own interest. As the argument goes, a woman will never have real power within the military because she will never command in combat, so there's no need to waste time and energy in promoting her career. Anthony Beevor reveals that within the British Army, many men still feel threatened when working alongside women:

> [M]ore depressing than the often infantile sexuality which the army seems to engender in men is the day-to-day professional prejudice [with] which both servicewomen and officers have to contend . . . To have a woman promoted over [a man] is seen as a humiliation.
>
> *(Beevor, 1990, p. 337)*

Male officers still assume that servicewomen will quit to get married and have children so they are seldom offered important courses or appointments. While British military policy currently offers women maternity leave, they come under pressure to leave if they are continually denied career advancements.

'NO *REAL* MAN WANTS A WOMAN TO DO HIS FIGHTING FOR HIM': ARGUMENTS AGAINST FEMALE COMBATANTS

As we have already seen, the issue of whether women *should* be allowed into combat may actually be quite academic. The dramatic displays of their participation in the Gulf War brought home the fact that, whatever sentiments are voiced to the contrary, women are on the front line in contemporary battles. The debate about women's entry into combat, as military expert Carolyn Becraft has said, has been overtaken by events (Wheelwright, 1991).

One of the most often cited and vigorously defended reasons for barring women from combat training are innate physiological differences between the sexes. It is often claimed that women's smaller stature and lack of 'upper body strength' make them less useful. Mitchell (1990) cites exhaustive Pentagon studies which reveal that women are 'smaller, weaker and slower than men, in general and this can put them at a disadvantage in many combat situations'. However, these arguments usually ignore the evidence offered by women in guerilla armies who have amply demonstrated their proficiency with weapons. To name only a few recent examples, women have fought with arms in the Tamil Tigers, in the FSLN in Nicaragua and with various armies in the Philippines, Ethiopia, Eritrea and Tigray.[5] None has reported concerns that lack of 'upper body strength' has made women less effective fighters (see also Article 2.1). Moreover, strength may bear little relation to stature and its relation to military performance is undoubtedly influenced by technology as increasingly sophisticated weaponry continually distances the soldier from the enemy forces (D'Amico, 1990, p. 11). In the US military, women are included in almost all areas of technological warfare, including holding the launching keys of nuclear missiles.

Even more revealing, however, Mitchell says women 'pose a serious threat to the honour and integrity of the services' (Mitchell, 1990). All other objections seem to stem from this central concern that women *per se* are incompatible with military structures. Although Mitchell and others rarely draw an explicit equation between masculinity and soldiering, it is assumed. A true soldier strives for the masculine ideal and therefore a woman can never be anything more than a poor imitation. In historical studies, female soldiers who served in all-male regiments identified themselves with 'masculine' values and denied any emotions that might be construed as feminine weakness (Wheelwright, 1989). Since the patriarchal nature of the military has not changed, it would seem that the equation remains intact. The eminent American General Westmoreland, who presided over the conflict in Vietnam, perhaps best describes this concept in his emblematic phrase, 'No *real* man wants a woman to do his fighting for him' (quoted in D'Amico, 1990).

Similar attitudes emerge from arguments that women soldiers on the front line would disrupt the process of 'male bonding'. A key element of this fraternal solidarity during times of war is an important sexual dynamic which always excludes women soldiers who simply cannot participate. A gun, in this context becomes more than a weapon: an American drill sergeant's song starkly reveals its phallic metaphor: 'This is my weapon, this is my gun/ This is for business, this is for fun' (quoted in Brownmiller, 1975, p. 85). In the 1989 film, *Casualties of War*, based on the true story of a Vietnamese woman's gang rape by US soldiers, a sergeant sings this ditty as he walks towards her, giving the words an even more sinister meaning. He grabs his crotch as he sings the word 'weapon' while he hoists his rifle on the line, 'this is for fun'. Killing becomes pleasure and sexual pleasure – rape – an act of war; a penis and an M-16 are interchangeable. Therefore, a woman with a gun has only half the equation since she lacks a real 'weapon'. Modern images are more 'romantic' or even erotic: see Plate 8.

Women's relationship to guns has always uneasily disrupted men's assumption of rape as a spoil of war. In Germany during the 1930s, a group of officers referred to the Russian women soldiers in the Red Army as rifle-women or *Flintenweiber*; according to historian Klaus Theweleit, the word *Flinte* in Germany was used from about 1919 on to designate guns or any description of weapons but also referred to the penis, prostitutes or a castrating woman. In Nazi propaganda the Soviet rifle-women were portrayed as sadistic, bestialized and devoid of all human feeling (Theweleit, 1987). Ironically, the universal fear that women soldiers are desexed or even dehumanized by combat experience is precisely what enables male soldiers to rape civilian women. To the US soldiers, Vietnamese women were a convenient target for all their frustration, hatred and unexpressed fear. Sex and murder became interchangeable.

Cynthia Enloe has written of how women are the counterpoint to 'male bonding' when it is instilled through collective actions such as visiting a brothel or gang rape. Women's presence on the battlefield would destroy the pretence that men are single-mindedly fighting for 'their women and children' at home. This would force the military to abandon the notion that men are entitled to a superior social position as defenders of the nation, peace, justice, freedom etc.

Intriguingly, sociologist Judith Hicks Stiehm has found that when women are defenders and no longer confined to the category of the 'protected', they are able to rid themselves of disabilities which attend dependency: low esteem, poor education and little sense of responsibility. Perhaps the only conclusion to be drawn from this particular objection to women's combat training is that if they can learn how to avoid becoming victims, men's power over them in other areas of society would be threatened (D'Amico, 1990, p. 11).

There are two final issues concerning the acceptance of women's integration. One is women's desire to combine career and having a family. Pregnancy is often cited as a compelling reason for the military not to train women for command positions. Studies, however, have found that US servicewomen lose less time off work, even when having a baby, than the average serviceman does through sickness, going absent without leave or substance-abuse problems (Beevor, 1990, p. 333). The second issue is sexual harassment. A Pentagon survey reported in the *Washington Times* (12 September 1990) found that 64 per cent of American military women who responded said they had been harassed in some way – from whistles and jokes to rape. A study of a Navy boot camp over an 18-month period, reported in the *Washington Post* (22 October 1990) showed 24 rapes or sexual assaults reported, while only one in 13 cases resulted in court-martial proceedings, thereby contributing to an atmosphere in the camp making women feel like second-class citizens. Investigation revealed that often the worst offenders were the commanding officers to whom women were supposed to report if they experienced any difficulties.

CONCLUSION

At the heart of the military's refusal to integrate women fully into the armed forces lies a number of unanswered questions about their relationship to combat, and to the technologies of combat. As we have seen, the military needs women to offset declining male recruitment. Concurrently, however, military policy sets artificial boundaries around definitions of combat to keep women from gaining real power and authority. Those who 'man' the latest equipment – worth millions of pounds – are still the nation's wartime heroes. Ideological considerations such as fears about women's sexuality, their need for maternity leave, their perceived physical limitations and their interference with the mysterious process of 'male bonding' have kept them out of the most technologically sophisticated occupations.

Notes

1   See Hacker (1981), Trustram (1984), Summers (1988) and Wheelwright (1989) for further information about the historical position of women within European militaries.

2   For more information about Vietnam nurses' experiences, see Saywell (1985) and Van Devanter (1983).

3   To mention but one example, Melissa A. Nealy, a Marine Specialist 4th Class with the 223rd Transport Company was taken as a prisoner of war by the Iraqi Army with her fellow driver David Lockhart at the Battle of Kafji in Saudi Arabia on 31 January 1991. It was the first time an American woman had ever been taken prisoner as a soldier and it shocked the Western media to realize how close to combat these servicewomen were working.

4   See also *Facts about Women in the Persian Gulf War*, Women's Research and Education Institute, Washington, DC, 1991. For more about Iraqi and Kuwaiti women casualties, see *Women in the Front Line* from Amnesty International (1991).

5   For further reading see 'Tamil Tigress', *Washington Times* (3 April 1990), Randall (1980) and Hammond (1990).

Article 3.7
SCIENCE, TECHNOLOGY AND DEVELOPMENT: THE IMPACT ON THE STATUS OF WOMEN
Radha Chakravarthy

The significant and largely unused reservoir of talent and work power of women needs to be placed in a position to make its contribution to the development process and to improve the standards of living and productivity of society. But this is not happening in the development process at present. While science and technology provide the foundations for wealth and development, the benefits of development have been generally unevenly distributed. In particular, benefits have not accrued equally with respect to aspects of the quality of life that are not normally included when measuring economic development. Women often have a keen sense of such unquantified measures of quality of life. In this context, the selection, design and development of technologies assume a great deal of importance. This relates largely to the selection of technologies in the rural context since rural development and the application of science and technology to further it is currently a priority item in many countries. This is not to say that there are technologies for women as such, but in formulating policies for development and shaping its direction it has to be kept in view that technologies and technological change affect large numbers of women.

Recognizing the need to apply science and technology so that it will benefit women, the Indian Sixth Plan document (Ch. 19) argues:

- The question of development activities related to women vis-à-vis Science and Technology has two aspects. First, there is the contribution by women to the development of Science and Technology. Second, one has to consider as to how Science and Technology can contribute to improvement in the life and status of women generally ...

- Application of Science and Technology to the improvement of the life and status of women will depend upon the development of home technologies, suitable agricultural technologies and technologies for improvement of productivity ...

- There is greater need to develop appropriate technologies for those working in the small and unorganized sector.

This is particularly applicable to women facing serious occupational hazards in several professions leading to avoidable health problems. There is also a need for co-ordinated research projects to find methods to improve the production efficiency and reduction of drudgery in the occupations of women.

(Planning Commission)

Technological change can have both favourable and unfavourable effects on the position of women. A substantial number of writers have brought home the fact that women suffer negatively from technological and socio-economic changes brought about by the development process (Jain, 1985; Dey, 1975; Palmer, 1975). While technological changes in general have benefited society in terms of its quality of life for the society as a whole, the significant forms of technological change affecting women are not innovations aimed directly at them. Rather they are the indirect consequences of planned and unplanned innovations in the production system.

WOMEN AND TECHNOLOGICAL CHANGE

The literature on technological change underlines an influential and important paradigm called the 'Employment, Productivity and Income Distribution paradigm' (Iftikhar, 1978a). Changes in technology have varied kinds of impact on different classes of workers. As an illustration, the effect on women of the introduction of high-yielding varieties (HYV) of crops has been examined by Palmer (1978). She points out that HYV innovations affect all points of a crop cycle, which includes land preparation, pre-harvest and post-harvest tasks in which both men and women engage at various points. She describes the effects of the introduction of this technology on women compared with men:

> The new technology has probably led to men doing some work on more days of the year – a fall in seasonal unemployment or a fall in underemployment on an annual basis. Hence, men's greater labour effort would entail a more even spread of work throughout the year with no extra physical strain. On an annual basis employed men would have experienced an increase in productivity, and if they use some machinery, an increase in hourly productivity. Peasant household women's greatest effort has to be seen in more hours in the fields on the days they do go into the fields, and probably more days in the week that they go into the field. Combined with their household tasks, peasant women do not usually experience seasonal unemployment (or any unemployment) and their

additional field work would rise but this, as with men's, would be due to more work effort. On an hourly basis there is no reason to believe there is any increase in women's labour productivity.

(Palmer, 1978, p. 8)

Some general conclusions can be drawn from Palmer's work and the existing literature. First, most significant forms of technological change affecting women may not be aimed directly at them. Rarely are interventions made in the kind of work that women do and the way they do it. For large numbers of women, the most significant forms of technological change are more likely to be the indirect consequences of both planned and unplanned innovations.

The second conclusion concerns the importance of conceptualizing the manner in which women's work is done and in particular the social relations that surround it. The division of labour is such that gender differentiation marks the allocation of social agents to work tasks and to the processes of work (Whitehead, 1980). Women's work is not always characterized by the same employment relations nor the social relations as for men. Palmer maintains that discussions of the employment effects of high-yielding varieties took place largely in terms of male employment because female labour was regarded as economically insignificant and *socially and politically invisible.*

The third essence of technological changes is that they have by and large strengthened the dominant position of the male head of household. Implied thereby is that there has been no attempt to deconstruct the family or household into constituent members for reckoning women's work. Two illustrations can be cited in support. With the introduction of technology for biogas[1] production in the rural areas, some simple, uncomplicated equipment was installed in the backyards of rural households which maintained reasonably good cattle population. While men control and operate the equipment women continue to collect the dung and pour it into the ponds as they were doing before. Men secure some training for repairing the equipment, but women are generally excluded from securing this simple knowledge. Similarly in urban areas in offices, equipment like electronic typewriters, Fax machines and computers are used, but it is men who are given access to training wherein replacement of parts, maintenance and repair are taught. Women employees no doubt use the equipment as they were using the traditional equipment, but it is men who exercise control over it in terms of maintenance and operational requirements. These two illustrations are evidence of the unfortunate reality that technological changes often bestow status and power on men leaving the women where they were.

The process of socio-economic change affects men and women differently and promotes a gender gap rather than gender equality. Much current empirical work confines itself to an analysis of class-based inequalities and not to dealing with gender-related questions. For instance, it does not cover the issues like the failure of women to benefit from increased production and productivity, the problems of uptake and of reaching women and the apparent intractability of the increasing differentiation between men and women in relation to the modern sectors of the economy (Griffin, 1974).

That women are potential independent producers rather than family members needs to be recognized. An essential requirement is for women to have unimpeded and secure access to productive resources. In most non-industrialized country situations, women do not have ownership rights to land. They have only use rights. Even where full rights of ownership exist, the size of the women's land holding is usually less than that of men. Their occupancy tends to be insecure. The socially dominant position of men has always been critical in determining access where there is competition for land. The household is by and large a set of social relationships for allocating resources differentially to its members, who occupy different positions within it.

A woman's status in the household creates a mediated relationship. Land, for instance, is allocated between men and women not on economic criteria but on social criteria. Very few women gain access to the cheap sources of credit. Many schemes hardly ever consider that women might be able to utilize credit; yet others stipulate conditions that they could not even fulfil. Government agencies treat the household as a unit with the husband as the economically active member and it is with him that they deal (Ward, 1970; Sridharan, 1975).

EFFECT OF AGRICULTURAL MODERNIZATION

Agarwal (1983) has examined the empirical evidence available on the effect of technological changes in agriculture particularly of modernization schemes on rural women in the Third World. She says that the commonality in the experience of women is striking in that the result of innovations in agricultural technology is that women are generally left worse off or less well off than the men of their culture and class. The innovations have an inherent gender bias which affects the distribution of costs and benefits between men and women. The introduction of rice-milling in Bangladesh and Java led to destitution among women who depended on manual rice-processing for their livelihood. Manual dehusking of rice is an important source of female wage employment in the rural areas of Bangladesh and often is the only source. The grain-processing mills which mechanize the process tend to employ only men; many women have been displaced and become destitute. A similar situation has been noted in Java.

Women's subordination manifests itself in inequalities in access to productive resources, in the roles that they assume in the private and public spheres, and in the sharing of the burden of work between male and female household members.

In joint male–female co-operative societies, women are seldom observed to participate in the actual management (Dixon, 1978). Women appear to receive a disproportionately small share of the resources generated by and through such co-operative ventures (Greeley, 1981). Women from poorer rural households need to have greater control over productive resources and over the product of their labour if many of the adverse effects suffered by them as a result of technological changes are to be stemmed. If the overall structure of a country is highly inegalitarian, achieving this control may be very difficult. Wider-based measures to promote greater material and ideological equality between the genders are necessary conditions in most Third World countries for bringing about a fairer distribution of the benefits and burdens of technological change.

WOMEN'S EMPLOYMENT IN INDUSTRY

As in the case of agriculture, the experience of development in the industrial sector has also been unfavourable to women. Technological progress in industry has no doubt widened women's employment opportunities but has generally pushed them into less skilled, laborious jobs. In areas like metal trading, textiles, clothing, leather, foot-wear, food and printing when a new machine is installed the tendency is to substitute male for female workers and to keep women workers on older and non-automatic machinery (Ela, 1985).

In developing countries scarcely one per cent of the industrial labour force is female. Women account for about 30 per cent of the industrial employment in Asia, 15 per cent in Latin America and 20 per cent in Africa. They form less than 20 per cent of the industrial labour force in India (UNIDO, 1984).

While women's industrial employment has increased in several countries in recent times, traditional social values often do not permit women to participate in economic activities outside their homes. Even when women are engaged in productive activities, they work mainly at home either in household activity or as home-based producers. The growth in women's industrial employment is selective, being confined mainly to those countries which are actively participating in the spurt in international trade in manufactured commodities. A large number of South East Asian countries – Taiwan, Hong Kong, Republic of Korea, Singapore, Thailand, Malaysia – fall into this category. This is true even of India, where growth in women's employment is confined to a group of light consumer goods industries, producing non-traditional manufactured goods for the export market. But the recent increase in women's industrial employment in developing countries is small compared to the size of the female population or the workforce in those countries. It has made no significant difference to women's status, since it has done little to break the isolation of women in the industrial work force. Women are still largely confined to a few 'woman-prone' industries where they form the overwhelming bulk of the workforce. Also this development has, as yet, not overcome the shortfall in women's earnings as compared to those of men (Benerjee, 1985, p. 18).

OUTLOOK FOR EMPLOYMENT

In the developing countries subsistence crafts are losing ground as communications improve and as local materials like wood, cane and grass become scarce. Women who have taken to traditional pro- cessing, manufacturing, services or repair operations are being gradually deprived of their occupations and employment. Even where they continue in such occupations, women continue to be ignorant of market prospects and mechanisms and therefore are subjected to greater exploitation than before. For example, Bengal's rough silk material, woven from yarn hand-spun from damaged cocoons, is now in demand and Bengal is importing damaged co- coons from all over India for the industry, but the women who spin the yarn continue to work in the traditional way, unaware of the changed market conditions.

Women's jobs have been susceptible to technological obsol- escence. This is because they are generally repetitive and have low skill and status. Machines can easily replace them. As an illustration, in the bidi industry in India, the preparation of the tobacco for rolling was originally done by women. Recently these operations have been mechanized and women's annual work-days have reduced from 200 million to 70,000 (*Economic Times*, 1984). Similarly, rationalization and modernization of the Indian textile industry led to the reduction of women's jobs by two-thirds between 1955 and 1965 (Benerjee, 1985, p. 26).

Certain lines of demarcation between male and female occu- pations are clearly visible:

1   The most important of these is the tendency to give women less than equal access to means of production. There is less capital input per unit of labour either in the form of improved tools or in the form of arrangements for using non-manual sources of power in women's occupations. Available information shows that, for oil grinding, the traditional Indian technique uses a wheel and animal power, but in French-speaking Africa it is done by women by hand

using rough stones. In Morocco women make pottery at home by hand and men do it with wheels in shops. In Indonesia women do 'batik' work at home by hand and men use screen printers and machine rollers (Trouve, 1980; Lewis, no date).

2   Women suffer from lack of access to technical training and knowledge opened up by modern science and from lack of proper tools. Women have thus become vulnerable to the onslaught of technological obsolescence. In East Africa the women's hand-made soap industry is facing extinction due to the popularity of imported soap because of its colour and smell. The latter is getting the better of the traditional technique for making soap with palm oil (Iftikhar, 1978b).

3   Women are not given adequate protection in occupations where the tasks are physically harmful. This is because they are not provided with adequate tools. In Africa women clean melons in a standing position and are required to bend 600 to 700 times a day to soak their cloth in a tub of water for which no tables are provided. Many women consequently have developed back problems and muscle soreness (ILO, 1978).

4   Women's jobs have no certainty in the future. Because of technical obsolescence or because of men taking jobs from women, an insecure future stares at women. Women's experience in India has been that on the upswing of the trade cycle, they got less than a proportionate share in the increased employment (Benerjee, 1985, p. 38).

5   Women are tied down to drudgery and hard work for very low returns because of poor techniques, inadequate tools and control by familial intermediaries. There is a consistent tendency to put a lower value on women's work and for women to accept it. The status of women in the labour market is a mirror reflection of their status in their families and societies. The tradition of women's submission to patriarchal control is still ingrained in most societies.

New technical equipment often results in the abolition of posts and work for women: for instance, in telecommunications the operator's job normally held by women is done away with after automation is introduced; computers eliminate clerical and book-keeping work for women. Thus, science which is designed to alleviate human misery has adverse consequences in practice for women. Ela Bhatt (1985) has forcefully argued: 'Unless women get organized against the onslaught of technology or in favour of suitable technology, the technology storm will sweep them away from the world of work.'

CONCLUSION

The relationship between technology and socio-economic systems is a complex one from the perspective of women. New technologies have often displaced women from their traditional avenues of employment and even where they have had access to improved employment in industries like electronics – export-oriented industries – they are confined to a limited range of occupations and skills. Women are usually hit adversely by technological development for several reasons. In most developing countries they are heavily represented in the subsistence crafts which are often an extension of household activities like dairy production, fish curing and so on. In areas like textiles and cane and wood products, women are an important part of the workforce. But in all these areas, women are provided with inadequate or crude tools and traditional techniques which leave them with the same status as before despite scientific and technological development. They have no access to technical training and knowledge. Where modernization takes place to meet the demands of growing markets, new skills and tools are made available to men and not to women.

Starting from the premise that technologies per se have no inherent gender bias, but that there is skewed distribution of assets, resources and knowledge between genders, the impact of the new technologies needs to be assessed in a total context. The magnitude of the problem is so large that isolated activities may not meet the requirements of women engaged particularly in the non-formal and unorganized sectors. If technology and women's employment are to be interwoven, there must be not only quantitative participation but equitable distribution of assets, wages and productivity, skill formation and training, and institutional and organizational support particularly with credit and marketing.

Note

1   Biogas technology involves the production of a gaseous fuel, methane, from dung. It can be done on a small scale, making it suitable for rural development.

4
CONSUMING SCIENCE AND TECHNOLOGY

This final chapter contains the most diverse selection of articles, diverse in terms of both content and style. Feminist social scientists have argued that activities which take place in the public arena, in particular in paid work, cannot be separated from activities which take place in the private arena of domestic life, and our attempt to make a somewhat similar separation in the organization of the material for this book demonstrates how permeable any boundary is between the two. The focus of this chapter is on women as the end-users of technological artefacts and systems, but the boundary between users and makers is not a clear-cut one: stove users, for example, become stove makers (Article 4.2), and computer users can become creative programmers (Article 4.4).

All women (and all men) are consumers of science and technology. In the developed world what is consumed is more often the product of high technology, and in the underdeveloped world, more often, but not exclusively, the product of low – or obsolete Western – technology. A comparison between the articles by Judy Wajcman (4.1) and Bina Agarwal (4.2) – both about domestic technology – highlights the gulf between women in industrialized and in non-industrialized countries in terms of material conditions and the technology available to them to act on these conditions.

Consumption is not a passive process, although it is sometimes presented as if it were by those who suggest that women are simply exploited by industrial capitalism. Such economic or technological determinism has a depressing view of human beings and gives no credit for the creative way in which we all interact with our material environment in order to optimize the conditions under which we live. In this process there are conflicts of interest between people, and between people and other aspects of the living world. The ecology and the animal rights movements (both of which involve many women) are examples of organizations trying to resolve these ethical conflicts and to have a significant impact on the technology of food production and distribution in particular.

Chapter 3 described how the social organization of science and technology combines with the way in which intellectual and manual skills are defined in order to erect barriers to women's involvement in creating science and technology; women were also

232

shown attacking these barriers and surmounting them. The articles in this chapter describe a similar process occurring in other areas of women's lives. Cat Cox (Article 4.5), for example, argues that the ecology movement has made the activity of consuming both public and political, in a way that enables women to influence the application of science and the development of technology.

The concepts of public and private as definitions both of geographical place and gendered spheres of action were developed in feminist theory of the 1970s. If the social division reflected by the phrase 'a woman's place is in the home' is repressive to women, why and how did it come about that women became restricted to the private sphere only? The social construction of these divisions is discussed in a companion volume (McDowell and Pringle, 1992). This book is concerned with questions about the nature of the physical and technological systems which are part of the social infrastructure. Architecture, for example, does not determine social relations but it organizes them physically and supports them symbolically. Domestic houses in particular embody ideology about gender in their design, as do domestic artefacts. Architecture is also a male profession. It was a group of feminist architects – Matrix – who analysed this ideology and described how it was reflected in the design of domestic architecture (Matrix, 1984).

Article 4.1 by Wajcman discusses the technology of housework, that labour which seems to belong to women everywhere in the world. Before the publication of *The Sociology of Housework* by Ann Oakley in 1974, housework *as work* was invisible with respect to social analysis. Household work was of more interest to historians who looked at the changes in the nature of the tasks, and the effect of social and technological change. Joan Vanek (1974) examined records of how much time housewives spent on their tasks (time-budgets) between 1920 and 1960 and found the hours worked little changed. Yet during that period a variety of technical developments had been applied in homes; these were presumed to have made housework easier and quicker. Why was it, then, that women reported no significant difference in their hours of housework?

In the 1980s the new feminist understanding of housework and the historical analysis of technological change came together in a number of books: *More Work for Mother* by Ruth Schwartz Cowan (1983) and *Never Done: a history of American housework* by Susan Strasser (1982) – both using US data, and *A Woman's Work is Never Done* by Caroline Davidson (1982), using UK data and illustrations. All, as their titles suggest, argued that technical developments applied to housework had not reduced the labour of housework but had somehow reinforced it. The conclusion being drawn by these writers is encapsulated in the folk song where a woman is bemoaning

233

her fate as she sweeps:

> 'Last night in my dreams I was stationed forever
>
> On a far little rock in the midst of the sea.
>
> My one chance of life was a ceaseless endeavour
>
> To sweep off the waves as they swept over me.
>
> Alas t'was no dream – ahead I behold it.
>
> I see I am helpless my fate to avert.'
>
> She lay down her broom, her apron she folded,
>
> She lay down and died and was buried in dirt.

Wajcman describes and analyses the changing feminist debate about the technology of housework. The household became a 'respectable' focus of non-feminist research and theory in the 1980s with work on the 'post-industrial' society. This has a strong 'futurist' element, and a 'technicist' bias, predicting a new industrial revolution for the home based on the introduction of information technology. This work contradicts feminist historical analysis since it argues that technology has increased the productivity of women's work in the home, whereas feminists have seen housework expanding to fill the time available, and domestic technology serving to reinforce a sexual division of labour in the home as well as an ideology of housework. Although supporting the feminist analysis, Wajcman suggests that it has, at times, erred in the opposite direction in refusing to acknowledge the power of technology to improve women's lives. It has remained a problem for many feminists that women have chosen, for example, to buy washing machines for individual family use rather than to wash clothes in communal facilities such as launderettes. In theory the launderette could reduce women's isolation and contribute to those neighbourhood support networks that feminism has complained have been lost in modern, individualized capitalism. However, perhaps a focus on the social relations has detracted from an understanding of the nature of the tasks themselves and the way in which women make choices that do, overall, lessen their physical labour and increase their personal flexibility. Wajcman argues for a more sophisticated analysis of the technology grounded in a theory of patriarchal and capitalist relations.

Agarwal's article, 'Cold hearths and barren slopes: the woodfuel crisis in the Third World', shows that an exclusive concern with the impact of technology on the domestic lives of women in industrialized countries can lead to conclusions which are questionable when applied to the lives of rural women in non-industrialized countries, where there is an absence of systems and resources. Where there is no infrastructure of services such as gas, electricity and water for domestic consumption, women's domestic work is arduous and physically debilitating, and providing fuel for cooking and heating is one of the most punishing tasks:

> Throughout the world, women are carrying loads up to 35 kilograms over distances as much as ten kilometres from home. The weight exceeds the maximum weights permissible by law in many countries, which typically prohibit manual carrying by women of loads greater than 20 kilograms. These heavy burdens damage the spine and cause problems with childbearing. The back-breaking work of collecting, cutting and transporting wood, exacerbated by poor nutrition, undermines women's health still further, and the longer they have to walk the more they are affected.

(Dankelman and Davidson, 1988)

Agarwal describes the problems of implementing technological developments which would improve the domestic lives of poor rural women, the greatest barriers tend to be ideological and social. Agarwal's case study illustrates in more detail some of the issues discussed by Chakravarthy in Article 3.7. She describes the use of a low-technology, participant design process which has produced successful, improved versions of domestic stoves that are within the resources available to the rural poor, and which are appropriate to the cultural needs of the community, in fact 'appropriate' technology. The participative process she describes, where women teach each other skills and so develop expertise both individually and within the community, would be regarded as exemplary by many feminists and others concerned to find ways to transfer technology to less industrialized countries in ways that take into account the needs and lifestyles of the users.

The poem 'Dry' by Jean Binta Breeze (Article 4.3) represents the voice of a poor woman who could be anywhere in the world from a ghetto in New York to a small Indian village. In it the problem of improving women's lives is seen as one about who controls access to technology and resources.

The notion of the post-industrial world described by Wajcman is based on a belief in the power of information technology to transform society in both the public and the private spheres. Article 4.4 reviews feminist writing on the gendered nature of computing and the ways in which women have – and have not – been involved with it. One of the sources of women's alienation from computers is that its genesis as a military device has produced a particular language and a culture of computing (a discourse). It is useful to read this article as a companion to Wheelright (Article 3.6) to get a sense of the military/information technology relationship from both sides. Initial feminist work on computers focused on their impact on women's employment. There seemed no good reason why this new technology should improve the employment conditions of women or transform the gendered inequality of the workplace. There seemed instead every reason to believe that conditions would worsen. In the early 1990s the most pessimistic predictions have not been fulfilled – work tasks have changed, new jobs and skills have appeared – but the gendered structure of the workplace remains basically unchanged. Fears about the technology have been replaced in some cases by grassroots enthusiasm as women try to come to grips with it. This has been paralleled by feminist writing which now attempts to analyse whether and how the technology can be transformed or developed to suit a feminist agenda. For example, since the early 1980s the London-based group, Microsyster, has concentrated on providing computer access and training for women's groups. Whether you believe a technology is capable of being transformed to purposes other than those for which it was intended, as Wajcman suggests happened with the telephone, depends on how embedded you believe values are in the technology itself.

Article 4.5, 'Ecofeminism' by Cat Cox, a member of the UK Women's Environment Network, is an example of the direction of some of the most recent, and still minority, feminist thinking on the relationship between the practice of science and technology and the sustainability of life on Earth. Article 4.2 illustrated the close relationship between environmental conditions and women's lives and showed how a deterioration in the first led directly to a deterioration in the second.

Ecofeminism and the Green Movement in general are Western in their origin but global in their focus; they also draw on the beliefs and practices of other cultures to illustrate some of the more exploitative facets of industrialized culture, and to illustrate that alternatives exist. The ecofeminist critique of scientific method is similar to those discussed in the first chapter of this book, although the references to Daly and Griffin as sources of inspiration demonstrate an essentialist position which sees women as having a special relationship to Nature. However, this relationship is revalued as positive and powerful, unlike the patriarchal versions of the same position which saw this relationship as one of weakness. As Cox explains, ecofeminism covers a range of positions: her own which is interested in the relationship between women's spirituality and a special relationship to Nature is different from that of more economically or technologically based positions. However, ecofeminism is also an umbrella which allows people with a variety of theoretical positions to use their combined strength. It is another demonstration of the more optimistic attitude of feminists in the 1990s that technology and science are not monolithic and determinist, and can be changed.

We have chosen a piece of fiction to end this volume. For many women who feel intimidated or ignorant with respect to science and technology, the only way to re-think what is desirable is through fictional narrative. Utopias and dystopias have been important in feminist fiction of the 1970s and '80s; often they deal with the effect of technological development on gender relations. We think of science fiction very much as part of Western literature but 'Sultana's dream' is a special example of this tradition: it was written by a Bengali woman at the turn of the century, a woman who cannot have read any other feminist Utopias, and who herself never wrote for publication in English again. But her imaginative solution to the problems of sexual oppression in nineteenth-century India contains the notion of a female science with non-aggressive purposes and methods on which a peaceful (but not pacifist) feminist society could be built. It reflects a Victorian faith in the power of science, used for good, as the basis of a just society, as well as one which would overthrow patriarchy. It is impossible in the industrialized world for feminists to have such a faith in the liberatory potential of science any longer. It reminds us that the debates by Harding and Fox Keller in Chapter 1 are now sophisticated and academic, but the seeds of the ideas have been in the heads of women in different cultures and historical periods. They may more easily be first expressed by many women through the imagination, before they can be realized in scientific theory and technological developments. But it is in the interaction of the two that women will reinvent their worlds.

Gill Kirkup

Article 4.1
DOMESTIC TECHNOLOGY: LABOUR-SAVING OR ENSLAVING?

Judy Wajcman

> Out there in the land of household work there are small
> industrial plants which sit idle for the better part of every
> working day; there are expensive pieces of highly
> mechanized equipment which only get used once or twice
> a month; there are consumption units which weekly
> trundle out to their markets to buy 8 ounces of this
> nonperishable product and 12 ounces of that one. There
> are also workers who do not have job descriptions, time
> clocks, or even paychecks.
>
> (*Cowan, 1979*)

The introduction of technology into the home has especially affected
women's lives and the work that goes on in the household. Indeed,
it has been suggested that we should conceive of an industrial
revolution as having occurred in the home too, that 'the change
from the laundry tub to the washing machine is no less profound
than the change from the hand loom to the power loom' (Cowan,
1976, pp. 8–9).

[· · ·]

This [article] begins by looking at feminist material on the
mechanization of housework and then considers the work of post-
industrialists on the impact of technological innovation in the home.
By way of challenge to these latter theorists, I go on to examine
some alternative approaches to individualized housework. In the
last section I look at some of the key factors operating in the design
process of specific household appliances. My aim is to explore the
way the design and promotion of domestic technologies have been
shaped by existing ideologies of gender.

INDUSTRIALIZATION OF THE HOME AND CREATION OF THE HOUSEWIFE

... [D]espite massive technological changes in the home, such as
running water, gas and electric cookers, central heating, washing
machines, refrigerators, ... studies show that household work in
the industrialized countries still accounts for approximately half of
the total working time ...

238

The conventional wisdom is that the forces of technological change and the growth of the market economy have progressively absorbed much of the household's role in production. The classic formulation of this position is to be found in Talcott Parsons' (1956) functionalist sociology of the family. He argues that industrialization removed many functions from the family system, until all that remains is consumption. For Parsons, the wife–mother function is the primary socialization of children and the stabilization of the adult personality; it thus becomes mainly expressive or psychological, as compared with the instrumental male world of 'real' work. More generally, modern technology is seen as having either eliminated or made less arduous almost all women's former household work, thus freeing women to enter the labour force. To most commentators, the history of housework is the story of its elimination.

Although it is true that industrialization transformed households, the major changes in the pattern of household work during this period were not those that the traditional model predicts. Ruth Schwartz Cowan (1983), in her celebrated American study of the development of household technology between 1860 and 1960, argued ... that ... the view that the household has passed from being a unit of production to a unit of consumption, with the attendant assumption that women have nothing left to do at home, is grossly misleading. Rather, the processes by which the American home became industrialized were much more complex and heterogeneous than this.

Cowan provides the following explanations for the failure of the 'industrial revolution in the home' to ease or eliminate household tasks. Mechanization gave rise to a whole range of new tasks which, although not as physically demanding, were as time-consuming as the jobs they had replaced. The loss of servants meant that even middle-class housewives had to do all the housework themselves. Further, although domestic technology did raise the productivity of housework, it was accompanied by rising expectations of the housewife's role which generated more domestic work for women. Finally, mechanization has only had a limited effect on housework because it has taken place within the context of the privatized, single-family household.

It is important to distinguish between different phases of industrialization that involved different technologies. Cowan characterizes twentieth-century technology as consisting of eight interlocking systems: food, clothing, health care, transportation, water, gas, electricity, and petroleum products. While some technological systems do fit the model of a shift from production to consumption, others do not.

Food, clothing, and health care systems do fit the 'production to consumption' model. By the beginning of the twentieth century, the purchasing of processed foods and ready-made clothes instead of home production was becoming common. Somewhat later, the health-care system moved out of the household and into centralized institutions. These trends continued with increasing momentum during the first half of this century.

The transportation system and its relation to changing consumption patterns, however, exemplifies the shift in the other direction. During the nineteenth century, household goods were often delivered, mail-order catalogues were widespread and most people did not spend much time buying goods. With the advent of the motor car after the First World War, all this began to change. By 1930 the automobile had become the prime mode of transportation in the United States. Delivery services of all kinds began to disappear and the burden of providing transportation shifted from the seller to the buyer (Strasser, 1982). Meanwhile women gradually replaced men as the drivers of transport, more and more business converted to the 'self-service' concept, and households became increasingly dependent upon housewives to provide the service. The time spent on shopping tasks expanded until today the average time spent is eight hours per week, the equivalent of an entire working day.

In this way, households moved from the net consumption to the net production of transportation services, and housewives became the transporters of purchased goods rather than the receivers of them. The purchasing of goods provides a classic example of a task that is generally either ignored altogether or considered as 'not work', in spite of the time, energy and skill required, and its essential role in the national economy.

In charting the historical development of the last four household systems, water, gas, electricity and petroleum, Cowan reveals further deficiencies in the 'production to consumption' model. These technological changes totally reorganized housework yet their impact was ambiguous. On the one hand they radically increased the productivity of housewives: 'modern technology enabled the American housewife of 1950 to produce singlehandedly what her counterpart of 1850 needed a staff of three or four to produce; a middle-class standard of health and cleanliness' (1983, p. 100). On the other hand, while eliminating much drudgery, modern labour-saving devices did not reduce the necessity for time-consuming labour . . . Thus there is no simple cause-and-effect relation between the mechanization of homes and changes in the volume and nature of household work.

Indeed the disappearance of paid and unpaid servants (unmarried daughters, maiden aunts, grandparents and children fall into the latter category) as household workers, and the imposition of the entire job on the housewife herself, was arguably the most

240

significant change... The disappearance of domestic servants stimulated the mechanization of homes, which in turn may have hastened the disappearance of servants...

This change in the structure of the household labour force was accompanied by a remodelled ideology of housewifery. The development in the early years of this century of the domestic science movement, the germ theory of disease and the idea of 'scientific motherhood', led to new exacting standards of housework and childcare[1] ... Housework began to be represented as an expression of the houswife's affection for her family.

With home and housework acquiring heightened emotional significance, it became impossible to rationalize household production along the lines of industrial production (Ravetz, 1965). Cowan graphically captures the completely 'irrational' use of technology and labour within the home, because of the dominance of single-family residences and the private ownership of correspondingly small-scale amenities. 'Several million American women cook supper each night in several million separate homes over several million stoves' (Cowan, 1979, p. 59) ... This is not an inevitable, immutable situation, but one whose transformation depends on the transformation of gender relations.

The relationship between domestic technology and household labour thus provides a good illustration of the general problem of technological determinism, where technology is said to have resulted in social changes. The greatest influences on time spent on housework have in fact come from non-technological changes: the demise of domestic servants, changing standards of hygiene and childcare, as well as the ideology of the housewife and the symbolic importance of the home.

GENDER SPECIALIZATION OF HOUSEHOLD TECHNOLOGY

If domestic technology has not directly reduced the time spent on housework, has it had any effect on the degree of gender specialization of household labour? ...

Available evidence suggests that domestic technology has reinforced the traditional sexual division of labour between husbands and wives and locked women more firmly into their traditional roles. Because technologies have been used to privatize work, they have cumulatively hindered a reallocation of household labour.

The allocation of housework between men and women is in fact much the same in households where the wife is employed and those in which she is not. Husbands in all social classes do little housework. Where men do undertake housework, they usually perform non-routine tasks at intervals rather than continually, and frequently the work is outdoors. This is in marked contrast to women's housework, the dominant characteristic of which is that it is never complete.

Task-specific technologies may develop in such a way that women can take over tasks previously done by other family members. For example, Charles Thrall (1982) found that in families which had a garbage disposal unit, husbands and young children were significantly less involved in taking care of the garbage and wives were more likely to do it exclusively. Similarly with dishwashers, which are cited as one of the few appliances that do the job better and save time, husbands were less likely to help occasionally with the dishes.

[· · ·]

The household division of labour is reflected in the differential use of technologies, as Cockburn's (1985) study confirms. Few of the women in her sample used a hammer or screwdriver for more than hanging the occasional picture or mending the proverbial plug. Fewer still would use an electric drill or even a lawnmower, as 'men were proprietorial about these tools and the role that goes with them' (p. 219). Generally, women used utensils and implements – the dishwasher, vacuum cleaner, car – rather than tools. The skills necessary to handle these utensils and implements are no less than the male skills of their husbands. But, as Cynthia Cockburn points out, women cannot fix these utensils and implements when they go wrong and are therefore dependent on husbands or tradesmen, so that finally 'it is men on the whole who are in control of women's domestic machinery and domestic environment' (p. 220).

Technologies related to housework are not the only technologies to be found in the home. Indeed the extent to which the meanings and uses of domestic technologies have a gendered character is perhaps even more clearly demonstrated with regard to the technology of leisure. While for women the home is primarily defined as a sphere of work, for men it is a site of leisure, an escape from the world of paid work. This sexual division of domestic activities is read onto the artefacts themselves. (See Plate 9.)

For example, television viewing reflects existing structures of power and authority relations between household members. In a study of white, working-class nuclear families in London, David Morley (1986) found that women and men gave contrasting accounts of their experience of television. Men prefer to watch television attentively, in silence, and without interruption; women it seems are only able to watch television distractedly and guiltily, because of their continuing sense of their domestic responsibilities. Male power was the ultimate determinant of programme choice on occasions of conflict. Moreover, in families who had a remote control panel, it was not regularly used by women. Typically, the control device was used almost exclusively by the father (or by the son, in the father's absence) and to some extent symbolized his domestic power.

Video recorders, like remote control panels, are the possessions of fathers and sons. Women's estrangement from the video recorder is no simple matter of the technical difficulty of operating it. 'Although women routinely operate extremely sophisticated pieces of domestic technology, often requiring, in the first instance, the study and application of a manual of instructions, they often feel alienated from operating the VCR' (Gray, 1987, p. 43). Rather, women's experience with the video has to be understood in terms of the 'gendering' of technology. When a new piece of technology arrives in the home it is already inscribed with gendered meanings and expectations. Assuming himself able to install and operate home equipment, the male of the household will quickly acquire the requisite knowledge. Along with television, the video is incorporated into the principally masculine domain of domestic leisure. Gray also points out, however, that some women may have developed what she calls a 'calculated ignorance' in relation to video, lest operating the machine should become yet another of the domestic tasks expected of them.

TECHNOLOGICAL INNOVATION AND HOUSEWORK TIME

Attempts by 'post-industrial Utopians' to conceive of the likely shape of the household in the future suffer from many of the intellectual defects that have misled analysts of domestic technology in the past... The British economist and sociologist, Jonathan Gershuny (1978, 1983, 1985, 1988), has made the most sustained attempt to give empirical weight to post-industrial predictions about the household ... [His] main thesis is that the economy is moving toward the provision of services within the household, that is, to being a self-service economy.

Although not drawing on the feminist literature, Gershuny shares with it a recognition that unpaid domestic production is in fact work and takes it seriously as such. He goes on to argue for a reorientation of the way we study technical change. Instead of starting from the workplace, as is typical for example in economics, sociology and economic history, in his view we should start from the household.

Households have a certain range of needs, a set of 'service functions' that they wish to satisfy, such as 'food, shelter, domestic services, entertainment, transport, medicine, education, and, more distantly, government services, "law and order" and defence' (1983, p. 1). Historically the means by which households satisfy these needs change. Gershuny describes a shift from the purchase of final services (going to the cinema, travelling by train, sending washing to a commercial laundry) to the purchase of domestic technologies (buying a television, buying a car, buying a washing machine). A degree of unpaid domestic work is necessary in order to use such commodities to provide services . . . In this way domestic technology is of enormous economic significance, affecting the pattern of household expenditure, the industrial distribution of employment and the division of labour between paid and unpaid work.

Like Cowan, Gershuny argues that people make rational decisions in this area. However, whereas her emphasis is on moral values and the social nature of human desires and preferences, his emphasis is on prices. The household will choose between alternative technical means of provision on the basis of the household wage rate, the relative prices of final services and goods, and the amount of unpaid time necessary to use the goods to provide the service functions . . .

Implicit in this analysis is the assumption that the household can be treated as a unity of interests, in which household members subordinate their individual goals to the pursuit of common household goals . . . What this approach overlooks is that there are conflicts of interest between family members over the differential distribution of tasks and money, and this may well influence how decisions actually come about.

Let us see how this theory explains the widespread purchase and use of washing machines, as opposed to commercial laundries. Gershuny argues that as the time needed to use a washing machine has fallen, and the price of washing machines relative to the price of laundry has fallen, so their popularity has increased. These developments are not linear, however. A central feature of Gershuny's model is that it predicts first a rise, then a plateau, and then a decline in the time spent on domestic labour.

The first phase constitutes the shift from the service to the goods – for example from commercial laundries to domestic washing machines. According to the model this is a rational decision because it is cheaper, even counting the housewife's labour. But clearly, the domestic time spent on laundry goes up at this point. And precisely because it is a cheaper form of washing clothes, it becomes rational to wash more clothes more often, to satisfy (high) marginal desires for clean laundry.

In the second phase, where washing machines are fairly widely diffused, competition between manufacturers at least partly takes the form of offering more efficient machines, replacing the twin tub with the automatic. At the same time, the desire for clean laundry will begin to stabilize – slowing the rate of growth in clothes to be washed. . . [E]ventually, time spent in laundry will start to fall. Thus, Gershuny argues, an effect of this move to a self-service

economy, is that the amount of time spent on housework has declined since 1960 (1983, p. 151).

Gershuny is so convinced that new technologies increase the productivity of domestic labour that, in a recent paper with Robinson (1988), he takes issue with the feminist 'constancy of housework' thesis. Whilst conceding that prior to the 1960s the time spent by women on domestic work did remain remarkably constant, he insists that a shift occurred at that point. Drawing on evidence from time-budget surveys in the USA and UK, as well as Canada, Holland, Denmark and Norway, he concludes that domestic work time for women has been declining since the 1960s, and even that men do a little more than previously . . .

In fact on closer inspection, these findings are more in line with feminist theories about constancy of domestic work than the authors would lead us to believe. Although the central argument is that domestic work time has been declining for women between the 1960s and the 1980s, this is only the case with respect to 'routine' domestic work. Unpaid work is subdivided into three categories: routine domestic chores (cooking, cleaning, other regular housework), shopping and related travel, and childcare (caring for and playing with children). While routine domestic work has declined, the time spent in childcare and shopping have substantially increased.

This finding . . . is entirely consistent with the feminist emphasis on the added time now devoted to shopping and childcare. Certainly the feminist concern with the constancy of housework has employed a broader notion that includes childcare and shopping. To argue that domestic labour time has reduced is only meaningful if it means that leisure or discretionary free time has increased. If, however, mechanization results in less physical work but more 'personal services' work in the sense of increased time and quality of childcare, then surely this does not mean a real decrease in work . . .

Indeed it seems that the preoccupation with increases in productivity due to technological innovation blinds many analysts to more fundamental social factors. For example, the presence or absence of children, their age and their number all have significantly greater effects on time spent in housework than any combination of technological developments. Similarly, the presence of men in a household increases women's domestic work time by at least a third. In contrast, for men, living with women means that they do less domestic work (Wyatt *et al.*, 1985, p. 39). Furthermore, it has repeatedly been found that the amount of time women spend on housework is reduced in proportion to the amount of time they spend in paid employment.

A major problem with most time-budget research is that it does not recognize that the essence of housework is to combine many things, usually concurrently. This has a profound bearing on the interpretation of time spent in childcare and the apparent growth of leisure time... Perhaps ... the private and gendered character of the household promotes the kinds of technological innovations that maximize the number of tasks that can be performed simultaneously ... Gershuny's focus on technological innovations and tasks *per se* seems indicative, once again, of a technicist orientation which sees the organization of the household as largely determined by machines.

A technicist orientation is also evident in much of the futuristic literature on 'home informatics' ... [Research] on the electronic, self-servicing home of the future remains remarkably insensitive to gender issues. In particular, it ignores the way in which the home means very different things for men and women. Many of the new information and communication technologies are being developed for the increasing trend towards home-centred leisure and entertainment. But leisure is deeply divided along the gender lines ... Furthermore, the possibilities of home-based commercial operations, from 'telebanking' and shopping to 'teleworking', are likely to involve more housework for women in catering for other home-based family members ...

ALTERNATIVES TO INDIVIDUALIZED HOUSEWORK

Even the most forward looking of the futurists have us living in households which, in social rather than technological terms, resemble the households of today. A more radical approach would be to transform the social context in which domestic technology applies. In view of what has been said about the shortcomings of domestic technology, one is prompted to ask why so much energy and expertise has been devoted to the mechanization of housework in individual households rather than to its collectivization.

During the first few decades of this century there were a range of alternative approaches to housework being considered and experimented with. These included the development of commercial services, the establishment of alternative communities and co-operatives and the invention of different types of machinery. Perhaps the best known exponent of the socialization of domestic work was the nineteenth-century American feminist Charlotte Perkins Gilman. Rather than men and women sharing the housework, as some early feminists and Utopian socialists advocated, she envisaged a completely professionalized system of housekeeping which would free women from the ties of cooking, cleaning and childcare.

The call for the socialization of domestic work was not unique to the early feminist movements. Revolutionary socialists such as Engels, Bebel and Kollontai also saw the socialization and collectivization of housework as a precondition for the emancipation of women. And they embraced the new forces of technology as making this possible. Writing in the 1880s, Bebel saw electricity as the great liberator: 'The small private kitchen is just like the workshop of the small master mechanic, a transition stage, an arrangement by which time, power and material are senselessly squandered and wasted' (1971, pp. 338–9). The socialization of the kitchen would expand to all other domestic work in a large-scale socialist economy.

The ... socialist states of Eastern Europe took up some of these ideas, establishing collective laundry systems in apartment blocks and communal eating facilities. Whilst these initiatives certainly represented a different use of technology, they did not challenge the sexual division of labour insofar as women remained responsible for the housework, albeit collectivized. These policies on domestic labour resulted from the economic necessity of drawing women into the workforce combined with the ideology of equality ... [Families using these facilities saved time on household tasks but saving time ... [was] not the sole motive as a housing crisis and overcrowded living conditions also encouraged this pattern.]

History thus provides us with many examples of alternatives to the single-family residence and the private ownership of household tools. Why then, in the USA in particular, has the individualized household triumphed?

[· · ·]

To argue that women just welcomed the new domestic technologies because they became available is to come perilously close to technological determination. On the other hand, how can women have consciously and freely chosen to embrace the new methods when they have been so discredited as a liberating force? It is tempting in these circumstances to see women as duped, as passive respondents to industrialization, and as victims of advertisers.

Cowan argues that women embraced these new technologies

Figure 4.1.1
An Edwardian (c. 1908) electric kitchen in which eight electrical appliances are installed, together with an electrically driven knife cleaner in the scullery

because they made possible an increased material standard of living for substantially unchanged expenditure of the housewife's time. To this extent women were acting rationally in their own and their families' interests.

However, as the following passage illustrates, Cowan seems to find the most convincing explanation of the paths chosen in a set of values to which women subscribed – the 'privacy' and 'autonomy' of the family.

> ... when decisions have to be made about spending limited funds, most people will still opt for privacy and autonomy over technical efficiency and community interest ... Americans have decided to live in apartment houses rather than apartment

> hotels because they believe that something critical to family life is lost when all meals are eaten in restaurants or all food is prepared by strangers; they have decided to buy washing machines rather than patronize commercial laundries because they prefer to wash their dirty linen at home . . . (*ibid., p. 150*)

Cowan does here depict women as active agents of their own destiny rather than passive recipients of the process. However, an approach that gives such primacy to values and to the symbolic importance of the home inevitably plays down the material context of women's experience. It may be that the effectiveness of the professional experts in imposing new notions of domestic life . . . has been overestimated, and the resistance they engendered ignored . . . The evidence . . . suggests that women negotiated the ideology of housewifery and motherhood according to their actual circumstances and that major contradictions underlay this attempt to rationalize domestic life . . .

In Britain in the 1930s, there already existed an 'infrastructure' for the communal provision of domestic appliances. There were municipal wash-houses and laundries, communal wash-houses in the old tenement blocks, and at this time several local authorities experimented with building blocks of flats, modelled on those built in Russia, and incorporating wash-houses, crèches and communal leisure areas. However, the communal provision of amenities was not always seen as progressive. It was associated in many people's minds with back-to-back houses with their shared water supply and sanitation, and a characteristic squalid view of rows of dustbins and WCs, and the tap at the end of the street. Interestingly, class differences emerged over this issue on the Women's Housing Sub-Committee, with some of the middle-class feminists on the committee more interested in the possibilities for communal childcare, laundries and other facilities. That working-class women favoured privacy and did not favour communal arrangements may have been based on their own experience of communal living in conditions of poverty.

It is important to recognize the extent to which individual choice is constrained by powerful structured forces. The available alternatives to single-family houses were extremely limited, especially for the working class. In fact, state policy in the area of housing and town planning played a key role in promoting privatism. Without the extensive provision of different options, it is not clear to what extent people freely chose private domestic arrangements.

It is even less clear to what extent women, as opposed to men, exercised the degree of choice available. Oddly Cowan separates this American preference for domestic autonomy from the sexual division of domestic labour. No role is granted to men in choosing this single-family home even though Cowan's own historical findings point to men being well served by the private domestic sphere.

The common feminist stress on the negative effects of domestic technology has contributed to the view that women have been duped. There is a tendency among some feminist scholars to assume an unqualified anti-technological stance and to imply that modern housewives are worse off than their grandmothers (Reiger, 1986, p. 110). This tendency is evident in those authors who stress the increasing isolation of the domestic worker and see domestic labour as having lost much of its creativity and individuality. Once we recognize that the mechanization of the home did bring substantial improvements to women's domestic working conditions, even while it also introduced new pressures, women seem less irrational. . .

Against this there is no doubt that people can be taken in by false promises, especially where advanced technology is involved. Wanting to save time and improve the quality of their housework and in turn the quality of their home life, housewives are susceptible to well-targeted advertising about the capacity of new appliances to meet their needs. The irony is that women have commonly blamed themselves for the failure of technology to deliver them from domestic toil, rather than realizing that the defects lie in the design of technologies and the social relations within which they operate.

MEN'S DESIGNS ON TECHNOLOGY

The forms of household equipment are almost always taken as given, rather than being understood in their social and cultural context. Yet there are always technological alternatives and any specific machine is the result of non-technological as well as technological considerations. A society's choices among various possible directions of technological development are highly reflective of the patterns of political, social and economic power in that society. Is it possible to detect these patterns in the design of domestic technology?

Gender relations are most obviously implicated in the development of domestic technology because of the extent to which the sexual division of labour is institutionalized. Most domestic technology is designed by men in their capacity as scientists and engineers, people remote from the domestic tasks involved, for use by women in their capacity as houseworkers . . .

It is not only gender relations that influence the structure of domestic technology. Like other technologies, domestic technology is big business . . . The design and manufacture of household appliances is carried out with a view to profit on the market. And the economic interests involved are not simply those of the manufacturers, but also those of the suppliers of the energy needed by these appliances.

Household appliances are part of technological systems, such as electricity supply networks. The interests of the owners of these systems have played an important part, along with those of the manufacturers, in shaping domestic technology. There is nothing the owner of an electricity supply system, for example, likes better than the widespread diffusion of an electricity-using household appliance that will be on at times of the day when the big industrial consumers are not using electricity. Residential appliances (including heating and cooling equipment) use about a third of the electricity generated in the US today; the refrigerator alone uses about seven per cent. Unlike most other household appliances, the refrigerator operates twenty-four hours a day throughout its life. In fact, many American kitchens now contain between 12 and 20 electric motors. Indeed the drive to motorize all household tasks – including brushing teeth, squeezing lemons and carving meat – is less a response to need than a reflection of the economic and technical capacity for making motors.

[· · ·]

An important dimension glossed over in the literature on the development of domestic equipment is the culture of engineering. After all, engineers do not simply follow the manufacturers' directives; they make decisions about design and the use of new technologies, playing an active role in defining what is technically possible. . . [T]he masculinity of the engineering world has a profound effect on the artefacts generated. This must be particularly true for the design of domestic technologies, most of which are so clearly designed with female users in mind.

When women have designed technological alternatives to time-consuming housework, little is heard of them. One such example is Gabe's innovative self-cleaning house (Zimmerman, 1983). Frances Gabe, an artist and inventor from Oregon, spent 27 years building and perfecting the self-cleaning house. In effect, a warm water mist does the basic cleaning and the floors (with rugs removed) serve as the drains. Every detail has been considered. 'Clothes-freshener cupboards' and 'dish-washer cupboards' which wash and dry, relieve the tedium of stacking, hanging, folding, ironing and putting away. But the costs of the building (electricity and plumbing included) are no more than average since her system is not designed as a luxury item. Gabe was ridiculed for even attempting the impossible, but architects and builders now admit that her house is functional and attractive. One cannot help speculating that the development of an effective self-cleaning house has not been high on the agenda of male engineers.

DOMESTIC TECHNOLOGY: A COMMERCIAL AFTERTHOUGHT

The fact is that much domestic technology has anyway not been specifically designed for household use but has its origins in very different spheres. Consumer products can very often be viewed as 'technology transfers' from the production processes in the formal economy to those in the domestic informal economy.

Typically, new products are at first too expensive for application to household activities; they are employed on a large scale by industry only, until continued innovation and economies of scale allow substantial reduction in costs or adaptation of technologies to household circumstances ... Gas and electricity were available for industrial purposes and municipal lighting long before they were adapted for domestic use. The automatic washing machine, the vacuum cleaner and the refrigerator had wide commercial application before being scaled down for use in the home. Electric ranges were used in naval and commercial ships before being introduced to the domestic market. Microwave ovens are a direct descendant of military radar technology and were developed for food preparation in submarines by the US Navy. They were first introduced to airlines, institutions and commercial premises before manufacturers turned their eyes to the domestic market.

... For this reason new domestic appliances are not always appropriate to the household work that they are supposed to perform, nor are they necessarily the implements that would have been developed if the housewife had been considered first or indeed if she had had control of the processes of innovation.

[· · ·]

Throughout this [article] I have been examining the way in which the gender division of our society has affected technological change in the home. A crucial point is that the relationship between technological and social change is fundamentally indeterminate. The designers and promoters of a technology cannot completely predict or control its final uses. Technology may well lead a 'double life', '. . . one which conforms to the intentions of designers and interests of power and another which contradicts them – proceeding behind the backs of their architects to yield unintended consequences and unanticipated possibilities' (Noble, 1984, p. 325).

A good illustration of how this double life might operate, and how women can actively subvert the original purposes of a technology, is provided by the diffusion of the telephone. In a study of the American history of the telephone, Claude Fischer (1988) shows that there was a generation-long mismatch between how the consumers used the telephone and how the industry men thought it should be used. Although sociability (phoning relatives and

friends) was and still is the main use of the residential telephone, the telephone industry resisted such uses until the 1920s, condemning this use of the technology for 'trivial gossip'. Until that time the telephone was sold as a practical business and household tool . . .

The people who developed, built and marketed telephone systems were predominantly telegraph men. They therefore assumed that the telephone's main use would be to directly replicate that of the parent technology, the telegraph. In this context, people in the industry reasonably considered telephone 'visiting' to be an abuse or trivialization of the service. It did not fit with their understandings of what the technology was supposed to be used for.

The issue of sociability was also tied up with gender. It was women in particular who were attracted to the telephone to reduce their loneliness and isolation and to free their time from unnecessary travel. When industry men criticized 'frivolous' conversation on the telephone, they almost always referred to the speaker as 'she'. A 1930s survey found that whereas men mainly wanted a telephone for business reasons, women ranked talking to kin and friends first (Fischer, 1988, p. 51).

Women's relationship to the telephone is still different to men's in that women use the telephone more because of their confinement at home with small children, because they have the responsibility for maintaining family and social relations and possibly because of their fear of crime in the streets (Rakow, 1988) . . . The telephone has increased women's access to each other and the outside world . . . However, the unintended consequences of a technology are not always positive. The diffusion of the telephone has facilitated the electronic intrusion of pornography into the home. Not only are abusive and harassing telephone calls made largely by men to women, but new sexual services are being made available. The French post office's Minitel service, which is a small television screen linked to the telephone, has seen a massive 'pink message service' arise. When it was introduced over ten years ago, the Minitel system was intended to replace the telephone directory. Since then it has developed thousands of services, the most popular being pornographic conversations and sexual dating via the electronic mail. When complaints have been made the French post office claim that they can do nothing to censor hardcore pornography as it is part of private conversations.

CONCLUSION: MORE WORK FOR SOCIAL SCIENTISTS?

I started this [article] by noting how belated has been the interest in domestic technology and household relations. There is now a substantial body of literature on the history of housework and the division of labour in the home. In recent years too there has been growing interest in domestic technology both among feminist theorists and, from a different perspective, among post-industrial society theorists. This work is still relatively underdeveloped and much of the literature shares a technicist orientation whether optimistic or pessimistic in outlook. Technology is commonly portrayed as the prime mover in social change, carrying people in its wake, for better or worse. But history is littered with examples of alternative ways of organizing housework and with alternative designs for machines we now take for granted. In retrieving these lost options from obscurity the centrality of people's actions and choices is highlighted and with them the social shaping of technology that furnishes our lives.

An adequate analysis of the social shaping of domestic technology cannot be conducted only at the level of the design of individual technologies. The significance of domestic technology lies in its location at the interface of public and private worlds. The fact that men in the public sphere of industry, invention and commerce design and produce technology for use by women in the private domestic sphere, reflects and embodies a complex web of patriarchal and capitalist relations . . . By refusing to take technologies for granted we help to make visible the relations of structural inequality that give rise to them.

Note

1   There is now quite an extensive feminist literature on the domestic science movement and its attempt to elevate the status of housekeeping. See, for example, Ehrenreich and English (1975, 1979) and Margolis (1985) on America; Davidoff (1976) and Arnold and Burr (1985) on Britain; and Reiger (1985) for Australia.

Article 4.2

COLD HEARTHS AND BARREN SLOPES: THE WOODFUEL CRISIS IN THE THIRD WORLD

Bina Agarwal

It costs as much to heat a pot as to fill it.

(*African proverb*)

It's not what's in the pot but what's under it that worries you.

(*Chinese saying*)

Every aspect of fires and fuels is the work of women in Kwemzitu [Tanzania], and no other task is considered to be as tiring or as demanding, or to have so little to show for itself.

(*Fleuret and Fleuret, 1978, p. 318*)

THE IMPORTANCE OF WOOD AS FUEL

One of the most important sources of renewable energy presently in use in large parts of the Third World is woodfuel. This includes wood burnt directly (termed 'firewood' or 'fuelwood') as well as fuels derived from wood, [such as] charcoal and methanol.

On the basis of Food and Agriculture Organization (FAO) figures, it is estimated that currently two-thirds of all energy in Africa, one-third in Asia, and one-fifth in Latin America comes from fuelwood and charcoal (Arnold and Jongma, 1977, p. 2). In many countries such as Benin, Chad, Ethiopia, Nepal, Rwanda, Uganda and [Burkina Faso], firewood and charcoal together provide close to 90 per cent or more of the total energy used, and for the majority of other countries in Africa, and many in Asia and Central America, the figure is well over 50 per cent.

The domestic consumption of fuelwood constitutes its primary use. Assessments for several countries indicate that 75–89 per cent of the fuelwood consumed is in the rural household sector, 7–9 per cent being used in cottage industries and 2 to 18 per cent in other

Note: This article has been condensed from Bina Agarwal's book of the same name (Zed Books, 1986). We have therefore not shown by ellipses and square brackets all the editorial changes that have been made.

industrial and service sectors.[1] Within the domestic sector, the primary use of fuelwood is for cooking.[2]

In most of the Third World, dependence on firewood as the primary source of fuel for domestic energy and particularly for cooking energy, is extremely high, especially in the rural areas. Firewood may be supplemented by agricultural residues and animal wastes, but typically these are of relatively much less importance except where woodfuel shortages have left few other options. In general, firewood constitutes the main, and for some the sole, source of energy.

Furthermore, a number of studies suggest that other renewable energy alternatives, such as solar and wind technologies or even biogas, are not yet at a stage of development where they can be adapted successfully to serve adequately the need that woodfuels currently serve. In India, for example, solar and wind power are not likely to provide viable options until at least the year 2000 (Prasad, 1979, p. 396).

FIREWOOD COLLECTION: FROM WHERE AND BY WHOM?

In most rural areas people usually depend on what they can themselves gather. Rural households with land can gather firewood from trees on their own land. The landless, however, have to depend on wood from common land or, where allowed to do so, gather it from other people's land – perhaps contributing labour in return. As incomes decline, the dependency for fuel collection from sources other than one's own increases.

The collection of firewood in most parts of the Third World is done primarily by women and children. The actual time taken for collection varies in different regions according to the availability of resources, but in most cases it is a strenuous and time-consuming task.[3]

IMPLICATIONS OF SHORTAGES

The availability of wood, even though it constitutes a *renewable* resource, is limited, and becoming increasingly so. Large tracts of land, which were earlier thickly wooded, today lie barren. By one estimate there will be virtually no forests left in the Third World countries in 60 years time, in the absence of serious measures to counteract this; and the present rate of reforestation is assessed to be less than 10 per cent of that necessary to supply the minimum needs of these countries by the year 2000 (Spears, 1978, ii, p. 15).

Deforestation, in turn, can have devastating consequences. At the social level these relate to the effects of soil erosion, flooding, climatic maleffects, the spread of deserts, the drying of previously perennial streams, an increased frequency of landslides, the rapid siltation of rivers and reservoirs and so on. As a result, there is also an adverse effect on agricultural production which has implications both for society and for those dependent on agriculture for their livelihood. The disappearance of forests produces a tendency for rain water to be released in floods during the wet season, with drought in other seasons.

For the individual, there is a substantial increase in the time and energy spent (especially by women and children) to gather firewood. In parts of Sudan, over the past decade or so, the time taken to collect firewood has increased over four-fold (Digerness, 1977, p. 15).

In India, in parts of Bihar where 7–8 years ago women of poor rural households could get enough wood for self-consumption and sale within a distance of 1.5 to 2 km, they now have to trek 8–10 km every day. Similarly, in some villages of Gujarat (India) the women, even after spending several hours searching, do not get enough for their needs, and have to depend increasingly on the roots of trees and on weeds and shrubs which do not provide continuous heat, thus increasing their cooking time as well (Nagbrahman and Sambrani, 1983, pp. 36,37). Given the already heavy working day of most rural women, any further increase in time spent on firewood collection and cooking becomes an overwhelming burden. Hoskins (1983) notes how in parts of Africa, because of the extra time needed to collect firewood, daughters are now taken out of school to help their mothers. For the mothers themselves there might be a resultant economic cost in terms of employment or other income-earning opportunities foregone. (See Plate 10.)

A related aspect is the greater time now spent by women in cooking because they have to adapt their cooking methods to economize on firewood. (See Plate 11.) In ecological zones where wood has generally been scarce, conventional cooking practices are already such as to conserve wood at the cost of greater time and effort spent on preparing the meal. For example, in parts of the Sahel, women light only the ends of logs and branches, placed like the spokes of a wheel, and cook with the heat generated from the ends of the spokes (Howe, 1977, p. 83). Where adequate fuel is not obtainable there have been noticeable changes in consumption patterns. In some areas families have had to reduce the number of meals cooked, as in Bangladesh (Hughart, 1979, p. 27) and the Sahel (Floor, 1977, p. 6). In other cases there is a shift to less nutritious foods.[4]

Necessity is also driving people in some areas to shift to food which can be eaten raw, or to eat partially cooked food (which could be toxic) or cold leftovers (with the danger of food rotting in a tropical climate) and so on (Hoskins, 1979, p. 7). All this increases the vulnerability to ill-health and infection. In some regions, adverse nutritional consequences result from the trade-off between time spent in gathering fuel and that spent in cooking.

Additionally, deforestation has been noted to lower the water table, making it much more difficult and time-consuming for women to obtain water, especially during the dry season, for instance in Senegal (Hoskins, 1983), India (Bahuguna, 1984) and Nepal (Dogra, 1984). As a woman of the Uttarkhand hills in India put it:

> When we were young, we used to go to the forest early in the morning without eating anything. There we would eat plenty of berries and wild fruits, drink the cold sweet (water) of the *Banj* (oak) roots. . . In a short while we would gather all the fodder and firewood we needed, rest under the shade of some huge tree and then go home. Now, with the going of the trees, everything else has gone too.

In some areas, such shortages are found to be linked crucially to life and death questions. In the above mentioned region of India, for example, Bahuguna (1984) has noted several cases during the past three years of young women committing suicide because of the growing hardship of their lives with ecological deterioration. Their inability to obtain adequate quantities of water, fodder and fuel leads to scoldings by their mothers-in-law (in whose youth forests were plentiful), and soil erosion has made it much more difficult for the women to produce enough grain for subsistence in a region of high male out-migration. In one year seven such cases of suicide were observed – four of them in a single village where shortages are especially acute.

Women in poor households bear an additional burden. First, as the main gatherers of fuel it is primarily *their* time and effort that is extended with shortages. Second, they face more severe nutritional consequences from such shortages than men because of biases against them in the distribution of food within the family, as has been noted in many parts of Africa and Asia. The extra energy expended by women of poor households to collect fuel is also unlikely to be made up in most cases by the required higher consumption of food.

THE SEARCH FOR SOLUTIONS

In technical terms, the 'solutions' most commonly outlined in current literature concern two categories of innovations:

(a) Woodfuel-related innovations, especially improved wood-burning stoves, and tree-planting schemes – the former representing a way of increasing the efficiency with which existing supplies of firewood can be used and thus of increasing the effective fuel energy available to the household, and the latter a way of increasing the existing supplies of firewood. Both these can be seen as having the potential for making a direct impact on the problem of woodfuel shortages faced in the rural areas.[5]

(b) Non-wood-related (renewable) energy technology such as solar cookers, biogas plants, etc.

However, such 'solutions' fail to come to terms with the central question: how can the successful adoption of these innovations be ensured? The problem of the diffusion of innovations in rural areas is not always easy to solve. A complex set of economic, social and political factors impinge on both the appropriateness of particular innovations and the feasibility of their adoption. For example, even though conceptually the process of innovation-generation (the technical aspect) can be separated from that of diffusion, such a separation is often not desirable in practice. *In practice* the degree to which the user is involved in innovation-generation itself can be significant in determining whether or not the innovation is adopted, or continues to be used when adopted. This is not merely because the user would then develop a personal interest, but also because the innovation is likely to be more closely moulded to the user's needs. These needs, which are often culturally and socially determined (as, for example, the method of cooking), can rarely all be anticipated or taken into account in the laboratory.

DIFFUSION OF INNOVATION
The social structure

Inequalities in social status and the unequal nature of power balances between different classes/castes etc., and between the sexes are likely to affect technology diffusion.

The status of women within the household could be a significant factor in household technology adoption, especially where adoption requires cash expenditure, by virtue of the fact that although women are the potential users of the innovation and therefore in the best position to assess its advantages and disadvantages, it is the men who usually handle the household cash and make decisions on how it is to be spent. Generally, rural women and men have differing priorities in household expenditure. For instance, in poor rural households if women have some independent earnings they are observed to spend them on the family's basic needs, while the men spend their earnings largely on their own needs. Hence where men make the decisions, the purchase of an improved stove may not get priority, especially where the only advantage perceived is greater leisure or convenience in cooking for the women. It is in fact noteworthy that in the heart of India's green revolution, viz. Punjab, while there have been considerable improvements in the technology handled by men – in the form of tractors, threshers, combines etc. – there has been little improvement in the women's kitchen apparatus, even in economically well-off families (Agarwal, 1984, A–49).

Likewise, the status of women within the community is an influencing factor in a number of significant ways. Rural women usually have no direct access to institutional credit or to independently disposable cash income to purchase new innovations/technologies. This has been found to constrain dissemination in several wood-stove diffusion programmes, for instance, in the Sahel and El Salvador.

Further, women seldom have access to information on new innovations. There is a strong ideological bias in extension services[6] which is likely to work against the direct involvement of, or consultation with, village women in the experimental designing of wood-stoves for their use – an involvement which was found to be a significant feature in effective diffusion in several case studies. Also, rural women are not usually given the training or the opportunity to undertake decision-making roles or responsibilities in the public sphere.

The balance of power between rural households which differ in their ownership and control of material assets and/or in their social status – political power and social status generally co-exist with the ownership of wealth – affects the ability of different households to purchase technologies and their access to information and to credit. Further, social hierarchies, whether based on differences in inter-household distribution of material assets, or on gender differences, or defined by some other criteria, are likely to make difficult the setting up of precisely those linkages between indigenous technical knowledge and skills and the more formalized research and development networks, and between the user (including the user-innovator) and the scientist/professional, important in the successful diffusion of rural innovations in general and wood-stoves in particular.

Typically, there is an absence of a two-way interaction – a dialogue – between the scientists/professionals, the village extension agents and the poor peasants or other underprivileged (in particular women) users of innovations. The bias of government extension workers, who enjoy a certain status in the village, in favour of rich land-owners and against the poor peasants, has been noted. But the problem is only partly one of economic inequalities. Underlying the divide between the scientists/professionals (usually urban-based) and the rural users of innovations (including the user-innovators) whose knowledge comes more from field experience than from formal education is also usually the divide between mental and physical labour, between town and countryside, and between the sexes.

This is not to say that examples of localized experiments to establish these links, manifesting a 'participative' (of the rural poor) rather than a top-down approach to diffusion, do not exist. In fact there are several success stories which serve to demonstrate what can be achieved through a dialogue between those seeking to diffuse innovations or innovative ideas and those whose lives are directly affected by the programme. At the same time, they also point to the need for more comprehensive social changes if these experiments are to become general and wide-based.

Improved wood-burning stoves

Attempts to develop improved wood-burning stoves have been ongoing in several countries in recent years. Improvements in the design of wood-burning stoves are aimed primarily at increasing the efficiency with which wood is burned. The most important aspect of this is reduction in the amount of firewood needed to cook the household's everyday meal, and additionally to improve the conditions under which cooking is done, especially by eliminating smoke.

While simple measures such as drying the firewood before burning can considerably raise its calorific value and so increase efficiency, improvements in stove and/or pot design (and in the skill of the person operating the stove) are necessary for more substantive efficiency increases. The idea is to improve the heating process which can be seen as involving three stages:

- efficient generation of heat through the efficient combustion of wood;
- efficient transmission of the heat to the heat-absorbing surfaces;
- conservation of heat in the heating appliance and minimization of heat dissipation.

Inefficiencies may usually be traced to aspects such as:

- incomplete combustion of wood due to inadequate or unevenly distributed air;
- heat loss from the stove due to conduction from the stove wall, convection of hot gases, and radiation from the hot surface of the stove;
- inadequate heat transfer from flame to pot due to the surface area, shape, size, colour etc. of the pot;
- other aspects such as the heat needed to warm the stove first, loss of heat if firewood is left to smoulder after cooking is complete etc.

261

The principle underlying the stove improvements is to regulate the inflow and outflow of air currents in such a way as to ensure the efficient combustion of wood and make maximum use of the heat generated.

Testing the effect of specific design improvements on stove efficiency when the stove is used *in practice* is by no means a straightforward procedure; and the way in which such tests are usually conducted often makes suspect many of the stated claims of improvement.

Consider, for instance, the two standard procedures for testing a stove: heating water to boiling point and cooking a 'typical' meal. The water heating test has the advantage that it is simple to perform and easy to replicate. However, determining the efficiency of wood-burning stoves, even with this simple test, can be complicated. The major problem lies in the difficulty of controlling the heating rate in the stove (which relates to how quickly and how high the flame temperature rises and the efficiency of heat transfer from the fuel to the pot). Technically, the higher the heating rate the less fuel is needed to heat water or to bring it to boil. But because the heating rate cannot be controlled easily (due to the difficulty of ensuring that the wood used is the same in all respects each time the experiment is performed, and that all other conditions are the same as well), even a standard operation such as heating a given quantity of water, in a given vessel, in a given stove, can give variable results.

It might be possible to establish, through a large number of tests, which stoves, on average, have a high heating rate and which a low one. But a second problem still remains, namely that a stove which might prove efficient in the water-heating test may not prove so in the cooking of a meal, since cooking a meal needs a range of heating rates. For example, in cooking rice a high heating rate would be desirable for boiling the water and a lower one would be adequate to keep it simmering. Hence a stove with a high heating rate which performs well in the water-heating test may not perform as well in cooking rice. In other words, two stoves, tested in terms of their relative efficiencies in water heating, can reverse their positions when tested in terms of a 'standard' meal. Ultimately stove efficiency needs to be established in terms of actual cooking performance.

Other complications in testing the efficiency by cooking a meal relate to variations in what constitutes a 'meal' and the way it is cooked. The type and variety of foods cooked, the sequence in which they are cooked, the degree to which they are cooked (e.g. well-cooked or lightly prepared), the form in which they are cooked (e.g. fried, baked or boiled), and the quantities in which they are cooked (a doubling of food quantity will not double fuel requirements) would all affect the amount of fuel needed. Additionally, the amount of fuel used can vary a good deal according to the skill of the operator. In other words, the concept of 'efficiency' as applied to wood-burning stoves is itself complicated and efficiency tests on such stoves are difficult to perform and do not give uniform results.

Relative to an open fire, stoves have other potential benefits such as a reduced risk of burns (from sparks) or scalds (due to spills from unstable pots); lesser fire risk in huts made of easily combustible material; the elimination of health problems associated with smoke-filled kitchens; the saving of labour otherwise needed to clean soot-blackened pots, walls and clothes, and so on.

A CASE STUDY

A close interaction between designers, users, local artisans and extension agents is likely to be a crucial element in the successful diffusion of wood-stoves. This is illustrated by an alternative, on-going experiment for diffusing wood-stoves in north-west India, where a highly personalized and participative approach to diffusion has been followed. Sarin, the principal initiator of this experiment, provides a detailed account of the process by which she helped construct her first 29 stoves (Sarin, 1981). Each stove, built from local clay, was made user-specific in terms of its location within the kitchen, its size, the cooking routine of the family, the number of pot holes, the size of the pots and the overall aesthetics of design. The stove was usually built jointly by Sarin and the female members of the household, with other village women sometimes helping or observing the process. Modifications were made after the user had utilized the stove for some time and found some aspects unsatisfactory. Each user's problems were resolved and their needs taken into account. It is apparent that many of the problems which cropped up could only have been resolved through the close participative interaction with the users that characterized the building of the stoves.

This method of stove development and diffusion has been found to have several advantages:

(a) Since the stoves are closely adapted to user needs, user-satisfaction is high, as expressed by 27 of the 29 households reviewed. The flexibility of the approach is especially advantageous for taking care of the needs of poor households: some of these cook only one item and need a certain economy of design to maximize the use of available fuel heat; others have only thatched roofs and need special care for reducing the fire hazard, such as sealing the chimney with rags or clay to prevent its hot contact with the thatch, etc.

(b)   As the women users are closely involved in building the stove and can thus gain familiarity with the basic principles involved: (i) they can carry out minor modifications and repairs themselves; (ii) some can even build the stove on their own – one woman built herself a second stove, and another built a fairly successful first one on her own merely after watching one being constructed in a neighbouring house; (iii) the stoves are looked upon by the women (who often decorate them) with pride, and as items to be shown to neighbours and relatives especially during festivals, weddings etc. This has a strong demonstration effect both within the village and in neighbouring villages from where requests for similar stoves often follow. In other words, there is an automatic propagation of the improved stoves in informal ways, which few official channels can easily duplicate.

(c)   Since the process of building usually involves close interaction with the household members it often helps to build support for the stove from husbands or other men in the household. This too facilitates the acceptance and dissemination of the stove.

Initial evaluations of the stove indicate a high degree of success in terms of providing clean cooking conditions. In the 29 households in the villages where the experiment was first conducted, women noted that the new stoves helped eliminate smoke and thus prevented the blackening of pots, walls and clothes and saved their time and effort in scrubbing and cleaning; it was also easier to start a fire. (Some men mentioned that it reduced their waiting time for meals, tea and bathing water due to the possibility of simultaneous heating and cooking.) Although no systematic tests were conducted on wood saving, 11 users mentioned that it did save wood. In another area, a woman worker who had received six days of intensive training under Sarin built 30 stoves using a similar approach. In all 30 cases there was fuel saving (Sarin and Winblad, 1983).

Notes

1   In Pura village of Karnataka (India) 90 per cent of the firewood consumed is for domestic purposes, 4 per cent for cottage industries and 6 per cent for other industries (Ravindranath et al., 1978).

2   In Pura village 82 per cent of total firewood consumed by the community is found to be for cooking (op. cit.). Surveys in Gambia and Thailand indicate that cooking (including water heating, baking and brewing beverages) accounts for over 75 per cent of total firewood consumption (Hughart, 1979).

3   Some existing studies indicate the time taken and distances

travelled in rural households for firewood collection. In a significant number of cases the time is 3–4 hours per day or more. In some areas, as in the Sahel, women have to walk up to 10 km for this purpose; in Gambia it takes from midday to nightfall to gather an evening's supply, while in parts of India women spend five hours per day on an average, travelling 5 km or more over difficult terrain.

4   In Guatemala, to conserve firewood, families are shifting away from beans (which were a part of the staple diet) because they take too long to cook (Hoskins, 1979, p. 7). In the Sahel, the diet of millet is rarely supplemented by meat, because a large quantum of firewood is needed in its preparation (Howe, 1977, p. 84); families in this region are shifting from millet to rice because rice takes less time to cook (Hoskins, ibid.). Again, in eastern [Burkina Faso], attempts by the government to introduce the cultivation of soyabeans is being resisted by the women because of the longer cooking time and greater quantity of fuel that soyabeans require relative to the traditional cowpeas (op. cit.).

5   Improved equipment for converting wood to charcoal or other secondary fuels is also sometimes emphasized but this constitutes only a small percentage of total woodfuel energy used in most Third World countries, and cannot be seen as having the same importance in the present context as stoves or tree-planting.

6   Extension services are performed by agents who are government-appointed as local disseminators of information and expertise in areas such as agriculture, home economy etc. They liaise with a centre of expertise, usually a government department (eds).

Article 4.3
DRY

Jean Binta Breeze

(i)
from a standpipe in a tenement
      yard
   days of
      dirty bundles
   squatted
      by a cistern
   altar

   swollen feet
      clawed on cracks
   in the hot gutter

      lizard eyes
   of women
     fixed in worship
       on the mouth
of god
      which coughed its
       chronic lumps
     of air
begging them for
   water
(ii)
back to a standpipe in a tenement
      yard
  we set drums
  to catch the rain

  it didn't rain
  we trekked miles
  to the river

  the river dried
  the trucks came
  once or twice

  then stopped

  we marched
  to see the councillor

  who told us 'sorry
  my party's not
  in power'

Article 4.4
THE SOCIAL CONSTRUCTION OF COMPUTERS: HAMMERS OR HARPSICHORDS?

Gill Kirkup

The 1980s was the decade of 'new' technology. For a good part of that time it was not necessary to include the word 'information' alongside the adjective 'new' because we were all aware of exactly what kind of technology 'new' referred to: computer-based systems of information processing, transmission and storage. Optimistic futurists predicted a society transformed radically for the better by information technology (IT) as a tool for liberation. Pessimistic critics saw it instead as a tool for increasingly inhumane and despotic capitalism. Both agreed that its social effects would be dramatic. However, the reality of the 'computer revolution' has been that, like all technological innovations, its impact has varied across different categories of people.

Governments, industry and individuals have invested in IT equipment (hardware), in the programs that run on it (software), and in training people to operate it (fleshware!). In 1988 the US Office of Technology Assessment estimated that 40 per cent of all new investment in plant and equipment in the US was in computers and communication technology (Perrolle, 1988). Western economies have been changing from manufacturing production to information production. But the new jobs created by this transformation have been unequally occupied by white men in the higher status, higher paid jobs of analyst, programmer and repairer and by women of all races in the lower status and lower paid jobs of computer operator and keyboarding (Banks and Ackerman, 1990). Few women have been actively involved in IT developments either in employment or at home, and it may be that women will be even more peripheral to developments in the 1990s than they have been in the 1980s.

In the United Kingdom 1982 was designated Information Technology Year and during the 1980s the Government promoted the use of micro-computers ('micros') generally. The Department of Trade and Industry funded a 'computers in schools' initiative which aimed to get micro-computers for classroom use in all British schools. The BBC became involved in promoting computer literacy through special television programmes and through having their name attached to a particular machine which became, for most of the 1980s, the UK school standard. By 1988, 18 per cent of all households in Britain owned something that could be classified as a 'home computer' (*Social Trends 21, 1991*).

Yet during this period the proportion of women entering UK universities to study computer science courses fell from 24 per cent in 1979 to 15 per cent in 1984 and to less than 10 per cent by 1989 (UCCA 25th Report and UFC), despite special schemes to train teachers and encourage pupil use. The statistics look even worse when they are seen against a background of the increasing participation of women in university undergraduate courses overall – from 42.4 per cent in 1985/6 to 44.4 per cent in 1989/90. A similar although later trend has happened in the United States and data from the US also shows that African-American and Hispanic women were only 5 per cent of all women getting computer science degrees (Banks and Ackerman, 1990).

Here is an example of an innovatory technology which during the last ten years has seen a significant reduction in the proportion of women interested in gaining professional expertise. Why? Politicians, journalists and researchers – who should have known better – speculated about the impact of IT in employment, the home and education without any acknowledgement that the experiences of women and men, girls and boys were quite different. Feminist critics were a minority voice, and it has been only in the latter part of the 1980s that there has been wider acknowledgement that gender is important in understanding this impact.

I begin this article by discussing the origins of the computer – how it was designed and manufactured with particular purposes and users in mind which produced a gendered social construction. This is reinforced by an educational system and an employment market which privileges men and masculinity. However, computers are different from other technological artefacts in that their function is to engage in particular logical and analytical processing. In the final section I discuss how reflecting on the ways in which people work with computers is providing a feminist critique that questions the privileging of formal analytical thinking and modern scientific method.

WOMEN AT THE BIRTH OF A NEW TECHNOLOGY

Before the 1980s computers existed in our imaginations and in reality as huge, powerful and mysterious machines, serviced by teams of people in white coats who worked in dust-free, temperature-controlled environments. The image is that of careful laboratory work, and in science fiction the villain was often a malfunctioning computer like HAL in the film *2001*. Developing the first 'mainframe' computers took the kind of funding that initially only governments could provide, and the organization of large teams of people that the military could provide.

Box 4.4.1 Computing development in the military

The first computer was the British Colossus, completed in 1943 to decode German radio transmissions. The first US computer was the Electronic Numerical Integrator and Computer (ENIAC) of a similar date which computed ballistic tables for targeted bombing. It can be argued that the US computer industry began as a military project of the Army's Ballistic Research Laboratory (Edwards, 1990). The US military and other government departments were almost the only sources of research funding until the mid-1950s as well as the major buyers of computers. Even COBOL, the renowned business-oriented language, was originally specified by the US Department of Defense. The importance of military needs in determining developments in computers is not unusual; it is perhaps simply more widely known than the military's role in other technologies. Unfortunately the language and imagery of computing retains an association with its military origins even when it is being used outside that context. Terms like 'crash', 'abort', 'terminate', 'kill', 'execute', 'violate', 'penetrate', 'degrade', 'disable' are part of a discourse which is deeply implicated with aggression and militarism. Paul Edwards (1990) perceives a 'cultural fit' between computer science, research and the military.

> The military itself, as an institution, already has the character of a microworld.[1] Its hierarchies, strict laws of conduct, chains of command, orders, uniforms and precise jargon all contribute to the game-like structure of a microworld.

(Edwards, 1990, p. 114)

For most people the relationship is not so explicit, but it is uncomfortably present.

Women were involved in these war-time and post-war developments since this was the kind of non-combat technical and clerical work that fitted women's role in the military (see Article 3.6). However, women were not to be found directing the work, designing the machines or specifying the problems to be solved. They were operators and programmers at a time when those activities were considered mundane, and, in the case of applications such as wartime code-breaking or calculating ballistics tables, were certainly tedious and repetitive, although less so than doing the same calculations using mechanical adding-machines.

The precursor of the modern computer is usually identified as Charles Babbage's unbuilt analytical engine. During the 1840s he was helped in his theoretical work by Ada, Countess Lovelace (1815–52). Lovelace was 'rediscovered' by feminists who reclaimed the importance of the work of various historical women. Something of a myth has now been embroidered around Lovelace, but her example is useful mainly for countering arguments that women do not have the intellectual capacity for the kind of disciplined, abstract logic needed for computer science.

More contemporary examples of the involvement of women in developing modern computing are Adelle Goldstine and Grace Hopper. Histories of computing tend to ignore the fact that Goldstine co-authored important papers with her husband who was one of the collaborators developing ENIAC, and that Hopper developed the concept of the compiler, thereby rendering the computer far easier to program than it had previously been. Hopper was also instrumental in developing COBOL (COmmon Business Oriented Language), one of the most widely used programming languages.

PERSONAL COMPUTERS: TOYS FOR MEN AND BOYS?

In the 1990s our image of the computer is most likely to be that of a small personal computer (PC) with multiple uses at work or at home: a sometimes helpful, sometimes irritating machine with foibles which we tend to anthropomorphize. Our new science fiction images of computers have human attributes and even human-looking bodies like Data in the television series *Star Trek*. Our nightmares are closer now to Mary Shelley's, but this time we have created an inhumanly perfect monster who is visually indistinguishable from us, like the androids in the film *Bladerunner*. We worry that artificial intelligence might turn out to be better than

the real thing. Although fiction might give substance to our dreams, and give voice to our discomfort about the value put on particular computer-like styles of thinking, there are pragmatic factors such as design, marketing and access to computers which mean that many women never get the chance to experience the technology.

Leslie Haddon (1988, 1991) has done extensive research on the product development of the PC in Britain. He argues that it was in the deliberate choices that companies made about what hardware and software to produce and how to market it that PCs were gendered. What he describes is the historical process of the social construction of a technology.

During the 1970s various computer companies had experimented with producing smaller machines for business, research and education, but these machines remained too expensive and specialized for any domestic market. A different market of electronic hobbyists was buying microprocessor chips to build into radio-controlled toys and gadgets. In 1980 Clive Sinclair began to create a domestic market out of a hobbyist market with the launch of his ZX80 computer. He had for some years been a typical (male) electronics hobbyist and small-time inventor. He sold various electronics gadgets for hobbyists through the many electronics magazines such as *Wireless World* that existed in the 1970s. Electronics has been an almost exclusively male pastime – buying resistors and transistors and building short-wave radio-sets and radio-controlled aeroplanes – and a mysterious one to most women.

In general male hobbies can be distinguished from female hobbies in that the latter need little capital outlay and have a useful end-product (they are often related to pre-industrial crafts), such as knitting, sewing, embroidery, even flower-arranging, whereas the former need a large capital outlay and produce little or no end-product, being done for the pleasure of the activity itself, for example fishing, photography, ham radio and electronics.

The amount of leisure time available for women and men is different. Survey data (*Social Trends 21*, 1991) shows that in 1989 women in Britain enjoyed 33 hours a week leisure time if they were in full-time work, 39 hours if they were in part-time work and 53 hours if they were full-time housewives. This compares with 44 hours a week for men in full-time employment. However, housewives who have the most leisure time have the least access to disposable income to spend on expensive hobbies for themselves.

The ZX80 was a hobbyists' machine or, as Haddon calls it, a 'self-referential' machine. It was cheap (roughly £50) and you could do little with it except learn about computing by assembling the kit and programming it; it had no external application. Sinclair's innovation was to market this machine and later versions through High Street stores, and to do that he needed to claim more for it

271

than it was an interesting gadget. He was helped by UK Government concern to raise general awareness about IT and stimulate development and production in the UK. This machine became one of the first 'home computers'; its name suggested that the mystique and some of the power of the old mainframe could now be afforded and 'tamed' for any home. Sinclair computers sold very well although the only people who could do anything with them were electronics hobbyists; others remained disappointed – until a market developed for games applications. Then children and adults who had not been interested in programming in machine code or BASIC (another programming language) could play a variety of animated games.

Companies other than Sinclair – in particular Acorn and Commodore – had a different concept of a domestic machine. They saw it as a software player, primarily for entertainment. In parallel with marketing their machines they developed a software market for games on cassettes. Skilled hobbyists, usually young men, could write their own games software, and some did. The media enjoyed stories of young boys making money from selling programs they had written, but most people were happy just to play with what others had produced. Unfortunately most games were miniature warfare games – from hand-to-hand fighting to 'Star Wars' – which fitted the interests of the men and boys who were the real market.

It was no accident that most of these early games were military simulations of some kind; they reflected the major software research and development of the time. Warfare simulation games are at least as old as chess, but computer games are new in that they simulate not only the tactics but the sight and sound of a 'kill'. The analogy for men between warfare and gaming and sport is strong: 'War is a brutal, deadly game, but a game, the best there is. And men love games' (Broyles, 1984; quoted in Edwards, 1990).

The relationship between games software and actual military electronics was brought home forcibly during the Gulf War in 1991, by the images of 'smart' bombs destroying their targets with dramatic accuracy. When these video images were broadcast it was hard to recognize them as images of real destruction and not as the computer-generated games graphics that we have all become so used to.

By the mid-1980s one of the most important variables connected with ownership of a micro-computer was having an 11–14 year old boy in the family. Culley (1986, 1988) in a survey of English school pupils found that computers were more likely to have been bought for boys than for girls and, even when children reported the machine as being bought for the family, it was more likely to be used by boys and fathers – almost exclusively for games-playing. For example, 85 per cent of boys in a family with a computer reported that it had been bought for them or for another male, and none said that it was for their mother or sister; while of the girls with a computer at home, only 14 per cent reported that it had been bought for them.

In the early 1990s the power expected of a personal computer in the home is now the same as that of a small business machine. In 1987 Amstrad marketed a machine compatible with an IBM personal computer but less than half the price. General business applications software is more expensive than games software but with a mass market in PCs it is becoming 'affordable'. However, the domestic PC, especially in the UK, retains the gendering of its predecessors, and no attempt has been made by manufacturers to appeal to women, except perhaps as parents.

IT AND WOMEN'S WORK

In the 1970s and 1980s most feminist writing about the potential impact of IT on women's jobs was very pessimistic. Juliet Webster summarizes it as follows:

> Two processes related to IT were seen as threatening the position of women in the workplace. Firstly, the routine and unskilled jobs in both factories and offices which were overwhelmingly filled by women were seen as particularly susceptible to automation and by implication job loss. Secondly, the application of IT to jobs was part of a managerial strategy to further degrade and deskill them, and thus to assert managerial control over them. An array of practices associated with the implementation of ITs was forecast, including job . . . fragmentation, pieceworking and output monitoring, and shiftwork which would enable capital to recoup its investment on the equipment. Thus although women would be particularly vulnerable to technological job rationalization and unemployment by virtue of being concentrated in jobs especially open to these processes, all employees remaining in work – whether male or female – would be subject to managerial strategies to use information technologies to bring the techniques of the assembly line to *all* jobs and to render *all* labour subordinate to the juggernaut of capital.

(*Webster, 1989*)

Employment statistics have not shown a dramatic job loss amongst women in Britain and Europe in the 1980s. Instead, there has been a steady increase in the numbers of women in employment. Industries have been restructured, but the famous examples of job loss due to new technology such as the printing industry – and Wapping in particular – were bastions of traditional, *male* craft skill. Jobs in secretarial, clerical and retail work, where women are

273

concentrated, have not changed structurally although the tasks that individuals carry out have been modified.

For example, working at a large supermarket check-out in the 1990s means working with an optical reader which registers the price and description of items, rather than keying prices in manually. The nature of the job – registering purchases, packing them and interacting with customers – has remained the same. The greater impact has been on the (usually female) customer who, while receiving the advantage of an itemized receipt, has a trolley full of purchases few of which have any indication of price on them for her future reference. The variety of IT adopted in secretarial work, from autonomous but networked work-stations to centralized, dedicated word-processing equipment, has changed the job but has *re-skilled* rather than *de-skilled* it. New skills include electronic page and document layout, producing and inserting graphical material and familiarity with new communications systems such as facsimile transmission (fax) and electronic mail. Some of the early predictions of how word processing would deskill typing read now as rather naive comments from people who did not use the technology themselves, and who accepted the popular notion that information technology was a black box demanding only the most limited kind of button pushing from the operator:

> Typing is a skill which requires some years to perfect. [It] . . . requires an ability to perform certain skills such as centring headings, tabulation, setting out documents neatly, as well as the attainment of high speeds. These functions can be carried out automatically by the word processor at the touch of a button.

> *(CSE Microelectronics Group, 1980; quoted in Webster, 1990, p. 10)*

A different and depressing fact is that despite the evidence that some women workers now have greater IT skills than before, jobs remain defined as women's work, low status and low paid. This should not be a surprise. Historical research, such as that of Cockburn (1983, and Article 3.4), demonstrates that what is credited as skill with respect to employment more often has to do with the gender of the person claiming the skill rather than proficiency in it. Prior to sex discrimination legislation, skilled trades were usually male trades, and often kept exclusively male by apprenticeship systems that excluded women. Such exclusion is no longer legal, and legislation attempts to compare work of 'equal value' in disputes between men and women over pay, so cutting through comparisons of skill. However, there remains an implicit association between masculinity and financial rewards for 'skilled' work.

Women have learned to use computer-based technology in their work, and some have become expert with aspects of it, and yet this expertise is not being transferred or developed to provide entry into jobs where they would be professionally involved with computers. From the 1970s to the 1980s, when the computer industry was restructuring and expanding, there were opportunities for enthusiastic, energetic and often self-taught women to break in and establish themselves as professionals (Deakin, 1984). There was also optimism that IT would provide the flexibility, especially for women, to work as professionals from networked computers in their own homes. For example, 'F International', a British company, was set up by women to provide consultancy work in programming and systems analysis for women largely working at home. However, IT homeworking has not expanded in anything like the way predicted by futurists, and the IT industry looks like most other industries in the 1990s, with centralized places of work, people occupying and moving through hierarchically-based jobs, and with recognized qualifications needed for entry. In 1991 high-level jobs in computing in the UK had very small proportions of women: for example, women were 3 per cent of data-processing managers, 20 per cent of senior systems analysts and 25 per cent of programmers (WIT, 1991).

It is no longer possible for enthusiasm and self-teaching alone to get anyone access to a high-level job, which is why the diminishing proportions of women choosing to study computer science combined with women's lack of time, money and enthusiasm for recreational computing suggest a spiral of an increasingly male industry developing an increasingly masculine technology.

COMPUTING IN THE EDUCATION SYSTEM

The low proportion of women entering undergraduate computing courses in the UK is paralleled by a decline in the proportion of girls studying A-level computer science: from 22 per cent in 1983 to 18 per cent in 1985 and from 30 per cent at O-level prior to 1985 to 9 per cent in GCSE in 1987/8 (Buckley and Smith, 1990). It certainly appears that the special nature of British recreational computing combined with gender reinforcement in the education system is producing an extremely high level of withdrawal of women. Research in Israel and the United States (Levin and Gordon, 1989; Kersteen et al., 1988) suggests that there is a positive relationship between using a computer at home and doing well in school and university. This relationship holds better for boys than for girls, partly because so few girls have experience at home.

National education systems have introduced computers into the school curriculum in order to give children at least a minimum experience of the technology, if not 'literacy' with it. But schooling has long been recognized as an arena where gender is reinforced. This has always discriminated against girls' involvement in science (see Article 3.2) and technical subjects. Computer science as an area of academic study has traditionally belonged with mathematics (and still does in The Open University, for example). This association has persisted despite the fact that some of the most interesting developments are in other areas:

> Metaphors for computer technology are moving away from the number-cruncher computer, away from the machine that can replace human action and decision making, and toward an understanding of computing as an interactive process in which the computer becomes an intelligent co-participant in and a facilitator of individual and group communication. This shift reflects the fact that creative computing now relies at least as much upon language, visual design, problem definition, and organizational skills as upon quantitative analysis.
>
> *(Kramer and Lehman, 1990, p. 171)*

A restricted number of computers in a school is likely to mean that priority is given to subjects like mathematics where computing is seen as essential.

It is not only the content of computer education that has been a problem for girls, so has the process of learning. Because most schools had only a few machines, teachers used group rather than individual computer activities. Evidence has accumulated from educational research over the years that in mixed-sex groups gender stereotyping is reinforced, so that in laboratory-type situations boys, who feel that they are expected to know what they are about, take over the direction of the activity and the physical manipulation of equipment. Girls play a passive role and record events. Similar interactions have been observed at computers (Culley, 1986, 1988). These early observations justified single-sex teaching groups in computers and other aspects of technology. However, recent research has suggested that in some situations single-sex groupings of girls attempting a computing task perform worse than a mixed group since their lack of confidence can lead to mutual recrimination and failure (Hughes *et al.*, 1988). Unfortunately the end-result of this classroom experience is that boys become more positive about computers and girls less so. 'Hacking' or being a computer 'junkie' remains a predominantly male obsession, while negative feelings about computers are not restricted to women (Levin and Gordon, 1989; Kersteen *et al.*, 1988).

A MACHINE TO THINK DIFFERENTLY WITH

Finally, one of the most interesting theoretical positions on the gendering of computing is found in the work of Sherry Turkle (1984b, 1990). She synthesizes feminist epistemology, object relations

theory and cognitive science. Her interest is in computers as 'objects to think with', and she argues that the present social construction of programming styles and computer culture encourages one particular style of thinking which is not only repressive for many women, but restricts the potential of computers. But she is an optimist in that she believes that the computer has the potential for other constructions.

Turkle's ideas are important because she not only addresses some of the deeper reasons why many women do not enjoy computing, she also proposes a potential for computing as a tool for alternative ways of thinking from the rational masculine paradigm of which there was a critique in Chapter 1. Turkle researched different styles of computer use from the perspective of the object relations school of psychoanalysis. Object relations theory suggests that, as we develop, we relate to the world by internalizing the people and objects we come into contact with, and then they become for us 'objects to think with'. This is true both of people and everyday artefacts. The computer is something of a special object because it can on another level be a tool to think with since it is a logic processing machine. Whether or not one enjoys working with a computer depends on developing a comfortable relationship with it.

In Turkle's first major research (1984b) she studied the different ways in which children and adults related to computers, and used them as tools in their work. She identified two different styles: 'hard mastery' which she defined as being about control, a style more comfortable with formal hierarchical programming techniques and those militaristic structures referred to earlier, and more usual among men and boys; and 'soft mastery' which she defined as being more a process of negotiation with the machine and found more often among women and girls. In her later work (1990) she has elaborated her categories and now she writes about a formal analytic approach (rather than hard mastery) versus 'bricolage' (rather than soft mastery). She has taken the term 'bricolage' from anthropology where it was used to describe ways of thinking in so-called 'primitive' societies. This style is more concrete than the analytical rationality favoured by the West and valued in modern science in particular. Turkle's work would not be innovatory if she had simply stopped at this critique. Much educational research on learning styles and intellectual development is based on the developmental scheme of Piaget, who postulated a hierarchy of stages of intellectual development from concrete ways of thinking to formal and abstract. In Piaget's scheme each stage is superior to the previous one. Turkle's more radical formulation is to accept the existence of Piaget's styles but deny that they are stages in a hierarchy. She argues that equally productive and creative thinking can be carried on by people using a concrete style, unless they are forced to adopt a formal style which is then likely to inhibit them. When you are next struggling unsuccessfully to plan a piece of writing or use an outlining program on your PC you might be as comforted by the following description of bricoleurs as I was when writing this chapter!

> Bricoleurs are also like writers who do not use an outline but start with one idea, associate to another and find a connection with a third. In the end, an essay 'grown' through negotiation and association is not necessarily any less elegant or easy to read than one filled in from an outline, just as the final program produced by a bricoleur can be as elegant and organized as one written with a top-down approach.
>
> *(Turkle, 1990, p. 40)*

Turkle argues that society has much to gain from valuing and encouraging bricoleurs.

In taking this position she allies herself with another important feminist theorist of the 1980s, Carol Gilligan. Gilligan's focus was on moral reasoning. She took a well-established model of moral development, that of Kohlberg, and argued that it was wrong with respect to her own research on women. Kohlberg's model, like that of Piaget, is hierarchical and prescriptive. Kohlberg asserted that ideally people should pass through concrete reasoning stages until they reach a stage of moral reasoning based on abstract analytic notions of justice. Gilligan argued that women's psycho-social development leads them to value context and caring above abstraction, and that this should not be devalued as less developed or less sophisticated than formal abstraction, but rather valued for the new insights it brings. Gilligan's work has become important for feminist educators who are interested in developing new teaching styles to support these alternative styles of thinking. Turkle sees that in claiming value for 'bricolage' she is reinforcing Gilligan's valuing of 'connection', and she relates them both to ideas about a potential feminist science developed by Fox Keller (see Article 1.3). The positions converge as a powerful theoretical critique of traditional epistemology, each position grounded in empirical evidence about women's styles of thinking.

> Several intellectual perspectives suggest that women would feel more comfortable with a relational, interactive and connected approach to objects, and men with a more distanced stance, planning, commanding and imposing principles on them. Indeed we have found that many women do have a preference for attachment and relationship with computers and compu-tational objects as a means of access to formal systems. Yet in our culture computers are associated with a construction of science that stresses aggression, domination, and competition.
>
> (*Turkle, 1990, p. 150*)

Turkle demonstrates from interviews and observation that many women (and some men) are alienated from the computer – which is actually flexible enough to be a tool for a variety of ways of thinking – because the computer culture imposes a particular 'correct' style of interaction, based on a formal, top-down method of working, in which the problem is dissected into separate parts and solved by designing sets of modular solutions. Turkle describes the alienation of Lisa, a non-science undergraduate student who wants to use a programming style similar to that she uses when composing poetry. She begins her computing course well but as she goes on she becomes increasingly alienated:

> Lisa wants to manipulate computer language the way she works with words as she writes a poem. There, she says, she 'feels her way from one word to another', sculpting the whole. When she writes poetry, Lisa experiences language as transparent, she knows where all the elements are at every point in the development of her ideas. She wants her relationship to computer language to be similarly transparent. When she builds large programs she prefers to write her own, smaller, building block procedures even though she could use prepackaged ones from a program library; she resents the opacity of prepackaged programs. Her teachers chide her, insisting that her demand for transparency is making her work more difficult; Lisa perseveres, insisting that this is what it takes for her to feel comfortable with computers.
>
> Two months into the programming course, Lisa's efforts to succeed are no longer directed toward trying to feel comfortable. She has been told that the 'right way' to do things is to control a program through planning and black-boxing, the technique that lets you exploit opacity to plan something large without

knowing in advance how the details will be managed. Lisa struggles against using them as the starting points for her learning. Lisa ends up abandoning the fight, doing things 'their way' and accepting the inevitable alienation from her work. She . . . begins to insist that the computer is 'just a tool'. 'It's nothing much', she says, 'just a tool'.

(*Turkle, 1990, pp. 133–4*)

Of course, writes Turkle, the computer is a tool: 'but is it more like a hammer or more like a harpsichord?'

The development of a new computer culture would require more than environments where there is permission to work with highly personal approaches. It would require a new social construction of the computer, with a new set of intellectual and emotional values more like those applied to harpsichords than hammers. (*ibid., p. 153*)

IF WE UNDERSTAND IT, WE CAN MAKE IT WORK FOR US...

Turkle postulates a more creative and liberatory role for computers than any other feminist writing in the area so far.

CONCLUSION

Turkle's theory suggests that feminists should feel optimism about the potential effect of computers in society, that their social construction can be modified, and that women should reject the computer culture's notions of how computing should be done, and negotiate with the computer ways that we find convivial. It is a position which endows individuals with power, but can perhaps be criticized for not acknowledging the investment that many powerful groups – such as the military and governments of rich countries – have in computing continuing to develop along those lines already set down. Her work – with that of Gilligan – is exciting in what it contributes to feminist theory, but it is the case that in the 1990s few women, even in developed countries, will get the chance to engage with a computer in the way the students whom Turkle observed did. Most women's relationship to computers will be limited to operating equipment controlled by a microprocessor or networked to a large computer and to manufacturing and assembling computer components in the underdeveloped world. Although the predictions of the pessimists summarized by Webster have not occurred, this innovatory technology has not so far been used as a tool to restructure established sexual divisions of labour, or unequal race or gender relations. Neither has IT contributed to a significant reduction in inequality between the rich and poor countries of the world.

Earlier I suggested that our new nightmares about computers were based on a worry that they may be better at rational thought than we are. If we value ourselves only in terms of our ability to process data and reason by analytical logic, then we must compare ourselves unfavourably with computers. This supports Turkle's thesis that computers are used to validate a particular mode of thinking which is not only predominantly male, but Western and middle-class. This model of thinking has permeated Western thought for some centuries now, and it may be the existence of 'thinking' machines that will draw our attention to the value of our other human attributes such as imagination, humour and love. When we validate these in ourselves and in others we may find new ways of breaking down boundaries other than those of gender.

Note

1   A microworld is the term given to a computer program which creates a simulated environment or situation with internally consistent rules of operation.

Article 4.5
ECO-FEMINISM
Cat Cox

Ecofeminism draws together environmental, feminist and women's spirituality movements; it describes the diverse range of women's efforts to save the Earth from ecological disaster and incorporates a new feminist view of women and nature. The term was first used by Françoise d'Eaubonne (1974) to describe women's potential to effect environmental change; it spans a broad range of women's concerns focusing on activism and demonstration. The underlying theme linking the many strands of activity is a sense of inter-relatedness: that a healthy life depends on a healthy environment, that humans exist in a symbiotic relationship with the Earth, and that to disregard this is destructive to both.

These views are explored in the science of ecology, a study of the relationship of living organisms to each other and to their environment. Global awareness, developed over the last few decades and now realized through worldwide communications and information systems, means that our environment is indeed the whole planet.

WOMEN'S RELATIONSHIP TO THE ENVIRONMENT

That women should take the lead in such a global movement is felt by some to be a natural expression of an intrinsic relationship between women and the environment – a relationship revalued over the last decade through the work of feminist poets, thinkers and historians. That such a movement is growing in the 1980s and 1990s is a result not only of such practical and intellectual revaluation of women and nature, but also of a movement towards a feminist spirituality.

The various ecological feminist perspectives, rather than being shades of green or varying expressions of feminism, represent a range of practical activities. Women concerned about environmental damage are voicing their concerns on issues ranging from dumping toxic waste to overpackaging and from uranium mining to nuclear testing.

Throughout India, Africa and the rest of the underdeveloped world, women are acting to preserve their environment. Deforestation is a vital issue for many women (see Article 4.2). The Chipko Movement of India, begun in the 1970s, has received attention and support as women have banded together to defend the forests. In Kenya the Green Belt Movement, founded by Wangari Maathai in

1977, now has 50,000 supporters, as women work to reforest the land.

In the developed world women, recognizing the relationship between consumerism and the environment, are finding expression through groups such as the Women's Environmental Network in the United Kingdom and similar groups in Canada, Switzerland and Malaysia. The Women's Environmental Network organizes actions to protest at overpackaging as a waste of resources, by ripping off excess layers of packaging at the supermarket check-out, and depositing the waste with the store manager. In Japan the woman-run Seikatsu Club Consumer Co-operative seeks to provide safe products for its members and conserve resources by collective purchasing.

Since 1988 Mothers and Children Against Toxic Waste has actively campaigned against the production and dumping of toxic waste in the UK. In the United States women protest at toxic waste dumping following the precedent of Lois Gibbs of the Love Canal Home-owners Association who demonstrated in 1978 that children's health was being seriously affected by a nearby toxic waste dump. Canadian and Australian women have demonstrated against uranium mining, Orkney women have campaigned against the Dounreay nuclear reactor, and in the Pacific region women have protested at nuclear testing carried out by developed countries. In viewing the nuclear industry as the most life-threatening technological advance of the scientific age, women around the world have spoken to protest against all aspects of nuclear technology. Through all these examples runs a common thread: a shared view of the need for a human-centred, equitable, sustainable and healthy lifestyle. Underlying this vision is a growing sense of the importance of women's relationship to the environment and recognition of the value of feminine perspectives.

WOMEN AND NATURE

The work of feminist poets, writers and historians in the last decade was fundamental in developing a new view of women and nature. The earliest work to reconsider the importance of archetypical feminine values was Françoise d'Eaubonne's *Les Femmes Avant le Patriarchie* (1975). A wave of writing followed which challenged and overrode the view that the association between women and nature was another form of patriarchal oppression. Mary Daly's *Gyn/Ecology* and Susan Griffin's *Women and Nature* (both 1978) were revolutionary texts demonstrating the widespread oppression of women under patriarchy and comparing this with the domination of nature.

In *Gyn/Ecology*, Daly synthesized a historical and global survey of women's oppression. Using a unique style which challenged the inherent bias of contemporary language, she described a vast and ancient patriarchal domination. Encompassing women's experience under the Church, during witchburnings, within modern American gynaecology and in Africa, India and China, she presented a view of women's physical, mental and spiritual domination by men. In response to such a monopoly of power, she argued for a revaluation of women's space, women's friendships and women's energy and took a radical feminist stance in advocating separatism in order to rediscover and revalue the feminine self.

Box 4.5.1
The new language of women and nature

Mary Daly felt restrained by contemporary language. In writing *Gyn/Ecology* she used a challenging style of prose, in order to provoke the recognition of the ubiquitous influence of patriarchy.

PRELUDE TO THE THIRD PASSAGE

The know-ing of this deadly intent has been necessary for our a-mazing process of exorcism. It is equally necessary for moving on the Labyrinthine Journey of Ecstasy, for this process is damaged/hindered by not knowing/acknowledging the dangers, traps, deceptions, built into the terrain. As long as 'knowledge' of the horrors of androcracy is fragmented, compartmentalized, belittled, we cannot integrate this into our knowing process. We then mistake the male-made maze for our Self-centering way

(Daly, 1978)

Susan Griffin also used poetic prose to create compelling, emotive imagery by juxtaposing images of women and nature, revealing their oppression under patriarchy through their dialogue with the voice of cultural authority.

PROLOGUE

He says that woman speaks with nature. That she hears voices from under the earth. That wind blows in her ears and trees whisper to her. That the dead sing through her mouth and the cries of infants are clear to her. But for him this dialogue is over. He says he is not part of this world, and that he was set on this world as a stranger. He sets himself apart from woman and nature. . . .

> . . .We are the bird's eggs, flowers, butterflies, rabbits, cows, sheep; we are caterpillars; we are leaves of ivy and springs of wallflower. We are women. We rise from the wave. We are gazelle and doe, elephant and whale, lilies and roses and peach, we are air, we are flame, we are oyster and pearl, we are girls. We are women and nature. And he says he cannot hear us speak.
>
> But we hear.
>
> (Griffin, 1978)

Susan Griffin in *Women and Nature* explored the pain of women's oppression and likened this to the domination of nature. Writing in poetic prose, she surveyed history, describing patriarchy's domination of women and the Earth. She presented the view that current developments of dualistic thought had created unnatural barriers and contrived separations as society had polarized into culture/nature, mind/body, man/woman – and placed unequal values on each aspect. In 'Her vision' she explores a holistic view of life attained through synthesis and a fundamental revaluation of the feminine in all its aspects – as woman, nature and physicality.

Griffin's work was followed by Carolyn Merchant's *The Death of Nature* (1980). This chronicled the progress of the scientific revolution from the sixteenth to eighteenth centuries and explored the effects of a mechanistic philosophy on women and nature, arguing that the end of an organic view of the world – prevalent till the end of the fifteenth century – constituted the death of nature. Women and nature had been disparaged, as a mechanistic view – promoting science and reason – had prevailed over an organic view; this prompted the nature/culture divide. Masculine values of mind, culture and reason were elevated at the expense of body, nature and feeling. Like Griffin, Merchant argued for a revision of the values upon which society and science were based, and suggested drawing on an holistic view with its sense of balance and interconnection that had been lost with the end of an organic view.

In exposing the links between women and nature under patriarchy, these feminist authors developed a theme which has been expanded by others. As feminism has drawn on the language of ecology to explore new paradigms, so feminism has contributed to the study of ecology by supplying political understanding of the role of patriarchy. Establishing the political parallels between women and nature has been fundamental for the development of ecofeminism, both in providing insight into the problems and in creating a vision for the path forward.

ENVIRONMENTAL AWARENESS AND WOMEN'S ROLE IN THE WORLD

Women are the major consumers in the developed world and the greatest producers of food and caretakers of the Earth in the underdeveloped world. As the environment movement has demonstrated the links between consumerism and the environment, women have recognized the strength of their role as consumers. Research by Irene Dankelman and Joan Davidson in the late '80s documented the direct relationship that Third World women have with their environment, as farmers, water collectors and fuel gatherers. They also participate in commerce. Evidence of increased daily hardship as a result of environmental degradation is an expression of these close links.

A second aspect of the relationship between women and the environment centres on women's role in biological reproduction. Considered to be closer to nature because of their capacity to bear children, this connection has been used as a symbol of oppression, yet it can be women's reproductive capacity which sensitizes us to the environment. Pregnant women, susceptible to miscarriage or foetal damage as a result of contact with otherwise seemingly benign environmental pollutants, have been made conscious of this relationship and thus motivated to environmental action.

Many women who have taken part in environmental activism have not needed to experience extreme physical effects of environmental contamination to know that the environment is threatening their health and that of their children. Women, in general, are sensitive and responsive to their children's health and welfare. Numerous women have responded intuitively to environmental conditions which have then been later acknowledged to be dangerous. For example, women at Sellafield claimed that the nuclear reprocessing plant was damaging the health of their children, and women in Arkansas campaigned to stop the incineration of Agent Orange before the dangers were acknowledged by governments.

One of the earliest women's voices speaking for the environment was Rachel Carson who recognized that indiscriminate technological advances were precipitating an ecological crisis. Her 1962 book *Silent Spring* caused a furore. It inspired many people to consider the effects of technology and scientific progress on the environment, and also engendered a massive response from the agrochemical industry who felt particularly threatened by such a raising of environmental awareness. Her book marked a watershed – not just for environmentalism which saw an unprecedented surge of support leading to the establishment of the US Environmental Protection Agency and of Earth Day in 1970 – but also for women's active involvement in the environment movement.

Box 4.5.2 Rachel Carson

Silent Spring was a pioneering and paradigmatic work chronicling the effects of increased use of pesticides on the environment. Synthetic chemicals discovered during weapons research in World War Two were developed as peace-time pesticides whose production and use escalated during the 1950s. Carson documented evidence of fish kills, bird loss, water contamination and human loss of life as the book traced the causal relationship between the vast quantities of poisonous chemicals sprayed on the land and the damage to the environment and human health. Carson received many medals during her lifetime both for her literary skills and her scientific research. She had trained in genetics and biology and studied marine life in particular. Her understanding of marine ecology combined with her passion for the sea prompted her to write *Under the Sea Wind* and then *The Sea Around Us*.

Silent Spring was her fourth book, provoked by the receipt of a letter from a friend, detailing the death of birds in a sanctuary following an aerial spraying with DDT. The book fused an understanding of the interconnected web of life described by ecology, the necessity for diversity which is essential to ecological balance and a far-sighted view of the chain of events which occur within ecosystems. With this holistic view, she recognized that synthetic chemicals, delivered as insecticides, were also agents of death throughout the whole ecosystem and she termed them biocides. She documented the ubiquitous presence of these chemicals worldwide and the range of their effects. Her holistic approach extended to her solutions. She advocated integrated pest control with the use of naturally occurring predators that would interact favourably with the ecosystem rather than chemicals that would destroy it. She recognized that this kind of work held no glamour for many scientists, as demonstrated in 1960, when 98 per cent of all entomologists worked on chemical controls and only 2 per cent on biological controls. Her aim in the book was twofold, firstly to educate the general public and the government to all aspects of the use of pesticides and, secondly, to regenerate a sense of respect for the Earth in arguing that the care of the environment is a moral issue.

Carson preceded modern feminism yet her work shows an holistic vision similar to that espoused by ecofeminists. She saw a connection between health and the environment when she demonstrated how widespread use of chemicals was poisoning the Earth and resulting in illness and death. *Nuclear Madness* by physician Helen Caldicott (1978) had a similar view of the effects of radioactive pollution on human health. This work has been substantiated and developed by both Rosalie Bertell and Alice Stewart, nuclear physicists studying the biological effects of low-level radiation who have recently presented evidence linking escalating levels of radioactivity with millions of human casualties. Pioneering work by Alice Stewart established the link between high degrees of radioactivity at Sellafield and congenital birth defects in the area, between X-rays and foetal damage and between the radioactive work environment of operatives at the Hanford (US) nuclear power plant and their higher incidence of cancer. Rosalie Bertell argues that the bland reassurance of 'no immediate danger' (also the title of her book, 1985) offered by governments in response to queries about radiation danger is inadequate and misleading – both about the safety of nuclear technology and about the motivation for its development. She calls for an end to seeking peace and economic prosperity through militaristic technology and looks to ecofeminism and the women's movement to provide an integrated and holistic approach to technology enabling a future healthy human existence.

A NEW ACTIVISM: THE GROWTH OF ECOFEMINISM

Whilst women have been involved in the environment movement throughout the '70s, it is only in the 1980s that women's groups such as Women For Life On Earth and the Women's Environmental Network have explored the links between women and the environment and have proposed a particular women's perspective of environmentalism.

The origins of Women For Life On Earth are intimately connected with the women's peace movement. Women came together in the United States in 1980 because of the nuclear accident at Three Mile Island, and in the United Kingdom in 1981 to explore the connection between militarism, healing and ecology. Many women wanted to overcome the divisions that had developed within the feminist movement and found that they shared a deep concern for the state of the planet. Many were especially concerned about the threat of annihilation from nuclear arms and the UK group was motivated to march to Greenham in the summer of 1981 under the Women For Life On Earth banner and to set up a peace camp. WFLE's concerns were not exclusively military. In making the connection between women and the fate of the Earth, they explored issues of chemical and radioactive pollution, alternative technology, alternative healing and women's spirituality, and in 1983 they published the first collection of ecofeminist writings, *Reclaim The Earth: women speak out for life on Earth* (Caldicott and Leland, 1983). WFLE embraced the ecological metaphor of interconnection and the web of life, and in taking the web as a symbol they made ecology a political issue.

The women's peace camp at Greenham, with its strong emphasis on political activism and its reliance on networking for information, inspired many to campaign for peace. WFLE was unable to reach a large audience with its message promoting women's role in the protection of the environment. It was not until the late '80s with the establishment of the Women's Environmental Network and the concept of consumer power as environmental action that the majority of women felt they could participate in environmental protection. The Women's Environmental Network was initiated in 1988 by women working in the mainstream environment movement who felt that women's issues were not fully addressed there. In establishing their mandate to inform, educate and empower women, the Women's Environmental Network was concerned both with women's ability to promote environmental change and also women's sensitivity to the environment. In researching and collating information on environmental issues concerning women and in campaigning to promote environmental change – focusing especially on consumer issues – WEN facilitated

---

Box 4.5.3
The Women's Environmental Network

The Women's Environmental Network is a campaigning pressure group which takes up major environmental issues that affect women. Most of the mainstream environmental groups exhibit elements of radicalism in their goals and their approach, but balance this with an endorsement of science and an ability to compromise on major issues, often fighting on the polluter's own terms rather than developing new ways of solving problems and creating change.

The Women's Environmental Network is conscious of the limitations of science whilst recognizing its value as a means of checking and accounting. WEN uses scientific language to convey and make information accessible but is critical of the way that science has been used to manipulate ideas and attitudes through complex and technical information. WEN voiced this

---

criticism in their 1988 book *The Sanitary Protection Scandal* in an appendix of organic chemical compounds:

> Too often science is regarded as threatening and beyond the comprehension of ordinary people. It can be used, intentionally or unintentionally, to prevent the public from questioning what is being produced, released into the environment, and the effects as a consequence. In order to fully understand the pollution caused by industrialization, we need to question technology, to challenge science and to appreciate the chemical balance of natural systems.

WEN's approach acknowledges that instinct and emotions are as crucial as scientific evidence and statistical data in saving the planet. WEN's ecofeminist philosophy elevates the feminine aspect of intuition as a leading mechanism for the preservation of life.

WEN's approach is to ask questions of industry and politicians until polluters are ready to confront long-term solutions instead of political compromises. WEN has found that often polluters do not know what they are doing or are not prepared to admit that a problem exists, and when they try to defend the indefensible they cannot convince the public of the truth of their argument.

The Women's Environmental Network has campaigned on sanitary products and on disposable soft paper. Spearheaded by the 1990 release of the book, *Tissue of Lies?: disposable paper and the environment*, the organization challenges the disposable paper industry, showing how products sold almost exclusively to women were invented by accident, design or greed and examining the environmental impact of this paper production. The Women's Environmental Network questions not just corporate negligence but the whole necessity of disposable paper use and argues that a one-use paper item is an irresponsible and short-sighted use of resources. WEN advocates the use of reusable and recycled alternatives to soft tissue paper such as cotton handkerchiefs instead of tissues or recycled toilet paper in encouraging a sustainable use of resources and an awareness of total environmental impact.

for many women an understanding of their relationship to the environment and empowered many to act.

As ecofeminism has developed in the North, similarly it has been developing in the South. In particular, the work of Vandana Shiva, an Indian nuclear physicist, has transformed the view of women, environment and development in defining the links between ecological crises, colonialism and the oppression of women. Her 1989 book, *Staying Alive*, appearing a year after Irene Dankelman and Joan Davidson's anthropological survey *Women and the Environment in the Third World*, provides the first clear insight into the relationship between women, environment and development in the South. Shiva argued that ecological destruction often results from the development process, and is legitimized by a patriarchal view of nature. She argues that development is the imposition of Western ideology and shows that, from the perspective of women in the Third World, science and development are not as inclusive or human-centred as they purport to be, but result in ecological destruction and the marginalization of women. Shiva believes that the efforts of women struggling for the survival of their environment in India express a growing belief in an holistic, inclusive approach to life which will be achieved through the intellectual recovery of the feminine principle.

The ecofeminist view is being promoted in the international political arena. Fifty women environmentalists from around the world, including Vandana Shiva and Rosalie Bertell, met together in New York in November 1990 to discuss the role of women in the environment internationally. The aims of the International Policy Action Committee established at this meeting are to inject a women's perspective into preparatory discussions for the 1992 United Nations Conference on Environment and Development. The group advocated the development of a code of Earth ethics, and will present a policy to the UN which promotes an holistic view of environment and development.

THE SPIRITUAL DIMENSION

An holistic vision of the Earth has been present in many communities, cultures and civilizations throughout history, and has often been allied with the belief in the Earth Mother, where the Earth was seen as a sacred, nurturing being. Indeed, a full discussion of ecofeminism requires not just a description of women's involvement in the environment movement, but also a discussion of the influence of women who are exploring Earth-based spirituality. For feminists in the '70s the experience of self-liberation was a consciousness-raising experience, and for some this entailed the significance of spiritual experience. Feminists have provided a critique of traditional religion as a vehicle of patriarchy and have responded to it with views ranging from total rejection of all patriarchal religion to seeking the ordination of women within the Church. However, it is only more recently, with women exploring their own views, that the women's spirituality movement is beginning to emerge independently of male models and male guidance. Some women have turned to Wicca and other Earth-based beliefs for inspiration

---

Box 4.5.4
The Masculine and Feminine Principles

The Chinese I Ching provides a powerful example of a philosophy of life which described the duality of existence based upon the masculine and feminine principles. The Chinese sought *harmony* through the *balance* of these complementary aspects. Threads of this philosophy have run through all cultures, finding expression in the religious and philosophical thought of the early Near Eastern civilizations and influencing Western mystical traditions and more recently the work of Carl Jung who applied these principles of duality to psychology and an understanding of the psyche. This philosophy is being explored by ecofeminists seeking environmental solutions which espouse balance between aspects of the masculine and feminine principles.

Masculine	Feminine
Yang	Yin
Dynamic	Passive
Firm	Yielding
Rigid	Fluid
Creative	Receptive
Active	Responsive
Order	Chaos
Competitive	Co-operative
Separation	Synthesis
Detachment	Connection

---

and as vehicles for expressing their developing awareness of feminine spirituality. Women are exploring the immanence and sacredness of the Earth through honouring the cycles of the Earth and connecting with the body in ritual and celebration, and through valuing and expressing the psyche and the imagination (Spretnak, 1982; King, 1989).

In the 1970s, the scientist James Lovelock developed the Gaia theory which through scientific analysis modelled the Earth as a self-regulating organism (Lovelock, 1979). This idea sparked a dialogue between the mainstream scientific ecological community and the burgeoning '70s spiritual movement which had been exploring alternatives to the rational scientific view of the world. However, Lovelock's model of the Earth did not include the dimension that women exploring Earth-based spirituality experienced – a sense of sanctity of the Earth. This has been explored more through religious and mystical ideas than in science.

The feminist rediscovery of the Goddess through archaeological and historical examination of prehistory by people such as Maria Gimbutas (1982), Merlin Stone (1976) and Riane Eisler (1987) has provided inspiration for many women. Some women worship the Goddess as a deity, others have drawn on her as a feminine symbol of the divine, in order to express their faith in the feminine principle. These women recognize that their spiritual needs include a quest for wholeness and integration and a wish to heal deep divisions within humankind. The veneration of the Earth becomes intrinsic to spirituality both in the celebration of nature and as an understanding of human integration with the Earth.

It is not by chance that this new spirituality should blend with environmental action in that both share an empowering holistic vision, a reverence for life and a commitment to a new form of community. As Starhawk in *Dreaming the Dark* (1980) shows, spirituality is not merely a personal quest for meaning and inwardness, but is often closely connected with acceptance of social responsibility and political activism. Ecofeminism has developed out of the revaluation of the feminine principle in all its aspects – women, the Earth, the body, the feminine aspect of the divine. Women's spirituality unites with feminism and ecology in providing a framework of action, understanding and meaning for a progressive ecofeminist vision that looks to redress the balance between masculine and feminine principles in seeking an equitable, healthy and sustainable world.

Article 4.6
SULTANA'S DREAM
Rokeya Sakhawat Hossain

Introduction by Frances Bonner

In 1516 Sir Thomas More published *Utopia*, a vision of an imaginary 'good' society, establishing and naming a form which was to be used in various types of political writing to the present day. Scientific Utopias, where the good society was premised on scientific understanding, are considered to have begun a century later with the publication of Francis Bacon's *New Atlantis*. Both these works, and most of those that followed them, failed to see any need to address the subordinate position of women. (Some Utopian communities actually established in the nineteenth century, Frances Wright's Nashoba, for example, attempted to incorporate feminist principles (see Bensman, 1984).)

The Utopian story, 'Sultana's dream', first published in 1905, is one of the earliest known feminist Utopias, preceding by ten years the better-known *Herland* by Charlotte Perkins Gilman. Its author, Rokeya Sakhawat Hossain, was a Bengali Muslim feminist who campaigned for women's education, established and ran schools and, as a journalist, wrote articles attacking the practice of purdah (see Hossain, 1988).

'Sultana's dream' is a scientific Utopia, in that the good society is based on scientific developments. It does not matter that the technology described is impossible; it is based on such scientific principles as were known to a (self-)educated Bengali woman at the turn of the century. At the time, the linking of science and progress was little questioned, but it is worth noting that Hossain recognizes that science can be used in morally diverse ways. The story provides a remarkably early instance of the identification of 'bad' male science with weaponry and 'good' female science with gardens.

Feminist Utopias were not very common before the 1970s when several were published in the wake of second-wave feminism. Most of these have some claim to be scientific Utopias, largely on the basis of their concern with alternative modes of reproduction. Marge Piercy's *Woman on the Edge of Time* (1976) is the most explicit of these, attempting to depict a society operating according to Shulamith Firestone's project to liberate women through the development of reproductive technology. A more recent example is Joan Slonciewski's *A Door into the Ocean* (1986), which depicts a female society predicated on a highly developed knowledge of biological sciences. Like most such second-wave feminist fiction, these can also be described as ecotopias – the good society is better not just politically and socially, but is ecologically sensitive as well.

■ ■ ■

[Sultana falls asleep while thinking about the condition of women in India. She dreams that she is invited to go walking with a friend.]

When walking I found to my surprise that it was a fine morning. The town was fully awake and the streets alive with bustling crowds. I was feeling very shy, thinking I was walking in the street in broad daylight, but there was not a single man visible.

Some of the passers-by made jokes at me. Though I could not understand their language, yet I felt sure they were joking. I asked my friend, 'What do they say?'

'The women say you look very mannish.'

'Mannish?' said I. 'What do they mean by that?'

'They mean that you are shy and timid like men.'

'Shy and timid like men?' It was really a joke . . .

She felt my fingers tremble in her hand, as we were walking hand in hand.

'What is the matter, dear, dear?' she said affectionately.

'I feel somewhat awkward,' I said, in a rather apologizing tone, 'as being a purdahnishin woman I am not accustomed to walking about unveiled.'

'You need not be afraid of coming across a man here. This is Ladyland, free from sin and harm. Virtue herself reigns here.'

By and by I was enjoying the scenery. Really it was very grand. I mistook a patch of green grass for a velvet cushion. Feeling as if I were walking on a soft carpet, I looked down and found the path covered with moss and flowers.

'How nice it is,' said I.

'Do you like it?' asked Sister Sara . . .

'Yes, very much; but I do not like to tread on the tender and sweet flowers.'

'Never mind, dear Sultana. Your treading will not harm them; they are street flowers.'

'The whole place looks like a garden,' said I admiringly. 'You have arranged every plant so skilfully.'

'Your Calcutta could become a nicer garden than this, if only your countrymen wanted to make it so.'

'They would think it useless to give so much attention to horticulture, while they have so many other things to do.'

'They could not find a better excuse,' said she with [a] smile.

I became very curious to know where the men were. I met more than a hundred women while walking there, but not a single man.

'Where are the men?' I asked her.

'In their proper places, where they ought to be.'

'Pray let me know what you mean by "their proper places".'

'Oh, I see my mistake, you cannot know our customs, as you were never here before. We shut our men indoors.'

'Just as we are kept in the zenana?'

'Exactly so.'

'How funny.' I burst into a laugh. Sister Sara laughed too.

'But, dear Sultana, how unfair it is to shut in the harmless women and let loose the men.'

'Why? It is not safe for us to come out of the zenana, as we are naturally weak.'

'Yes, it is not safe so long as there are men about the streets, nor is it so when a wild animal enters a marketplace.'

'Of course not.'

'Suppose some lunatics escape from the asylum and begin to do all sorts of mischief to men, horses, and other creatures: in that case what will your countrymen do?'

'They will try to capture them and put them back into their asylum.'

'Thank you! And you do not think it wise to keep sane people inside an asylum and let loose the insane?'

'Of course not!' said I, laughing lightly.

'As a matter of fact, in your country this very thing is done! Men, who do or at least are capable of doing no end of mischief, are let loose and the innocent women shut up in the zenana! How can you trust those untrained men out of doors?'

'We have no hand or voice in the management of our social affairs. In India man is lord and master. He has taken to himself all powers and privileges and shut up the women in the zenana.'

'Why do you allow yourselves to be shut up?'

'Because it cannot be helped as they are stronger than women.'

'A lion is stronger than a man, but it does not enable him to dominate the human race. You have neglected the duty you owe to yourselves, and you have lost your natural rights by shutting your eyes to your own interests.'

'But my dear Sister Sara, if we do everything by ourselves, what will the men do then?'

'They should not do anything, excuse me; they are fit for nothing. Only catch them and put them into the zenana.'

'But would it be very easy to catch and put them inside the four walls?' said I. 'And even if this were done, would all their business – political and commercial – also go with them into the zenana?'

Sister Sara made no reply. She only smiled sweetly. Perhaps she thought it was useless to argue with one who was no better than a frog in a well.

By this time we reached Sister Sara's house. It was situated in a beautiful heart-shaped garden. It was a bungalow with a corrugated iron roof. It was cooler and nicer than any of our rich buildings. I cannot describe how neat and nicely furnished and how tastefully decorated it was.

We sat side by side. She brought out of the parlour a piece of embroidery work and began putting on a fresh design.

'Do you know knitting and needlework?'

'Yes: we have nothing else to do in our zenana.'

'But we do not trust our zenana members with embroidery!' she said laughing, 'as a man has not patience enough to pass thread through [the eye of a needle] even.'

'Have you done all this work yourself?' I asked her, pointing to the various pieces of embroidered teapoy cloths.

'Yes.'

'How can you find time to do all these? You have to do the office work as well? Have you not?'

'Yes. I do not stick to the laboratory all day long. I finish my work in two hours.'

'In two hours! How do you manage? In our land the officers, magistrates, for instance, work seven hours daily.'

'I have seen some of them doing their work. Do you think they work all the seven hours?'

'Certainly they do!'

'No, dear Sultana, they do not. They dawdle away their time in smoking . . . They talk much about their work, but do little . . .'

We talked on various subjects; and I learned that they were not subject to any kind of epidemic disease, nor did they suffer from mosquito bites as we do. I was very much astonished to hear that in Ladyland no one died in youth except by rare accident.

'Will you care to see our kitchen?' she asked me.

'With pleasure,' said I, and we went to see it. Of course the men had been asked to clear off when I was going there. The kitchen was situated in a beautiful vegetable garden. Every creeper, every tomato plant, was itself an ornament. I found no smoke, nor any chimney either in the kitchen – it was clean and bright; the windows were decorated with flower garlands. There was no sign of coal or fire.

'How do you cook?' I asked.

'With solar heat,' she said, at the same time showing me the pipe, through which passed the concentrated sunlight and heat. And she cooked something then and there to show me the process.

'How did you manage to gather and store up the sun['s] heat?' I asked her in amazement.

'Let me tell you a little of our past history, then. Thirty years ago, when our present Queen was thirteen years old, she inherited the throne. She was Queen in name only, the Prime Minister really ruling the country.

'Our good Queen liked science very much. She circulated an order that all the women in her country should be educated. Accordingly a number of girls' schools were founded and supported by the Government. Education was spread far and wide among women. And early marriage also was stopped. No woman was to be allowed to marry before she was twenty-one. I must tell you that, before this change, we had been kept in strict purdah.'

'How the tables are turned,' I interposed with a laugh.

'But the seclusion is the same,' she said. 'In a few years we had separate universities, where no men were admitted.

'In the capital, where our Queen lives, there are two universities. One of these invented a wonderful balloon, to which they attached a number of pipes. By means of this captive balloon, which they managed to keep afloat above the cloudland, they could draw as much water from the atmosphere as they pleased. As the water was incessantly being drawn by the university people, no cloud gathered and the ingenious Lady Principal stopped rain and storms thereby.'

[· · ·]

'When the other university came to know of this, they became exceedingly jealous and tried to do something more extraordinary still. They invented an instrument by which they could collect as much sun heat as they wanted. And they kept the heat stored up to be distributed among others as required.

'While the women were engaged in scientific researches, the men of this country were busy increasing their military power. When they came to know that the female universities were able to draw water from the atmosphere and collect heat from the sun, they only laughed . . . and called the whole thing "a sentimental nightmare"!'

'Your achievements are very wonderful indeed! But tell me how you managed to put the men of your country into the zenana. Did you entrap them first?'

'No.'

'It is not likely they would surrender their free and open air life of their own accord and confine themselves within the four walls of the zenana! They must have been overpowered.'

'Yes, they have been!'

'By whom? – by some lady warriors, I suppose?'

'No, not by arms.'

'Yes, it cannot be so. Men's arms are stronger than women's. Then?'

'By brain.'

'Even their brains are bigger and heavier than women's. Are they not?'

'Yes, but what of that? An elephant also has got a bigger and heavier brain than a man has. Yet man can enchain elephants and employ them, according to his own wishes.'

'Well said, but tell me, please, how it all actually happened. I am dying to know it!'

'Women's brains are somewhat quicker than men's. Ten years ago, when the military officers called our scientific discoveries "a sentimental nightmare", some of the young ladies wanted to say something in reply to those remarks. But both the Lady Principals restrained them and said they should reply not by word but by deed, if ever they got the opportunity. And they had not long to wait for that opportunity ... And now the proud gentlemen are dreaming sentimental dreams themselves.

'Soon afterward certain persons came from a neighbouring country and took shelter in ours. They were in trouble, having committed some political offence. The King, who cared more for power than for good government, asked our kindhearted Queen to hand them over to his officers. She refused, as it was against her principle to turn out refugees. For this refusal the king declared war against our country.

'Our military officers sprang to their feet at once and marched out to meet the enemy.

'The enemy, however, was too strong for them. Our soldiers fought bravely, no doubt. But in spite of all their bravery the foreign army advanced step by step to invade our country.

'Nearly all the men had gone out to fight; even a boy of sixteen was not left home. Most of our warriors were killed, the rest driven back, and the enemy came within twenty-five miles of the capital.

'A meeting of a number of wise ladies was held at the Queen's palace to advise [as] to what should be done to save the land.

'Some proposed to fight like soldiers; others objected and said that women were not trained to fight with swords and guns, nor were they accustomed to fighting with any weapons. A third party regretfully remarked that they were hopelessly weak of body.

"If you cannot save your country for lack of physical strength", said the Queen, "try to do so by brain power."

'There was a dead silence for a few minutes. Her Royal Highness said again, "I must commit suicide if the land and my honour are lost."

'Then the Lady Principal of the second university (who had collected sun heat), who had been silently thinking during the consultation, remarked that they were all but lost; and there was little hope left for them. There was, however, one plan [that] she would like to try, and this would be her first and last effort; if she failed in this, there would be nothing left but to commit suicide. All present solemnly vowed that they would never allow themselves to be enslaved, no matter what happened.

'The Queen thanked them heartily, and asked the Lady Principal to try her plan.

'The Lady Principal rose again and said, "Before we go out the men must enter the zenanas. I make this prayer for the sake of purdah." "Yes, of course," replied Her Royal Highness.

'On the following day the Queen called upon all men to retire into zenanas for the sake of honour and liberty.

'Wounded and tired as they were, they took that order rather for a boon! They bowed low and entered the zenanas without uttering a single word of protest. They were sure that there was no hope for this country at all.

'Then the Lady Principal with her two thousand students marched to the battlefield, and arriving there directed all the rays of the concentrated sun light and heat toward the enemy.

'The heat and light were too much for them to bear. They all ran away panic-stricken, not knowing in their bewilderment how to counteract that scorching heat. When they fled away leaving their guns and other ammunitions of war, they were burned down by means of the same sun heat.

'Since then no one has tried to invade our country any more.'

'And since then your countrymen never tried to come out of the zenana?'

'Yes, they wanted to be free. Some of the Police Commissioners and District Magistrates sent word to the Queen to the effect that the Military Officers certainly deserved to be imprisoned for their failure; but they [had] never neglected their duty and therefore they should not be punished, and they prayed to be restored to their respective offices.

'Her Royal Highness sent them a circular letter, intimating to them that if their services should ever be needed they would be sent for, and that in the meanwhile they should remain where they were.

'Now that they are accustomed to the purdah system and have ceased to grumble at their seclusion, we call the system *mardana* instead of zenana.'

'But how do you manage,' I asked Sister Sara, 'to do without the police or magistrates in case of theft or murder?'

'Since the mardana system has been established, there has been no more crime or sin; therefore we do not require a policeman to find out a culprit, nor do we want a magistrate to try a criminal case . . .

'Now, dear Sultana, will you sit here or come to my parlour?' she asked me.

'Your kitchen is not inferior to a queen's boudoir!' I replied with a pleasant smile, 'but we must leave it now; for the gentlemen may be cursing me for keeping them away from their duties in the kitchen so long.' We both laughed heartily.

'How my friends at home will be amused and amazed, when I go back and tell them that in the far-off Ladyland, ladies rule over the country and control all social matters, while gentlemen are kept in the mardanas to mind babies, to cook, and to do all sorts of domestic work; and that cooking is so easy a thing that it is simply a pleasure to cook!'

'Yes, tell them about all that you see here.'

'Please let me know how you carry on land cultivation and how you plough the land and do other hard manual work.'

'Our fields are tilled by means of electricity, which supplies motive power for other hard work as well, and we employ it for our aerial conveyances too. We have no railroad nor any paved streets here.'

'Therefore neither street nor railway accidents occur here,' said I. 'Do not you ever suffer from want of rainwater?' I asked.

'Never since the "water balloon" has been set up. You see the big balloon and pipes attached thereto. By their aid we can draw as much rainwater as we require. Nor do we ever suffer from flood or thunderstorms. We are all very busy making nature yield as much as she can. We do not find time to quarrel with one another as we never sit idle. Our noble Queen is exceedingly fond of botany; it is her ambition to convert the whole country into one grand garden.'

'The idea is excellent. What is your chief food?'

'Fruits.'

'How do you keep your country cool in hot weather? We regard the rainfall in summer as a blessing from heaven.'

'When the heat becomes unbearable, we sprinkle the ground with plentiful showers drawn from the artificial fountains. And in cold weather we keep our rooms warm with sun heat.'

She showed me her bathroom, the roof of which was removable. She could enjoy a shower bath whenever she liked, by simply removing the roof (which was like the lid of a box) and turning on the tap of the shower pipe.

'You are a lucky people!' ejaculated I. 'You know no want. What is your religion, may I ask?'

'Our religion is based on Love and Truth. It is our religious duty to love one another and to be absolutely truthful. If any person lies, she or he is . . .'

'Punished with death?'

'No, not with death. We do not take pleasure in killing a creature of God – especially a human being. The liar is asked to leave this land for good and never to come to it again.'

'Is an offender never forgiven?'

'Yes, if that person repents sincerely.'

[· · ·]

'That is very good. I see Purity itself reigns over your land. I should like to see the good Queen, who is so sagacious and farsighted and who has made all these rules.'

'All right,' said Sister Sara.

[The two women travel by a hydrogen-powered flying machine to the Queen's garden.]

[· · ·]

I had seen from the air-car the Queen walking on a garden path with her little daughter (who was four years old) and her maids of honour.

'Halloo! you here!' cried the Queen, addressing Sister Sara. I was introduced to Her Royal Highness and was received by her cordially without any ceremony.

I was very much delighted to make her acquaintance. In [the] course of the conversation I had with her, the Queen told me that she had no objection to permitting her subjects to trade with other countries. 'But,' she continued, 'no trade was possible with countries where the women were kept in the zenanas and so unable to come and trade with us. Men, we find, are rather of lower morals and so we do not like dealing with them. We do not covet other people's land, we do not fight for a piece of diamond though it may be a thousandfold brighter than the Koh-i-Noor, nor do we grudge a ruler his Peacock Throne. We dive deep into the ocean of knowledge and try to find out the precious gems [that] Nature has kept in store for us. We enjoy Nature's gifts as much as we can.'

After taking leave of the Queen, I visited the famous universities, and was shown over some of their factories, laboratories and observatories.

After visiting the above places of interest, we got again into the air-car, but as soon as it began moving I somehow slipped down and the fall startled me out of my dream. And on opening my eyes, I found myself in my own bedroom still lounging in the easy chair!

REFERENCES

ABERDEEN, COUNTESS (1990) *The International Congress of Women of 1899*, London, Unwin Publishers.

ABIR-AM, P.G. and OUTRAM, D. (eds) (1987) *Uneasy Careers and Intimate Lives: women in science 1789–1979*, New Brunswick and London, Rutgers University Press.

ADAS, M. (1990) *Machines as the Measure of Men: science, technology and ideologies of Western dominance*, Ithaca, NY, Cornell University Press.

AGARWAL, B. (1983) *Mechanisation in Indian Agriculture: an analytical study based on Punjab*, New Delhi, Allied Publishers.

AGARWAL, B. (1984) 'Rural women and the high yielding variety rice technology', *Economic and Political Weekly, Review of Agriculture*, Vol. 19, No. 13 (March).

ALIC, M. (1986) *Hypatia's Heritage: a history of women in science from antiquity to the late nineteenth century*, London, The Women's Press.

AMARA, J. (1990) 'The double dilemma of the science education of girls in developing countries: a case study of schools in Sierra Leone', contribution to GASAT 1990 Conference, Jönköping, Sweden.

AMNESTY INTERNATIONAL (1991) *Women in the Front Line*.

ARDENER, E. (1975) 'Belief and the problem of women', in Ardener, S. (ed.) *Perceiving Women*, London, Malaby.

ARDITTI, R., BRENNEN, P. and CAVRAK, S. (eds) (1980) *Science and Liberation*, Boston, MA, South End Press.

ARDITTI, R., DUELLI-KLEIN, R. and MINDEN, S. (eds) (1984) *Test-tube Women: what future for motherhood?*, Boston, MA, Pandora Press.

ARNOLD, E. and BURR, L. (1985) 'Housework and the appliance of science', in Faulkner, W. and Arnold, E. (eds).

ARNOLD, J.E.M. and JONGMA, J.H. (1977) 'Fuelwood and charcoal in developing countries', *Unasylva*, Food and Agriculture Organisation, Vol. 29, No. 118.

ASSESSMENT OF PERFORMANCE UNIT (1988) *Science at Age 11: a review of APU findings*, 1980–84, London, HMSO.

BABCOX, D. and BELKIN, M. (eds) (1971) *Liberation Now*, New York, Dell Publishing.

BAHUGUNA, S. (1984) 'Women's non-violent power in the Chipko Movement', in Kishwar, M. and Vanita, R. (eds) *In Search of Answers: Indian women's voices from Manushi*, London, Zed Books.

BAKER, E.F. (1964) *Technology and Women's Work*, New York, Columbia University Press.

BANKS, M.E. and ACKERMAN, R.J. (1990) 'Ethnic and computer

employment status', *Social Science Computer Review*, Spring, Vol. 8, No. 1, pp. 75–82.

BEBEL, A. (1971) *Women Under Socialism*, New York, Schocken Books.

BEEVOR, A. (1990) *Inside the British Army*, London, Chatto and Windus.

BELLER, A.S. (1977) *Fat and Thin: a natural history of obesity*, New York, Farrar, Straus and Giroux.

BENERJEE, N. (1985) *Women and Industrialization in Developing Countries*, Centre for Studies in Social Science, Calcutta.

BENSMAN, M. (1984) 'Frances Wright: Utopian feminist', in Rohrlich, R. and Baruch, E. Hoffman (eds) *Women in Search of Utopia: mavericks and mythmakers*, New York, Schocken Books.

BENSTON, M. LOWE (1982) 'Feminism and the critique of scientific method', in Miles, A. and Finn, G. (eds) *Feminism in Canada*, Montreal, Black Rose Books, pp. 47–66.

BENTLEY, D. and WATTS, M. (eds) (1989) *Learning and Teaching in School Science: practical alternatives*, Buckingham, Open University Press.

BERNDT, C.H. (1981) 'Interpretations and "facts" in Aboriginal Australia', in Dahlberg, F. (ed.), pp. 153–203.

BERTELL, R. (1985) *No Immediate Danger: prognosis for a radioactive world*, London, The Women's Press.

BINFORD, L.R. (1981) *Bones, Ancient Men and Modern Myths*, New York, Academic Press.

BIRKE, L. (1992) 'Transforming biology' in Crowley, H. and Himmelweit, S. (eds) *Knowing Women: Feminism and Knowledge*, Cambridge, Polity Press/The Open University. (Book 1 in this series.)

BLEIER, R. (1984) *Science and Gender: a critique of biology and its theories on women*, New York and Oxford, Pergamon Press.

BLOOR, D. (1977) *Knowledge and Social Imagery*, London, Routledge and Kegan Paul.

BORDO, S. (1987) *The Flight to Objectivity*, Albany, NY, University of New York Press.

BOSTON WOMEN'S HEALTH COLLECTIVE (1971) *Our Bodies, Our Selves*, New York, Simon and Schuster.

BRADSHAW, J.L. (1989) *Hemispheric Specialization and Psychological Function*, Chichester, John Wiley.

BRAYBON, G. (1981) *Women Workers in the First World War*, London, Croom Helm.

BRAYBON, G. and SUMMERFIELD, P. (1987) *Out of the Cage: women's experiences in two World Wars*, London, Pandora.

BRIGHTON WOMEN AND SCIENCE GROUP (eds) (1980) *Alice Through the Microscope: the power of science over women's lives*, London, Virago.

BROCK, W.H. (1973) *H.E. Armstrong and the Teaching of Science, 1880–1930*, Cambridge, Cambridge University Press.

BROWNE, N. (1991) *Science and Technology in the Early Years*, Buckingham, Open University Press.

BROWNMILLER, S. (1975) *Against Our Will: men, women and rape* (Harmondsworth, Penguin, 1986).

BROYLES, W. JR. (1984) 'Why men love war', *Esquire*, November.

BUCKLEY, P. and SMITH, B. (1991) 'Opting out of technology: a study of girls' GCSE choices', in Lovegrove, G. and Segal, B. (eds) *Women into Computing Selected Papers 1988–1990*, Springer Verlag.

BURN, E. (1989) 'Inside the Lego house', in Skelton, C. (ed.).

CALDICOTT, H. (1978) *Nuclear Madness*, New York, New English Library.

CALDICOTT, L. and LELAND, S. (1983) *Reclaim the Earth: women speak out for life on Earth*, London, The Women's Press.

CAPRA, F. (1982) *The Turning Point: science, society and the rising culture*, London, Wildwood House.

CARSON, R. (1954) *The Sea Around Us*, New York, NAL-Dutton (Special Edition, New York, Oxford University Press, 1991).

CARSON, R. (1962) *Silent Spring*, Boston, MA, Houghton Mifflin (Twenty-fifth Anniversary Edition, 1987).

CARSON, R. (1991) *Under the Sea Wind*, New York, NAL-Dutton.

CARTER, R. and KIRKUP, G. (1990) *Women in Engineering: a good place to be?*, London, Macmillan.

CHAYTOR, M. and LEWIS, J. (1982) Introduction to Clark, A.

CHERNIN, K. (1981) *The Obsession: reflections on the tyranny of slenderness*, New York, Harper and Row.

CHODOROW, N. (1978) *The Reproduction of Mothering: psychoanalysis and the sociology of gender*, Berkeley, CA, University of California Press.

CHRISTENSEN, D.B. and BUSH, P.J. (1981) 'Drug prescribing: patterns, problems, and proposals', *Social Science and Medicine*, Vol. 15A, pp. 343–55.

CLARK, A. (1982) *Working Life of Women in the Seventeenth Century*, London, Routledge and Kegan Paul. (First published in 1919.)

COCKBURN, C. (1983) *Brothers: male dominance and technological change*, London, Pluto Press.

COCKBURN, C. (1985) *Machinery of Dominance: women, men and technical know-how*, London, Pluto Press.

CONRAD, P. and SCHNEIDER, J.W. (1980a) *Deviance and Medicalization: from badness to sickness*, St Louis, MO, C.V. Mosby.

CONRAD, P. and SCHNEIDER, J.W. (1980b) 'Looking at levels of medicalization: a comment on Strong's critique of the theses of medical imperialism', *Social Science and Medicine*, Vol. 14a, pp. 75–9.

COOPERSTOCK, R. and PARNELLE, P. (1982) 'Research on psychotropic drug use: a review of findings and methods', *Social Science and Medicine*, Vol. 16, pp. 1179–96.

COWAN, R. SCHWARTZ (1976) 'The "Industrial Revolution" in the home: household technology and social change in the twentieth century', *Technology and Culture*, Vol. 17, pp. 1–23.

COWAN, R. SCHWARTZ (1979) 'From Virginia Dare to Virginia Slims: women and technology in American life', *Technology and Culture*, Vol. 20, No. 1, pp. 51–63.

COWAN, R. SCHWARTZ (1983) *More Work for Mother: the ironies of household technology from the open hearth to the microwave*, New York, Basic Books.

CRAWFORD, R. (1980) 'Healthism and the medicalization of everyday life', *International Journal of Health Service*, Vol. 10, pp. 365–89.

CSE MICROELECTRONICS GROUP (1980) *Microelectronics, Capitalist Technology and the Working Class*, London, CSE Books.

CULLEY, L. (1986) *Gender Differences and Computing in Secondary Schools* (unpublished report, available from the Department of Education, Loughborough University of Technology).

CULLEY, L. (1988) 'Girls, boys and computers', *Educational Studies*, Vol. 14, No. 1.

CURIE, E. (1938) *Madame Curie*, Sheean, V. (trans.), New York, Doubleday.

DAHLBERG, F. (ed.) (1981) *Woman the Gatherer*, New Haven, CT, Yale University Press.

DALTON, K. (1977) *The Premenstrual Syndrome and Progesterone Therapy*, Chicago, IL, Year Book Medical Publishers.

DALY, M. (1978) *Gyn/Ecology: the metaethics of radical feminism*, Boston, MA, Beacon Press.

D'AMICO, F. (1990) 'Women at arms: the combat controversy', *Minerva Quarterly Report*, Summer.

DANKELMAN, I. and DAVIDSON, J. (1988) *Women and the Environment in the Third World*, London, Earthscan Publications.

DARWIN, C. (1936) *The Descent of Man and Selection in Relation to Sex*, New York, Modern Library. (First published in 1871.)

DARWIN, C. (1936) *The Origin of Species*, New York, Modern Library. (First published in 1859.)

DAVIDOFF, L. (1976) 'The rationalization of housework', in Barker, D.

and Allen, S. (eds) *Dependence and Exploitation in Work and Marriage*, London, Longman.

DAVIDSON, C. (1982) *A Woman's Work is Never Done: a history of housework in the British Isles, 1650–1950*, London, Chatto and Windus.

DAVIES, M.L. (1978) *Maternity: letters from working women*, New York, Norton.

DAWKINS, R. (1982) *The Extended Phenotype*, San Francisco, W.E. Freeman.

DEAKIN, R. (1984) *Women and Computing: the golden opportunity*, London, Macmillan.

D'EAUBONNE, F. (1980) 'Feminism or death', in Marks, E. and de Coutivron, I. (eds) *New French Feminisms: an anthology*, Amherst, MA, University of Massachusetts Press.

DEETZ, J. (1968) 'Hunters in archeological perspective', in Lee, R.B. and Devore, I. (eds), pp. 281–5.

DEFOE, D. (1796) *Tour*, cited by Pinchbeck, I. (1981).

DELANEY, M., LUPTON, J. and TOTH, E. (1976) *The Curse*, New York, E.P. Dutton.

DEY, J. (1975) *The Role of Women in Third World Countries*, Agricultural Extension and Rural Development Centre, University of Reading.

DICKSON, D. (1974) *Alternative Technology and the Politics of Technical Change*, London, Fontana.

DIGERNESS, T. HAMMER (1977) 'Wood for fuel: the energy situation in Bara, the Sudan', mimeo. (July), Department of Geography, University of Bergen, Norway.

DIXON, R.B. (1978) *Rural Women and Work: strategies for development in south Asia*, London, Johns Hopkins University Press.

DOGRA, B. (1984) *Forests and People*, Bharat Dogra, A-2/184 Janakpuri, New Delhi.

DONAHUE, T. and JOHNSON, N. (1986) *Foul Play: drug abuse in sports*, Oxford, Basil Blackwell.

DOOLITTLE, W. FORD (1981) 'Is nature really motherly?', *Co-Evolution Quarterly*, Spring, pp. 58–63.

DYE, N.S. (1980) 'History of childbirth in America', *Signs: Journal of Women in Culture and Society*, Vol. 97, pp. 97–108.

DYER, K. (1982) *Catching up the Men: women in sport*, London, Junction Books.

EASLEA, B. (1978) *Liberation and the Aims of Science*, London, Chatto and Windus.

EASLEA, B. (1981) *Science and Sexual Oppression*, London, Weidenfeld and Nicolson.

ECONOMIC TIMES (1984) 'Perils of modernisation', 1 April.

EDWARDS, P.N. (1990) 'The army and the microworld: computers and the politics of gender identity', *Signs: Journal of Women in Culture and Society*, Vol. 16, No. 1.

EHRENREICH, B. and ENGLISH, D. (1973) *Complaints and Disorders: the sexual politics of sickness*, Old Westbury, NY, Feminist Press.

EHRENREICH, B. and ENGLISH, D. (1975) 'The manufacture of house-work', *Socialist Revolution*, Vol. 26, pp. 5–40.

EHRENREICH, B. and ENGLISH, D. (1979) *For Her Own Good: 150 years of the experts' advice to women*, Garden City, NY, Anchor (London, Pluto Press).

EISENSTEIN, H. (1983) *Give us Bread but Give us Roses*, London, Routledge and Kegan Paul.

EISLER, R. (1987) *The Chalice and the Blade*, San Francisco, Harper and Row.

ELA BHATT, R. (1985) 'Women's employment and technology', in Jain, S.C. (ed.).

ELIAS, S. and ANNAS, G.J. (1987) 'Routine prenatal genetic screening', *The New England Journal of Medicine*, Vol. 317, pp. 1047–9.

EMERY, A. (1984) *An Introduction to Recombinant DNA*, Chichester, John Wiley and Sons.

ENGELS, F. (1972) *Origin of the Family, Private Property and the State*, New York, Pathfinder Press.

ENLOE, C. (1989) *Does Khaki Become You?: the militarisation of women's lives*, London, Pandora Press.

ESTIOKO-GRIFFIN, A. and GRIFFIN, P.B. (1981) 'Woman the hunter: the Agta', in Dahlberg, F. (ed.), pp. 121–51.

ETTORE, B. (1985) 'Psychotropics, passivity and the pharmaceutical industry', in Henman, A., Lewis, R. and Malyon, T. (eds) *Big Deal: the politics of the illicit drug business*, London, Pluto Press.

EVANS-PRITCHARD, E.E. (1965) *Theories of Primitive Religion*, Oxford, Clarendon Press.

FAIRWEATHER, H. (1976) 'Sex differences in cognition', *Cognition*, Vol. 4, pp. 231–80.

FARRANT, W. (1985) 'Who's for amniocentesis? The politics of prenatal screening', in Homans, H. (ed.) *The Sexual Politics of Reproduction*, Aldershot, Gower.

FAULKNER, W. and ARNOLD, E. (eds) (1985) *Smothered by Invention: technology in women's lives*, London, Pluto Press.

FAUSTO-STERLING, A. (1987) *Myths of Gender: biological theories about women and men*, New York, Basic Books.

FERRIS, E. (1980) 'Attitudes to women in sport', International Congress on Women and Sport, July, Rome.

FEYERABEND, P. (1975) *Against Method*, London, Verso.

FEYNMAN, R.P. (1988) 'The value of science', text of a 1955 lecture printed in *'What do you care what other people think?': further adventures of a curious character*, London, Unwin Paperbacks.

FINGER, A. (1984) 'Claiming all of our bodies', pp. 281–97 in Arditti, R. *et al.*, (eds).

FIRESTONE, S. (1980) *The Dialectic of Sex: the case for feminist revolution*, (new edn) London, The Women's Press.

FISCHER, C. (1988) '"Touch someone": the telephone industry discovers sociability', *Technology and Culture*, Vol. 29, No. 1, pp. 32–61.

FLEURET, P.C. and FLEURET, A. (1978) 'Fuelwood use in a peasant community: a Tanzanian case study', *The Journal of Developing Areas*, Vol. 12.

FLOOR, W.M. (1977) 'The energy sector of the Sahelian countries', mimeo. (April), Policy Planning Section, Ministry of Foreign Affairs, The Netherlands.

FLORMAN, S.C. (1984) 'Will women engineers make a difference?', *Technology Review*, Vol. 87, No. 8 (November/December), pp. 51–2.

FLORMAN, S.C. (1991) 'Cosmic promises', *Technology Review*, Vol. 94, No. 1, (January).

FOSSEY, D. (1984) *Gorillas in the Mist*, Boston, MA, Houghton Mifflin.

FOUCAULT, M. (1973) *The Birth of the Clinic: an archeology of medical perception*, New York, Pantheon.

FOX, R. (1977) 'The medicalization and demedicalization of American society', *Daedalus*, Vol. 106, pp. 9–22.

FRANKLIN, I. (1988) 'Services for sickle cell disease: unified approach needed', *British Medical Journal*, Vol. 296.

FREEMAN, L., JR. (1968) 'A theoretical framework for interpreting archeological materials', in Lee, R.B. and Devore, I. (eds), pp. 262–7.

FRIEDAN, B. (1963) *The Feminine Mystique*, New York, Dell.

FRIZE, M. (1991) 'Women in engineering in Canada', Proceedings of the Ninth International Conference of Women Engineers, University of Warwick.

FROW, E. and FROW, R. (1982) *Engineering Struggles*, Working Class Movement Library.

GARNER, D.M., GARFINKEL, P.E., SCHWARTZ, D. and THOMPSON, M. (1980) 'Cultural expectations of thinness in women', *Psychological Reports*, Vol. 47, pp. 483–91.

GENOVA, J. (1989) 'Women and the mismeasure of thought', in Tuana, N. (ed.).

GERSHUNY, J. (1978) *After Industrial Society: the emerging self-service economy*, Basingstoke, Macmillan.

GERSHUNY, J. (1983) *Social Innovation and the Division of Labour*, London, Oxford University Press.

GERSHUNY, J. (1985) 'Economic development and change in the mode of provision of services', in Redclift, N. and Minigione, E. (eds) *Beyond Employment: household, gender and subsistence*, Oxford, Basil Blackwell.

GERSHUNY, J. and ROBINSON, J. (1988) 'Historical changes in the household division of labour', unpublished ms.

GILLIGAN, C. (1982) *In a Different Voice: psychological theory and women's development*, Cambridge, MA, Harvard University Press.

GILMAN, C. PERKINS (1979) *Herland: a lost feminist Utopian novel*, London, The Women's Press (New York, Pantheon). (First published in 1905.)

GIMBUTAS, M. (1982) *The Gods and Goddesses of Old Europe, 6500–3500 BC: myths and cult images*, Berkeley, CA, University of California Press.

GLUCKMAN, M. (1984) 'Women and the "new industries": changes in class relations in the 1930s', paper to the Economic and Social Research Council Seminar on Gender and Stratification, July, University of East Anglia, Norwich.

GOODALL, J. (1979) *In the Shadow of Man*, London, New English Library, Collin (London, Weidenfeld and Nicolson, rev. edn, 1989).

GORDON, L. (1976) *Woman's Body, Woman's Right: a social history of birth control in America*, New York, Penguin Books.

GOULD, R.A. (1981) 'Comparative ecology of food-sharing in Australia and Northwest California', in Harding, R.S.O. and Teleki, G. (eds), pp. 422–54.

GRAY, A. (1987) 'Behind closed doors: video recorders in the home', in Baehr, H. and Dyer, G. (eds) *Boxed In: women and television*, London, Routledge and Kegan Paul.

GREED, C. (1991) *Surveying Sister: women in a traditional male profession*, London, Routledge.

GREELEY, M. (1981) *Rural Technology, Rural Industries and the Rural Poorest: the case of rice processing in Bangladesh*, January, New Delhi, IARI.

GREEN, B. (1990) 'Women in combat', *Air Force Magazine*, June.

GRIFFIN, K. (1974) *The Political Economy of Agrarian Change: an essay on the Green Revolution*, Basingstoke, Macmillan.

GRIFFIN, S. (1978) *Women and Nature: the roaring inside her*, New York, Harper and Row (London, The Women's Press, 1984).

GRIFFIN, S. (1982) *Made from This Earth*, New York, Harper and Row.

GROBICKI, A. (1987) 'Barbara McClintock: what price objectivity', in McNeil, M. (ed.) *Gender and Expertise*, London, Free Association Books.

GROSS, H.S., HERBERT, M.R., KNATTERUD, G.L. and DONNER, L. (1969) 'The effect of race and sex on the variation of diagnosis and disposition in a psychiatric emergency room', *Journal of Nervous and Mental Disease*, Vol. 148, pp. 638–43.

HAAS, V.B. and PERRUCCI, C.C. (eds) (1984) *Women in Scientific and Engineering Professions*, Ann Arbor, MI, University of Michigan Press.

HACKER, B.C. (1981) 'Women and military institutions in early modern Europe: a reconnaissance', *Signs: Journal of Women in Culture and Society*, Vol. 6 (Summer), pp. 643–71.

HACKER, S. (1989) *Pleasure, Power and Technology: some tales of gender, engineering and the co-operative workplace*, London, Unwin Hyman.

HACKING, I. (1984) *The New York Review of Books*, 28 June, pp. 17–20.

HADDON, L. (1988) 'The home computer: the making of a consumer electronic', *Science as Culture*, No. 2, pp. 7–51.

HADDON, L. and SKINNER, D. (1991) 'The enigma of the micro: lessons from the British home computer boom', *Social Science Computing Review*, Fall, Vol. 9, No. 3.

HALL, D.L. (1976) 'Biology, sex hormones and sexism in the 1920s', in Gould, C.C. and Wartotsky, M.W. (eds) *Women and Philosophy: toward a theory of liberation*, New York, G.P. Putnam's.

HAMILTON, W.D. (1975) 'Innate social aptitudes in man: an approach from evolutionary genetics', in Fox, R. (ed.) *Biosocial Anthropology*, New York, John Wiley.

HAMMOND, J. (1990) *Sweeter than Honey*, London, Link Publications.

HARAWAY, D. (1986) 'Primatology is politics by other means', in Bleier, R. (ed.) *Feminist Approaches to Science*, Elmsford, NY, Pergamon Press, pp. 77–118.

HARDING, S. (1986) *The Science Question in Feminism*, Ithaca, NY, Cornell University Press.

HARDING, R.S.O. and TELEKI, G. (eds) (1981) *Omnivorous Primates: gathering and hunting in human evolution*, New York, Columbia University Press.

HARPER, P. (1983) 'Genetic counselling and prenatal diagnosis', *British Medical Bulletin*, Vol. 39, pp. 302–9.

HARRISON, M. (1982) *Self-Help for Premenstrual Syndrome*, Cambridge, MA, Matrix Press.

HARTSOCK, N. (1983) 'The feminist standpoint: developing the ground for a specifically feminist historical materialism', in Harding, S. and Hintikka, M. (eds) *Discovering Reality: feminist perspectives on epistemology, metaphysics, methodology and philosophy of science*, Dordrecht, The Netherlands, Reidel Publishing, pp. 283–310.

HAWKESWORTH, M.E. (1989) 'Knowers, knowing, known: feminist theory and claims of truth', *Signs: Journal of Women in Culture and Society*, Vol. 14, No. 3, pp. 533–57.

HAYDEN, B. (1981) 'Subsistence and ecological adaptations of modern hunter-gatherers', in Harding, R.S.O. and Teleki, G. (eds), pp. 344–421.

HEARN, J. and PARKIN, W. (1987) *Sex at Work: the power and the paradox of organisation sexuality*, Brighton, Wheatsheaf.

HEGEL, G.W.F. (1979) *Phenomenology of Spirit*, Miller, A.V. (trans.), New York, Oxford University Press.

HERRNSTEIN, R. (1971) 'IQ', *Atlantic Monthly*, Vol. 228, pp. 43–64.

HINTON, J. (1981) *The First Shop Stewards' Movement*, London, George Allen and Unwin.

HMSO (1991) *Social Trends 21*, London, HMSO.

HORNIG, L.S. (1984) 'Women in science and engineering: why so few?', *Technology Review*, Vol. 87, No. 8 (November/December), pp. 31–41.

HOSKINS, M. (1979) 'Women in forestry for local community development: a programming guide', paper prepared for the Office of Women in Development, December, Washington, DC, Agency for International Development.

HOSKINS, M. (1983) 'Rural women, forest outputs and forestry projects', discussion draft paper No. MISC/83/3, Rome, Food and Agriculture Organisation.

HOSSAIN, R. SAKHAWAT (1988) *Sultana's Dream and Selections from The Secluded Ones*, Jahan, R. (ed. and trans.) (afterword by Papanek, H.), New York, The Feminist Press at the City University.

HOWE, J.W. and STAFF OF THE OVERSEAS DEVELOPMENT COUNCIL (1977) *Energy for the Villages of Africa: recommendations for African governments and outside donors*, Overseas Development Council, Washington, DC.

HOWE, LADY (chair) (1990) *Report of the Hansard Society Commission on Women at the Top*, London, Hansard Society.

HUBBARD, R. (1979) 'Have only men evolved?', in Hubbard, R., Henifin, M.S., and Fried, B. (eds).

HUBBARD, R. (1981) 'The politics of women's biology', lecture given at Hampshire College, October.

HUBBARD, R. (1982) 'Legal and policy implications of recent advances in prenatal diagnosis and fetal therapy', *Women's Rights Law Reporter*, Rutgers, Vol. 7, pp. 201–18.

HUBBARD, R. (1983) 'Women and biology', lecture at annual conference, New England Women's Studies, Keene State College, Keene, NH.

HUBBARD, R. and LOWE, M. (eds) (1983) *Women's Nature: rationalization of inequality*, New York, Pergamon Press.

HUBBARD, R., HENEFIN, S. and FRIED, B. (eds) (1979) *Women Look at Biology Looking at Women*, Cambridge, MA, Schenkman Publishing Co.

HUGHART, D. (1979) 'Prospects for traditional and non-conventional energy sources in developing countries', World Bank Staff Working Paper No. 346, Washington, DC, World Bank.

HUGHES, M., BRACKENRIDGE, A., BIBY, A. and GREENHOUGH, P. (1988) 'Girls, boys and turtles: gender effects in young children learning with Logo', in Hoyles, C. (ed.) *Girls and Computers*, Bedford Way Papers 34, London Institute of Education, University of London.

HUTCHINS, B.L. (1978) *Women in Modern Industry*, Wakefield, E.P. Publishing Ltd. (First published in 1915.)

HYNES, P. (1984) 'Women working: a field report', *Technology Review*, Vol. 87, No. 8 (November/December).

IFTIKHAR, A. (1978a) *Technology and Rural Women: conceptual and empirical issues*, London, George Allen and Unwin.

IFTIKHAR, A. (1978b) *Technical Change and the Conditions of Rural Women*, Technological and Employment Programme, No. 39, Geneva, ILO.

ILLICH, I. (1976) *Medical Nemesis: the expropriation of health*, New York, Pantheon.

INTERNATIONAL LABOUR ORGANISATION (1978) *Participation of Women in Economic Activities and their Working Conditions in African Countries*, November, Geneva, ILO.

ISAAC, G. (1978) 'The food-sharing behavior of protohuman hominids', *Scientific American*, Vol. 238, pp. 90–106.

ISAAC, G. (1980) 'Casting the net wide: a review of archeological evidence for early hominid land use and ecological relations', in Konigsson, L.K. (ed.) *Current Argument on Early Man*, Oxford, Pergamon Press, pp. 226–51.

ISAAC, G. (1982) 'Models of human evolution' (letter), *Science*, Vol. 221, p. 295.

ISAAC, G. (1984) 'The archeology of human origins: studies of the lower Pleistocene in East Africa 1971–1981', in Wendorf, F. and Close, A.E. (eds) *Advances in World Archeology*, Orlando, FL, Academic Press, pp. 1–87.

JACKSON, L. (1986) 'Prenatal genetic diagnosis by chorionic villus sampling', in Porter, I., Hatcher, N. and Willey, A. (eds) *Perinatal Genetics: diagnosis and treatment*, London, Academic Press.

JAIN, S.C. (ed.) (1985) *Women and Technology*, Jaipur, Rawat Publications.

KAHLE, J.B. (1985) 'Retention of girls in science: case studies of secondary teachers', in Kahle, J.B. (ed.) *Women in Science: a report from the field*, Brighton, Falmer Press.

KELLER, E. FOX (1983) *A Feeling for the Organism: the life and work of Barbara McClintock*, New York, W.H. Freeman.

KELLER, E. FOX (1984) Untitled article, *Technology Review*, Vol. 87, No. 8 (November/December), pp. 45–7.

KELLER, E. FOX (1985) *Reflections on Gender and Science*, New Haven, CT, Yale University Press.

KELLER, E. FOX (1986) 'How gender matters, or, why it's so hard for us to count past two', in Harding, J. (ed.) *Perspectives on Gender and Science*, Brighton, Falmer Press. (Edited version printed as Article 1.3 in this volume.)

KELLY, A. (ed.) (1981) *The Missing Half: girls and science education*, Manchester, Manchester University Press.

KELLY, A. (ed.) (1987) *Science for Girls?*, Buckingham, Open University Press.

KELLY, A., WHYTE, J. and SMAIL, B. (1984) *Girls into Science and Technology*, Department of Sociology, Manchester, University of Manchester.

KERMODE, F. (1967) *The Sense of an Ending*, London, Oxford University.

KERSTEEN, Z.A., LINN, M., CLANCY, M. and HARDYNCK, C. (1988) 'Previous experience and the learning of computer programming: the computer helps those who help themselves', *Journal of Educational Computing Research*, Vol. 4, No. 3.

KESSLER-HARRIS, A. (1982) *Out to Work: a history of wage-earning women in the United States*, New York, Oxford University Press.

KEVLES, D.J. (1986) *In the Nature of Eugenics*, Harmondsworth, Penguin Books.

KING, U. (1989) *Women and Spirituality*, London, Women in Society.

KOUMJIAN, K. (1981) 'The use of valium as a force of social control', *Social Science and Medicine*, Vol. 15E, pp. 245–9.

KRAMARAE, C. (ed.) (1988) *Technology and Women's Voices: keeping in touch*, London and New York, Routledge.

KRAMER, P. and LEHMAN, S. (1990) 'Mismeasuring women: a critique of research on computer ability and avoidance', *Signs: Journal of Women in Culture*, Autumn, Vol. 16, No. 1.

KROPOTKIN, P. (1902) *Mutual Aid*, Boston, MA, Extending Horizon Books.

KUHN, T. (1962) *The Structure of Scientific Revolutions*, Chicago, IL, Chicago University Press.

LANDAU, M. (1984) 'Human evolution as narrative', *American Scientist*, Vol. 72, pp. 262–8.

LEACOCK, E. BURKE (1981) *Myths of Male Dominance*, New York, Monthly Review Press.

LEAKEY, R.E. (1981) *The Making of Mankind*, New York, Dutton.

LEAVITT, J.W. (1980) 'Birthing and anaesthesia: the debate over twilight sleep', *Signs: Journal of Women in Culture and Society*, Vol. 6, pp. 147–64.

LEE, R.B. (1968) 'What hunters do for a living, or, how to make out on scarce resources', in Lee, R.B. and Devore, I. (eds), pp. 30–48.

LEE, R.B. and DEVORE, I. (eds) (1968) *Man the Hunter*, New York, Aldine.

LEIBOWITZ, L. (1983) 'Origins of the sexual division of labor', in Hubbard, R. and Lowe, M. (eds), pp. 123–47.

LÉVI-STRAUSS, C. (1949) *The Elementary Structure of Kinship*, Boston, MA, Beacon Press.

LEVIDOW, L. (1988) 'Non-Western science, past and present', *Science as Culture*, Vol. 3, pp. 101–17.

LEVIN, T. and GORDON, C. (1989) 'Effect of gender and computer experience on attitudes towards computers', *Journal of Educational Computing Research*, Vol. 5, No. 1.

LEWIS, B. (N.D.) *Invisible Farmers: Women and the Crisis in Agriculture*, Washington, DC, Agency for International Development.

LINTON, S. (1971) 'Woman the gatherer: male bias in anthropology', in Jacobs, S.E. (ed.) *Women in Perspective: a guide for cross-cultural studies*, Urbana, IL, University of Illinois Press, pp. 9–21.

LONG, J. and DOWELL, J. (1989) 'Concepts of the discipline of HCI: craft, applied science and engineering', in Sutcliffe, A. and Macaulay, L. (eds) (1989) *People and Computers V – HCI '89*, Cambridge, Cambridge University Press, pp. 9–32.

LOVEJOY, C.O. (1981) 'The origin of man', *Science*, Vol. 211, pp. 341–50.

LOVELOCK, J. (1979) *Gaia: a new look at life on Earth*, London, Oxford University Press.

LYMAN, F. (1989) 'What Gaia hath wrought', *Technology Review*, Vol. 92, No. 5 (July), pp. 55–61.

MACINTYRE, S. (1987) 'Women's experiences and attitudes to screening', in *Screening for Fetal and Genetic Abnormality*, King's Fund Forum, London, November/December.

MACKINNON, C. (1982) 'Feminism, Marxism, method and the state, Parts 1 & 2', *Signs: Journal of Women in Culture and Society*, Vol. 7, No. 3, pp. 515–44.

MALOIY, G.M.O., HEGLUND, N.C., PRAGER, L.M., GAVAGNA, G.A. and TAYLOR, C.R. (1986) 'Energetic costs of carrying loads: have African women discovered an economic way?', *Nature*, Vol. 319, pp. 668–9.

MARGOLIS, M. (1985) *Mothers and Such: views of American women and why they changed*, Berkeley, University of California Press.

MARTIN, M.K. and VORHEES, B. (1975) *Female of the Species*, New York, Cambridge University Press.

MARX, K. (1954) *Capital*, Vol. I, London, Lawrence & Wishart. (First published in 1887.)

MASON, J. (1991) 'A forty years' war (1880–1920): the admission of women to the Fellowship of the Chemical Society', *Chemistry in Britain*, Vol. 27.

MATRIX (1984) *Making Space: women and the man-made environment*, London, Pluto Press.

MCGUINESS, D. (1976) 'Sex differences in the organisation of perception and cognition', in Lloyd, B. and Archer, J. (eds) *Exploring Sex Differences*, London, Academic Press.

MCKINLAY, J. (1981) 'A case for refocussing upstream: the political economy of illness', in Conrad, P. and Kern, R. (eds) *The Sociology of Health and Illness*, New York, St. Martin's Press, pp. 613–33.

MCLAREN, A. (1987) 'Can we diagnose genetic disease in pre-embryos?', *New Scientist*, 10 December.

MERCHANT, C. (1980) *The Death of Nature: women, ecology and the scientific revolution*, San Francisco, Harper and Row.

MILLMAN, M. (1980) *Such a Pretty Face: being fat in America*, New York, Berkley Books.

MILLMAN, M. and KANTER, R. MOSS (1975) 'Editors' introduction', in their edited collection, *Another Voice: feminist perspectives on social life and social science*, New York, Anchor Books.

MITCHELL, B. (1990) 'Should women serve in combat?', *The American Legion*, May.

MODELL, B. (1983) 'Screening for carriers of recessive disease', in Carter, E.O. (ed.) *Developments in Human Reproduction and their Eugenic and Ethical Implications*, London, Academic Press.

MOHR, J.C. (1978) *Abortion in America: the origins and evolution of national policy, 1800–1900*, New York, Oxford University Press.

MOIR, A. and JESSEL, D. (1989) *Brain Sex: the real difference between men and women*, London, Michael Joseph.

MOOS, R.H. (1963) 'The development of a menstrual distress questionnaire', *Psychomatic Medicine*, Vol. 30, pp. 853–67.

MORLEY, D. (1986) *Family Television: cultural power and domestic leisure*, London, Comedia.

MORRIS, J. (1974) *Conundrum*, London, Faber and Faber.

MOSKOS, C. (1990) 'Army women', *Atlantic Monthly*, August.

MUMFORD, L. (1934) *Technics and Civilization*, London, Routledge and Kegan Paul.

MURRAY, E.M. (1991) 'Current statistical data for women engineers and scientists in the USA', Proceedings of the Ninth International Conference of Women Engineers, University of Warwick.

NAGBRAHMAN, D. and SAMBRANI, S. (1983) 'Women's drudgery in firewood collection', *Economic and Political Weekly*, 1–8 January.

NATIONAL CURRICULUM COUNCIL (1989) *NCC Non-statutory Guidelines*, York, Department of Education and Science.

NEFF, W.F. (1966) *Victorian Women*, London, Frank Cass.

NEWMAN, E. (1985) 'Who controls birth control?', in Faulkner, W. and Arnold, E. (eds).

NEWTON, I. (1687) *Mathematical Principles of Natural Philosphy*; quoted in Brody, B.A. and Capaldi, N. (eds) (1968) *Science: men, methods, goals*, New York, W.A. Benjamin, p. 78.

NOBLE, D. (1979) *America by Design: science, technology and the rise of corporate capitalism*, London, Oxford University Press.

NOBLE, D. (1984) *Forces of Production: a social history of industrial automation*, New York, Knopf.

NOTELOVITZ, M. (1986) 'Interrelations of exercise and diet on bone metabolism and osteoporosis', in Winick, M. (ed.) *Nutrition and Exercise*, Chichester, Wiley-Interscience.

OAKLEY, A. (1972) *Sex, Gender and Society*, London, Temple Smith.

OAKLEY, A. (1974) *The Sociology of Housework*, London, Martin Robertson.

O'DRISCOLL, K. and FOLEY, M. (1983) 'Correlation of decrease in perinatal mortality and increase in Caesarean section rates', *Obstetrics and Gynecology*, Vol. 61, pp. 1–5.

OGILVIE, M.N. BAILEY (1986) *Women in Science: antiquity through the nineteenth century*, Cambridge, MA, MIT Press.

PALMER, I. (1975) *Women in Rural Development*, Geneva, ILO.

PALMER, I. (1978) *Women and Green Revolutions*, Institute of Development Studies, University of Sussex.

PANKHURST, E.S. (1931/1977) *The Suffragette Movement*, London, Longman/Virago, London.

PARSONS, T. (1956) 'The American family: its relations to personality and the social structure', in Parsons, T. and Bales, R., *Family, Socialisation and Interaction Process*, London, Routledge and Kegan Paul.

PELLING, H. (1976) *A History of British Trade Unionism*, Basingstoke, Macmillan.

PENNY, V. (1869) *Think and Act*, cited in Meyer, A.N. (ed.) (1972) *Woman's Work in America*, Salem, NH, Arno. (First published in 1891.)

PENTAGON (1990) *Special Edition – Equal Opportunity*, April, Pentagon.

PERROLLE, J.A. (1988) 'The social impact of computing: ideological themes and research issues', *Social Science Computer Review*, Winter, Vol. 6, No. 4, pp. 469–81.

PIERCY, M. (1976) *Woman on the Edge of Time*, London, The Women's Press (New York, Fawcett, 1972).

PILBEAM, D. (1980) 'Major trends in human evolution', in Konigsson, L.K. (ed.) *Current Argument on Early Man*, Oxford, Pergamon Press, pp. 261–85.

PINCHBECK, I. (1981) *Women Workers and the Industrial Revolution, 1750–1850*, London, Virago. (First published in 1930.)

POSTAN, M.M. (1975) *The Medieval Economy and Society*, Harmondsworth, Penguin Books.

POTTS, R. (1984) 'Home bases and early hominids', *American Scientist*, Vol. 72, pp. 338–47.

PRASAD, N.B. (1979) *Report of the Working Group on Energy Policy*, Ministry of Energy, Department of Power, Government of India, New Delhi.

QUINN, N. (1977) 'Anthropological studies on women's status', *Annual Review of Anthropology*, Vol. 6, pp. 181–225.

RAKOW, L. (1988) 'Women and the telephone: the gendering of a communications technology', in Kramarae, C. (ed.).

RAGHUWANSHI, C. (1990) 'Status of women in science and technology in India: current trends', contribution to GASAT 1990 Conference, Jönköping, Sweden.

RANDALL, M. (1980) *Sandino's Daughters*, Vancouver, BC, New Star Press.

RAVETZ, A. (1965) 'Modern technology and an ancient occupation:

housework in present-day society', *Technology and Culture*, Vol. 6, pp. 256–60.

RAVINDRANATH, N.H., SOMASHEKHAR, H.I., RAMESH, R., REDDY, A., VENKATRAM, K. and REDDY, A.K.N. (1978) *The Design of a Rural Energy Center for Pura Village, Part I: its present pattern of energy consumption*, Bangalore, India, ASTRA, Indian Institute of Science.

REDSTOCKINGS (1971) 'The politics of housework', in Babcox, D. and Belkin, M. (eds).

REID, R. (1978) *Marie Curie*, London, Paladin.

REIGER, K. (1985) *The Disenchantment of the Home: modernizing the Australian family 1880–1940*, Melbourne, Oxford University Press.

REIGER, K. (1986) 'At home with technology', *Arena*, Vol. 75, pp. 109–23.

REVERBY, S. (1981) 'Stealing the golden eggs: Earnest Amory Codman and the science and management of medicine', *Bulletin of the History of Medicine*, Vol. 55, pp. 156–71.

ROGAN, H. (1981) *Mixed Company: women in the modern army*, Boston, MA, Beacon Press.

ROGERS, L. (1988) 'Biology, the popular weapon: sex differences in cognitive function', *Crossing Boundaries: feminisms and the critique of knowledges*, Sydney, Allen and Unwin.

ROGGENCAMP, V. (1984) 'Abortions of a special kind: male sex selection in India', in Arditti, R. *et al.* (eds).

ROSE, H. (1983) 'Hand, brain and heart: a feminist epistemology for the natural sciences', *Signs: Journal of Women in Culture and Society*, Vol. 9, No. 1, pp. 73–90.

ROSENBERG, N. (1982) *Inside the Black Box: technology and economics*, Cambridge, Cambridge University Press.

ROSENBERG, N. and BIRDZELL, L.E., JR (1990) 'Science, technology and the Western miracle', *Scientific American*, Vol. 263, No. 5 (November), pp. 18–25.

ROSENBERG, R. (1982) *Beyond Separate Spheres: intellectual roots of modern feminism*, New Haven, CT, Yale University Press.

ROSSER, S.V. (1990) *Female-friendly Science: applying women's studies methods and theories to attract students*, Oxford, Pergamon Press.

ROSSITER, M. (1982) *Women Scientists in America: struggles and strategies to 1940*, Baltimore, MD, Johns Hopkins University Press.

ROTHMAN, B. KATZ (1986) *The Tentative Pregnancy*, New York, Viking Press.

ROTHSCHILD, J. (ed.) (1983) *Machina Ex Dea: feminist perspectives on technology*, New York, Pergamon Press.

RUBLE, D. (1977) 'Premenstrual symptoms: a re-interpretation', *Science*, Vol. 197, pp. 291–2.

RUSSETT, C.E. (1989) *Sexual Science: the Victorian construction of womanhoods*, Cambridge, MA, Harvard University Press.

SACKS, K. (1982) *Sisters and Wives*, Chicago, IL, University of Chicago Press.

SAHLINS, M.D. (1960) 'The origin of society', *Scientific American*, Vol. 203, pp. 76–86.

SARIN, M. (1981) *Chulha Album*, mimeo. (July), Delhi, The Ford Foundation.

SARIN, M. and WINBLAD, U. (1983) *Cook Stoves in India: a travel report*, mimeo. (May), Delhi, Swedish International Development Agency.

SAYERS, J. (1980) 'Psychological sex differences', in Brighton Women and Science Group (eds).

SAYWELL, S. (1985) *Women in War: from World War II to El Salvador*, Harmondsworth, Penguin Books.

SCHRIRE, C. (1980) 'An inquiry into the evolutionary status and apparent identity of San hunter-gatherers', *Human Ecology*, Vol. 8, pp. 9–32.

SEAGER, J. and OLSON, A. (1986) *Women in the World: an international atlas*, London, Pluto Press.

SELLERS, M. (1987) 'Unanswered questions on neural tube defects', *British Medical Journal*, Vol. 294, pp. 1–2.

SHARP, E. (1926) *Hertha Ayrton 1854–1923: a memoir*, London, Edward Arnold.

SHIELDS, S.A. (1987) 'The variability hypothesis: the history of biological model of sex differences in intelligence', in *Sex and Scientific Inquiry*, Chicago, Chicago University Press.

SHIVA, V. (1989) *Staying Alive: women, ecology and survival in India*, London, Zed Books.

SKELTON, C. (1989a) 'And so the wheel turns . . . gender and initial teacher education', in Skelton, C. (ed.).

SKELTON, C. (ed.) (1989b) *Whatever Happens to Little Women*, Buckingham, Open University Press.

SLONCIEWSKI, J. (1986) *A Door into the Ocean*, London, The Women's Press.

SMITH, D. (1987) *The Everyday World as Problematic: a feminist sociology*, Boston, MA, Northeastern University Press.

SOLDEN, N. (1978) *Women in British Trade Unions 1874–1976*, Dublin, Gill and Macmillan.

SPALLONE, P. and STEINBERG, D. (eds) (1987) *Made to Order: the myth of reproductive and genetic progress*, Oxford, Pergamon Press (Elmsford, NY, Pergamon Press; 1987).

SPEARS, J.S. (1978) 'Wood as an energy source: the situation in the developing world', paper for the 103rd Annual Meeting of the American Forestry Association (October), USA.

SPENDER, D. (1980) *Man Made Language*, London, Routledge and Kegan Paul.

SPRETNAK, C. (1982) *The Politics of Women's Spirituality*, New York, Anchor Press.

SRIDHARAN, S. (1975) 'In Chatera', *Indian Farming*, November, New Delhi, ICAR.

STANLEY, A. (1981) 'Daughters of Isis, daughters of Demeter: when women reaped and sowed', *Women's Studies International Quarterly*, Vol. 4, No. 3.

STANLEY, A. (1983) 'Women hold up two-thirds of the sky: notes for a revised history of technology', in Rothschild, J. (ed.).

STARHAWK (1980) *Dreaming the Dark*, Beacon Press, Boston.

STARK, E. and FLITCRAFT, A. (1982) 'Medical therapy as repression: the case of battered women', *Health and Medicine*, Vol. 1, pp. 29–32.

STARR, P. (1983) *The Social Transformation of American Medicine*, New York, Basic Books.

STEPHEN, A. (1990) 'Mom's army breeches in the Gulf', *The Observer*, August.

STIEHM, J. HICKS (1989) *Arms and the Enlisted Woman*, Philadelphia, PA, Temple University Press, pp. 34–41.

STONE, M. (1976) *When God was a Woman*, New York, Harcourt Brace Jovanovich.

STRACHEY, R. (1928) *The Cause* (London, Virago, 1978).

STRANDH, S. (1979) *A History of the Machine*, New York, A. & W. Publishers, Inc.

STRASSER, S. (1982) *Never Done: a history of American housework*, New York, Pantheon.

SUMMERS, A. (1988) *Angels and Citizens: British women as military nurses 1854–1914*, London, Routledge.

TESART, A. (1978) 'Les sociétés de chasseurs-cueilleurs', *Pour la Science*, Vol. 16, pp. 99–108.

THEODORE, C.N. and SUTTER, G.E. (1966) *Distribution of Physicians in the US*, Department of Survey Research, Management Services Division, American Medical Association.

THEWELEIT, K. (1987) *Male Fantasies*, New York, Polity Press.

THORNE, B., KRAMARAE, C. and HENLEY, N. (eds) (1983) *Language, Gender and Society*, Rosley, MA, Newbury House.

THRALL, C. (1982) 'The conservative use of modern household technology', *Technology and Culture*, Vol. 23, pp. 175–94.

TRAWEEK, S. (1984) 'High-energy physics: a male preserve', *Technology Review*, Vol. 87, No. 8 (November/December), pp. 42–3.

TROUVE, J. (1980) *Rural Industries in French-speaking Black Africa*, Rural Industrialisation and Employment Project, Geneva, ILO.

TRUSTRAM, M. (1984) *Women of the Regiment*, Cambridge, Cambridge University Press.

TUANA, N. (1989a) 'The weaker seed: the sexist bias of reproductive theory', in Tuana, N. (ed.).

TUANA, N. (ed.) (1989b) *Feminism and Science*, Bloomington, IN, University of Indiana Press.

TURKLE, S. (1984a) 'Women and computer programming', *Technology Review*, Vol. 87, No. 8 (November/December), pp. 48–50.

TURKLE, S. (1984b) *The Second Self: computers and the human spirit*, London, Granada.

TURKLE, S. and PAPERT, S. (1990) 'Epistemological pluralism: styles and voices within the computer culture', *Signs: Journal of Women in Culture and Society*, Vol. 16, No. 1.

TUTEN, J.M. (1982) 'The argument against female combatants', in Loring, N. Goldman (ed.) *Female Soldiers – Combatants or Noncombatants? Historical and contemporary perspectives*, Westport, CT, Greenwood Press, pp. 237–65.

UNIDO (1984) *Report of the Asian Regional Workshop on Integration of Women in Industrial Development Process*, July, Vienna.

UNIVERSITY FUNDING COUNCIL (1990) *Annual Report*.

UNIVERSITY GRANTS COMMITTEE (1988) *UCCA 25th Report 1986/87*, Cheltenham.

VAN DEVANTER, L. (1983) *Home before Morning: the story of an army nurse in Vietnam*, New York, Beaufort Books.

VANEK, J. (1974) 'Time spent in housework', *Scientific American*, Vol. 231, No. 5, pp. 116–20.

VARE, E.A. and PTACEK, G. (1987) *Mothers of Invention – from the Bra to the Bomb: forgotten women and their unforgettable ideas*, New York, Quill, William Morrow.

VERBRUGGE, L.M. and STEINER, R.P. (1981) 'Physician treatment of men and women patients: sex bias or appropriate care?', *Medical Care*, Vol. 19, pp. 609–32.

WARD, B. (1970) 'Women and technology in developing countries', *Impact of Science on Society*, Vol. 20, No. 1, Paris, UNESCO.

WASHBURN, S.L. and DEVORE, I. (1961) 'Social behaviour of baboons and early man', in Washburn, S.L. (ed.) *Social Life of Early Man*, Chicago, IL, Aldine, pp. 91–103.

WASHBURN, S.L. and LANCASTER, C.S. (1968) 'The evolution of hunting', in Lee, R.B. and Devore, I. (eds), pp. 293–303.

WASHINGTON TIMES (1990) 'Tamil Tigress', 3 April.

WATSON, J.D. (1968) *The Double Helix: a personal account of the discovery of the structure of deoxyribonucleic acid*, (rev. edn, Stent, G.S.; London, Weidenfeld and Nicolson, 1981).

WEATHERALL, D. (1985) *The 'New Genetics' and Clinical Practice*, London, Oxford University Press.

WEBSTER, J. (1989) 'Gender, paid work and information technology', paper presented to the PICT Gender and ICT Workshop, May, Brighton, Brighton Polytechnic.

WEBSTER, J. (1990) *Office Automation: the secretarial labour process and women's work in Britain*, Hemel Hempstead, Harvester Wheatsheaf.

WEMPLE, S.F. (1981) *Women in Frankish Society: marriage and the cloister 500–900 AD*, Philadelphia, PA, University of Pennsylvania Press.

WERTZ, R.N. and WERTZ, D.L. (1979) *Lying in: a history of childbirth in America*, New York, The Free Press.

WHEELWRIGHT, J. (1989) *Amazons and Military Maids: women who dressed as men in pursuit of life, liberty and happiness*, London, Pandora Press.

WHEELWRIGHT, J. (1991) 'Women at war', *The Guardian*, 24 January.

WHITE, L. JR (1962) *Medieval Technology and Social Change*, London, Oxford University Press.

WHITE, M.J.D. (1973) *The Chromosomes* (6th edn), London, Chapman and Hall.

WHITEHEAD, A. (1980) 'A conceptual framework for the analysis of the effects of technological change on rural women', unpublished ms., University of Sussex.

WHITELOCK, D. (1952) *The Beginnings of English Society*, Harmondsworth, Penguin Books.

WHYTE, J. (1986) *Girls into Science and Technology*, London, Routledge and Kegan Paul.

WHYTE, J., DEEM, R., KANT, L. and CRUICKSHANK, M. (eds) (1985) *Girl-friendly Schooling*, London, Methuen.

WILKINSON, B. (1969) *The Later Middle Ages in England 1216–1485 AD*, Harlow, Longman.

WILLIAMS, G.C. (1966) *Adaptation and Natural Selection*, Princeton, NJ, Princeton University Press.

WILLIAMS, R. (1990) 'How the West misjudges the rest', *Technology Review*, Vol. 93, No. 4 (May/June).

WILSON, D.S. (1983) 'The group selection controversy: history and current status', *Annual Review of Ecological Systems*, Vol. 14, pp. 159–87.

WINNER, L. (1991) 'A post-modern world's fair', *Technology Review*, Vol. 94, No. 2 (February/March).

WITCHER, H. (1985) 'Personal and professional: a feminist approach', in Whyte, J. *et al.* (eds).

WOMEN INTO INFORMATION TECHNOLOGY FOUNDATION (1991) *Progress Report*, June.

WOMEN'S ENVIRONMENTAL NETWORK (1988) *The Sanitary Protection Scandal*, London, WEN.

WOMEN'S ENVIRONMENTAL NETWORK (1990) *Tissue of Lies?: disposable paper and the environment*, London, WEN.

WOMEN'S RESEARCH AND EDUCATION INSTITUTE (1990) *Facts about Women in the Military: 1980–1990*, Washington, DC, WREI.

WOMEN'S RESEARCH AND EDUCATION INSTITUTE (1991) *Facts about Women in the Persian Gulf War*, Washington, DC, WREI.

WURDERMAN, L.E. (1980) *Physician Distribution and Medical Licensure in the US, 1979*, Center for Health Services Research and Development, American Medical Association.

WYATT, S., THOMAS, G. and MILES, I. (1985) 'Preliminary analysis of the ESRC 1983/4 time budget data', Science Policy Research Unit, Brighton, University of Sussex.

YOXEN, E. (1986) *Unnatural Selection? Coming to terms with the new genetics*, London, Heinemann.

ZEITLIN, J. (1979) 'Craft control and the division of labour: engineers and compositors in Britain 1890–1930', *Cambridge Journal of Economics*, No. 3.

ZIHLMAN, A.L. and TANNER, N. (1978) 'Gathering and the hominid adaptation', in Tiger, L. and Fowler, H.T. (eds) *Female Hierarchies*, Chicago, IL, Beresford, pp. 163–94.

ZILSEL, E. (1942) 'The sociological roots of science', *American Journal of Sociology*, Vol. 47, pp. 544–62.

ZIMMERMAN, J. (1983) *The Technological Woman: interfacing with tomorrow*, Praeger, New York.

SOURCE LIST OF ARTICLES

Article 1.1 'Discovering and doing: science and technology, an introduction' Laurie Smith Keller
Commissioned article.

Article 1.2 'Women's voices/men's voices: technology as language' Margaret Lowe Benston
from Kramarae, C. (ed.) (1988) *Technology and Women's Voices: keeping in touch*, London, Routledge and Kegan Paul (pp. 15–28).

Article 1.3 'How gender matters, or, why it's so hard for us to count past two' Evelyn Fox Keller
from Harding, J. (ed.) (1986) *Perspectives on Gender and Science*, Brighton, Falmer Press (pp. 168–83).

Article 1.4 'How the women's movement benefits science' Sandra Harding
from *Women's Studies International Forum*, Vol. 12, No. 3, pp. 271–83 (1989).

Article 2.1 In pursuit of difference: scientific studies of women and men Lynda Birke
Commissioned article.

Article 2.2 The changing role of women in models of human evolution Linda Marie Fedigan
from *Annual Review of Anthropology*, Vol. 15, pp. 25–66 (1986).

Article 2.3 Women and medicalization: a new perspective Catherine Kohler Riessman
from *Social Policy*, Summer, pp. 3–17 (1983).

Article 2.4 Detecting genetic diseases: prenatal screening and its problems Lynda Birke, Susan Himmelweit and Gail Vines
from Ch. 7 in Birke, L., Himmelweit, S. and Vines, G. (1990) *Tomorrow's Child: reproductive technologies in the 1990s*, London, Virago (pp. 157–201).

Article 3.1 Hertha Ayrton: a scientist of spirit Joan Mason
Commissioned article.

Article 3.2 Girls in science education: of rice and fruit trees Liz Whitelegg
Commissioned article.

Article 3.3 A feeling for the organism: Fox Keller's life of Barbara McClintock Gill Kirkup and Laurie Smith Keller
Commissioned article.

Article 3.4 Technology, production and power Cynthia Cockburn from Cockburn, C. (1985) *Machinery of Dominance: women, men and technical know-how*, London, Pluto Press (pp. 15–43).

Article 3.5 The Secretary Chant Marge Piercy
from *To Be of Use: poems by Marge Piercy*, New York, Doubleday, 1973 (p. 5).

Article 3.6 'A brother in arms, a sister in peace': contemporary issues of gender and military technology Julie Wheelwright
Commissioned article.

Article 3.7 Science, technology and development: the impact on the status of women Radha Chakravarthy
Commissioned article.

Article 4.1 Domestic technology: labour-saving or enslaving? Judy Wajcman
from Wajcman, J. (1991) *Feminism Confronts Technology*, Cambridge, Polity Press (pp. 81–109).

Article 4.2 Cold hearths and barren slopes: the woodfuel crisis in the Third World Bina Agarwal
from Agarwal, B. (1986) *Cold Hearths and Barren Slopes: the woodfuel crisis in the Third World*, London, Zed Books Ltd, pp. 5–6, 11–17, 20–27, 38–9, 45–53, 83–5, 97–100.

Article 4.3 Dry Jean Binta Breeze
from Morris, M. (ed.) (1988) *Riddym Ravings and Other Poems*, London, Race Today Publications (pp. 18–19).

Article 4.4 The social construction of computers: hammers or harpsichords? Gill Kirkup
Commissioned article.

Article 4.5 Eco-feminism Cat Cox
Commissioned article.

Article 4.6 Sultana's dream Rokeya Sakhawat Hossain
from Hossain, R. Sakhawat (1988) *Sultana's Dream and Selections from the Secluded Ones*, Jahan, R. (ed. and trans.) (afterword by Papanek, H.), New York, The Feminist Press at the City University of New York.

SHORT BIOGRAPHIES OF THE CONTRIBUTORS

Bina Agarwal is Professor of Agricultural Economics at the Institute of Economic Growth, Delhi University. She has published extensively on technological change in agriculture, the political economy of the fuelwood and environmental crisis, poverty and land rights, and the position of women in south Asia. She is currently working on her fifth book on *Gender and Land Rights in South Asia* (forthcoming: Cambridge University Press). She was awarded a McArthur research and writing grant, 1990–91.

Margaret Lowe Benston taught in the Computing Science Department and the Women's Studies Program at Simon Fraser University in Canada. Her research area was women and technological change. Sadly she died early in 1991, before she knew that her article would be part of this collection.

Lynda Birke is a biologist in the Department of Continuing Education at the University of Warwick. She has long had an interest in feminist questions about science and was part of the Brighton Women and Science Group which produced *Alice Through the Microscope* (Virago, 1980). She authored *Women, Feminism and Biology* (Wheatsheaf, 1986) and co-authored *Tomorrow's Child: reproductive technologies in the '90s* (Virago, 1990). Apart from feminism, her other passion is animals and she lives with lots of them.

Jean Binta Breeze is a black poet who both performs and publishes her poetry. Her collection, *Riddym Ravings* (Race Today, 1988), shows concern with both humour and tragedy in the black experience.

Radha Chakravarthy is a scientist at the National Institute of Science and Technology and Department Studies (NISTADS) in New Delhi, India. She has done research into international comparisons of the productivity of women in the science and technology professions. She has published in numerous journals and presented papers at many international conferences.

Cynthia Cockburn spent some years as a freelance journalist followed by twenty years in research, first at the Centre for Environmental Studies London, then at City University, London, at the Centre for Research in Gender, Ethnicity and Social Change. Her main political commitments are to the women's movement, particularly women's peace activities and international links. She is the author of a number of books on education, the state and technology and gender. Her most recent book is *In the Way of Women: men's resistance to sex equality in organizations* (Macmillan Education and ILR Press, Cornell University, Ithaca, NY, 1991). She has two adult daughters and has been *un*married many years.

Cat Cox has a degree in pharmacology and a particular interest in the effects of chemicals in diet and health. She lives in North London and works at the Women's Environmental Network as a specialist researcher and writer, currently working on food issues. Her work on the global effects of the pulp and paper industry contributed to the publication of *A Tissue of Lies?: disposable paper and the environment* (Women's Environmental Network, 1990). She has also written on ecofeminism for various magazines and journals.

Linda Marie Fedigan has worked at the Department of Anthropology at the University of Alberta, Canada since 1974. Her research interests include sexual selection theory, life histories of female primates and the role of women in science. She has a field site in Costa Rica where she studies Japanese monkeys. She has written two books: *Primate Paradigms* and *The Monkeys of Arashiyama*. Her home is near the Rocky Mountains where she goes cross-country skiing and cycling.

Sandra Harding is Professor of Philosophy and Director of Women's Studies at the University of Delaware. She authored *The Science Question in Feminism* (Open University Press and Cornell University Press, 1986) which won the Jessie Bernard Award of the American Sociological Association 1987. She edited *Feminism and Methodology: Social Science Issues* (Open University Press and Indiana University Press, 1987) and co-edited two other collections on gender and methodology in science. Her most recent book is *Whose Science? Whose Knowledge? Thinking from women's lives* (Open University Press and Cornell University Press, 1991).

Susan Himmelweit teaches economics and women's studies at The Open University. She was a founder member of the journal *Feminist Review* and has written on the political economy of women, the place of reproduction in society and new reproductive technologies. She is co-editor with Helen Crowley of another book in this series, *Knowing Women: feminism and knowledge* (Polity, 1991).

Rokeya Sakhawat Hossein (1880–1932) was the first and most important feminist of Bengali Muslim society. She wrote extensively, campaigning against the oppression of women in Bengali society. She founded the Bengali Muslim Women's Society in 1916 and all her life was interested in the education of Muslim girls and women.

Evelyn Fox Keller originally trained and worked as a mathematical biophysicist but she is best-known for her feminist writing on gender and science. Her most influential books are *A Feeling for the Organism: the life and work of Barbara McClintock* (Freeman, 1983) and *Reflections on Gender and Science* (Yale University Press, 1985). She lives and teaches in the United States.

Laurie Smith Keller is a lecturer in computer science at The Open University. Her first degree was in English Language and Literature but in the 1960s she began to work with computers and worked as a systems engineer for a variety of organizations before becoming an academic. She is a member of the British Computer Society and a chartered engineer. She has had a lifelong interest in science and technology and enjoys reading, walking and cooking.

Gill Kirkup is a senior lecturer in educational technology at The Open University. Her research interests are in new technologies for teaching and learning, and feminist pedagogy as well as gender and technology. She is the author (with Ruth Carter) of *Women in Engineering: a good place to be?* (Macmillan and New York University Press, 1990) and numerous articles. When not working she enjoys time with her two sons, and reading paperback fiction late into the night.

Joan Mason is a former Reader in chemistry at The Open University, which she joined in 1970. After post-doctoral research and teaching in the 1950s at the Universities of Southern California, London (University College) and Ohio (Columbus), she dropped out for eight years, encountering problems of discrimination, then of combining science with raising a family. She returned to research and teaching when her youngest child was four. Her good fortune in 'surviving' made her decide to make time for women in science.

Marge Piercy is a poet and novelist best known in feminist circles for her brilliant Utopian novel *Woman on the Edge of Time*.

Catherine Kohler Riessman, Professor of Sociology and Professor of Social Work at Boston University, is both a sociologist and a social worker. She received her PhD from Columbia University. Her interest is in medical sociology, with special emphasis on women and health, and in the family, especially gender differences in the experience of marriage and divorce. Her recent book is *Divorce Talk: women and men talk about personal relationships* (Rutgers University Press, 1990).

Gail Vines is a science journalist with an abiding interest in the interplay between science and society. Trained in biology, and now features editor of *New Scientist*, she has focused particularly on the debates now raging round the 'new genetics', reproductive technologies and animal experimentation. She is co-author of *The Evolution of Life* (Collins, 1986) and *Tomorrow's Child* (Virago, 1990).

Judy Wajcman is a senior lecturer in sociology at the University of New South Wales, Sydney, Australia. She has been active in the women's movement and on the left in both Britain and Australia since the early 1970s. She is the author of *Women in Control: dilemmas* *of a workers' cooperative* (Open University Press, 1983), *Feminism Confronts Technology* (Polity, 1991) and co-editor of *The Social Shaping of Technology* (Open University Press, 1985). She lives in a low-tech, inner-city apartment and has just discovered the joys of owning a dishwasher.

Julie Wheelwright is a Canadian author and journalist who lives in London. She has written for several feminist magazines, reviews for *The New Statesman and Society* and contributes regularly to *The Guardian* women's page. Her interest in female soldiers began with research for her MA in history, which led to her first book *Amazons and Military Maids* (Pandora, 1989). Her second – *Fatal Lovers: Mata Hari and the myth of women in espionage* – will be published in 1992.

Liz Whitelegg chose to specialize in physics and maths at her single-sex grammar school, and went on to study physics at university where she began to realize that other people felt that she had made a strange choice for a woman. She has worked at The Open University in women's studies and science education and is currently involved in developing in-service training courses for teachers. Through this work she encourages teachers to develop strategies to increase opportunities for girls to study science.

ACKNOWLEDGEMENTS

Grateful acknowledgement is made to the following sources for permission to reproduce material in this book:

Text

Chapter 1: Benston, M. Lowe 'Women's voices/men's voices: technology as language', from Kramarae, C. (ed.) (1988) *Technology and Women's Voices: keeping in touch*, Routledge; Keller, E. Fox 'How gender matters, or, why it's so hard for us to count past two', from Harding, J. (ed.) (1986) *Perspectives on Gender and Science*, Falmer Press; Harding, S. 'How the women's movement benefits science', from *Women's Studies International Forum*, Vol.12, No.3, 1989, Pergamon Press PLC.

Chapter 2: Riessman, C. K. 'Women and medicalization: a new perspective', from *Social Policy*, Summer 1983, published by Social Policy Corporation, New York, New York 10036, copyright © 1983 by Social Policy Corporation; Birke, L., Himmelweit, S. and Vines, G. 'Detecting genetic diseases: prenatal screening and its problems', from Birke, L., Himmelweit, S. and Vines, G. (1990) *Tomorrow's Child: reproductive technologies in the 1990s*, Virago Press.

Chapter 3: Extracts from Keller, Fox. E. *A Feeling for the Organism: the life and work of Barbara McClintock*, copyright © 1983 by W. H. Freeman and Company. Reprinted by permission; Cockburn, C. 'Technology, production and power', from Cockburn, C. (1985) *Machinery of Dominance: women, men and technical know-how*, Pluto Press; Piercy, M. 'The Secretary Chant' from *Circles on the Water* by Marge Piercy, copyright © 1979. Reprinted by permission of Alfred A. Knopf, Inc.

Chapter 4: Wajcman, J. 'Domestic technology: labour-saving or enslaving?' from Wajcman, J. (1991) *Feminism Confronts Technology*, Polity Press; Agarwal, B. (1986) *Cold Hearths and Barren Slopes: the woodfuel crisis in the Third World*, Zed Books Ltd, London, extracts from pp. 5-6,11-17,20-27,38-9,45-53,83-5,97-100, reproduced by permission of the publisher; Breeze, Binta, J. 'Dry' from Morris, M. (ed.) (1988) *Riddym Ravings and Other Poems*, Race Today Publications; Hossein, R. Sakhawat 'Sultana's dream' translation © 1988 by Roushan Johan from the book Hossein, R. Sakhawat (1988) *Sultana's Dream and Selections from the Secluded Ones*. Published in 1988 by The Feminist Press at the City University of New York. All rights reserved.

Illustrations

p. 22: '*Una epidemia que se creia olvidado, reparece*'. Reproduced from *Semana*, No. 469; p. 44: Reproduced with permission from James Deese, *General Psychology*, 1967, Allyn and Bacon; p. 84, Figure 2.1.2: from Williams, R. H., *Textbook of Endocrinology*, W.B. Saunders Co. Inc., 1981; p. 86: from Jacky Fleming, *Be a Bloody Train Driver*, Penguin Books Ltd, Copyright © Jacky Fleming, 1991; p. 87, Figure 2.1.3: based on data from Marshall, W.A. and Tanner, J.M. (1969) 'Variations in the pattern of pubertal change in girls', *Archives of Disease in Childhood*, Vol. 45, pp. 291-303, and (1970) 'Variations in the pattern of pubertal change in boys', *Archives of Disease in Childhood*, Vol. 45, pp. 13-23; p. 89, Figure 2.1.4: from Figure 26 in J.M.Tanner, *Foetus into Man: physical growth from conception to maturity*, © J.M.Tanner 1978, originally from Tanner, Hughes and Whitehouse, unpublished;

p. 90, Figure 2.1.5 and p. 93, Figure 2.1.7: adapted from material in Dyer, K. F, *Challenging the Men,* University of Queensland Press; *pp. 163, 280:* cartoons by Anne S. Walker. Reproduced from 'Women and new technologies', *The Tribune,* No. 44, by permission of the International Women's Tribune Center, New York; *pp. 190-91:* Reproduced from M. J. D. White, *The Chromosomes* (6th edn), 1973, Chapman and Hall, Figures 2, 8 and 14, by permission of Isobel White; *p. 210:* cartoon by Liz Mackie; *p. 237:* Reproduced by permission of Recycled Images; *pp. 245, 253:* from Cecil Meadows, *Victorian Ironmonger,* 1978, Shire Publications, by permission of the publisher and Mrs Meadows; p. 248: Reproduced from Bob Gordon, *Early Electrical Appliances,* 1984, Shire Publications, by permission of the author; *pp. 270, 277:* Reproduced by permission of David Shenton.

Black and White Plate Section

Plate 1: Ann Ronan Picture Library, caption adapted from Londa Schubinger, *The Mind Has No Sex,* London, Harvard University Press, 1989; *Plates 2 and 9:* Advertising Archives, London; *Plate 3:* copyright © Nobel Foundation, Stockholm. Photo: Inge Holm; *Plate 4:* Girton College Archives. Reproduced by permission of the Mistress and Fellows, Girton College, Cambridge; *Plate 5:* Illustrated London News. Reproduced from Evelyn Sharp, *Hertha Ayrton: a memoir,* 1926, Edward Arnold; *Plate 6:* Chicago Historical Society, Photo: William Walton; *Plate 7:* Imperial War Museum; *Plate 8:* Photo: Eric Roberts; *Plates 10 and 11:* Tom Learmonth.

Colour Plate Section

Maps 1-4: Maps 8: Contraception, 10: Birth and Death, 26: Illness and Health, 32: Military Service from Joni Seager and Ann Olson, *Women in the World,* 1986, Pluto. Reproduced by permission of Swanston Publishing Ltd.

INDEX

*(Note: Page numbers in **bold** indicate articles by these authors.)*

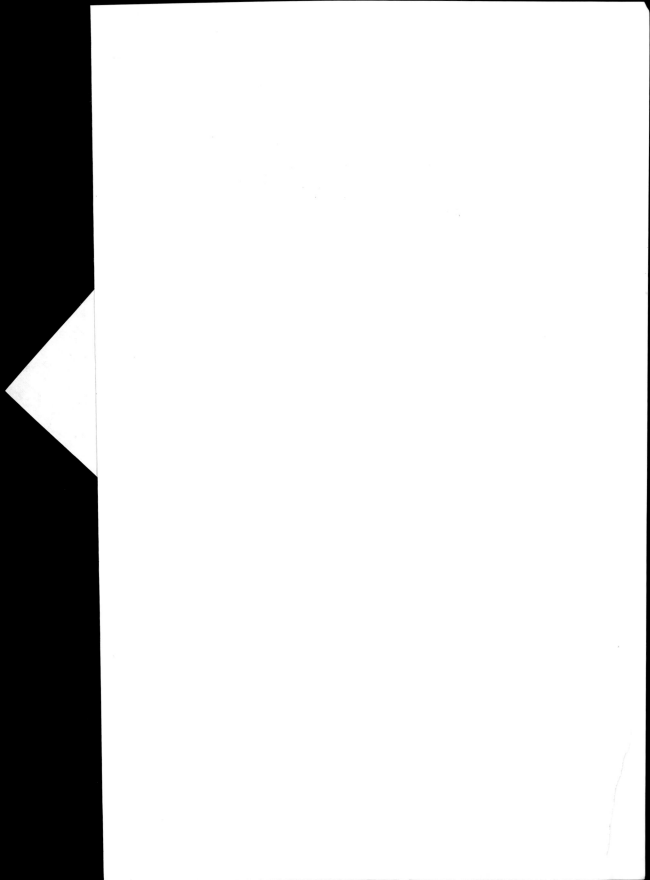